Phillip Kerman

Macromedia®
Flash® 8

@work

PROJECTS AND TECHNIQUES TO GET THE JOB DONE

SAMS

800 East 96th Street, Indianapolis, Indiana 46240

Macromedia® Flash® 8 @work: Projects You Can Use on the Job

Copyright © 2006 by Phillip Kerman

International Standard Book Number: 0-672-32828-3

Library of Congress Catalog Card Number: 2005903522

Printed in the United States of America

First Printing: January 2006

09   08   07   06   4   3   2   1

Trademarks

All terms mentioned in this book that are known to be trademarks or service marks have been appropriately capitalized. Sams Publishing cannot attest to the accuracy of this information. Use of a term in this book should not be regarded as affecting the validity of any trademark or service mark.

Warning and Disclaimer

Every effort has been made to make this book as complete and as accurate as possible, but no warranty or fitness is implied. The information provided is on an "as is" basis. The author and the publisher shall have neither liability nor responsibility to any person or entity with respect to any loss or damages arising from the information contained in this book or from the use of the programs accompanying it.

Bulk Sales

Sams Publishing offers excellent discounts on this book when ordered in quantity for bulk purchases or special sales. For more information, please contact

U.S. Corporate and Government Sales

1-800-382-3419

corpsales@pearsontechgroup.com

For sales outside the United States, please contact

International Sales

international@pearsoned.com

Snowboard image courtesy of www.deepplay.com/sites/m399/.

Acquisitions Editor
Linda Bump Harrison

Development Editor
Alice Martina Smith

Managing Editor
Charlotte Clapp

Project Editor
Dan Knott

Production Editor
Megan Wade

Indexer
Erika Millen

Proofreader
Brad Engels

Technical Editors
Aria Danika
Larry Drolet
David Vogeleer

Publishing Coordinator
Vanessa Evans

Multimedia Developer
Dan Scherf

Book Designer
Gary Adair

Page Layout
Michelle Mitchell

Contents at a Glance

Table of Contents

Contents

We Want to Hear from You!

As the reader of this book, *you* are our most important critic and commentator. We value your opinion and want to know what we're doing right, what we could do better, what areas you'd like to see us publish in, and any other words of wisdom you're willing to pass our way.

You can email or write me directly to let me know what you did or didn't like about this book—as well as what we can do to make our books stronger.

Please note that I cannot help you with technical problems related to the topic of this book, and that due to the high volume of mail I receive, I might not be able to reply to every message.

When you write, please be sure to include this book's title and author as well as your name and phone or email address. I will carefully review your comments and share them with the author and editors who worked on the book.

Email: graphics@samspublishing.com

Mail: Mark Taber
          Associate Publisher
          Sams Publishing
          800 East 96th Street
          Indianapolis, IN 46240 USA

Reader Services

For more information about this book or another Sams Publishing title, visit our website at www.samspublishing.com. Type the ISBN (excluding hyphens) or the title of a book in the Search field to find the page you're looking for.

Introduction

A lot of books claim that they're unique, but this one really is. The *@ work* series leads you directly into building the kinds of practical projects you're likely to encounter in a professional environment. That promise has appeal because readers have a very clear idea of what they want to build. The projects in this book are definitely in demand. (I know because all these projects have come up more than once in my job.) However, the idea that you can bypass details and learn just the facts is a potential fallacy that threatens the premise of this book series. In fact, I'd argue that there are only a few ways to learn difficult subjects and, unfortunately, none are "quick and easy."

In case you think I'm a walking contradiction, let me explain how this book *can* be to the point without being so "lite" that the projects aren't useful. It might sound terrible, but in this book you won't learn the Flash skills needed to build complex projects. But the projects you'll build aren't lightweight either. Rather, for each chapter, I've built adaptable support files that serve as engines that display your content. What you'll learn here is how to adapt and extend these engines for your projects. (Of course, you'll be able to investigate the files to see how I built them, but the focus is on using these files.)

These engines are not merely templates that you fill with your own content, switch a few colors, and then put your logo on. In fact, the engines are invisible. For example, when you add captions to a video (in Chapter 3,

"Creating a Video with Synchronized Captions"), you create the text display and supply the actual captions. The engine handles the bulk of the timing and programming tasks and then simply sends a message to your display when a new caption should appear. Here's a wild analogy to illustrate how it works: Think of how you're insulated from the details involving exactly how your car works. You only have to interface with the steering wheel, gas pedal, and brakes. Now imagine if your car had modular components enabling you to change and modify everything in the interior. As long as you always included some sort of steering wheel, gas pedal, and brakes, the whole system would work.

I know the engines in this book work because I've already seen them customized and extended by several book reviewers. Furthermore, after writing the chapters, I began creating more and more templates that work within the engines (and you can download these from www. samspublishing.com). I also expect readers will develop even more templates and email them to me to share. (Making templates for the engines is easy; that's one of the main things you'll be doing in this book.)

Let me conclude with a few contrasting notes about what this book is and isn't, and who it's written for. This book is appropriate for a wide range of readers; some of you *will* simply replace a few colors and add your logo to the finished files I supply, while others will create very advanced templates that adapt and extend my engines. You'll definitely get a lot more out of the book if you're familiar enough with Flash that you're not fighting with its interface. I

explain every step in detail, but I also know that it's easy to get lost if you've never touched Flash. The target audience for this book is an accomplished novice or intermediate Flash user. A lot of people learn how to create animations and projects with simple interactivity but then hit a wall that blocks them from tackling advanced projects. I'm writing for the reader who's at that wall but who wants to learn only how to get over the wall at hand—the projects at hand in your work today.

This book is not a guide to Object Oriented Programming (OOP). Although all the code in my engines uses OOP as well as ActionScript 2 (AS2), you can build the projects using any style you want: You can do everything in the Flash timeline or make your own class files (that is, use AS2). You don't need any AS2 experience. The only AS2-specific task you must complete is to copy .as files into the folders in which you're building the projects. All my source files are open for your perusal (which, for me, is a lot like appearing in public in my underwear—not that I've done that). I'm not a hack programmer by any means, but don't expect the source files to be the most elegant examples of OOP you've ever seen. They will, of course, work for the task at hand and won't have a negative impact on performance.

Every project in this book assumes you're delivering content to Flash Player 8. I suppose that's not totally practical because many clients don't want to require their users to have the latest version of the Flash plug-in until after it has been out a while. (However, in Chapter 1, "Exploring Flash 8," I give you evidence for why the adoption rate is likely to occur quickly with Flash Player 8.) The reason the projects use features that require

Flash Player 8 is not arbitrary. In every case, I'm embracing new features that either provide results previously unavailable or because they make the development of the project much easier.

The engines in this book are not Flash components. You won't receive a library of advanced UI components. Nor are the engines standalone applications. However, I did build a few helper applications that turned out very cool. For example, one tool lets you add cue points to video and audio in a very natural manner during video playback. I should also add that you won't find a bunch of clipart in the files I've made available for you to download from the accompanying CD-ROM. I hope I don't see a real project in which a reader uses my prototype graphics. Not that I mind, but they're pretty rough.

You are welcome to use any of the code from this book in your real projects. You have no further obligation to me and, similarly, there's no stated or implied guarantee that I will support the files (beyond maintaining the book errata). My point is simply that the projects really are ready for primetime and I expect you to use them.

Finally, for the third time, I'll reiterate that the projects are not lightweight. While I was writing them, I refused to build something that wasn't representative of a real project (and therefore was impractical). I've yet to persuade a client that we should remove a useful feature just because I found it hard to build, so I didn't use excuses here either. Having said that, it's possible you will want a specialty feature added to one of the engines. Realize that you'll learn how to make pretty significant changes to the projects throughout this book. I wouldn't be surprised if you

wanted to insert an additional feature I didn't think of. In such cases, feel free to email me at work@phillipkerman.com, and I might be motivated to actually build it—at worst, I can point you in the right direction to help you build it yourself.

Organization of This Book

This book is divided into three parts:

▶ Part I, "Getting Started," introduces Flash 8 and provides your basic training for building projects in Flash. The two chapters in this part are really the prerequisites for the rest of the book; don't skip them.

▶ Part II, "Projects," contains a variety of practical projects that are sure to come up in some form during your Flash career. They're not in any particular order and have little overlap or cross referencing. Therefore, you can read them in any order. For example, if you need to add captions to a video, start with Chapter 3, "Creating a Video with Synchronized Captions." If you need to make a PowerPoint-like presentation, jump directly to Chapter 7, "Creating a PowerPoint-style Slide Presentation." In each chapter you'll start by building a basic working version of the project and then go on to add enhancements and variations as you wish. For example, you'll create a quiz in Chapter 5, "Creating an Assessment Quiz," and have the opportunity to add all kinds of question types (such as multiple-choice and drag-and-drop). The chapters in this portion of the book contain the projects you can use on the job.

In Part III, "Appendixes," you'll find Appendix A, "Resources," which provides links and information about third-party products for Flash, important links on the Macromedia website, Flash community websites, plus some tips for accessing various Flash preferences on your own computer. Appendix B, "Components," can be thought of as the CliffsNotes version of a book called *Learn How to Use Flash V2 Components in 24 Seconds* (if it existed). There you'll learn the important highlights for using Flash components. Finally, the Glossary lists and defines the key terms used throughout the book.

Accessing the Book's Project Files

The chapter-by-chapter project and media files are available on this book's CD.

Remember to visit the author's website at www.phillipkerman.com/at-work to access additional templates. You can even upload your successful template files to make them available to other readers of this book.

Go to www.samspublishing.com/register to register your book so you will be notified of future updates and errata or corrections.

> **! CAUTION**
>
> Be sure you extract all the files from each Zip file with the Use Folder Names option (for PC users) selected so you can get the same folders on your computer as included in each Zip file. Mac users can simply double-click the Zip file, and the folder structure should appear intact, as named.

Conventions Used in This Book

This book uses the following conventions:

▶ *Italic* is used to denote key terms when they first appear in the book.

 TIP

Tips provide shortcuts to make your job easier or better ways to accomplish certain tasks.

 NOTE

Notes provide additional information related to the surrounding topics.

! **CAUTION**

Cautions alert you to potential problems and help you steer clear of disaster.

 @work resources

▶ This indicates specific files that are available on the accompanying CD-ROM.

PART I: Getting Started

This chapter and the one that follows are intended to orient you to the projects that follow. Here you'll learn about the core new features in Flash 8 and—more importantly—how these features influence the kinds of projects you can build.

You'll need to have Flash 8 installed on your computer because I'm certain you'll frequently want to put the book down and check out some of the features mentioned in this chapter. If you only have Flash 8 Basic installed, I suspect you'll want to upgrade to Flash 8 Professional by the end of this chapter.

What's New in Flash 8

I've been using Flash since version 2, and with each successive version I say it's the biggest upgrade yet. That's true once again, but with Flash 8 I can add that it's the *best* version yet. From the features supported in the Flash player to the stability and usability of the Flash authoring environment, the features in Flash 8 have been honed. This chapter highlights my favorite features and why they're important.

Expressive Features

Macromedia's buzzword for Flash 8 is *expressiveness*. Flash 8 was designed to win back visual designers who were alienated by features in recent versions geared toward programmers. The big features that will attract graphic folks are *filters* and *blends*. Filters (such as drop shadow, glow, and blur) have traditionally been available only in bitmap editing tools such as Photoshop. What's cool about filters in Flash is that they are applied at runtime (while your movie plays). This approach to filters makes them nondestructive, meaning they can be added or removed from a particular image without permanently changing that image. The fact that filters are applied at runtime also means they contribute almost nothing to the file size, so your creations can download quickly. As you'll see later in this chapter, you can add and modify filters both manually (while authoring) as well as using the *ActionScript programming language*. Lastly, filters can be *tweened* over time. For example, you can move a Drop Shadow filter to make it appear as if the sun was setting while your video clip is playing.

A lot of people think filters are simply gratuitous special effects that distract users. That's simply not the case when they are strategically applied. For example, if you add a Drop Shadow filter to a tile while a user drags it, you will add dimension and make the tile feel as if it were floating above the screen, as Figure 1.1 shows. In addition to the Drop Shadow filter you can see in the figure, I've also applied a Bevel filter to the tile and then applied a second Bevel filter (offset by 180°) on the target (the area to which the tile is being dragged) to make the target look pushed in.

FIGURE 1.1   Filters aren't just for special effects. The Drop Shadow and Bevel filters used here demonstrate a way to add a realistic sense of dimension.

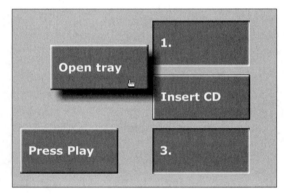

> **⚑ NOTE**
>
> Although filters come up in several chapters, you'll find them covered in the most detail in Chapter 9, "Creating Special Effects."

Blends (such as Invert, Hard Light, and Lighten) should also be familiar to Photoshop users. Blends perform compositing effects by combining the colors from one image layered on top of another image underneath. (Although Flash's timeline does have layers, I'm using the term *layer* more generally; the idea is that multiple movie clip instances can be stacked in layers, and you can use a blend to merge two or more of these layers together artistically.) Blends can be as simple as setting a black shape to Invert, causing the image underneath that black shape to appear like a photographic negative. More complex effects are possible, such as using a yellow radial gradient set to the Hard Light blend so the gradient adds punch to some headlights on a car image underneath. As are filters, blends are applied at runtime (meaning they are nondestructive and optionally controllable using ActionScript). However, there's no way to smoothly tween from one blend type to another. Only one blend can be applied at once, and there are no gradations; they're either on or off.

Flash 8 has a new text rendering technology called *FlashType*. With past versions of the software, you really had no way to control antialiasing except to turn it on or off. The added variations now available with FlashType mean you can select from a series of presets (such as Anti-alias for Readability or Anti-alias for Animation) to make it more legible. Additionally, you can fine-tune the thickness and sharpness manually instead of using the presets. No more tiny fonts that look blurry—unless, of course, that's what you're into.

Except for video (which I cover in the next section), the rest of the so-called expressive features are easy to overlook. However, I'd call many of these features subtly awesome. One of my favorites is the Scale option for strokes. Normally, when you put a stroke around a shape in a movie clip, that stroke thickens as you resize the clip, as shown on the left side of Figure 1.2.

FIGURE 1.2   The Normal stroke in the clip at the upper left thickens when the clip is scaled (bottom left). Compare that to a clip containing strokes set not to scale (upper right). The scaled version of the clip retains the original stroke thickness (bottom right).

Scale: Normal   Scale: None

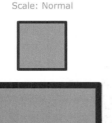

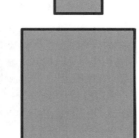

If you want to resize a clip without having the contained stroke resize at all, simply use the Properties panel to change the stroke's Scale option to None. There are also Scale options for Vertical and Horizontal, meaning the stroke grows in proportion only to how much vertical or horizontal scaling you apply to the clip.

You'd think strokes wouldn't need so many upgrades, but there are actually two additional important new features: Cap and Join.

It's easiest to understand the Stroke Cap options if you realize that a line connecting two points doesn't really have any thickness until you apply a stroke to it. Strokes are applied to thicken an infinitely thin line. A 10-point stroke fattens the line by 5 pixels on each side of the otherwise invisible line. In the

previous versions of Flash, the endpoint of a 10-point stroke would have a 5-pixel radius half-circle protruding past the end point. If you wanted the end of the line you had stroked to be square, you must select Modify, Shape, Convert Lines to Fills and then cut off the offending round end point. In Flash 8, the stroked line has a rounded end only when the Round Cap setting is applied to the stroke. Figure 1.3 shows the all the stroke Cap options now available.

NOTE

Just to be complete, let me point out that strokes can now contain *gradient* colors. Instead of a solid black-colored stroke, you can make the stroke outline around your clip gradually go from black to silver, adding a sheen. Gradients in strokes are definitely subtle when the stroke is thin.

FIGURE 1.3   It's easiest to see the difference between the Cap options by selecting a thick stroke with the Subselection tool.

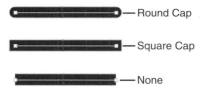

Although the Cap options affect only the endpoint of a line, the Join options affect strokes connected to other strokes—that is, they control how the strokes join. Similar to the extra rounded endpoint that used to accompany every stroke, the corners of a square would have the same rounded effect. Flash 8 adds two additional Join options (besides the Round Join): Miter Join creates sharp corners, and Bevel Join flattens the corners by effectively cutting off the corners at 45° angles. Figure 1.4 shows the Join options.

📌 TIP

If your Miter Join appears like a bevel, you probably need to increase the Miter Limit setting in the Properties panel. This setting specifies how many times thicker than the stoke thickness the joined portion can grow.

FIGURE 1.4 **The Join options let you control how the corners of adjoining strokes appear.**

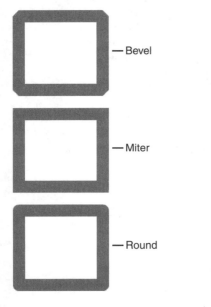

— Bevel

— Miter

— Round

Video Improvements

An improvement to video in Flash 8 is support for the VP6 codec from a company named On2. (*Codec* is short for compressor/decompressor, which is the technology that first compressed video into a smaller file size and then decompressed it during playback.) Bottom line: The VP6 codec results in much better quality at a target file size than the old Spark codec that was first added to Flash MX (and, I should note, you must select Spark when you deliver video content to users with Flash Player 6 or Flash Player 7). The quality of the video compressed with VP6 is really stunning. Alas, the increased hardware demands to play VP6 videos means your project can appear sluggish on slower computers.

Another great addition to the Flash 8 video features is the ability to encode an *alpha channel*. Alpha channels let you shoot a character on a solid-colored background and perform a *chroma key effect* (like the TV news meteorologist who appears "on top of" the weather map). (You'll need a video editing tool such as Adobe After Effects to create the alpha channel in the video before you bring it into Flash.) I suppose this means we've entered an era of video characters appearing on top of your website pointing to user interface elements. In any event, the alpha channel is a huge enhancement. Before, you could put things on top of video; with Flash 8, you have the option to see *through* the video.

Flash 8 also includes a much-improved video import wizard that makes Flash video deployment easier. Integrated in the import process is a new component called FLVPlayback. Basically, you just point to a source video, make a few compression setting selections, pick a *skin* for the FLVPlayback component (there are a number of skins from which you can choose), and the wizard does the rest. Figure 1.5 shows one of the Mojave skins.

In addition to using Flash 8 to convert videos to the Flash video file format (.flv), you can also export .flv files directly from one of several third-party video editing tools. This involves using the Flash Video Exporter, which is included when you install Flash 8. The benefit is simply that you can output a .flv file directly from your video editor instead of first creating a temporary video file (in a format such as QuickTime) that Flash can then convert to a .flv.

Another new option I want to mention is that you can use the standalone Flash Video Encoder that ships with Flash Professional 8. This barebones application lets you do one thing: create .flv files (and without the help of the video import wizard). The advantage of the Flash Video Encoder is that you can automatically encode a sequence of files (that is, a *batch*) at once.

Another profound addition to the video features in Flash 8 is the support for embedded *cue points*. Cue points let you inject the .flv file with information such as captions. Think of it this way: Normally, there's information on every frame of a video with the

picture and sound. Cue points let you add text information to each frame as well. You'll learn all about cue points and other approaches to making things happen in synch with your video, such as fading in a static photograph that's not in the video, in Chapter 3, "Creating a Video with Synchronized Captions."

NOTE

Although many video editors can encode video files in .flv format, they all use the same Flash Video Encoder that Flash does. This is nice in that the interface (and quality) is identical regardless of which video editor you use; however, it doesn't mean you'll get the *best* quality possible. To get the absolute best-quality .flv files from your source video files, use Sorenson Media's Squeeze 4.2 for Flash with the On2 VP6 Pro Plug-in (www.sorensonmedia.com) or On2's Flix 8 (www.on2.com). Both tools add support for *deinterlacing* and *multipass* encoding as well as other features that improve quality.

Workflow Improvements

If you've used Flash before, you'll find a lot of new workflow improvements in Flash 8 that range from cosmetic to profound. For example, the Library panel stays where you put it (minor, but it was frustrating when it used to have a mind of its own). The Library also has a new drop-down menu that gives you easy access to libraries from other open files. I could go on, but these sorts of changes are details only noticeable to Flash veterans. (You can find a complete list of changes by selecting Help, What's New in Flash 8.)

There are a few notable changes regardless of your level of Flash experience. There's now a Preferences setting that changes the way the

Undo command works (the Undo feature is accessible by pressing Ctrl+Z). The default, Document-level Undo, means that every time you undo (by pressing Ctrl+Z), you go back to the state before the last change. Perhaps this is the most intuitive behavior. However, the other option, Object-level Undo, is very useful. With this option, if you make changes while inside one movie clip and then make changes to another movie clip, you can return to the first clip and press Ctrl+Z to undo the last thing you did in *that* clip! It's the way Flash used to work (before version MX2004), and it's back as a preference.

The margins for your text fields are also easier to modify in Flash 8. You can now grab any one of the six handles, as shown in Figure 1.6. In previous editions, there was only one special margin-changing handle; dragging any other handle scaled and stretched the *text* rather than the text field. In Flash 8, if you want to scale the text, you can use the Free Transform tool or the Properties panel's W (width) and H (height) fields.

FIGURE 1.6   **Drag any handle on a text field to modify the margin width in Flash 8.**

A block
of text

In addition to the previously mentioned fact that gradients can be applied to strokes, gradients also sport a new overflow setting (accessible in the Color Mixer panel). An

Overflow setting of Extend makes your gradient fade off infinitely; a setting of Repeat lets the gradient fade from the beginning to the end and then repeat and fade from the beginning to the end; a setting of Reflect fades the gradient from the beginning to the end, fades it back up to the beginning, and continues to fade it up and down. Another change to the way gradients work in Flash 8 is that radial gradients support a focal point, which means you can create oblong off-center radial gradients.

Some of the new Flash 8 features appear subtle or esoteric—and they are. Although the 9-slice feature can be hard to see initially, it's quite powerful. When you select the Enable Guides for 9-slice Scaling option in a movie clip's Symbol Properties dialog box (shown in Figure 1.7), you are given four special guides that make a tic-tac-toe pattern on the clip's contents. (The guides are editable only while you're editing the symbol from the Library— that is, not by double-clicking an instance on the stage.)

The contents of your clip in the four outer squares don't get scaled when the clip is scaled. The midsections stretch as needed but not the corners. This means you can use a single symbol scaled to multiple sizes and dimensions, but the corners won't stretch or appear distorted. You can see the difference between shapes scaled in various ways with 9-slice scaling in Figure 1.8. Notice how the word close doesn't appear stretched even though the clip's width and height vary.

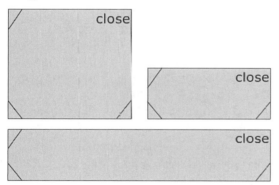

FIGURE 1.8 The same symbol scaled to different dimensions, yet the corners don't scale.

Flash Player

Interestingly, it took a separate team about the same size as the team that built Flash 8 Professional just to build the new Flash player! Flash (the authoring tool) just creates .swf files, but the Flash player has to render those .swf files—plus work with all kinds of browsers on different operating systems. And it does all this with a file size under 1MB. My point is that the Flash player makes many of the new features possible. For example, Flash player 8 now lets you load .png or .gif files. You don't even need to author your application in Flash 8 to take advantage of this feature, but your users will need the Flash player 8 to properly load the content of your files.

This also means that, if you want to employ one of the new Flash 8 features, your users must have the Flash player 8 plug-in

📌 NOTE

One drawback of the Enable Guides for 9-slice Scaling option is that it doesn't work when your clip contains nested clips. Everything inside the movie clip on which you want 9-slice scaling to work must be plain shapes (not clip instances).

installed. One nice new feature when planning to deliver to an earlier version of the Flash Player is that you're given feedback (as to which features are not available) while authoring. Say you select File, Publish Settings; click the Flash tab; and pick an older target Flash player version (such as Flash player 7). In that case, any newer Flash 8 features that don't work in the older Flash player version you selected are grayed out. In fact, if, after you select an older Flash player, you attempt to access a grayed-out, off-limits feature such as 9-slice, you are presented with a dialog box and the option to revisit your Publish Settings (as shown in Figure 1.9).

FIGURE 1.9   Flash informs you when a feature is off-limits to the Flash player you're targeting.

Although you, the developer, undoubtedly want to require your users to upgrade to Flash player 8 so you can use all the cool new features, your boss, client, or customers might not be so eager to upgrade their browser plug-ins to Flash player 8. On one hand, I understand this reality. It's going to be a matter of time before Flash player 8 is an accepted minimum requirement for websites. However, it's also important that you educate your boss, client, or customers.

Two ways to face the prospect of forcing a plug-in upgrade on your users are to look at which new features you want (or need) and to look at the upgrade experience the users will have to endure. Every Flash version has some killer feature that—for the right project—makes an upgrade requirement worthwhile. I'd imagine the video quality or alpha channels will be enough to convince many users to make the leap to Flash player 8. Only you can answer whether a new feature is profound enough or saves you enough time in production to require Flash 8—but there's a lot of new stuff that could easily tip the scale.

The upgrade process to Flash player 8 has been *vastly* improved through what's called Express Install. If your user has Flash player 6.0r65 or later, he already has an integrated feature you can trigger to install Flash player 8 inline. That is, the user doesn't have to download something, quit the browser, run an installer, and so on. He simply clicks Yes in a security dialog box that appears right inside the Flash application (shown in Figure 1.10); a new browser window opens with your content, and Flash player 8 has been installed!

FIGURE 1.10   The inline Express Install dialog box appears inside your Flash application.

Express Install is not the only upgrade approach and has its drawbacks, such as needing to first check which version the user has and creating a Flash player 6 .swf to perform the Express Install. Just read the 25-page document and associated sample files in the Flash Deployment Kit (www.macromedia.com/go/fp_detectionkit), and you'll learn all the available options. I predict that this Express Install feature, along with the killer features such as filters and video, will greatly accelerate the adoption rate for Flash 8 (historically taking 12 months for a new player version to reach 80% of all Internet users).

> **📌 NOTE**
>
> The express install is simply the most advanced option available because it performs the install from within the older Flash player. Traditional ways of upgrading users still exist. For example, the default .html generated when you publish automatically presents the user with a traditional Active X install dialog box in Internet Explorer or the Missing Plug-ins button in Netscape and Firefox.

Flash Professional 8 and Flash Basic 8

I suppose this is a bit of a sour way to end an otherwise exciting section about what's possible with Flash 8, but I have to explain the differences between the two versions of the Flash 8 product. Unlike the confusing and subtle differences between Flash MX 2004 and Flash MX 2004 Professional, the split between Flash Professional 8 and Flash Basic 8 is profound. In a nutshell, the only reason to purchase Flash Basic is if you need supplemental copies for machines dedicated for some sort of Flash assembly line. Macromedia says Basic is for the "occasional user," which is accurate if you don't plan on using most of the new Flash 8 features, including using the

Flash interface to control filters or blends, producing videos that use the new On2 VP6 codec, and using advanced FlashType text settings—none of which are fully supported in Flash Basic.

Granted, Flash Basic is almost half the price of Flash Professional. But it's not even that easy to purchase it. You can't purchase Basic as part of Macromedia Studio 8 (the bundle that also includes Dreamweaver, Fireworks, and Contribute). And all upgrades from any older version of Flash lead to Flash Professional. Ultimately, the only good feature in Flash Basic is the fact there's an integrated upgrade system to turn your version of Basic into Flash Professional 8.

ActionScript Additions

ActionScript hasn't gotten the same facelift it did when AS2.0 was introduced in Flash MX2004. Nevertheless, there are some pretty major additions to the ActionScript feature list—too many, in fact, to list them all here. However, I'll list the major new features in the following sections because most appear in later chapters (even if the appearance is often hidden away in the support files).

A Programming Primer

Because the section that follows this section covers new ActionScript features, you'll find it peppered with terms such as *variables*, *instances*, and *properties*. If this kind of information is familiar to you, feel free to skip ahead to the next section (on the flash.filters package). If such terms *are* new to you, you'll find additional definitions for such terms in the Glossary (as well as in

Chapter 2). However, instead of having you keep one thumb in the Glossary while you read this chapter, here's a narrative definition of the terms that appear throughout the rest of this chapter and the book. Let me stress two things before I start: First, if you find this material basic, don't worry, I promise you'll get plenty of opportunities to adapt the projects in this book and flex your programming skills. (I won't treat anyone like a baby.) If, on the other hand, this material is totally new to you, this explanation will only provide an introduction to the terms I use in this book. I don't suspect this quick lesson will turn you into a hardcore programmer, but at least you can follow along when I explain the code behind the scenes of each project. You don't *have* to add any custom programming to build the projects, but you can. And for me to explain what's going on, I have to use a programmer's vocabulary.

It's easiest to start with the most common object type, movie clips, because they have a visual representation on stage. A movie clip symbol on stage is called an *instance*. You can give each instance on stage a unique instance name by using the Properties panel. The instance name is used in your ActionScript code to refer to the clip—or, more technically, to *address* the clip. The reason you don't use the symbol name (from the master Movie Clip symbol in the Library) is because you might have multiple instances of that same symbol on stage and you want to address each one individually. Why would you want to address a clip? Usually to change one of its *properties* such as its position on stage (either its _x property or _y property, although there are many other properties and they don't always have an

underscore in their names). Movie clip instances are the easiest type of object to understand because you can see them. But there are also instances of the Sound and Date classes—just to name two.

> **📌 NOTE**
>
> I capitalized Sound and Date because, when you create an instance of these object types, you must use the exact, case-sensitive spelling.

Think of this analogy: People have properties (such as hair color, weight, and age) and cars have properties (such as horsepower, make, and model). Interestingly, sometimes two different object *types* share the same property. Cars and humans both have a weight property. Similarly, movie clip instances and button instances both have a width property. Often, however, the available properties depend on the type of object you're working with. Sound instances have a duration property, but movie clip instances don't.

The good news is that the code you write to address clips and their properties uses the same form (or *syntax*) in every case regardless of the object type. Namely, the syntax to refer to an instance's property always looks like this: myInstance.myProperty (or "object dot property"). I use the prefix my to indicate something I made up so you don't think the terms myInstance or myProperty are built in to ActionScript. Note that sometimes you want to *set* a property (perhaps set a clip instance's _rotation property to make it spin); other times you'll just need to *get* a property's value to use within a larger *statement*. (A statement is a complete

instruction—basically one line of code.)
Check out this example:

```
myClip._x = otherClip._x
```

When Flash encounters this line of code, it interprets the code and *executes* the instructions (meaning it does what the code says to do). In this example, the instance called myClip gets its _x property set to a value equal to the _x property of another instance called otherClip. (Anytime you see a single equals sign, it's an *assignment* meaning "is now equal to," as in "myClip's _x is now equal to otherClip's _x".) Notice that you're setting the _x property of myClip but only getting the property of otherClip.

Another important concept is *methods*. Methods are like processes or procedures applied to a single instance. You can also think of methods as the capabilities a particular object type supports. Back to the human analogy: walk, talk, and comb your hair are all methods—they're all things an instance of a human being is capable of doing. Methods you can apply to movie clip instances include play(), stop(), and gotoAndPlay(). I like to compare properties to methods because their syntaxes are nearly identical. It's always "object dot method," as in myClip.play(). An easy way to distinguish methods is that they always have parentheses. Some methods accept *parameters* (also called *arguments*) that provide needed additional details. For example, when you say myClip.gotoAndPlay(1), 1 is a parameter indicating which frame you want to go to.

Events are things that happen while a Flash movie plays. The most intuitive event types are things the user does, such as clicks, drags,

or presses a key. Naturally, there are all kinds of events, and like properties and methods, events vary depending on the object type. For example, Sound instances *trigger* or *fire* events when the event onSoundComplete is encountered (that is, when the sound ends). A button instance has an onPress event (but no onSoundComplete event). Just as trees can fall in the woods without anyone to hear them, events can fire in Flash and—unless your code is *listening* for that event—they go unnoticed. You have to write code to *trap* (or listen for) an event and define exactly how you want to *handle* that event. What's a little freaky is that events are really properties to which you assign a value. Just as you might say myClip._x = 100 (to make the clip appear at the x position of 100), you could say myClip.onEnterFrame = myAnimationFunction—that says the myClip's onEnterFrame event (which fires every 1/12 of a second if your frame rate is 12 fps) is now equal to something called myAnimationFunction. In both cases, a property (_x or onEnterFrame) is assigned a value. In this case, the value of the _x property is assigned a value in the *data type* Number. If you were to assign the label property for a Button component, you would want to use a value of the data type String. The value you assign to an event is of the type Function.

You can create variables as a way to store data for later use. For example, you could assign a variable's value with this code: myName = "Phillip" (which means the variable named myName is now equal to the string "Phillip"). You can change the value of a variable by simply reassigning a value, but at any one instant, a variable has a single value. You can store any data type in your variable, but you'll often want to *type* your variables—that is, to define the variable with the data type it is allowed to contain. Here is an example of typing the myName variable as a String data type:

```
var myName:String = "Phillip";
```

The reason you type a variable is simply so that Flash will give you a warning when you publish if you write code that tries to assign a value that doesn't match the data type you declared. That way, Flash helps you uncover mistakes in your code.

> **NOTE**
>
> In future versions of the Flash player, typing your variables will make your projects perform much faster.

Finally, terms such as *object* and *class* are thrown around a lot, but they're actually quite simple. I've been talking about movie clip instances because they're so common, but they're actually instances of the *class* MovieClip. You could say that their object type is MovieClip. Instances of the class MovieClip are easy to understand because you make an instance by simply dragging the symbol from the Library onto the stage. For most other object types, you must formally *instantiate* them (as in "make an instance of"). You always instantiate an instance of a class by using this syntax:

```
myInstance = new MyClass()
```

You replace MyClass with the class you're instantiating. (By convention, all class names begin with an uppercase character.)

Sometimes the class you instantiate is part of Flash and other times the definition for its behavior resides in a class file (MyClass.as, for example). For instance, I created an EventChannel class (in a file named EventChannel.as) for Chapter 3. You create an instance by using the following syntax:

```
myECInstance = new EventChannel();
```

After you have an instance of a class stored in a variable, you can do anything you want with that instance. That is, the class will probably expose public methods, which are methods you're allowed to access and trigger. Just as you can say myMovieClip.play(), you can also say myECInstance. startMonitoring() because I defined a public method called startMonitoring(). (Exactly what happens when that method gets triggered depends on what the programmer designed the class to do.) I should note that *private* methods can be triggered only from within the class itself; they are like internal utilities to help the class do its work.

Many times, you need to reference a class's complete path, as in this example:

```
myInstance = new
foldername.subfolder.MyClass()
```

I'll discuss class paths in Chapter 2, but just realize that there may be a MyClass class in the previous path shown and another—completely different—version of the same name in another path. There's no conflict because the code doesn't refer to MyClass but rather to foldername.subfolder.MyClass. Think how we have a president (like the president of the United States), but you can also have the Portland Cactus Collectors President—and they reference different positions. A class path is like a qualifier.

With your ActionScript primer out of the way, we will move onto the key new ActionScript features in Flash 8.

The flash.filters Package

Filters can be applied using the Filters panel (while authoring) or using ActionScript code. This enables you to write *scripts* that modify a filter's effect at runtime. For example, you could make some text get blurrier as the user moves the mouse away and sharper as the mouse moves closer. Writing the code to apply a filter at runtime is a two-step process. First, you create a filter instance and store it in a variable. Second, you apply the filter to a movie clip instance through its filters *property*. If you want to change the filter applied to a clip, you simply modify the filter or create another filter with different properties and (in either case) overwrite the clip's filters property. Here's a simple example in which we apply a blur filter to a movie clip instance named myClip:

```
myFilter = new flash.filters.BlurFilter();

myClip.filters = [ myFilter ];
```

Notice that the filters property is assigned an *array* that contains just one item (myFilter). By putting more filters in the array you can apply more than one filter. In addition, you can set various parameters when you first call the BlurFilter() function to affect how much of a blur you want. For example, this code applies a BlurFilter with a factor of 50 to a clip instance named myClip when the user clicks the stage; it then applies a different filter, with a factor of 5, when the user lets go:

```
onMouseDown = function(){
  var veryBlurry =
  new flash.filters.BlurFilter(50,50);
  myClip.filters = [ veryBlurry ];
}
onMouseUp = function(){
  var lessBlurry =
  new flash.filters.BlurFilter(5,5);
  myClip.filters = [ lessBlurry ];
}
```

The flash.filters package lets you create any kind of filter the Filters panel can create, but you do it with ActionScript so it can respond to any event, such as the user's mouse movement. One other thing to note is that movie clip instances in Flash 8 have a filters property.

In addition to ActionScript equivalents to all the filters in the Filters panel, ActionScript offers three other classes (in the flash.filters package) for even more advanced effects—namely, ColorMatrixFilter, DisplacementMapFilter, and ConvolutionFilter. You'll learn more about these in Chapter 9, "Creating Special Effects." They're identical to the flash.filters package in that you still apply them to the filters property, but the way in which you create them is much more involved.

The flash.display.BitmapData Class

There's just one class in the `flash.display` package, and it's a powerful one. Many people believe the BitmapData class is the biggest improvement in Flash 8. Basically, it's a way to store *raster images*, which are really just grids of pixels, into variables. You can create a bitmap image from scratch (for example, you can create a grid of 10 × 10 white pixels); you can load a bitmap from an image in your library (effectively copying the pixels from an imported image); or you can copy pixels from an area or a clip on stage. After the bitmap data is stored in a variable, you can modify it—for example, you can change its contrast or shape—and then display it on stage. This key step (necessary to *see* a BitmapData instance) is the MovieClip class' `attachBitmap()` method. This method works just like `attachMovie()`, as you can see in the following example:

```
myClip.attachBitmap(myBitmap, 0);
```

For some reason, I often forget that second parameter (the level number), but this parameter works the same way as how `attachMovie()` places a clip into a level number. Every object, `BitmapData` or `MovieClip`, that you create dynamically is placed into its own *level* within another movie clip—even if that movie clip is the main Timeline. The higher level numbers make the object appear above objects in lower-numbered levels. For the preceding code to work, you'd have to have previously created the `myBitmap` instance. Chapter 2 shows a simple example using the `BitmapData` class.

I use the `BitmapData` class constantly to effectively take a snapshot of part of the screen. For example, if I need to fade out one image while another image fades in, I simply make a `BitmapData` instance by copying the pixels from the outgoing image. Then I attach that `BitmapData` copy to a new clip (that I place on top of the old clip) and then load a new image into the old clip. When the new image is fully loaded, I can fade out the clip with the `BitmapData` instance. This is the same technique used in Chapter 4, "Creating a Portfolio."

The flash.geom Package

On the surface, you might think the classes in the `flash.geom` package would be attractive only to a true geometry nerd. And, in fact, when you look at `flash.geom.Point` and `flash.geom.Rectangle`, they're pretty much as you might expect: They offer methods for such things as calculating the distance between two points or determining the union between two rectangles. First, doing those sorts of operations in the past was *much* harder—so this package actually makes things easier. In the past, for example, calculating the distance between two clips (say, instances mc1 and mc2) required you to remember the Pythagorean Theorem (you know, a squared plus b squared equals c squared—except to solve for c you need to take the square root) and this not-so-lucid code:

```
a = mc1._x - mc2._x;
b = mc1._y - mc2._y;
cSquared = (a * a) + (b * b);
c = Math.sqrt( cSquared );
trace("distance is " + c);
```

Using the new flash.geom.Point class makes it much clearer, I believe:

```
a = new flash.geom.Point(mc1._x, mc1._y);
b = new flash.geom.Point(mc2._x, mc2._y);
c = flash.geom.Point.distance(a, b);
trace("distance is " + c);
```

In addition to helping you solve geometry problems, you'll also end up using the classes in the flash.geom package because several other classes require that you pass parameters with the data type Point or Rectangle. In fact, every project in this book uses this package!

Like the new filters property for movie clip instances, movie clips have new properties related to the flash.geom package. For example, there's a new scrollRect property you can set equal to a Rectangle instance. This is like a *mask* because it reveals a rectangular portion of the clip, but the scrollRect property is more like panning (or

scrolling) a camera's view of an object. For example, this code makes it appear as though the myClip instance's contents are shifting to the left when in fact it's just the scrollRect that is moving to the right:

```
var panX Number = 0;
onEnterFrame = function (){
  panX++
  myClip scrollRect =
  new flash.geom.Rectangle(panX,
                           0,
                           200,
                           200);
}
```

Another movie clip property related to the flash.geom package is transform. This property actually contains several other properties, but I'll start with just transform.matrix. The transform.matrix property is a way to store all of a clip's properties (such as _x, _y, and _xscale) in a single array (really, a *matrix* of six numbers). In fact, you never have to use _x or _y again if you don't want—all you have to do is modify the clip's transform.matrix property. The transform.matrix can get very complicated.

I have a simple and practical example in case you think matrixes are necessarily more complex than properties such as _x and _y. Suppose you want to set all the properties of one clip (instance name oneClip) to match another clip (with an instance name otherClip). The "old" way would look like this:

```
oneClip._x = otherClip._x;
oneClip._y = otherClip._y;
oneClip._xscale = otherClip._xscale;
oneClip._yscale = otherClip._yscale;
//and so on ad infinitum
```

The first line of code says, "the _x of the oneClip instance is now equal to the _x property of the otherClip instance." Then it continues for every property. Not only is that wordy, but there's no property for skew or tint.

Check out the "new" way that uses only one line:

```
oneClip.transform.matrix =
otherClip.transform.matrix;
```

Because the transform.matrix property only reflects a clip's scaling, rotation, and position (called the *translation* on a clip), you must use the transform.colorTransform property to grab any tinting applied to the otherClip instance. You could add this line to copy the tint as well:

```
oneClip.transform.colorTransform =
otherClip2.transform.colorTransform;
```

Like I said, classes from the flash.geom package (and, perhaps more to the point, movie clip properties such as scrollRect and transform) appear in most of the projects in this book. After you grasp the core concepts of using these classes in your ActionScript programming, you'll find that they will drastically simplify your ActionScript code.

The flash.external.ExternalInterface Class

This class provides an easy way for Flash to trigger JavaScript code (contained in the HTML web page that is hosting your .swf file) or for JavaScript code to trigger ActionScript code in your .swf file. Although you could send messages between JavaScript and ActionScript in the past, doing so wasn't very consistent and always required that the values being passed back and forth be of the String data type. Now you can pass any data type, such as an Array or a Number. In addition, calls are synchronous now, meaning you can call a remote method and get an immediate response.

Going from Flash ActionScript code to JavaScript code is really simple: Just use the call() method and pass the function name you want to trigger as a string followed by any parameters, which, incidentally, don't have to be strings. Listing 1.1 shows the basic form of the call() method, and Listing 1.2 shows specifically how to trigger JavaScript's built-in alert() method.

LISTING 1.1 **Triggering JavaScript from Inside Flash**

```
flash.external.ExternalInterface.call("methodName","parameter");
```

LISTING 1.2 **Triggering JavaScript's alert() Method from Inside Flash**

```
flash.external.ExternalInterface.call("alert", "hello");
```

In Chapter 6, "Saving and Evaluating Quiz Results," you'll see the ExternalInterface class used as a way for a .swf file to ask JavaScript to *parse* a query string in the HTML.

Going from JavaScript to Flash ActionScript isn't much more difficult, but because we don't do it in any projects in this book, it's worth detailing here. Letting JavaScript talk to Flash involves two steps: Make the call from inside JavaScript and, from inside your Flash file, identify the methods you want to expose to JavaScript. Here's how: In the HTML file, you must include the code in Listing 1.3.

Line 8 is the main call to Flash. It triggers a homemade function called exposedFunction() and passes an array called myArray. The thisMovie() method gets a reference to the Flash object. You can see in lines 12–17 that the exact way Internet

Explorer gets a reference to the Flash object (line 13) is different from how it is for Netscape or Firefox (line 16). This code assumes just two items not shown. First, the object and embed tags for your Flash movie need to contain id='example" and name="example", respectively, because that's the object name being referenced in line 8. (Those tags are added automatically if you publish a file called example.swf.) In addition, somewhere in the HTML file, you need to trigger the doit() function. For example:

```
<form>
  <input type="button" onclick="doit()"
              value="doit" />
</form>
```

The Flash ActionScript side of this example is shown in Listing 1.4.

LISTING 1.3 JavaScript Triggering a Function Inside Flash		

```
1   <script>
2   function doit() {
3     var myArray = new Array();
4     myArray.push("this");
5     myArray.push("that");
6     myArray.push("the other");
7
8     thisMovie("example").exposedFunction(myArray);
9   }
10
11  function thisMovie(movieName) {
12    if (navigator.appName.indexOf("Microsoft") != -1) {
13      return window[movieName]
14    }
15    else {
16      return document[movieName]
17    }
18  }
19  </script>
```

LISTING 1.4   How Flash Exposes a Function for JavaScript to Trigger

```
function exposedFunction(data:Array){
    var total = data.length;
    results_txt.text = "got an array with " +total + " items";
}

var methodName:String = "exposedFunction";
var methodReference:Function = exposedFunction;
flash.external.ExternalInterface.addCallback(methodName,
                                             null,
                                             methodReference);
```

The exposedFunction() method is plain old Flash code. The last three lines of code are the steps you need to take to grant access to exposedFunction(). That is, JavaScript can't just reach in and trigger Flash code without the formal step of using the addCallback() method.

The ExternalInterface class is a huge step forward for any project that needs to pass data back and forth to a hosted environment. This time I said *hosted environment* instead of *JavaScript* to draw attention to the fact that ExternalInterface is not limited to working only with JavaScript. As you'll see in Chapter 8, "Creating a CD-ROM Front End," there are third-party projector-making tools, and these can benefit from the ExternalInterface class.

The flash.net Package

The flash.net package lets you present a standard file open dialog box that viewers can use to browse to and select a file they want to upload. Then your code can upload that file. This process is secure for the user because the Flash player prevents the .swf file

(that is, your code) from seeing the file's full path. A user won't want to reveal her computer's folder structure to your application because that information could get sent back up to your server. Because of this security feature, you can't ask the user to select a file, such as an .mp3, and then immediately play that music file for her. (You could upload it and then play it, but that's totally different and a very slow prospect considering how large files can be.)

When the user points to a file, she's granting you access to copy that onto your server.

There's also a download() method that shows the user a save as dialog box to allow her to download files from your server to her hard drive.

Integrating this sort of file upload/download functionality into a Flash project in the past required complex and, ultimately, clunky use of multiple HTML windows. Now you can do it all from inside a Flash application. In fact, you will do exactly that in Chapter 10, "Building a Photo Share Application," where you make a photo-sharing application.

Here's a tiny addition that's not documented and doesn't really fit into any of the chapters in this book—but it's quite useful and officially supported. The `setTimeout()` and `clearTimeout()` methods are just like the existing `setInterval()` and `clearInterval()` methods, but `setTimeout()` fires only once. `setInterval()` lets you trigger the same code repeatedly on a specified time interval—say, every 2 seconds. You can use it to animate something across the screen. Although that's great for something that continues indefinitely, it's a bit of a chore to keep track of all your intervals and clear them using `clearInterval()`—but that's just the way it works. For the situations when you want something to happen, but not right away, and you want it to happen only once, you can use the new `setTimeout()` function. For example, if you want a display that reads `time's up` to appear after 10 seconds, you can use this code:

```
clip._visible = false;
setTimeout(function(){
        clip._visible = true;
        }, 10000);
```

The last parameter is in milliseconds.

Final Thoughts

I'm sorry if this chapter sounded like a sales job, but I actually restrained myself. The rest of the book is more matter of fact. The project-based chapters are all focused on specific tasks. Throughout the project chapters, I point out potential pitfalls and an occasional opinion based on my experiences. But in this chapter, my purpose was to get you psyched for the sorts of stuff you can do with Flash 8.

CHAPTER 2: Producing a Flash Project

There are three general things you do in Flash: create graphics, animate in the timeline, and add programming (which, in addition to making your project behave differently based on data or user input, can in turn produce graphics and animations). This chapter focuses on the programming. However, I want you to see how the graphics, animations, and programming elements are all connected. The most important question answered in this chapter is, "Where do I put stuff to make it behave the way I want?"

I hope that most of the basic Flash information covered in this chapter is familiar to you. But, even if it seems too straightforward, please read it anyway because I make many statements about what I believe are best practices. My recommendations should help you avoid frustration. It's alright if you don't agree with my preferences, but at least hear where I'm coming from. Everything is based on my experience teaching Flash to many students over the years. Besides, the content here is very concise.

In the last section of this chapter, you'll get a good sense of exactly how you'll be creating the projects that follow in the remaining chapters. Although each project chapter is different, they all draw from a few general frameworks. I'm sure that after you build a few projects, you'll begin to see similarities; this chapter introduces everything more formally.

You can download the source and starter files from the accompanying CD-ROM.

Flash's File Structure

Flash is unlike many document-creation tools in that you don't have a "document" (what the user sees) and the "tools" required to create or modify the document. It's fair to say Flash's *stage* is the document and the various panels (all accessible from the Windows menu) are the creation tools. But there's so much more when you consider such facts as these: The timeline can have multiple frames; movie clips have their own timelines and can contain nested movie clips; and the scripts you write can cause the movie to jump around the different frames in a timeline in a nonlinear fashion, as well as change the appearance of any movie clip. Let's discuss some of the big concepts and the pitfalls to avoid.

> **Scripting, Programming, Coding**
>
> **All three of these terms refer to the same thing. All you're doing is writing instructions you want Flash to follow. The instructions you write when you program for Flash must be very specific and use the ActionScript language.**

Timeline Animation

Some programmers have a disdain for the timeline. However, it's important to realize that animation can be a powerful way to communicate an idea or suggest a theme.

Flash's timeline automatically plays from frame 1 through to the last frame you create. Naturally, you can write a *script* to `stop()` on any frame you want or choose to create everything in just a single frame. Compare the timeline to a flip book that has a different picture on each page; the frames in the timeline are like the various pages in the flip book. However, in Flash, only frames that are *keyframes* display something new. The timeline in Figure 2.1 shows a keyframe in frame 1 followed by additional *frames*. Something new such as a background image appears on the first keyframe, but then nothing changes in that layer for the following 10 frames.

FIGURE 2.1 This timeline shows a keyframe (the circle) at the 1-second marker, followed by additional frames.

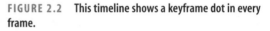

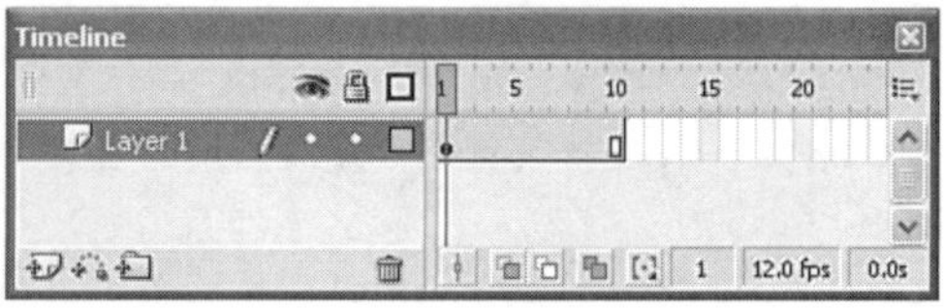

The timeline shown in Figure 2.2 has dots in every frame, meaning each frame is a keyframe. That would be the case if you drew a unique image on every frame using a traditional frame-by-frame animation technique. If the dot is filled in, it simply means something is present on the stage at that frame. Hollow dots mean that nothing is in the keyframe, as might be the case when you want to remove something from the screen (perhaps a blinking effect where every other frame is blank).

FIGURE 2.2 This timeline shows a keyframe dot in every frame.

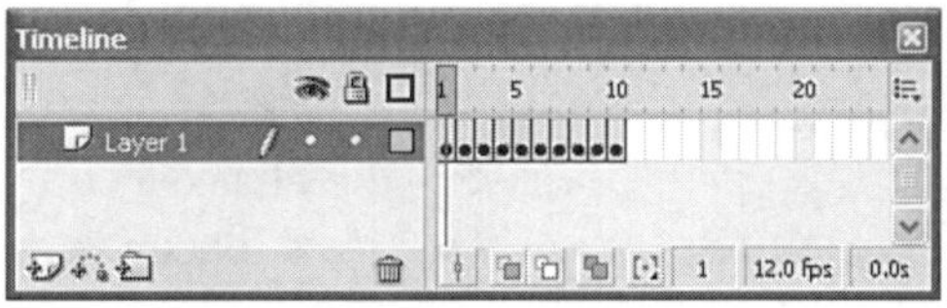

What you draw into each keyframe is up to you. But be sure to avoid adding a keyframe unless there's going to be something different or new in that frame. That is, if you want a title graphic to appear and then go away after a few seconds, you need one keyframe when it first appears followed by 36 frames (not keyframes). On frame 37, you can add another keyframe in which you delete the title, thus making the keyframe a blank—and therefore changed—frame.

I came up with 36 frames based on the default frame rate of 12 frames per second (fps). As a reference, conventional movies use 24 fps and television is approximately 30 fps. You can change the file's frame rate to make the animation appear to move faster or slower by selecting Modify, Document and changing the fps value there, but that's not the only way to make something appear to move faster or slower in Flash. If you want a ball to move across the screen more quickly, you can simply make the object move a bigger distance from frame to frame, thus making the trip across the screen take less time. Realize, too, that using a higher frame rate can mean more work if you're drawing something unique into each frame.

The flip book analogy is great, but you probably don't want to draw every keyframe yourself. For this, Flash has *tweening*. To tween, you put an object in one keyframe and then add a keyframe to a later frame (not the very next frame) that contains the object in a different location or physical state. Select the first frame and use the Properties panel to set the Tweening values. In the first keyframe, you tell Flash how to interpolate the in-be*tween* frames so your object ends up looking like the object in the ending keyframe. You draw two frames, and Flash tweens the difference.

There are two kinds of tweens: Motion and Shape. Motion tweens require you to have a *symbol instance* (usually a movie clip) in both the first and last keyframes. Flash can tween any property of that clip, including its position, scale, rotation, tint, and the new filter effects such as a drop shadow. Shape tweens require that you have no symbol instances (only shapes) in the two keyframes. Shape tweens can morph between any odd shapes you want, such as between a man and a werewolf. Given a choice, you should choose motion tweens over shape tweens because motion tweens are much simpler to manage and generally produce smaller files.

Tweening is nice because it can relieve you from the otherwise meticulous work of frame-by-frame animation. However, frame-by-frame animation is often the best option. Just a few strategically designed frames in your frame-by-frame animation can often communicate a feeling or message much better than a long, drawn-out tween the computer has created. A 1-second animation with 12 carefully created frames playing at 12 fps can look better than 36 frames played at 36 fps. Plus, your animation will appear much snappier if you use fewer frames.

Figure 2.3 shows a simple example in which the frame-by-frame version uses half as many frames as the motion tween.

FIGURE 2.3 Sometimes just a few frames in a frame-by-frame animation (bottom) is more effective than a long, drawn-out tween (top).

The example in Figure 2.3 might be an exaggeration, but my point is that drawing a few carefully crafted frames can be more effective than having Flash tween.

You probably already know that the Flash timeline supports the concept of *layers*.

Objects in higher layers appear in front of the objects in lower layers. In addition, special layer options are accessible from the Layer Properties dialog box shown in Figure 2.4. You can specify one of the following types of layers:

- **Normal layer**—Anything you draw in a Normal layer (the default) appears in your final movie as it appears while authoring.

- **Guide layer**—You can draw reference images that won't export with the movie.

- **Guided layer**—A motion tween follows a path drawn in a Guide layer.

- **Mask layer**—Objects serve to reveal what's in a lower layer that is set to the Masked layer type. If you wanted to create a round window port looking out on the ocean moving by, you'd draw a circle in a Mask layer.

- **Masked layer**—You draw the content you want to reveal only where the content of the parent Mask layer appears. For example, you could animate an image of the sea in a Masked layer as it's revealed through the circular window shape in the Mask layer.

To specify which type of layer you are working with, select Modify, Timeline, Layer Properties.

In addition to how layers stack images (and arguably more importantly), each layer contains a single animation track. So, if you want to make a motion tween with two things moving at the same time, you can use two layers. One layer's motion tween could

depict the first object and its change from the first keyframe to the last keyframe; the second layer would treat the second object the same way. When played together, the two layers would show the two objects moving in possibly different directions (such as two balls bouncing). To put one ball in front of the other, you'd simply change the order of the layers in the timeline.

FIGURE 2.4   Each layer has its own set of properties, as defined in the Layer Properties dialog box.

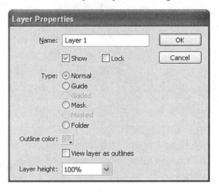

Movie Clip Hierarchy

After all this talk about the things you can do with multiple frames in the timeline, you might be surprised to discover that every project in this book uses just one frame! That's true because there are two ways, other than using multiple frames, to make something animate: You can use code to set a movie clip's properties such as _x and _y (the x and y coordinates to see it change position on stage), or you can use the timeline contained in every movie clip. Try this: Create a movie clip by drawing a shape; selecting it; and then selecting Modify, Convert to Symbol. Then click the Movie Clip option and click OK. In place of the shape you drew you'll have an instance of the clip you just created;

double-click it to edit its contents to see that it contains a timeline of its own.

Notice in Figure 2.5 that the Edit bar shows you are inside the movie clip symbol named Box. The content of this symbol is simply a drawn shape, the dark square in the lower-left corner (when a shape is selected, the Properties panel says Shape). The other objects on stage appear faded because, although you're inside the Box clip, you're editing it in the context of other objects on the stage. Alternatively, if you open the Library and select a symbol to edit, you won't see anything except that clip's contents.

What you must take away from this overview is that you must always know where you are in your movie. The Edit bar, shown in Figure 2.5, shows you where you are at all times. Because you can nest instances of other symbols inside a symbol, the hierarchy can get tricky; however, the Edit bar tracks the nesting of the symbols and helps you determine just where you are. The Edit bar helps you maintain your bearings when creating complex symbols such as a car with rotating wheels—you'd have a car symbol instance that animates across the screen, with its wheels also rotating. First draw a wheel with spokes; select it; and select Modify, Convert to Symbol. Then select the Movie Clip option, and click OK. Select the instance of the Wheel now on stage and select Modify, Convert to Symbol to nest the Wheel inside a new symbol; this time, though, call the movie clip Animating Wheel. Go inside the instance of Animating Wheel by double-clicking it, where you'll find an instance of Wheel. While inside Animating Wheel, click

the *cell* in frame 20 (underneath the 20 in the timeline but inside your layer) and press F6 to insert a keyframe. Finally, select the first keyframe in Animating Wheel and use the Properties panel to select Motion from the Tween drop-down list. Also, select CW to make the Wheel instance rotate once between frames 1 and 20. Return to the main timeline and create another instance of the Animating Wheel symbol by copying the instance on stage or by dragging a new one from the Library panel. Now draw a car body around the two wheels, select everything, and press F8 to create another movie clip—this time called Car. You'll be able to use an instance of the Car symbol to make a motion tween in the main timeline, perhaps making the car move across the screen. When you publish it, not only will the car move, but its contained rotating wheels will also move.

Instances Versus Symbols

It's important to understand that, when you make one master symbol, you can create multiple instances of that symbol anywhere in the movie except inside the master symbol itself. The terms *symbol* and *instance* are *not* interchangeable. Equally important is the fact that a symbol always has a name that appears in the Library. Each instance of that symbol on stage can be given an instance name that certainly doesn't have to match the original symbol's name. Because you can have many instances of a particular master symbol, the instance names let you address each instance independently using ActionScript. So, you don't say, "set the height of the box symbol to 100," but rather you say, "set the height of the instance of the box symbol with the instance name *littleBox* to 100." (The actual code is easier to read: littleBox._height = 100.)

FIGURE 2.5 The Edit bar is
the best indication that
you're inside the Box symbol,
editing its contents.

Symbol name   Edit bar

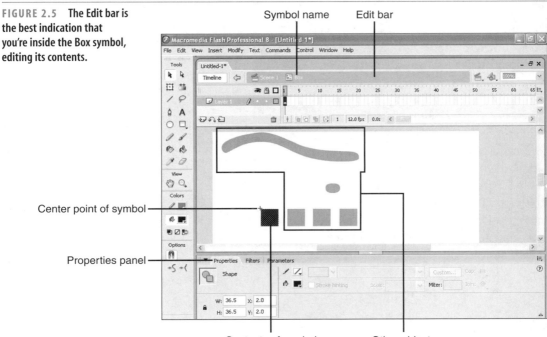

Center point of symbol

Properties panel

Contents of symbol
(selected shape)

Other objects
(not in this symbol)

Selecting

Here are just a few pointers on how to select objects. You can conveniently select all the objects on stage in a particular keyframe by simply clicking that keyframe on the timeline. Realize, though, that if you then select Cut or Delete, you'll remove the items *on stage* but won't remove the keyframe. If you click a layer's name, you select all the frames in that layer. If, while you have multiple frames selected, you press F6 or F7, you convert all the selected frames to keyframes or blank keyframes, respectively. Often you'll want to convert just one frame to a keyframe; in that case, you simply click a single *cell* in the timeline.

To remove a keyframe, it's easiest to right-click the cell in the timeline and select Remove Frames from the context menu, as

shown in Figure 2.6. Alternatively, you can select Edit, Timeline; Insert, Timeline; or Modify, Timeline—all of which demonstrate why the right-click approach is easiest.

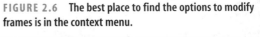

FIGURE 2.6 The best place to find the options to modify frames is in the context menu.

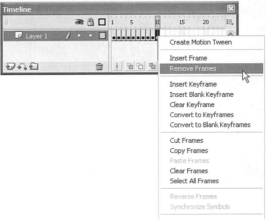

You can deselect an object by either clicking on the stage or pressing the Esc key. I recommend getting into the habit of pressing V to switch to the Selection tool (not the white Subselection tool). It's common to think you're about to select an object when, in fact, you have a drawing tool selected and you begin drawing on stage again.

You can select objects by clicking them. In fact, you can click a keyframe to select everything on stage in that frame. You double-click a shape to select both the fill and the stroke of a shape. Double-clicking also lets you select all the connected segments in an outline. You can always hold down the Shift key and click repeatedly to select multiple objects. The Marquee technique is also powerful; just use the Selection tool, click where no objects are present, and drag to encircle all the objects you want to select.

A great help is the way the mouse pointer's icon always tells you what will happen if you click. Check out Figure 2.7 to see a variety of the mouse pointer shapes that appear depending on what you're working on.

FIGURE 2.7   Here are just a few of the mouse pointer icons that communicate what will happen when you click.

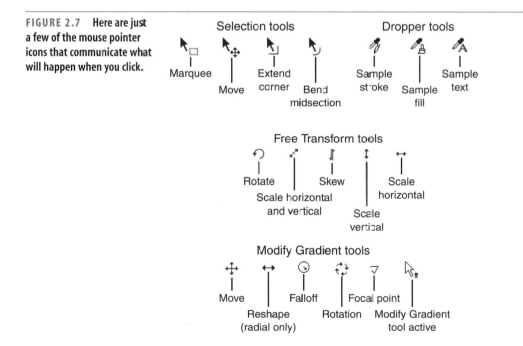

Finally, I should note that Flash 8 has a new option called Object Drawing. It's an alternative to the default Merge Drawing mode. You can turn on Object Drawing from the Options area in the Tools panel when a drawing tool is active, and you can toggle between Object and Merge drawing by pressing J. The difference between these two modes is that shapes which overlap in Merge mode, merge. That is, you can't have two shapes occupying the same space. You can actually use this behavior of one shape "eating away" another to your advantage. For example, you can quickly create a semicircle by drawing a circle and then drawing a vertical line through the shape. *Drawing Objects* are shapes created while in Object Drawing mode, are effectively grouped so that they don't eat away at each other, and can be stacked within a single timeline layer. You can't nest Drawing Objects within Drawing Objects—they're only one hierarchy deep. Even when you're working with only one level, you should pay attention to the Edit bar, just as you do when editing the contents of a movie clip (see Figure 2.8).

Neither drawing mode is better; you just need to know what's going on while you're drawing. By the way, you can turn a selected shape into a Drawing Object by selecting Modify, Combine Objects, Union.

Modular Delivery

A Flash project usually involves the creation of more than one file. I'm not talking simply about the fact that you'll always publish your .fla source file to create a .swf file and then post it on the Web along with a .html file to host the .swf file. Rather, there are several ways to modularize your project, and you might end up with multiple .swf files, external image files (.jpg, .gif, or .png), sound files (.mp3), Flash video files (.flv), and text data files (.xml).

FIGURE 2.8 **When you double-click a Drawing Object, the Edit bar indicates you're inside the object, in the same way as when you enter a movie clip.**

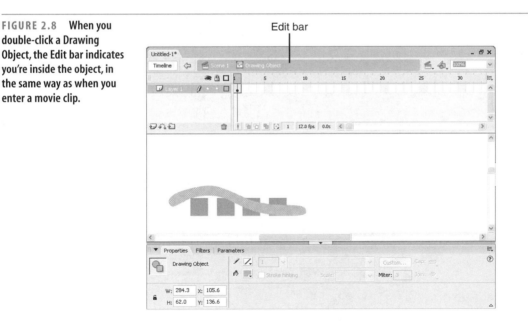

There are several reasons to break your project up into multiple files. First, modularizing lets you more easily work on smaller segments of a project. A single, complex, monolithic .fla file can quickly become difficult to manage. Also, if there's just one source file, you can't let team members work on different sections independently.

Another reason to modularize a project is so you can control when typically heavy media will download. For example, if you have 100 photographs, you can download only the images the user requests when he requests them. Similarly, by keeping media files external to your Flash file and in their native file formats (such as .jpg or .mp3), you can easily update the media files by replacing single files with new versions with the same names. With this organization approach, your script might simply read, "load the file named music.mp3"—and you change the MP3 file that Flash uses by simply renaming any MP3 file to music.mp3.

> **📌 NOTE**
>
> All these modular behaviors occur at *runtime*, and not while you're editing the .fla file. If you want to see how your .fla file makes use of the external media files as you're developing, select Control, Test Movie or Publish to see the media load.

The projects in this book almost always rely on multiple .swf files that are loaded using the loadMovie() method (actually, we'll use the MovieLoader helper class that's part of Flash). There are several tricky parts to designing a system that loads .swf files—or any media type, actually. First, every function in Flash that can load external content is *asynchronous*. That means one line of code makes the initial request to begin downloading, but Flash doesn't wait until it's complete; it keeps playing. Even if it could, you wouldn't want Flash to load external files *synchronously* because Flash would have to freeze while a potentially long download completes. The reason asynchronous functions are tricky is that you have to write two pieces of code: the code that waits until the media is downloaded and the code that makes the request.

In the case of .flv videos and .mp3 audio, Flash can begin playing the first part while the remainder downloads. Provided that the last bits of the file arrive by the time the playhead reaches the end of the file, everything works great. This is called a *progressive download*, and inaccurately called *streaming* by many people—true streaming involves a server that can send bits from any portion of the video. For example, if a user wants to jump to the middle of the video, a streaming server begins to send just those bits. With progressive downloading, which works on any standard HTTP web server, the bits can only download starting at the beginning of the video and continuing progressively to the end.

When loading .swf files or text data files, you must wait until they're fully loaded before you can do things such as jump to a particular frame in the .swf or parse the text data in, say, a .xml file.

Waiting for data to fully load is difficult because the ActionScript code to load data runs asynchronously, meaning the rest of your code continues to execute instead of waiting for the data to load. So, you can't just say "load the data" and then on the next line of code say "okay, take that data and proceed." As much as possible, I've insulated you from asynchronous code by handling that work in support files instead of the files you'll be creating. However, you *do* have to work within the reality of asynchronous operations. For this, you'll have to set up *event listeners*, which work the same way as the Flash V2 components (both of which are covered in more detail in Appendix B, "Components"). Here's what the code might look like:

```
myListener = new Object();
myListener.ready = function(){
 //we're ready, so you're free to continue
}
myInstance  = new MyClass();
myInstance.addEventListener ("ready",
                            myListener);
myInstance.loadMedia("myVideo.flv");
```

Basically, the first thing that happens is the last line, where the `loadMedia()` function is invoked and passed `myVideo.flv` for a parameter. All the code above that line sets up a listener that lies dormant, waiting to fire until the process has completed and the ready event is called. The code `myInstance = new MyClass()` creates an instance of the `MyClass` class and stores it in a variable called `myInstance`.

The code `addEventListener()` effectively says "I want to listen for when the `myInstance` variable broadcasts the ready event; when it does, send the notification to the `myListener` object." Incidentally, you'll often see an alternative version such as this:

```
myInstance.addEventListener("ready", this);
```

In this version, the `addEventListener()` method tells the `myInstance` to look for a function called `ready()`—even though it's specified as a string—in the same timeline (not in an object called `myListener` as in the previous example). That is, when the `myInstance` wants to broadcast the fact that it's ready, it triggers a function called `ready()` in every object that's listening, whether that's an object variable like `myListener` or simply a timeline like `this`. Continuing with the example of adding the listener called `this`, here's the code you'd have in your main timeline:

```
function ready(){
}
```

If you understand the concept behind listeners, that's great. If the concept is still hazy, check out the following, more conversational, steps:

1. Create a variable called `myListener` and set its value to a generic ActionScript object.

2. Add a property called `ready` and set its value to a function (that will act on any values received).

3. Create a variable called `myInstance` and set its value to a new instance of the `MyClass` class.

4. Before you tell the `myInstance` variable to actually do anything, you must subscribe to the ready event. Namely, you use `addEventListener()` to tell `myInstance` that the ready event should be broadcast to your `myListener` (which must have a `ready()` function to work).

5. Finally, tell the `myInstance` variable to do something by triggering its `loadMedia()` function. It doesn't matter how long it takes to finish that task. When the task is complete, the `myListener` variable's `ready()` function is triggered.

Although these steps provide just an example, the `ready` event would probably tell you that you can now tell the `myInstance` variable to `play()` or `stop()`. If you had just called `loadMedia()` and immediately followed that call with the `play()` function, the media file might not have been fully downloaded before the `play()` function tried to access the incomplete file.

ActionScript

You'll get a crash course in programming with ActionScript 2.0 (AS2) later in this chapter, but I want to cover exactly where you'll be putting your ActionScript code. While inside a `.fla` file, you always type ActionScript into the Actions panel. But, like any panel, the Actions panel reflects actions attached to the currently selected object. So,

if you select a keyframe, the Actions panel reflects the code on that frame. But you're also allowed to attach code to movie clip instances and button instances. I feel strongly that you should put code only in keyframes, so I'll only show code that you apply to a keyframe. That is, you'll read the instructions to "select the first keyframe, open the Actions panel, and type this code" repeatedly in the projects in this book. It's just too messy and complex to have to hunt down code you've attached to buttons and clips. Figure 2.9 shows how the Actions panel includes several indicators that you are indeed editing the code for a keyframe. Most notably, the Actions panel's tab has an icon that looks like a keyframe and the keyframe in the timeline has a letter *a* indicating that there's an action on it.

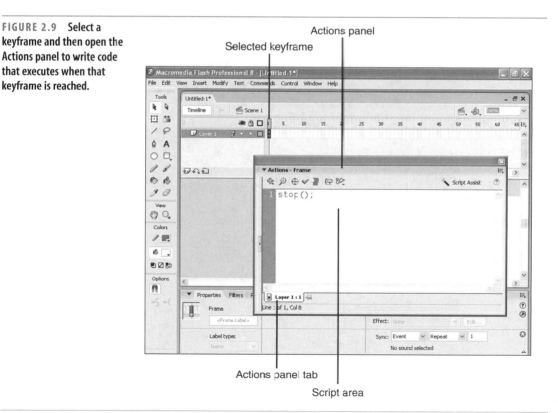

FIGURE 2.9 Select a keyframe and then open the Actions panel to write code that executes when that keyframe is reached.

Library Items

In the section "Movie Clip Hierarchy," earlier in the chapter, I discussed creating movie clip symbols, but here I want to talk about Library items in general. In addition to symbols (of type movie clip, button, or graphic), you can store symbols of type bitmap (really, any raster graphic that you import), sound, video, and font. If there's something in your Library and you're not using it on stage, it won't export with your movie (and, therefore, is not added to the .swf file size). However, you can override this behavior by setting a Library item's Linkage, which is accessible from the Library's options menu. Therefore, if you want to use ActionScript to make the item appear on stage—for example, to display a loading animation while something else loads—you must first select the Library item and select Linkage or Properties from the Library panel's options menu (see Figure 2.10).

FIGURE 2.10 You can access any Library item's Linkage setting or Symbol properties from the Library panel's options menu.

Setting an item's Linkage means selecting the Export for ActionScript check box and providing a linkage identifier in either the symbol's Linkage Properties dialog box or the Advanced portion of the Symbol Properties dialog box (shown side-by-side in Figure 2.11).

FIGURE 2.11 You can get to the Linkage settings from the Symbol Properties dialog box (left) or from the symbol's Linkage Properties dialog box (right).

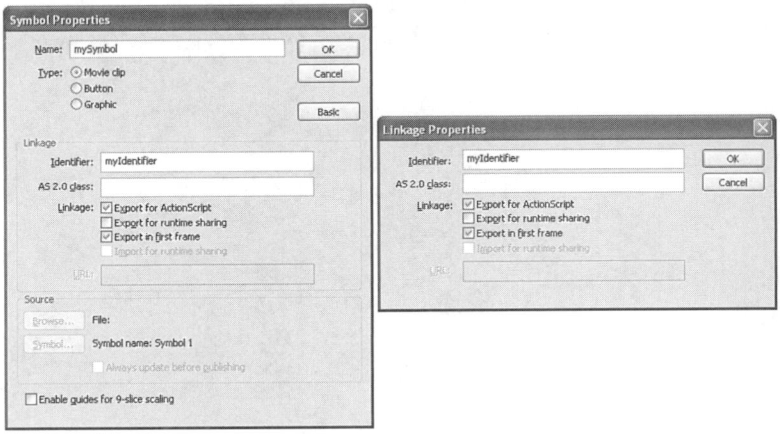

You'll do this a lot in the book: You'll enable the Export for ActionScript option and then give the item a unique linkage identifier. After a Library item has a linkage identifier, you can use code to effectively drag the item from the Library during runtime. Naturally, setting the Linkage option means the item will add to the overall file size.

When you enable the Export for ActionScript option, the Export in First Frame option is automatically selected as well (refer to Figure 2.10). The easiest and safest approach is to simply leave this option selected. This option means that, before the user sees anything and before your code begins to execute, the item downloads in its entirety. That's the safest route because it ensures that the media is downloaded before your ActionScript attempts to create an instance on stage (which would fail if the media wasn't fully loaded). However, selecting Export in First Frame also means the user sees nothing but a blank screen while the media file downloads. You can create a loading screen, which is a screen displaying the percentage of the file downloaded. However, the user won't even see *that* screen until after all the items with their Linkage values set to Export in First Frame have downloaded.

You can disable the Export in First Frame option, but then it's up to you to ensure that the media is downloaded before it's needed. I'll show you how to do that in the following section. But the projects in this book assume that either you must leave the Export in First Frame option selected or you must properly follow the manual process outlined next. The reason I don't instruct you how to do this in all the projects is that, as you'll see, the process is a bit detailed (you have to set up a preloader in frame 1, put all the items that

have the Linkage condition into frame 2, and move the primary project code to frame 3).

Disabling Export in First Frame

Follow these steps to both see the problem that occurs when you disable the Export in First Frame option as well as the steps to overcome the issue.

Step 1: See It Work with Export in First Frame Enabled

Select File Import, Import to Library and point to the photo.jpg file in the source_media folder you downloaded for this chapter. Open the Library to see the imported bitmap item (any raster image type—such as .jpg, .gif, .png, .pct, or .bmp—is called a *bitmap item* after it's imported into Flash). Select that item and open the Properties dialog box either from the Library panel's options menu or by clicking the little blue *i* button at the bottom left of the Library panel. Make sure the Properties dialog box is fully expanded by clicking the Advanced button if the dialog box is not fully expanded. Enable the Export for ActionScript option and change the linkage identifier to be just pic Leave the Export in First Frame option selected.

✒ NOTE

Flash 8 adds the capability to set the linkage for a bitmap item. In a minute you'll see how nicely this feature works with the new loadBitmap() method of the BitmapData class to effectively drag the bitmap item onto the stage at runtime.

You shouldn't have anything in your timeline. In frame 1, draw a rectangle; select it; and then select Modify, Convert to Symbol.

Name the symbol **Bar**, select the Movie clip Type option, make sure that the upper-left Registration option is selected (as shown in Figure 2.12), and then click OK.

FIGURE 2.12 Select the upper-left Registration position when creating the Bar symbol (don't make any Linkage settings).

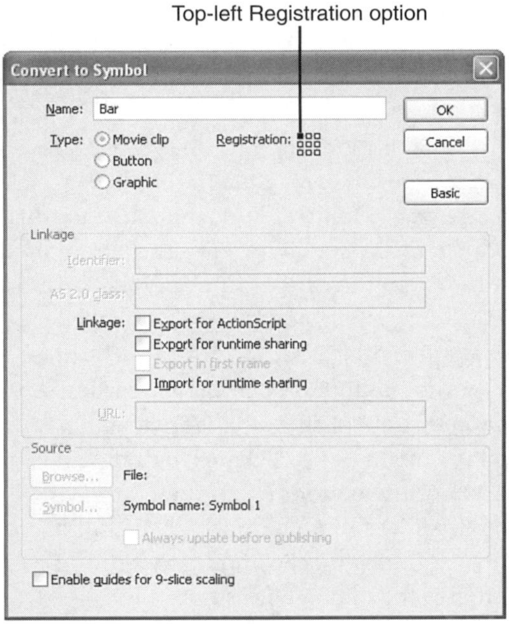

Top-left Registration option

Use the Properties panel to select the instance of your Bar symbol now on stage. Give it the instance name **bar**.

Select frame 1, open the Actions panel, and type or paste the following code (available in the step1_export_in_first_frame_selected.fla file in the finished_source folder you downloaded):

```
stop();
onEnterFrame = function(){
   bar._xscale = getBytesLoaded()/
                getBytesTotal() * 100;
```

```
if ( getBytesLoaded() ==
      getBytesTotal()    ){
   gotoAndStop(2);
   delete onEnterFrame;
   }
}
```

This code sets the bar instance's _xscale property proportional to how much of the file has downloaded; when the amount downloaded equals the total file size, the code jumps to frame 2.

Select frame 2 and press F7 to insert a blank keyframe at that point. Select the blank keyframe in frame 2, open the Actions panel, and type this code:

```
var bd =
flash.display.BitmapData.loadBitmap("pic");
attachBitmap(bd,0);
```

This code loads your Library item's contents into the homemade variable bd, which is attached to the main timeline into level 0.

Select Modify, Test Movie and you'll see the photo you imported without any delay. But, when online, it will take longer to download. To simulate how it will perform when online, select View, Download Settings, 14.4 (1.2KB/s), as shown in Figure 2.13.

Select View, Bandwidth Profiler so you can inspect what's going on. Finally, select View, Simulate Download and you'll see the Bandwidth Profiler in Figure 2.14.

The Bandwidth Profiler shows you how much of the file has downloaded, but you won't see your progress bar until after the Library item downloads because its Export in First Frame option was enabled. It would be nice to see the progress bar during the entire download process.

Step 2: See It Fail with Export in First Frame Disabled

Now I want you to see how the download progresses when the Export in First Frame option is disabled. Select the imported photo

in the Library and revisit the Linkage Properties dialog box by clicking the blue *i* button. Disable the Export in First Frame option, as shown in Figure 2.15.

Select Control, Test Movie. The image won't appear because it hasn't fully downloaded by the time you reach frame 2.

Step 3: Ensure the Item Downloads when Needed

The way to make sure a Library item that doesn't have the Export in First Frame option enabled actually downloads is to place the item in the timeline. Flash ensures that every piece of media in a frame is downloaded before it displays that frame. Our fix is pretty easy: Move the code that dynamically displays the image to frame 3; put a copy of the Library item in frame 2; and adjust the code so that, when 100% of the movie has downloaded, the code jumps to frame 3 (that is, past frame 2).

Click frame 1 and press F5 to insert a frame. Click the cell in frame 2 and press F7 to convert the frame to a blank keyframe. Drag an instance of the photo item (photo.jpg) onto frame 2.

Select the first keyframe, open the Actions panel, and change the `gotoAndStop(2)` method to `gotoAndStop(3)`. The finished code is shown here:

```
stop();
onEnterFrame = function(){
    bar._xscale = getBytesLoaded()/
                  getBytesTotal() * 100;
    if ( getBytesLoaded() ==
        getBytesTotal() ){
        gotoAndStop(3);
        delete onEnterFrame;
    }
}
```

Select Control, Test Movie and select View, Simulate Download. You'll see the progress bar grow while all the media downloads, including the imported photo.

As a review, you need to put all Library items (with their Export for ActionScript option selected, a linkage identifier specified, and the Export in First Frame option disabled) into a keyframe that you're going to jump past.

Authortime Versus Runtime

Most people understand the difference between *authortime* (the time you spend editing and developing your `.fla`) and runtime (when the `.swf` file runs for the user). During authortime, you can import many different media types and make detailed edits to all your assets. During playback (runtime), Flash is limited to playing what's in the `.swf` file and executing ActionScript code. Although ActionScript enables you to do things such as import and display images or sounds, you're limited to using a few file types. In addition,

ActionScript can modify things onscreen. Nothing during runtime permanently changes your `.swf` file.

In addition to authortime and runtime, there's another "time" that I call *offline time*, in which you create a Flash application solely for your own use in development. For example, I built an offline *cue point* and captioning tool that you'll use in Chapter 3, "Creating a Video with Synchronized Captions." The offline tool lets you listen to the music in a sound file and click every time you want to capture the current time in the song. When you're done using the tool, you can export the `.xml` file the tool created, which is loaded in at runtime by the `.swf` file the user visits. Imagine a player piano factory that had a special piano that punched holes in a paper scroll while a professional pianist played—that's the offline version where you collect the cue points and put them in an XML file. Then you take the scroll and load it into the consumer's player piano, similar to how Flash loads the XML file full of data.

Offline production tools can vary in sophistication. For example, select the first frame of a new movie, open the Actions panel, and type this code:

```
onMouseDown = function(){
    locX = new Array();
    locY = new Array();
    onEnterFrame = function(){
        locX.push( _xmouse );
        locY.push( _ymouse );
    }
}
onMouseUp = function(){
    trace ("locX = [ " + locX + " ]");
    trace ("locY = [ " + locY + " ]");
}
```

Select Control, Test Movie. When the .swf file begins to play, click, drag around the stage a bit, and then let go. When you let go, the Output panel displays a bunch of numbers (see Figure 2.16). Select the entire output, right-click it, and select Copy from the context menu (note that pressing Ctrl+C doesn't work in the Output panel).

FIGURE 2.16 In the offline mode, you'll see the collected coordinates in the Output panel.

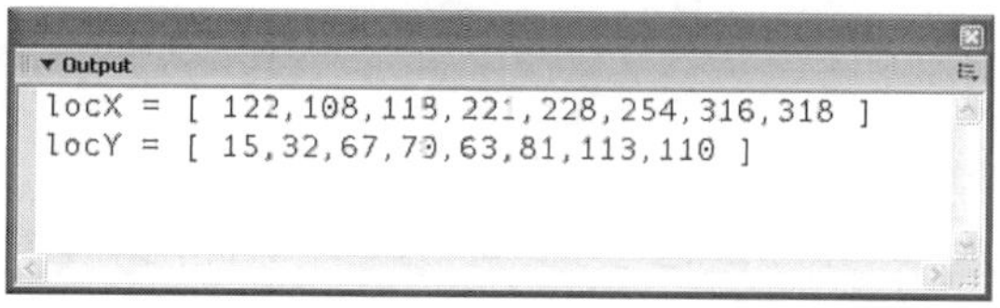

```
▼ Output
locX = [ 122,108,115,221,228,254,316,318 ]
locY = [ 15,32,67,79,63,81,113,110 ]
```

In a new Flash file, draw any small shape. Select it and select Modify, Convert to Symbol. Be sure you select the Movie Clip option and click OK. Select the instance on stage and use the Properties panel to give this symbol an instance name of clip. Select the first frame in this new movie, open the Actions panel, and paste what you copied from the Output panel of the other movie. Below the text you pasted, type the following code:

```
var step = 0;
onEnterFrame = function(){
    clip._x = locX[step];
    clip._y = locY[step];
    step++;
    if(step > locX.length){
        step = 0;
    }
}
```

The beginning of the first two lines you pasted into the Actions panel should look something like this:

```
locX = [ 6,7,9 …
locY = [ 21,21,23 …
```

When you test the movie, you'll see the clip move around exactly as you moved your mouse while dragging in the offline movie. This example shows how you can collect data in a real-time and natural way (based on mouse movements in this case) and then use the results in your finished application.

This offline application example was both simple and not particularly practical. You can create much more formal offline applications. In fact, there's a branch of ActionScript called JavaScript Flash (JSFL), which is ActionScript that runs as a command from a text file or a .swf file but only while you're in the Flash authoring tool. If the JSFL code resides in a text file, you can simply select Commands, Run Command and point to that text file. The advantage of creating a .swf file that contains JSFL code is that you can build an *interface* where the "user" (really the author running your command) can select options to change how the command is executed.

We won't create or use any JSFL in this book, but it can be useful in case you want to extend one of the offline applications I built.

📌 **TIP**

You can learn more about JSFL by selecting the Extending Flash help category (in the Help panel, select the Extending category from the drop-down menu). You can also download a few handy finished commands from the free extensions section at www.potapenko.com.

An ActionScript 2 Primer

This section can't and won't try to teach you everything about ActionScript 2.0 (AS2). I'm only going to highlight the details that affect how you assemble the projects in this book.

Typing Variables

One attribute of AS2 is assigning data types to variables. When you create a variable using the keyword var plus the variable name, you can specify the data type that variable should contain. Here are three examples:

```
var myName:String;
var myAge:Number = 40;
var aClip:MovieClip;
```

String, Number, and MovieClip are all data types. Notice in the second line that I both assign the data type Number to the myAge variable and also populate the variable with the value 40. If you don't know the value for a variable at the time you create the variable, you can still give the variable a data type. Although assigning data types to variables often makes the code more readable, its practical purpose is that, when you select Control, Test Movie to compile the project, you'll receive errors for any data type conflicts. The two possible kinds of conflicts are using a variable of one type where another type was expected and attempting to populate a variable of one type with a value of a different type. The error messages simply help you track down likely bugs because your project won't compile until you resolve all the variable type conflicts.

Flash's Classpath

Another, more significant, characteristic of AS2 is support for *class files*. The primary reason to use class files is to define a custom data type with behaviors you define. You can then make instances of your classes just as you can with any of the built-in ActionScript classes—but yours will behave uniquely because you define them. Class files are text files with the extension .as. Their filenames match their class names (or interface names). By convention, class filenames always begin with an uppercase letter, so MyClass.as is the definition for the MyClass class. Class files must adhere to very restrictive syntax rules.

You won't need to do much with class files if you don't want, except to place them where your application can find them. To create an instance of a class that is actually defined in the external file MyClass.as and store that instance in a variable called myInstance, you would put this code in your .fla file:

```
var myInstance:MyClass = new MyClass();
```

Your .fla file simply needs to know where to find the MyClass.as file where the class is defined. Flash will look for the file and, if it can't find it, display an error in the Output panel. Where does Flash look? In the *classpath*. Actually, Flash uses a default classpath, which you can edit, and each .fla file can have its own classpath. In fact, the classpath can include multiple locations to search. It's sort of like when the post office receives a letter with an incomplete address. Naturally, you don't have to include *USA* in every letter you write because the first place they look is in the United States. But if you say *Joe Smith, 123 Street, Portland*, the post office wouldn't know whether you meant Portland, Oregon, or Portland, Maine. Flash's classpath clears this up because it defines not only which folders to look in, but also the order in which to search those folders (in case two class files with the same class name appear in two folders).

Select Edit, Preferences or press Ctrl+U to display the Preferences window and select the ActionScript category in the left pane. Then click the ActionScript 2.0 Settings button to display the ActionScript 2.0 Settings dialog box, shown in Figure 2.17.

FIGURE 2.17   You can modify and add classpaths in the ActionScript category of Flash's Preferences window.

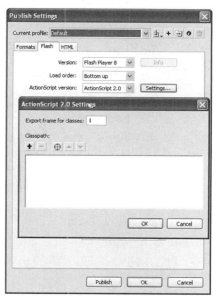

By default, you'll find two classpaths listed in the order that Flash will search: The first is represented by a dot (.), which means the same folder where your .fla file is saved. The second is $(LocalData)/Classes, which points to a folder called Classes inside the LocalData wildcard path. LocalData is a user directory (detailed in the Flash help system if you search for "localdata") where Flash can find the classes that ship with Flash. That first classpath (the .) means you can place class files in the same folder where you save your .fla file. If you build a general-purpose class,

you'll probably store the class files in the LocalData folder so you can use the classes in any of your projects. For this book, we'll store all classes in the same folder as the .fla simply to make it easier. This is reasonable for a class with a truly unique behavior.

In addition to the default classpath preference, you can set a classpath for each .fla file by selecting File, Publish Settings; clicking the Flash tab; and then clicking the Settings button adjacent to the ActionScript Version drop-down list, as shown in Figure 2.18. The dialog box that appears to set a file-specific classpath looks the same as the global ActionScript 2.0 Settings dialog box shown previously in Figure 2.17, except that you can also edit the export frame (which I'll come back to later in this section).

FIGURE 2.18   You can access a file-specific classpath under the Flash tab in your Publish Settings dialog box.

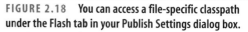

Every project in this book works by placing all the .as files in the same directory as your

.fla file. I'll direct you to copy class files into the same folder in which you're working. However, many people don't like doing this because it's messy having all the .as files in the same folder as the .fla and .swf files. A nice alternative is to store the support files in a folder called classes. Then when the directions say "put the .as files into your working directory where your .fla file is saved," you can put the .as files in a folder you create called classes within your working directory. To make this alternative work, you must add a new path to Flash's ActionScript 2.0 Settings dialog box. Press Ctrl+U to open the Preferences window, select the ActionScript category in the left pane, and click the ActionScript 2.0 Settings button. Then click the + button and type this classpath on a new line:

```
./classes
```

Earlier I showed you how to avoid enabling the Export in First Frame Linkage option. Although the advantage of that setting is that the media definitely loads before you need it, the disadvantage is that the user won't see anything (not even a progress bar) while the media loads "in the first frame" (actually, before the first frame appears). The same issue applies to AS2.0 class files. Notice that in the Publish Settings dialog box shown in Figure 2.18, the default setting is to export class files in frame 1. In fact, all class files (that is, all the code in those class files) download before frame 1 appears. Normally, this is not an issue because, compared to media files, class files tend to be very small. However, because I showed you the technique to control where symbols with linkage download, I'll show you how to do the same

with class files—it's actually much easier with class files.

Simply select a frame other than the first frame as the time you want the class files to load. That is, select File, Publish Settings; click the Flash tab; and then click the Settings button (you'll see the ActionScript 2.0 Settings dialog box from Figure 2.14). Change the Export Frame for Classes value at the top of the dialog box to 2. For this option to work, you can't attach ActionScript code that uses any class files to a frame before frame 2. Alternatively, you can write a loading script similar to the one from the section "Disabling Export in First Frame," earlier in this chapter. That means that only after the whole movie has loaded can you use the class files. I won't walk you through the steps for each project; you can do them if you want—but, really, the steps to export class files in a frame other than frame 1 can be a lot of work considering that the size of the class files is usually small compared to everything else (such as images, sounds, and video).

The Import Statement and Namespaces

Using the import statement is actually very simple; it reduces how much code you need to enter. I'll often make you type something like this in the project code:

```
import flash.display.BitmapData;
```

Without that statement, you can still use all the methods in the BitmapData class. However, unless you include the import statement, every time you want to access methods in the BitmapData class you have to specify the full path for the method (called the *namespace*), as in `flash.display.BitmapData.methodName()`. If you first issue an import statement, however, you can cut that statement down to `BitmapData.methodName()`. The import statement simply reduces the amount of code you have to enter.

The `import` statement tells Flash which classes you want to use without having to include the full path to the class file in each reference you make. Keep in mind that the file `BitmapData.as` is in a folder called `display` that's inside the folder called `flash`. But the `flash` folder needs to be in the classpath. The classpath is the starting folder; many classes are organized in subfolders (called *packages*), hence the long namespace.

The concept of namespaces is related to the `import` statement. Namespaces are similar to people's last names. Provided that you're alone with me, if you say "Phillip," I'll know you're talking to me. However, if we're in a crowd with several other Phillips, you'll have to say "Phillip Kerman" to address me, specifically. Classes, such as `BitmapData`, are similarly further qualified with a namespace. That is, it's not `BitmapData` but rather `flash.display.BitmapData`, which is different from any other `BitmapData` class that might be present.

Consider this analogy: The bedtime routine is likely different here at my residence than in

your home. I have my own process for getting ready for bed (for the sake of argument, this can be defined in a class called `BedReadyClass`). To ensure that my version of `BedReadyClass` doesn't get mixed up with your version of `BedReadyClass`, I'd be wise to qualify my class name by calling it `com.phillipkerman.BedReadyClass`. Because I own the domain phillipkerman.com, the classes built by everyone else who uses this convention won't conflict with mine. (Yes, the domain is reversed and com goes first.) If you want to refer to the `BedReadyClass()` method within the `BedReadyClass` class without using an import statement, you might say this:

```
var temp:com.phillipkerman.BedReadyClass =
new com.phillipkerman.BedReadyClass();
```

Instead, I'd probably want to say this:

```
import com.phillipkerman.BedReadyClass;
var temp:BedReadyClass = new BedReady-
Class();
```

Although the `import` statement ultimately reduces code when you reference multiple methods within a single class, it also affects namespaces. So, you might have your own `BedReadyClass` that you've called something else, in which case there would be no conflict. But what if you wrote a class and called it `BedReadyClass` and wanted to use both classes (my `BedReadyClass` and your `BedReadyClass`) in the same project? There would be a conflict, except that I was smart and didn't really name my class `BedReadyClass` but rather `com.phillipkerman.BedReadyClass`. In fact, the class file is called `BedReadyClass.as` but is stored in a folder called `phillipkerman`, which is in the folder com (and that com folder must be in Flash's classpath). A serious conflict would occur if you tried putting your `BedReadyClass.as` file in the same folder as my `BedReadyClass.as` file.

There won't be any conflicts if everyone selects a unique prefix to their classnames; `com.phillipkerman` is guaranteed to be unique if everyone else follows a similar convention, which most developers do. Even if you're not sharing classes with other people, you need to come up with a convention so you don't have internal conflicts. If I decide that I'm going to store this `BedReadyClass` class in the folder `com/phillipkerman`, inside the actual `.as` file the first line must read `class com.phillipkerman.BedReadyClass`, not just `class BedReadyClass`.

None of the projects in this book use namespaces, meaning packages in which related classes are stored in a hierarchy of folders. You might wonder why I just discussed this topic if it doesn't apply to this book. It's simple: If you want to use the class files from the projects in this book in other projects, you need to make sure that my class names don't conflict with your class names.

Sample Project Template

The following sample project gives you a sense of the larger and more complete projects in the following chapters. The focus here is to understand the thought process used for all the projects in the book. In addition, you'll see where you, the reader, fit into these projects. You'll understand what parts are ready-built and what parts you'll have to create. It turns out that this Clock Widget mini-project is actually pretty useful as it is, but that's more a serendipitous result of a

valid structure than the design I had in mind.

Planning for the End Product First

In any project, you should start by visualizing the end result. In the case of the projects in this book, there's the end product that the user sees, but there's also the process you must take to adapt and customize the project. For the user, the projects are very straightforward: video captions, a photo portfolio, a quiz, and so on. But the first thing I looked at with each one was what would I have to explain in the text and the steps readers would need to take to complete the project. In both cases, I wanted these steps to be easy and concise.

As far as the Clock Widget project goes, the end product for the user is a simple clock that appears on top of a Flash project. I can sort out all the steps I'd normally take to create such a project: the graphic interface for the user; the code that has to continually check the time; and some formatting to turn the raw time information into a nice presentation, such as 1:39 p.m. But because this is a project in this book, I chose to separate the parts you would want to (or have to) customize from the parts I had developed that work without requiring any additional code from you. For example, I thought you'd want to be able to choose the font style for the digital display, but I didn't think you'd want to get your hands dirty calculating the current hour, minute, and second. But if I assumed that you were going to be creating the display, the project framework would also need to support your ability to create an analog clock if you so choose. In addition, I had to consider the range of features you might want to add: Some people might want the clock to display AM and PM while others might prefer a 24-hour clock that displays 13:39 instead of 1:39 PM. I could have invested a lot of time and work building in options for all kinds of wild features. Instead, my goal was to simply build a platform on which you can easily add features without changing the underlying support class files.

Let's return to the features in the Clock Widget project. Here are the final features the project will support:

▶ The ability to create different inter-changeable templates for the clock face, such as analog or digital or a cartoon character clock face if you want.

▶ The ability to instantiate as many clocks as you want and to place them on stage at will.

▶ Finally, the ability to create any kind of clock you want without having to touch the underlying code in the class files.

The solution I came up with is very similar to other projects in this book and is presented in Figure 2.19.

FIGURE 2.19 This class diagram shows the flow of the sample project.

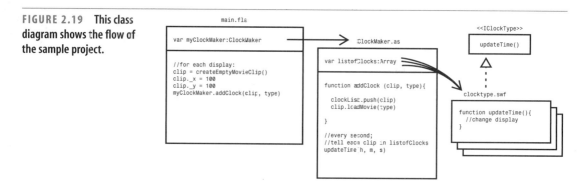

Your project file is the main.fla file, where you create one instance of the ClockMaker.as class (stored in a variable such as myClockMaker). Then, for every clock you want on stage, you create an empty clip and issue the addClock() method on the myClockMaker instance and pass both a clock type and a reference to the clip you just created—really just the clip's instance name. This clip will hold the clock display and the type of clock you want. The type is simply the name of the clocktype.swf template you want to use. (I use the term clocktype.swf

template to mean any .swf you generate that can be used in this project, such as an analog display or a digital display.) You must create the clocktype.swf template; for example, you'll create analog.swf or digital.swf. Each of these templates must implement the IClockType interface. Because the ClockMaker.as class will be sending updates every second by issuing the updateTime() method, each of your templates must support that method. An interface is a special kind of class file that lists methods—not their code but just the parameters and return values.

When you create another class and say it's going to implement a particular interface, the class must include each of the methods listed. It's just a formal way of ensuring that all the templates support the minimum set of methods.

Your work in your `main.fla` file is very minimal: Just create clips, position them on stage, and ask the `ClockMaker` class to create the clocks. The code for your `main.fla` file will look like the code in Listing 2.1.

The work you'll have to do to create the various `clocktype.swf` templates is a bit more involved. But realize that after you have a few templates, you can recycle them in new `main.fla` files. The basic work in your `clocktype.swf` templates is to take the parameters received in a method called `updateTime()` and use them to create a display. For example, to create the `digital.swf` file referenced in the `main.fla` file, you'd use the code in Listing 2.2.

You simply need a dynamic text field on stage with the instance name time_txt (as I'll instruct you to do in the next section).

> **📌 NOTE**
>
> There are two types of variables in Flash: reference and value (also called *primitive*). When you copy a value variable's value, you make a duplicate. This is like copying a file on your computer. Reference variables don't get copied; you can only get a reference to them. This is like making a shortcut or an alias to a file. The important difference appears when you change a variable's value. If it's an actual copy (that is, a value), the original is unaffected—just like changing a file you copied on your computer. If you think you have a copy of a variable and it's actually a reference, changing the reference also changes the original. `String` and `Number` data types are value types, whereas `Object`, `Array`, and `MovieClip` are reference data types. Suppose you have a clip on stage with the instance name `someInstance`. If you say `myClip = someInstance` and then say `myClip._x = 100`, you'll actually move the `someInstance` clip because `myClip` was only a reference.

LISTING 2.1 The Code in the `main.fla` File

```
var myClockMaker:ClockMaker = new ClockMaker();
var holder:MovieClip = createEmptyMovieClip("holder", 0);
var theTemplate:String = "digital.swf";
myClockMaker.addClock(holder, theTemplate);
```

LISTING 2.2 How the Digital Clock Template Displays the Time

```
function updateTime(hour, minute, second, twelveHour){
    time_txt.text = hour + ":" + minute + "." + second;
}
```

The hard work is all handled by the `ClockMaker.as` class, and you never have to edit the contents of this class file. You simply tell it what it needs to know. Namely, you must provide a clip into which it can load the template type and provide the template type you want to load. The `ClockMaker` class file handles loading the `clocktype.swf` file that you build next and telling it when the time changes.

If you step back a bit, you'll notice that, although you'll have to do a little bit of work to create the `clocktype.swf` template, once you have a few, you can use them in any project you want (including any `main.fla` file you want). There's almost no code in the `main.fla`, which makes it easy to reuse this clock widget in any project where you need a clock.

Building a Template

We'll go from the inside out starting with the `digital.swf` file, which serves as a `clocktype.swf` template. Create a new Flash file and immediately save it as **digital.fla** into a working directory. Select Modify, Document and set the dimensions of the file to 200 pixels wide by 200 pixels high. Use the Text tool to create a block of text with margins wide enough to accommodate at least eight digits. Use the Properties panel to set the field type to Dynamic Text and then give the field the instance name **time_txt**. Select the first keyframe, open the Actions panel, and type the code in Listing 2.3.

LISTING 2.3 How to Pad the Minutes with Zeros So They Always Appear As Two Digits

```
time_txt.text = "";

function updateTime(hour, minute, second, twelveHour){

    if(minute<10){
        minute = "0"+minute;
    }
    if(second<10){
        second = "0"+second;
    }
    time_txt.text = hcur + ":" + minute + "." + second;

}
```

I added some code in Listing 2.3 to ensure that the minutes and seconds are always displayed as two digits. Also note that the unused `twelveHour` parameter contains the hours as a number between 1 and 24. Before continuing, select Control, Test Movie to create the `digital.swf` file that you'll reference next.

For the main file, create a new Flash movie and immediately save it as **main.fla** into your working folder. Select the first keyframe, open the Actions panel, and type the following code:

```
var myClockMaker:ClockMaker =
            new ClockMaker();
var holder:MovieClip =
createEmptyMovieClip("holder", 0);
var theTemplate:String = "digital.swf";
myClockMaker.addClock(holder, theTemplate);
```

Copy the `ClockMaker.as` file from the `finished_source` folder and put the copy next to the `main.fla` file. Inside `main.fla`, select Control, Test Movie to view the basic clock, as shown in Figure 2.20.

You can change anything you want in the `clocktype.swf` template, such as font styles. You can also modify the code, such as the replacement code shown in Listing 2.4, which you'd insert into `digital.fla`.

FIGURE 2.20 The `main.fla` file directs the `ClockMaker` class to load your `digital.swf` template; then it displays the time.

9:57.05

Just remember to export a `.swf` file by selecting Control, Test Movie before you run the `main.fla` file again. You always run

main.fla, but it needs to find the template `.swf` (in this case, `digital.swf`) for you to see the time.

Now, I'll show you how to make an entirely different `clocktype.swf` template. You can open the finished `analog.fla` file, which is in the `finished_source` folder you downloaded for this chapter. Listing 2.5 shows the code you'll find in the first frame of the file.

On stage are three instances: `hour_mc`, `minute_mc`, and `second_mc`. These clips simply rotate into place depending on the current time. Select Control, Test Movie to produce a file called `analog.swf`. Go back to the `main.fla`, select the first keyframe, open the Actions panel, and edit the code to read as shown in Listing 2.6.

LISTING 2.4 Take Advantage of the `twelveHour` Parameter to Display AM or PM

```
time_txt.text = "";

function updateTime(hour, minute, second, twelveHour){

    if(minute<10){
        minute = "0"+minute;
    }
    if(second<10){
        second = "0"+second;
    }
    if(twelveHour<12){
        var meridian = "AM";
    }else{
        var meridian = "PM";
    }
    time_txt.text = hour + ":" + minute + "." + second + meridian;
}
```

LISTING 2.5 Rotate Three Clips (Based on the Time) to Create an Analog Display

```
function updateTime(hour, minute, second, twelveHour){
    hour_mc._rotation = (hour/12) * 360;
    minute_mc._rotation = (minute/60) * 360;
    second_mc._rotation = (second/60) * 360;
}
```

LISTING 2.6 How main.fla Tells the ClockMaker to Make Two Clocks: One Based on digital.swf and One Based on analog.swf

```
var myClockMaker:ClockMaker = new ClockMaker();
var holder:MovieClip = createEmptyMovieClip("holder", 0);
var theTemplate:String = "digital.swf";
myClockMaker.addClock(holder, theTemplate);

var holder2:MovieClip = createEmptyMovieClip ("holder2", 1);
holder2._x = 200;
var theSecondTemplate:String = 'analog.swf';
myClockMaker.addClock(holder2, theSecondTemplate);
```

Here you simply make another empty movie clip (called holder2) and set its _x location to 200 so that it doesn't cover the other clock. Then you issue the addClock() method with the type parameter set to "analog.swf".

Perhaps this sample isn't the most impressive project you've ever seen; it's certainly the simplest in this book. But the overall framework is what I want you to ponder. Look at the ClockMaker.as class file if you're interested, but the point here is that you don't have to know how it works; you just have to know how to work *with* it.

Understanding Other Project Variations

I approached each project in this book differently. They all involve at least one custom class file. They are all also based on the principle demonstrated in the preceding clock example: You build the templates that control how the display will behave and appear. For each project, I've created class files that handle as much of the complex and tedious code as possible. However, you won't always be creating a main file that tells a class which templates to load, as was the case with the clock example. Let's discuss the main variations.

The biggest difference in classes used in the projects is that some classes use the concept of *composition* while others employ *inheritance*. In my projects, a class that uses composition is given a reference to a movie clip instance, which it then modifies. That means the class is composed with a reference to a movie clip. The ClockMaker.as class uses composition because it has a reference to each holder clip—the first parameter in addClock() is a clip reference.

A class that uses inheritance actually *extends* the MovieClip class.

> **NOTE**
>
> Although we'll only be extending MovieClip, inheritance can be used for other data types.

The class initially has all the features of the MovieClip class (that's the class on which all movie clip symbols in the Library are based). By extending the class, you can add functionality to the MovieClip class. This way you can create a movie clip and put graphics or nested symbols inside it. Then you can say, "This clip will be based on this custom class file." The mechanical step you need to perform to cause a movie clip symbol to get extended by a class file is to specify that class file in the Symbol Properties dialog box.

Here's a simple example of inheritance. Let's say you hate the fact that you always need to set both the _xscale and _yscale of a clip instead of simply being able to set the "_scale"—a property that, by default, doesn't exist. (The new Flash 8 `MovieClip` transformation property lets you use a matrix to transform it, but that's another story....) In Flash, select File, New and select ActionScript File (instead of Flash Document). Then type this code into the script window:

```
class MyClip extends MovieClip {

    function MyClip(){
    }

    function set _scale(toWhat:Number){
        this._xscale = toWhat;
        this._yscale = toWhat;
    }

    function get _scale():Number{
        return (this._xscale);
    }
}
```

The set scale() and get scale() functions effectively create a new property called _scale that every movie clip based on this class will support.

Save the file as **MyClip.as** in a working folder. Now create a new Flash document—not an ActionScript file. Draw a square; select it; and select Modify, Convert to Symbol. Make sure you're looking at the expanded view of the Convert to Symbol dialog box (as shown earlier in Figure 2.11). Select the Movie Clip option and enable the Export for ActionScript option. Specify a linkage identifier of MyClip. Also, set the AS2.0 Class option to be **MyClip**; this makes Flash look for the MyClip.as class file when it runs. Click OK and save the file

in the same folder where MyClip.as resides. Select the first keyframe, open the Actions panel, and type this code:

```
onMouseDown = function(){
    box._scale = 300;
}
onMouseUp = function(){
    box._scale = 100;
}
```

Finally, use the Properties panel and select the instance of your symbol on stage (drag one from the Library if you don't have one) and give it the instance name **box**. Select Control, Test Movie. Now you have a .swf file containing a movie clip symbol that is everything a MovieClip is with the extended feature of supporting the homemade _scale property.

I should note that a lot of people pooh-pooh the idea of exposing a property in your class by using the get and set function types. The property is "exposed" because—from outside the class—it can be seen and edited. An alternative (and, arguably better) way is to create so-called getter/setter functions that give access to the property through standard methods. Here's a variation of the MyClip.as file, but this time using getter/setter functions:

```
class MyClip extends MovieClip {
    private var scale:Number;

    function MyClip(){
    }

    public function setScale(toWhat:Number){
        scale = Math.max(0, toWhat);
        this._xscale = scale;
        this._yscale = scale;
    }
```

```
public function getScale():Number{
    return scale;
  }
}
```

Notice three things: The variable `scale` is private, meaning that code from outside this class can't get or set it directly; the two getter/setter functions (`setScale()` and `getScale()`) provide an indirect way to change `scale` and are designated `public`; and the `scale` variable can never be set lower than 0. I'm preventing the `scale` variable from being lower than 0 to demonstrate that you can ensure that a property stays within a desired range regardless of what the user "attempts" when he invokes the setter method.

In a perfect world, you should choose composition over inheritance. For one thing, inheritance means the instructions are more detailed and therefore easier to mess up because I have to explain the AS2.0 class setting in the Symbol Properties dialog box. Having said this, nearly everything you do in a Flash project will go inside a movie clip, so extending the `MovieClip` class is often convenient.

To wrap up the difference between composition and inheritance, think about how you would verbally describe the framework. You can refer to a class that extends another by saying the child "is a" parent. That is, your class "is a" movie clip if it extends the `MovieClip` class. When verbalizing a class that employs composition, you can say the class "has a" reference to some other class. For example, the `ClockMaker.as` class "has a" reference to the holder into

which it loaded the `clocktype.swf` template. You can use the "is a" or "has a" test to distinguish inheritance from composition.

Final Thoughts

This chapter was one of the last things I wrote for the book so that I would have a good idea of what you need to know before you really start rolling. Ideally, each project stands on its own. In fact, you should be able to jump straight to any project and crank something out. Along the way, however, I have included a lot of tips that couldn't be left out. This chapter collects some of the most important and useful tips that I will expand later in the book.

PART II: Projects

CHAPTER 3: Creating a Video with Synchronized Captions

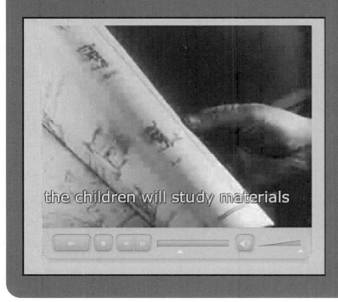

About the Projects

The projects in this chapter are the most universally practical projects in a book full of practical projects! At the core, you'll build text *captions* for video content. You'll also learn to create any kind of *synchronization*. For example, you can display bits of trivia on top of the video (like the old VH1 music video show *Pop Up Video*). Although you can always include such content right inside the video, keeping it separate in the Flash movie lets you easily modify it or even temporarily turn it off. Everything here also applies to audio. Not only are the synchronization concepts identical for video and audio, you can use what you build here for any audio-only projects you develop.

Prerequisites

You'll need Flash Professional 8 (not Flash Basic). There are no other prerequisites for this project. Ideally, you will have your own video and audio content—a short piece with narration or dialogue is best for testing. If you understand XML, that's great, but it's not required.

@work resources

Download the `chapter_3_downloads.zip` file for this chapter from the accompanying CD-ROM.

Planning the Projects

Almost all the work for these projects is done in the preproduction stage. If you do a good job preparing everything, the projects will go more smoothly than a television cooking show (where everything is measured and chopped up in advance). The preparation here involves gathering the transcript of the captions that will appear and identifying the places at which those captions should appear.

After you have your captions prepared, you'll move on to creating a few text display templates. On the surface, this is nothing more than selecting a variety of fonts to use; however, you'll also add an animation effect for when the text changes. The text display templates you create can be used with any future project you build where you want captions. The rest of the chapter shows you how to implement the support class I built called `EventChannel`. It handles all the grunt work of reading in the captions and making them appear in synch with your audio or video.

I should note that captions are good for much more than simply displaying the movie's dialogue for hearing-impaired folks (although captions obviously do that well, too). I've used the techniques from this chapter to display captions in multiple languages for a museum kiosk. I've also used the techniques in this chapter to display the lyrics for music where the singer might not annunciate the words clearly. The projects you build in this chapter can apply to any situation in which you want something to appear (such as text) in synch with your audio or video.

Cue Points and Captions

There's one huge chore when captioning audio or video: transcribing—someone needs to type in all the text. Plus, that text needs to be segmented into blocks that both fit within a given screen space and match the tempo of the video. Preparing a transcript for cue points is nothing more than creating a text file with every block of text on its own line, as in this example:

```
There once was a man who loved a woman.
She was the one he ate that apple for.
and so on...
```

You simply want to make sure that each line fits in the space you're allotting for the captions and that, when synched with the audio, the captions appear on screen long enough to read. For example, if you have space for only one or two words to appear at a time, they'd have to fly by so fast no one could read them.

The final step of synchronizing the captions with the media goes very quickly after you have the transcript prepared. With the tools I built for this chapter, you'll see that you can identify *cue points* in real time while watching the video. All the investments you make to prepare the captions will make this otherwise tedious process go smoothly.

Cue Point Types

There are no fewer than five types of video cue points: Event, Navigation, ActionScript, Caption, and Marker. Although each has its respective benefits depending on your application, they're mostly equivalent. The idea of any cue point is the same: to associate a block of information you want to appear—or, at least, get sent to your application—at a specific time in the video. Generally, the exact content for a cue point is whatever you decide. However, the exact form and where the cue point information resides are what vary in the different cue point types.

Videos produced in Flash Professional 8 (or the accompanying Flash Video Encoder) can be permanently injected with Event or Navigation cue points. The difference with Navigation cue points is that they are seek-able (unlike Event cue points). That is, the Encoder places a *keyframe* in the video at the exact frame you place a Navigation cue point. This way, users can navigate directly to such keyframes by clicking the Next or Previous button in the FLVPlayback compo-nent shown in Figure 3.1 (which triggers the seekToNextNavCuePoint() and seekToPrevNavCuePoint() methods). You can find the FLVPlayback component by selecting Window, Components.

FIGURE 3.1   The FLVPlayback **component lets the user seek to the next or previous Navigation type cue point.**

ActionScript cue points aren't permanently embedded into the FLV, which makes them different from all the other types of cue points. I'll talk about the advantages or disadvantages of this approach in the next section. For now, just realize that ActionScript cue points are set at runtime; therefore, they require additional scripting before the video starts. (As an added bonus, the project "Implement Code for Audio-only Captions" shows you how to use ActionScript cue points with an audio source instead of a video source.)

Each of these three Macromedia cue point types (Event, Navigation, and ActionScript) have properties for time and name. The time corresponds to where the cue point appears in the video, and the name is an arbitrary string you specify. You can include any text you want, such as a caption or a description of what's happening onscreen. Plus, each cue point has room for additional *parameters*—namely, as many name/value pairs as you want. In this way, you can associate more than just a single line of text with a particu-lar cue point. For example, you could store captions in different languages such as the following name/value pairs:

```
name:value
en:"Hello Friends"
es:"Hola Amigos"
fr:"bonjour amis"
```

Remember that you're packing information into a moment in time; you can store just a name or as many other parameters as you want.

Finally, although the third-party product Captionate (shown in Figure 3.2) is needed to inject Caption and Marker cue points, these cue point types are definitely worth including in this list. Captionate Markers are simple: They're just text labels associated with a moment in time. However, Captionate Captions are similar to Macromedia cue points because they have room for additional, optional information (in addition to the caption itself). Captionate Captions also let you identify a speaker (that is, the person talking) with each caption.

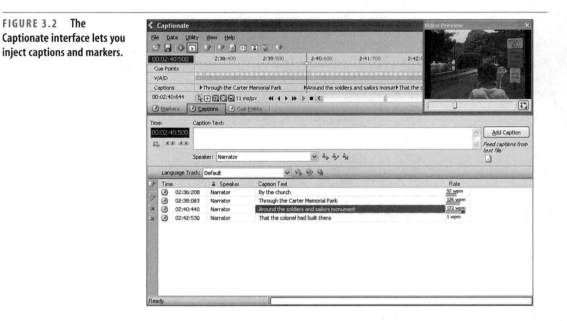

FIGURE 3.2 **The Captionate interface lets you inject captions and markers.**

In fact, Captionate's Caption type of cue point supports multiple tracks for multilingual applications. You could probably squeeze this same kind of information into the Macromedia cue point format (Event, Navigation, or ActionScript), but the logical and convenient structure is already built in to the Captionate Caption cue point. (If nothing else, you'll want to get Captionate because it lets you modify any cue points—including Macromedia ones—embedded in the .flv file; otherwise, these are uneditable.)

You can use any or all of these cue point types in a single video. You can also write code that responds to each type differently, perhaps displaying Caption cue points in a text field and then using Event cue points to jump to a different frame in a movie clip. Instead of learning the different syntaxes to handle all the cue point types, the projects in this chapter channel all the cue points through a single clearinghouse: the EventChannel class. This class triggers events in your project for every cue point type you want to listen for.

Embedded Cue Points Versus Separate Text Files

One of the coolest features in Flash Professional 8 is that, during the video encoding stage, you can embed cue points right into the video. As great as this feature is, though, it does have some disadvantages.

The biggest problem with embedding cue points into the video is that they're uneditable after the .flv file is encoded. (Well, the excellent third-party application called Captionate does let you edit cue points.) Although embedded cue points might be convenient because the data and video stay together, the data isn't left open for easy access. The alternative is to keep all the details of your cue points in an external source, such as an XML text file.

Saving cue point information in XML (a separate file from your video) can have its advantages. For example, if you have the same video encoded for different bandwidths, you can use a single XML file for the cue points. After all, the captions are the same for each bandwidth, so making an edit involves just one file instead of each .flv file. Plus, as you'll see in the tool I built for adding cue points, there are more convenient ways to specify cue points than through the Flash video encoder's interface. For one thing, when specifying cue points in Flash, you can't hear the audio track, which makes finding cue points very difficult indeed.

As great as storing cue point information in separate files is, if you choose that approach, you have to perform the additional step of importing and parsing the data. Also, although the FLVPlayback component has an addASCuePoint() method (to inject ActionScript cue points at runtime), you're pretty much taking a home-grown approach that might not match other developers' ways of working. I should note that, even though

the only logical format for an external file containing cue point information is XML, the exact structure of that file (that is, its schema) is up to you. As long as you leave room for all the cue point types, the exact schema is completely subjective. However, for this project to work, you have to use a single format. The structure I'm using is based on the output from Captionate—which, I suppose makes this format "better" only because it's consistent with another product.

Project:
Navigation Cue Points in a .flv File

In this project, you'll create a .flv video file you can use in the remaining projects in this chapter. You'll also use Flash to insert Navigation cue points into the video. You'll use an excerpt from a public domain video called *The Children Must Learn*. View the source file the_children_must_learn.mov (located in the source_media folder you downloaded for this chapter) to get a sense of where the captions might appear.

STEPS ▼

1. Creating a new .fla file
2. Importing the source video
3. Choosing video options
4. Adding the first navigation cue point
5. Adding more navigation cue points
6. Skinning the video
7. Navigating the video

STEP 1▼
Creating a New .fla File

Create a new Flash document and immediately save it as **working.fla**.

STEP 2▼
Importing the Source Video

Now, import a video clip into the new .fla file. Select File, Import, Import Video to launch the Import Video wizard, as shown in Figure 3.3.

Click the Browse button and select the the_children_must_learn.mov video (located in the source_media folder). Click Next.

STEP 3▼
Choosing Video Options

In the Deployment page of the Video Import wizard, leave the Progressive Download from a Web Server option selected, as shown in Figure 3.4, and click Next. The other options on this page of the wizard include two ways to stream a video from the Flash Media Server (formerly called Flash Communication Server) plus an option to embed the video into your .swf (neither of which we want to do here). Using the Flash Media Server (or a service provider) is an additional expense. Embedding the video into your .swf results in lower quality and audio that drifts out of synch over time.

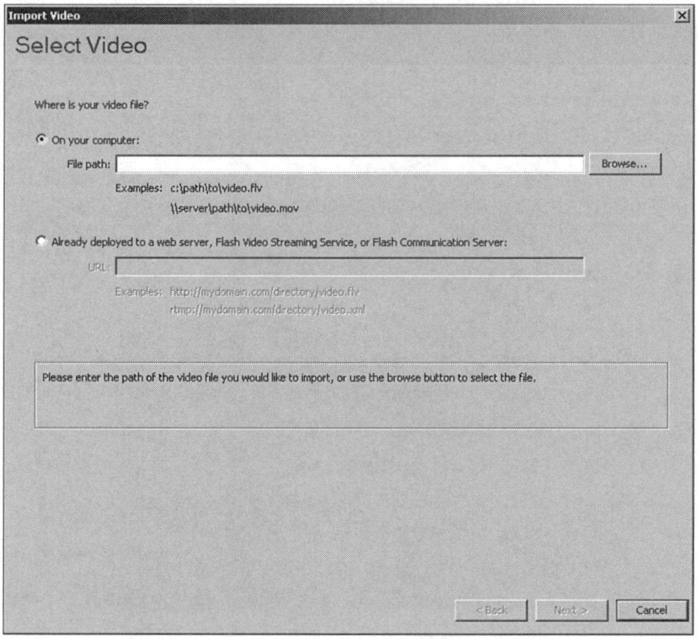

FIGURE 3.3   The first screen in the Import Video wizard asks you to browse to your source video.

In the Encoding page of the Import Video Wizard, select the Flash 8—Medium Quality (400kbps) encoding profile from the drop-down menu. Click the Show Advanced Settings button to expand the window so it shows additional options, and then click the Cue Points tab in the newly exposed section of the window. Figure 3.5 shows the dialog box you should be viewing.

STEP 4▼
Adding the First Navigation Cue Point

At this time, because Flash unfortunately provides no audio preview, you'd be hard pressed to set cue points for captioning. Instead, let's just insert Navigation cue points. Specifically, we'll insert them every time the video image displays a new page of the "Let's Learn About Goats" booklet.

Scrub the video to as close to 3.187 seconds as you can (displayed as 00:00:03.187); then click the plus button in the upper-left corner of the Cue Points list to add a cue point at this location in the video file. A new entry is created for this cue point in the Cue Points list. Set the cue point type to Navigation by selecting this option from the Type column. Next, type a name for the cue point in the Name column—for this example, use the name **The Goat Family** because that's the title of the page of the booklet displayed in the video (see Figure 3.6).

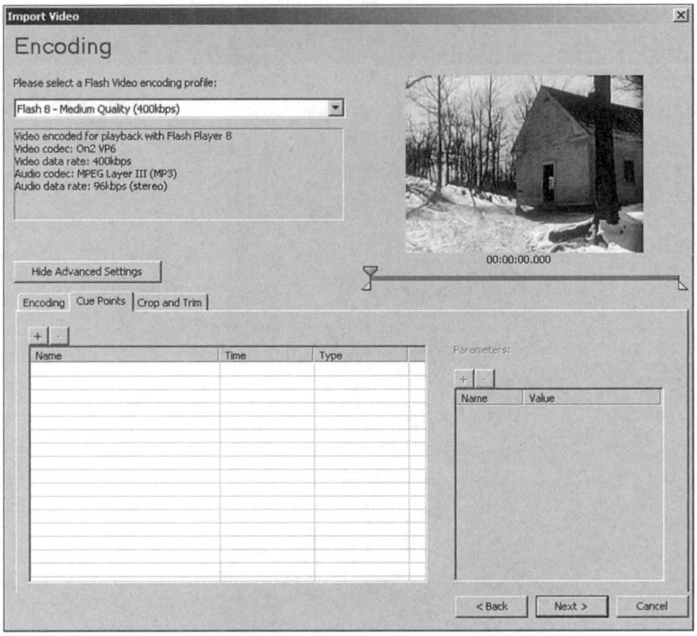

FIGURE 3.5 The Encoding dialog box, shown here with the Cue Points portion of the Advanced Settings.

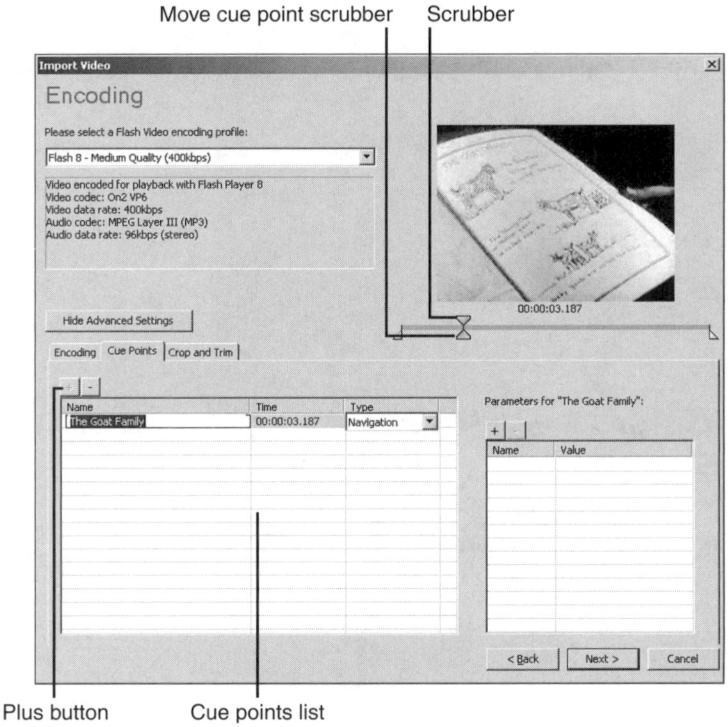

FIGURE 3.6 The advanced settings of the Import Video Wizard let you insert cue points.

Move cue point scrubber   Scrubber

Plus button   Cue points list

STEP 5 ▼
Adding More Navigation Cue Points

Scrub the video to 5.247 seconds (where the booklet in the video reads *TYPES OF GOATS*), and click the plus button to add another cue point. Name this cue point **Types of Goats** and remember to select Navigation from the Type column. Add three more Navigation cue points at the times shown in Figure 3.7.

FIGURE 3.7 These are all the Navigation cue points you'll insert.

Name	Time	Type
The Goat Family	00:00:03.187	Navigation
Types of Goats	00:00:05.247	Navigation
Uses of Goats	00:00:07.307	Navigation
Uses of Goat Milk	00:00:08.778	Navigation
Tomato Poem	00:00:13.191	Navigation

STEP 6 ▼
Skinning the Video

Click Next to arrive at the Skinning page in the wizard, as shown in Figure 3.8.

Here you can select a general theme for the look and feel of the video controls. There are themes for Artic (cool blue), Clear, Mojave (beige), and Steel (gray). Each skin has one version where the controls appear on top of the video (these skins have *Over* in their names), and one version where the controls appear underneath the video (these skins are identified with *External* in their names). Although we're only working on producing the .flv file at this point, select one of the skins with a name that ends in *All*—just so you can see the navigation feature at work. Click Next and then, at the last step, click Finish.

FIGURE 3.8 You can select the look and feel for your video controls in this Skinning dialog box.

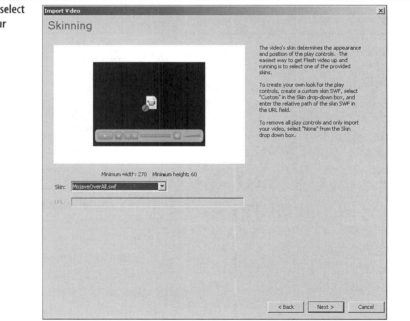

Navigating the Video

It should take a minute or so to compress the video file, depending on your computer. When it's complete, the progress bar disappears and you should see that, next to your `working.fla` file, a `.flv` file is present and named `the_children_must_learn.flv`. Select Control, Test Movie; the `.swf` will load the `.flv` you just created at runtime. It's sort of magical the way the `FLVPlayback` component gets configured automatically. You can pause and click the double-arrows in the video controller to jump to the Navigation cue points we added.

You can add the text for captions using the same technique we just used to add Navigation cue points. However, we're not going to do that because it's too difficult to select the times without an audio preview, which is simply not supported in Flash. We'll use another technique to create captions in the projects that follow. Realize that the primary goal of this project is to create a `.flv` file you can use in subsequent projects—and to see how you can use Flash to inject cue points.

Project:
ActionScript Cue Points for Captions in an XML File

In this project, we'll create an XML document containing cue point information. Namely, we'll specify the text captions and when—in the video—they should appear. The process involves using a separate application I built just for this purpose called `gathering_tool.swf`. The data you collect will become ActionScript cue points that get added at runtime simply because they won't be embedded in the `.flv` video; rather they'll be stored in an XML document.

STEPS▼

1. Preparing to use the offline gathering tool
2. Loading the video and transcript into the gathering tool
3. Setting cue points while the video plays
4. Exporting the XML file

Preparing to Use the Offline Gathering Tool

Copy the `gathering_tool.swf` file from the `gathering_tool` folder you downloaded and place a copy next to the `.flv` file produced in the first project (automatically named `the_children_must_learn.flv`). (You can also find a finished version of `the_children_must_learn.flv` in the `finished_source` folder you downloaded for this chapter.)

Copy the `video_captions.txt` file from the `starter_files` folder and place a copy of that file in your working directory.

Loading the Video and Transcript into the Gathering Tool

Double-click the gathering_tool.swf file to launch it in the Flash player. Type the name of the caption file (in this case, **video_captions.txt**) into the Transcription field and click the Load Text button. The contents of that text file appear in a list on the right, and the first row of that list is selected as shown in Figure 3.9.

Type the name of the .flv video file to which you want to add the captions (in this case, type **the_children_must_learn.flv**) into the Media field and click the Load button.

Next, you'll be using the gathering_tool.swf to collect cue points. Familiarize yourself with this tool (see Figure 3.10).

FIGURE 3.9   The gathering_tool.swf **can load the entire transcript from a text file.**

Setting Cue Points While the Video Plays

Now for the fun part. Click the Play button to watch the video as many times as needed to get an idea of when the captions are supposed to appear. You can scrub the video (drag the upward-pointing triangle), but when you let go, the video will jump to the closest keyframe. That is, when you encode a video, it automatically embeds keyframes where significant changes occur onscreen. The in-between frames contain only the parts that have changed. Therefore, you can only seek to keyframes (not to the in-between frames).

When you're ready, make sure the first row of the transcription list is still selected. Rewind the video and then click the Play button to start the video playing. Get ready to click the Add button! When the narrator says, "Next year," click the Add button to create a cue point and automatically advance to the next line in the transcription list (which is, "the children will study materials"). Then, at the right moment, click the Add button again to insert a cue point for the second line in the transcript. Because the captions appear quickly, you might need a few tries to get it right. If you accidentally add a cue point, you can click its triangle and then click the Remove button. Just remember that if you're coming back through to add more cue points, you need to first select the row in the

transcription list for the text you want to insert next.

FIGURE 3.10 **The** gathering_tool.swf **has a bunch of handy features.**

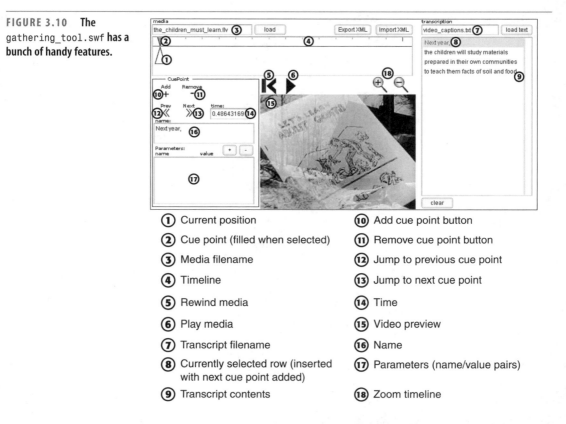

1. Current position
2. Cue point (filled when selected)
3. Media filename
4. Timeline
5. Rewind media
6. Play media
7. Transcript filename
8. Currently selected row (inserted with next cue point added)
9. Transcript contents
10. Add cue point button
11. Remove cue point button
12. Jump to previous cue point
13. Jump to next cue point
14. Time
15. Video preview
16. Name
17. Parameters (name/value pairs)
18. Zoom timeline

After you insert the cue points, rewind and then click the Play button to watch the captions appear in the cue point area. See whether the synchronization is close. For your reference, my five cue points were inserted at 3.239 seconds, 4.257 seconds, 5.825 seconds, 8.071 seconds, and 11.311 seconds. However, it's not as though you need to have those exact numbers because no one will notice if the caption appears a fraction of a second too early or late.

Don't close gathering_tool.swf because we still have to export the cue points! (Note that we haven't actually injected the caption cue

points into the .flv file the way we did with the Navigation cue points in the project "Navigation Cue Points in a .flv File.") In the next step, you will take the cue point information and export it to a text file.

STEP 4▼
Exporting the XML File

In gathering_tool.swf, click the Export XML button. Press Ctrl+C to copy the XML string the tool just generated for you. Create a new text file using Notepad or a similar program,

CHAPTER 3: Creating a Video with Synchronized Captions

and paste the contents of the XML string you just copied. Save the file as **video_captions.xml** in your working directory (we'll use it in the upcoming projects). You might want to view the XML file in a tool such as Internet Explorer (shown in Figure 3.11).

FIGURE 3.11   The XML file is much easier to read when viewed in Internet Explorer.

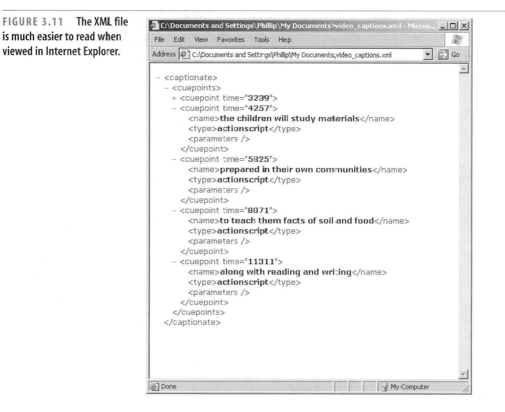

Now you have an XML file containing both the captions' values (the text) and the exact moment during the video when those captions should appear. You can use `gathering_tool.swf` for any video or audio file. Just import a different `.flv` video file (or `.mp3` file) and a corresponding transcript of the captions you want to add. The advantage of this tool is that you can identify the cue points in a natural manner—while the video plays.

Project:
Basic Caption Display Template

A video can contain a lot of cue points, but you need a vehicle to display them, such as a text field. In this project, we'll build a simple text display area that serves as a template from which you can create other styles and layouts. In the next project, we'll link the video to this .swf template file so the cue points from the video are sent to this text display area.

STEPS▼

1. Creating a captionType1.fla file
2. Adding the minimum code
3. Creating the .swf file

Creating a captionType1.fla File

Create a new Flash file and save it in your working directory with the name **captionType1.fla**. Select Modify, Document from the menu bar and set the width to **320** and the height to **50**. These settings change the .fla file to match the video's width and give you enough room for two lines of text—which should hold the caption text nicely.

Select the Text tool and create a block of text that fills the 320 × 50 stage. Use the handles on the text block to resize the text field area, as shown in Figure 3.12 (not the Properties panel's W and H fields because they scale the text).

FIGURE 3.12 Resize the text field using the handles, not the Properties panel.

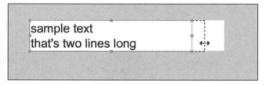

Next, use the Properties panel to set the Text Type to Dynamic Text. Set the instance name to **_txt** and set the Line Type to Multiline.

Finally, choose a font that will accommodate two lines of text (you can just type the longest caption in your project to see whether it fits in the newly adjusted text field). Next, set the text color to White.

To make the white text stand out on top of any background video, add a filter effect. With the block of text selected (not the characters *in* the text) select, Window, Properties, Filters and add the Drop Shadow filter—in fact, add two. For both, set the Blur X and Blur Y options to 0, the Strength to 100%, the Quality to Low (for better performance), and the Distance to 1. The default black color for the shadow will work fine. However, set one of the filter's angles to 225 and leave the other at the default angle of 45.

Finally, for the filter to really look great, return to the Properties panel and, with the text field instance selected, click the Embed button. Click the Basic Latin row and then click OK. This step adds to your .swf the font outlines for the font you chose. This way, the user won't need to have installed the font you selected. In addition, the filters have higher-quality results when the font is embedded.

STEP 2▼
Adding the Minimum Code

Each .swf file you create for this project can be used to display the text for a video. To do that, each .swf must implement the same minimum set of three functions: clear(), showText(), and getSize(). (They're formally defined in the ICaption.as interface file.) We'll add those functions now. Select the first keyframe in captionType1.fla and open the Actions panel. Type the code shown in Listing 3.1.

LISTING 3.1 **This Code Displays Captions in the** `captionType1.swf` **File**

```
function clear(){
    _txt.text = "";
}
clear();

function showText(name:String, wholeObject:Object, speed:String){
    _txt.text = name;
}

function getSize():Object{
    return {width:320, height:50};
}
```

Although you need all three of these functions in any template, you'll be able to modify how they're handled if you want to extend this project. (For now, use the code I provided here.) The `clear()` function is called immediately, and here we're just clearing the text field of any text that might already be there. The `getSize()` function returns (to the custom `CaptionHolder` class I built for this chapter) the size of this window so it can be masked out. Notice that 320 and 50 match the width and height of your movie. By providing the `getSize()` method, the `CaptionHolder` class can load any sized `captionType.swf` you create. (By the way, don't use Flash's `Stage.width` and `Stage.height` here because they won't report the correct values—the `captionType1.swf` file is ultimately loaded into a larger file that contains your video and `Stage.width` reflects the width of that file.) Finally, the `showText()` function is where you'll do the most modification in the more advanced variations of this project. Right now, it's very simple: When the video reaches a cue point, the cue point name is passed to the `showText()` function. In this case, we simply

display it in the _txt field instance onstage. There are additional parameters that we won't use until the "Advanced Captioning Template" project, later in this chapter.

STEP 3 ▼
Creating the .swf File

Finally, save the `captionType1.fla` file and select Control, Test Movie to generate the file `captionText1.swf`, which we will associate with the video in the next project. (The `.swf` we generate here has a blank screen.)

Project:
Channeling Cue Points to the Caption Display

Now we'll pull things together. Namely, we'll play the `the_children_must_learn.flv` video file we generated earlier while sending the captions gathered using the `gathering_tool.swf` to the `captionText1.swf` file we just built.

STEPS▼

1. **Creating the** `main.fla` **file**
2. **Creating the** `CaptionHolder` **symbol**
3. **Assembling support class files**
4. **Implementing the final code**
5. **Alternative 1: making the video play automatically**
6. **Alternative 2: adding a second** `captionText1.swf` **that supports navigation cue points**

STEP 1▼
Creating the main.fla File

For this project, we need to create a simple movie file that contains an `FLVPlayback` component that points to our `.flv` file.

Create a new Flash file and save it as **main.fla** in the same directory in which you've been working—the one that contains the video file `the_children_must_learn.flv`.

Select Window, Components and drag onto the stage an `FLVPlayback` component (from the FLVPlayback - Flash 8 category). Use the Properties panel to give the component an instance name of **playback**.

STEP 2▼
Creating the CaptionHolder Symbol

Select Insert, New Symbol. Click Advanced to expand the dialog box if isn't already expanded. Make sure the Type is set to Movie Clip and name it **CaptionHolder**. Next, enable the Export for ActionScript check box, which automatically enables the Export in First Frame check box. Then fill in both fields (Identifier and AS 2.0 Class) with the name **CaptionHolder** so your dialog box looks like the one in Figure 3.13. Click OK.

Now this empty symbol will be associated with the class file `CaptionHolder.as`.

FIGURE 3.13 **When you create the empty** `CaptionHolder` **movie clip, you can associate it with an ActionScript class file (**`CaptionHolder.as`**—but you don't type the** `.as`**).**

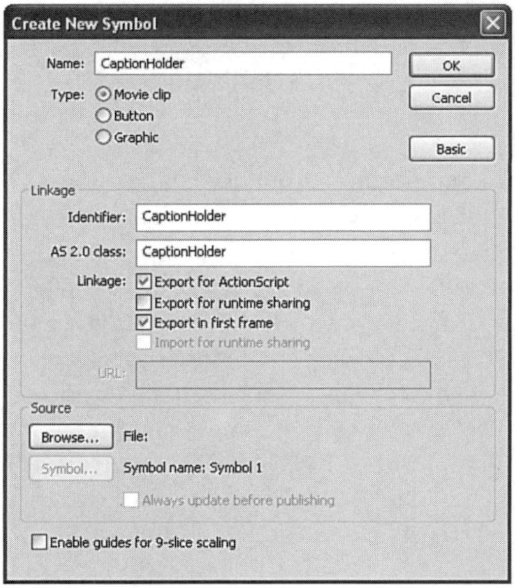

After you click OK, you are taken inside this new clip. Although you don't have to put anything here (the `captionText1.swf` file is loaded at runtime), draw a rectangle that's exactly 320 × 50 pixels (the space your captions need). Use the Info panel to ensure the rectangle's upper-left corner is aligned with the center of the clip (the plus sign), as shown in Figure 3.14.

FIGURE 3.14 The rectangle you draw inside the CaptionHolder symbol should have its upper-left corner aligned with the symbol's center (where the plus sign is shown).

Select your drawn rectangle and then select Modify, Convert to Symbol. Make sure the Movie Clip option is selected and name it **Rectangle**. After you click OK, use the Properties panel to give the Rectangle symbol an instance name of **preview**. Finally, click the first keyframe—still inside the CaptionHolder symbol—and type this code:

```
preview._visible = false;
```

This way, the preview instance is visible only while authoring.

Return to the main timeline of main.fla and drag an instance of CaptionHolder onto the stage. Because it contains the rectangle shape, you can position it below the playback instance or right on top—wherever you want. Use the Properties panel to give the CaptionHolder symbol on stage an instance name of **captions_clip**.

STEP 3 ▼
Assembling Support Class Files

You'll need to add two class files for the code to work. Copy the two homemade class files I created, named CaptionHolder.as and EventChannel.as, from the starter_files folder to your working directory. The following is a list of the minimum set of files that need to be in the same folder as main.fla:

- ▶ the_children_must_learn.flv
- ▶ video_captions.xml
- ▶ captionType1.swf
- ▶ CaptionHolder.as
- ▶ EventChannel.as

The FLVPlayback skin you selected, such as MojaveOverNoVol.swf, must also be adjacent to main.fla. (You're welcome to move the video, the XML, and the captionType1.swf files into a subfolder—just remember to add the path to that subfolder when specifying filenames in the next step.)

The CaptionHolder.as class file is needed by the CaptionHolder symbol you created in step 2. It handles loading the captionType1.swf file (or whatever template you specify). The EventChannel.as class does a lot of work, as detailed at the end of this chapter. It has three primary features:

- ▶ It takes all the events broadcast by the different cue point types in an FLVPlayback and channels them through a single, consistent event broadcast. That is, the cue point types all fire off different events (with different parameters and such), and the EventChannel.as class makes them all consistent.

- ▶ It handles the task of loading an optional XML file full of cue point information and injecting that information (as ActionScript cue points) at runtime.

- ▶ It supports the Sound object. This means that nearly everything you do with the FLVPlayback component and video you can do with an audio clip. (And you will in the next project.)

In doing all this work, the EventChannel.as class insulates you from the tedious code and keeps the code you have to write for each new project to a minimum.

STEP 4▼
Implementing the Final Code

Inside main.fla, select the first keyframe and open the Actions panel. Type the code in Listing 3.2.

There's very little code here, but it's worth digging into. The first three lines simply set up the FLVPlayback instance (playback), the same as using the Parameters panel but with script instead. Notice that you must set autoPlay to false because you need to wait for video_captions.xml to fully load. (I'll show you alternative code that makes the video start playing automatically in the next step.)

Line 5 creates an instance of the EventChannel class (saved in the variable myEventChannel). Next, we pass three parameters when triggering the init() method on the captions_clip instance (the CaptionHolder symbol you put on the stage—and therefore an instance of the CaptionHolder class). Those parameters are the path to the captionType1.swf template file we created earlier, a reference to the myEventChannel instance, and an array (eventList) that specifies which event types you want sent to the captionType1.swf template. (This array can include any of the following caption types: "event", "navigation", "actionscript", "caption", or "marker". In this example, though, because the array contains just "actionscript", we want to display only the cue points from the XML file.)

LISTING 3.2 **This Code Associates the** EventChannel **Class with Your** captionType1.swf **File**

```
1   var playback:mx.video.FLVPlayback;
2   playback.autoPlay = false;
3   playback.contentPath = "the_children_must_learn.flv";
4
5   var myEventChannel:EventChannel = new EventChannel();
6
7   //send init() function to the CaptionHolder instance
    //on stage (captions_clip)
8   var url = "captionType1.swf";
9   var eventList = ["actionscript"];
10  captions_clip.init(url, myEventChannel, eventList);
11
12  myEventChannel.init(playback, "video_captions.xml");
```

Finally, in the last line, we initialize myEventChannel by specifying the media source—in this case, it's the playback, which is an FLVPlayback component, but it could also be a Sound instance—and the XML file where ActionScript cue points can be found. The second parameter is optional, meaning you don't have to load cue points from the file if you don't want to.

Select Control Test Movie and then click the Play button on the FLVPlayback component to view the video. Figure 3.15 shows what mine looks like: The captions are on top of the video as if they were there the whole time.

FIGURE 3.15   The finished video with overlaying captions.

STEP 5 ▼
Alternative 1: Making the Video Play Automatically

There are two quick variations to this project worth examining. First, you might not like the fact that the video didn't automatically start playing. Add the following code *before* the last line, which triggers init() on myEventChannel:

```
function ready(){
    playback.play();
}
```

```
myEventChannel.addEventListener("ready",
                                this);
```

If this code looks familiar, that's because the myEventChannel instance supports every event supported by the FLVPlayback component (that is, our playback instance). Here, when the ready event fires, you tell the playback instance to play(). The myEventChannel class's ready event fires only after the XML has safely loaded *and* the playback instance has fired its ready event.

Select Control, Test Movie to confirm that the video begins playing automatically.

STEP 6 ▼
Alternative 2: Adding a Second captionText1.swf That Supports Navigation Cue Points

Just to see how versatile this application is, let's view those Navigation cue points you injected into the video back in the first project. One way you could do this is by simply passing ["navigation", "actionscript"] (instead of just ['actionscript']) for the third parameter when invoking init() on the captions_clip (lines 9–10 of Listing 3.2). But seeing both cue point types in the sole captionsType1.swf would get messy.

Do this instead: Create a duplicate of the captions_clip instance on stage and give it an instance name of **captions_clip2**. Move it to another area, such as above the video. Add the following code directly below where you call init() on captions_clip (line 10 of Listing 3.2):

```
var url = "captionType1.swf";
var eventList = ["navigation"];
captions_clip2.init( url,
                     myEventChannel,
                     eventList );
```

It's the same as the original call, except you're calling init() on captions_clip2 (not on captions_clip) and passing a different list of event types to support. (Well, just one type, but notice that it's an array, so you can specify more types. In fact, if you omit this parameter all cue point types are sent to the clip.)

> **📌 NOTE**
>
> By the way, if you were showing only Navigation or Event cue points, you wouldn't need to import the XML file because the cue point information would be in the .flv file. In that case you'd change
>
> ```
> myEventChannel.init(playback,
> "video_captions.xml");
> ```
>
> to simply read
>
> ```
> myEventChannel.init(playback);
> ```

Now when you test the movie, you'll see both ActionScript cue points (the captions in the XML file) and the names of the Navigation cue points embedded in the video.

Project:
Code for Audio-only Captions

To make a project like the one we just completed, but with audio this time, you use a nearly identical process. The only difference this time is that you can't inject the .mp3 file with Navigation cue points. You can only use ActionScript cue points.

STEPS▼

1. **Capturing the cue points**
2. **Creating the** main_audio.fla **file**
3. **Assembling support files**
4. **Writing the code**
5. **Alternative: using the** MediaPlayback **component**

STEP 1▼
Capturing the Cue Points

Follow the steps for the second project, "ActionScript Cue Points for Captions in XML File," but this time grab the file the_children_must_learn.mp3 from the source_media folder and the audio_captions.txt file from the starter_files folder. Enter those filenames when you run the gathering_tool.swf file, as shown in Figure 3.16.

When you're done gathering cue points, be sure to click the Export XML button. Then copy and paste the XML string into a text file you save as **audio_captions.xml**.

> **📌 NOTE**
>
> By the way, there's a long pause after the narrator says, "Some of them live a long way off." If you want the text to go away during the pause, simply insert an extra cue point and enter an empty string into the Name field.

FIGURE 3.16 You'll use the same `gathering_tool.swf` but this time for an audio track only.

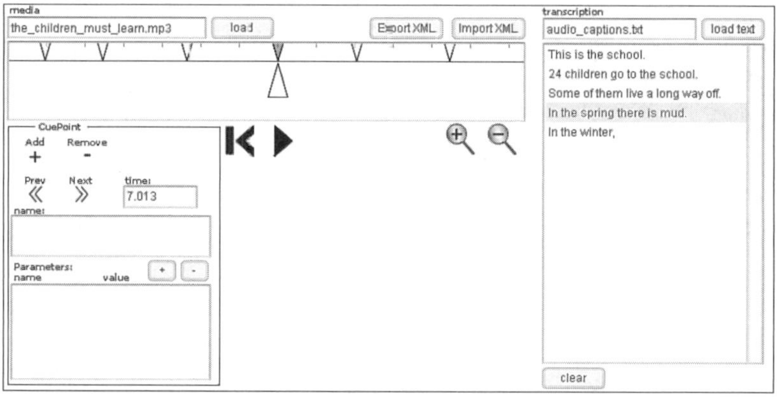

media			transcription	
the_children_must_learn.mp3	load		Export XML	Import XML	audio_captions.txt	load text

This is the school.
24 children go to the school.
Some of them live a long way off.
In the spring there is mud.
In the winter,

CuePoint
Add   Remove
  +   -

Prev   Next   time:
  «   »   7.013

name:

Parameters:
name   value   + -

clear

STEP 2 ▼
Creating the main_audio.fla File

Create a new Flash file and save it in your working directory as **main_audio.fla**. Either copy an instance of the `CaptionHolder` symbol created in the last project, "Cue Points in the Caption Display," or repeat step 1 of the preceding project.

Place on stage an instance of `CaptionHolder` and give it an instance name of **captions_clip** (just like before).

STEP 3 ▼
Assembling Support Files

Ensure that your working directory has, at least, the following support files in addition to `main_audio.fla` (you'll find the .as files in

the `starter_files` folder and the .mp3 in the `starter_media` folder—you need to create the .swf and .xml files yourself):

- ▶ `the_children_must_learn.mp3`
- ▶ `audio_captions.xml`
- ▶ `captionType1.swf`
- ▶ `CaptionHolder.as`
- ▶ `EventChannel.as`

STEP 4 ▼
Writing the Code

In the `main_audio.fla` file, select the first keyframe and open the Actions panel. Type the code shown in Listing 3.3.

```
1   var myEventChannel:EventChannel = new EventChannel();
2
3   var url = "captionType1.swf";
4   var eventList = ["actionscript"];
5   captions_clip.init( url, myEventChannel, eventList );
6
7   var mySound:Sound = new Sound();
8
9   function ready(){
10      mySound.loadSound( "the_children_must_learn.mp3", true );
11   }
12  myEventChannel.addEventListener( "ready", this );
13
14  myEventChannel.init( mySound, "audio_captions.xml" );
```

In Listing 3.3, I was extra careful not to start the audio until the ready event fires. If you don't have any captions at the start of the sound, you can safely start playing the sound anytime you want and forgo lines 9–12. The only critical sequence issues are that myEventChannel is instantiated before you invoke init() on the captions_clip (because you're passing a reference to the myEventChannel instance) and that the mySound instance is instantiated before you invoke init() on myEventChannel (because you're passing a reference to the mySound instance).

Save and test the movie.

STEP 5 ▼
Alternative: Using the MediaPlayback Component

Before I show you how to use the MediaPlayback component for this audio-only project, I want to tell you about the two advantages it offers. The first benefit is that it works with .mp3 audio files as well as .flv videos. Second, because the FLVPlayback component requires Flash Player 8, you'll want to use the MediaPlayback component if you're delivering a project to Flash Player 6 or 7.

Using the MediaPlayback component instead of the FLVPlayback component is simple. Open the Components panel and drag a MediaPlayback instance onstage (from the Media - Player 6-7 category). Give it an instance name of **myMediaPlayback**. Replace the code you wrote in step 4 with the code in Listing 3.4.

Basically, you can pass an FLVPlayback instance, a Sound instance, or—as shown here—a MediaPlayback component instance. The cool part about this version shown in Figure 3.17 is that, because you're using the MediaPlayback component, you automatically get a bunch of features, such as pause, play, and scrubbing. Remember that, although the FLVPlayback component also supports these features, it works only with video.

Additional Support for Sound Objects

Originally, I thought adding support for the Sound object made the `EventChannel.as` class particularly useful, which it does. However, programming a scrub bar for audio involves a fair bit of code, in addition to requiring you to temporarily disable the `EventChannel` instance from continuing to broadcast events. I added two public methods to the `EventChannel` class to do this: `stopMonitoring()` and `startMonitoring()`. In addition, while the user is scrubbing you can call `scrubTo(milliseconds)` to fire off the closest cue point to a given time—my class even prevents the same cue point from firing repeatedly. I mention all this for two reasons: First, if you want to dig into the code, you can (for that matter, I included a sample file called `bonus_scrub_audio.fla` in the download files). The second reason is that I wanted you to see my rationale behind adding support for the `MediaPlayback` component (which is explained in the next step). The `MediaPlayback` component works when delivering audio or video to Flash Player 6 or 7 (whereas the `FLVPlayback` component requires Flash Player 8). The `MediaPlayback` is definitely not my favorite component because it's next to impossible to skin and it's not consistent with other components. However, it's still compelling and hard to resist, especially now that you can easily add cue points in the same manner you've done for the `FLVPlayback` component and `Sound` class.

FIGURE 3.17   The `MediaPlayback` component is hard to resist when playing audio because it includes playback controls and is easy to use.

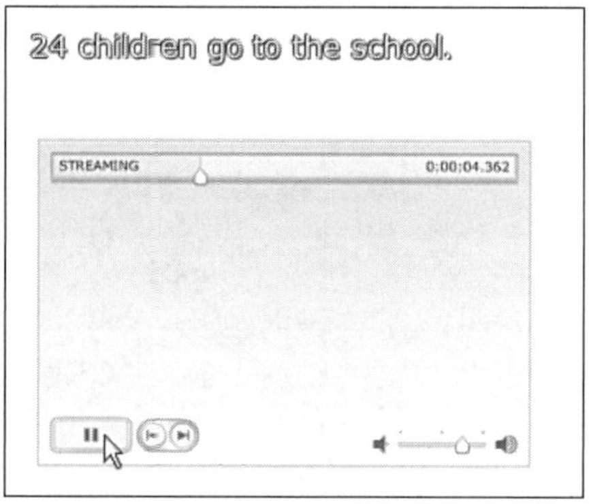

LISTING 3.4 This Code Plays a `.mp3` (and Its Captions) Through the `MediaPlayback` Component

```
import mx.controls.MediaPlayback;
var myMediaPlayback:MediaPlayback;
myMediaPlayback.contentPath = "the_children_must_learn.mp3";

var myEventChannel:EventChannel = new EventChannel();

var url = "captionType1.swf";
var eventList = ["actionscript"];
captions_clip.init(url, myEventChannel, eventList);

myEventChannel.init(myMediaPlayback, "audio_captions.xml");
```

Project:
Advanced Captioning Template

The projects in this chapter have thus far showed you various ways of collecting cue point information and then implementing the code to work with the accompanying class files. The only Flash file where you got to do any sort of layout work was the basic template from the third project, "Basic Caption Display Template." Now you'll get to see how that template can be expanded. That is, you can make as many template types as you want. For example, you can change the overall theme by modifying colors and fonts. In addition, your template doesn't have to show text at all. As long as your template includes a minimum set of features (namely, functions for `clear()`, `showText()`, and `getSize()`), you can make it perform however you want.

The features added to the basic display template in this project make the template more effective at displaying captions. In the next project, you'll make a template for a synchronized Flash display instead of captioning *per se*. The first feature you'll add here is a subtle transition animation that runs anytime the text updates. Although this might seem gratuitous, I think it's an effective way to cue the user that the text has updated because her attention might have drifted to the images in the video. The second feature you'll add is a hide/close feature. Some users might not want to view the captions, so allowing the viewer to turn off the captioning is a nice option to include.

STEP 1 ▼
Creating the captionType2.fla File

If you have `captionType1.fla` handy from the earlier project, just open that and immediately select File, Save As. Then, name the new file **captionType2.fla**. (Use the version of `captionType1.fla` from the `finished_source` folder if you don't have your own. But remember to save it as **captionType2.fla** in your working directory.)

STEP 2 ▼
Nesting the Text in a Clip

To easily duplicate and move the text, select the `_txt` instance on stage and then select Modify, Convert to Symbol. Select the Movie Clip option and name the symbol **clip**. Also be sure you select the upper-left registration option. Click OK and then use the Properties panel to set the instance name to **clip**.

Modifying the Code to Move the Text

Select the first keyframe and open the Actions panel. Completely replace the existing code with the code in Listing 3.5 (which, by the way, you can copy and paste from captionType2.fla in the finished_source folder):

LISTING 3.5 This Code Displays Captions by Moving the Old Captions Offstage

```
1   function clear(){
2       clip._txt.text = "";
3   }
4   clear();
5
6   var dupe:MovieClip = clip.duplicateMovieClip( "dupe", 0 );
7   dupe._txt.text = clip._txt.text;
8
9   var initialLocation = clip._y;
10
11  function showText( name:String,
                       wholeObject:Object,
                       speed:String ){
12      if(speed == "fast"){
13          var duration = 0.2;
14      }else{
15          var duration = 0.5;
16      }
17      dupe._txt.text = clip._txt.text;
18      clip._txt.text = name;
19      var endTop =    initialLocation - clip._height;
20      var endBottom = initialLocation + clip._height;
21
22      clip._y = initialLocation;
23
24      new mx.transitions.Tween(dupe, "_y",
25              mx.transitions.easing.Regular.easeOut,
26              initialLocation, endTop, duration, true );
27
28      new mx.transitions.Tween(clip, "_y",
29              mx.transitions.easing.Regular.easeOut,
30              endBottom, initialLocation, duration, true );
31  }
32
33  function getSize():Object{
34      return { width:320, height:50 };
35  }
```

As different as this code seems from the original `captionType1.fla`, it's essentially doing the same thing: It's code to clear the text, code to show new text, and code that returns the stage size. Let's walk through it because it is more involved than the original. The `clear()` function is nearly identical as before, but notice that it's clearing the `text` property of the `_txt` instance nested inside the instance `clip`. Lines 6 and 7 create a duplicate of the clip so the user will see two blocks of text animate: the old text (in the `dupe` instance) going up offscreen and the new block appearing from the bottom. The `initialLocation` variable simply saves a reference to the default location for the clip with text.

Inside `showText()` is where most of the work is done. First, notice that this time we do use the third parameter (`speed`) and set a local variable, `duration`, accordingly (lines 12–16). You'll see how the `wholeObject` parameter is used in the next project, but because we want access to the third parameter, we need to leave `wholeObject` in line 11. The animation sequence goes like this: Copy the text from `clip` into `dupe` (line 17), put the new text (`name`) into `clip` (line 18), figure out the destination for text moving offscreen and ending at the top (line 19), figure the starting location below the stage for text moving up (line 20), make sure `clip` is in its initial location (line 22), and then create a new `mx.transitions.Tween()` for both `dupe` (lines 24–26) and `clip` (lines 28–30). It's easiest if you can visualize new text arriving onstage (in `clip`) and old text moving off (in `dupe`), as Figure 3.18 shows.

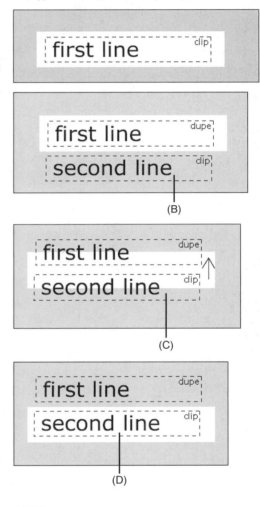

FIGURE 3.18 When a new line of text arrives, the `dupe` clip is placed onscreen (with `clip`'s old text) and `clip` is moved offscreen to the bottom (b). Then they both move up (c). When the animation is over, `dupe` is offscreen and the new text appears on `clip`, which is in place (d).

STEP 4 ▼
Publishing and Testing

While in your `captionText2.fla` file, select Control, Test Movie to produce `captionText2.swf`. You'll just get a blank `.swf` for now, which you can close. Reopen one of your main files (`main.fla` or `main_audio.fla`) and change the first parameter in the `init()` method on the instance of the `CaptionHolder` symbol. You want to point to `captionText2.swf` and not to `captionText1.swf`. You'll see that change in line 7 of Listing 3.6.

LISTING 3.6 This Code Uses `captionType2.swf` **Instead of** `captionType2.swf`

```
1   var playback:mx.video.FLVPlayback;
2   playback.autoPlay = false;
3   playback.contentPath = "the_children_must_learn.flv";
4
5   var myEventChannel:EventChannel = new EventChannel();
6
7   var url = "captionType2.swf";
8   var eventList = ["actionscript"];
9   captions_clip.init(url, myEventChannel, eventList);
10
11  myEventChannel.init(playback, "video_captions.xml");
```

Here's one last touch before you test: Select Modify, Document and set the frame rate to 31. This makes the `mx.transitions.Tween()` methods appear much smoother. Finally, make sure all the support files, such as the actual video, class files, and `video_captions.xml` data, are present. Then select Control, Test Movie.

The captions seem to appear from below and roll up offscreen as they depart. Plus, while you're scrubbing, the captions still animate but much more quickly.

STEP 5 ▼
Adding Code for the Hide/Reveal Feature

To support the hide/reveal feature, go to `captionText2.fla`, select the first keyframe, open the Actions panel, and add this code below all the existing code:

```
var showing = true;
var owner = this;
hide_btn.onPress=function(){
    var duration = 1;
    if(showing){
        //move down
        dupe._txt.text = "";
        showing = false;
        var destination = getSize().height;
        var startPosition = 0;
    }else{
        //move up
        showing = true;
        var destination = 0;
        var startPosition = getSize().height;
    }
    new  mx.transitions.Tween(     owner,
                                    "_y",
        mx.transitions.easing.Regular.easeOut,
                                   startPosition,
                                   destination,
                                   duration,
                                   true );
}
```

We'll create the `hide_btn` next. Anytime the user clicks this button, the entire caption template (owner) moves down or back up again.

STEP 6▼
Creating the Hide/Reveal Button

Inside captionText2.fla, draw a down arrow that is the full height of the stage. Above it, draw an up arrow, but make sure it's just above the stage (but not on stage at all) as Figure 3.19 shows. Select both arrows and select Modify, Group so they don't get wiped away.

FIGURE 3.19   The user will see only one arrow at a time (currently the arrow pointing down). After everything moves down, she'll see the up arrow.

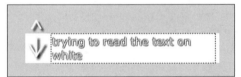

Nudge the clip instance over to the right if you need to make room for the arrows. You might also need to go inside the clip symbol to change the text margins or to modify the stage size. If you do change the stage size, remember to update the width and height properties in the object returned by the getSize() function that appears in the first frame's ActionScript.

Finally, draw a rectangle that's large enough to cover the two arrows. Convert the rectangle shape to a Button symbol by selecting it, pressing F8, and selecting the Button behavior. Name the new button symbol **Invisible** and click OK. Next, double-click the Invisible symbol and click once on the first keyframe; then click and drag the keyframe to the Hit

frame. The button's timeline should look like the one in Figure 3.20.

FIGURE 3.20   A Button symbol with nothing in any frame except the Hit frame will be invisible to the user but will remain clickable.

Return to the main timeline of captionText2.fla and be sure to give the Invisible symbol an instance name of **hide_btn** to match the code you added in step 5.

Select Control, Test Movie and then go back to and test the main file. Because only the template has changed, you could instead simply double-click the main.swf generated the last time you tested.

Project:
Synchronized Images Template

This project is simply another template that works with all the code you've produced so far. Specifically, the CaptionHolder.as class loads the .swf file you'll create in this project just like it does captionText1.swf and captionText2.swf. However, the purpose of this template isn't solely for captions. Rather, you'll specify frame labels that contain images, or any Flash graphic or animation, that you want to appear at synchronized times during the video. This project also incorporates the option of adding parameters to cue points (discussed earlier) to stuff even more information into each cue point.

STEPS▼

1. Encoding the video
2. Preparing to gather cue points
3. Creating an animated sequence
4. Gathering the cue points
5. Implementing the ActionScript in `imagesTemplate.fla`
6. Entering the ActionScript in `main_coffee.fla`
7. Testing `main_coffee.fla`

STEP 1▼
Encoding the Video

Create a new file in Flash and save it as **main_coffee.fla**. Select File, Import to Stage and then select the `coffee_house_1969.mov` public domain excerpt, located in the `source_media` folder. Step through the video import process, accepting all the defaults to produce `coffee_house_1969.flv`. You won't be injecting Event or Navigation cue points during this phase.

STEP 2▼
Preparing to Gather Cue Points

Select Control, Test Movie and then click Play to watch the video a few times, noting when the subject says the following phrases:

- ▶ "Circumscribed clientele"
- ▶ "cool people on campus"
- ▶ "not meaning derogatorily"
- ▶ "swinging" (and then "swinging" again)

- ▶ "coffee house"
- ▶ "place to be and the place to be seen"

STEP 3▼
Creating an Animated Sequence

Create a new file and save it in your working directory as **imagesTemplate.fla**. Select Modify, Document and set both the width and height to **250**. Select Insert, New Symbol. Make sure that the Movie Clip option is selected and name the symbol **Content**. Click OK and you'll be inside this clip. To see the edges of the stage, draw a rectangle that's 250×250 pixels. Position the rectangle inside the Content symbol so the upper-left corner of the rectangle aligns with the center of the Content symbol. Select Modify, Timeline, Layer Properties and then name the layer **Content**, click the Lock option, and change the layer type option to Guide (see Figure 3.21). Because we want the outline to guide us over several frames, click the cell in frame 25 and press F5 to insert frames.

FIGURE 3.21 The Outline layer simply helps you see the edge of the stage from inside the `Content` symbol.

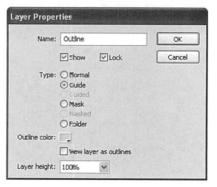

Here's where you can get creative. We'll create a graphic or an animation to correspond with each of the phrases the nice young man says. Open the file `imagesTemplate.fla` in the `finished_source` folder and investigate the contents of the `Content` symbol to see how I created the sequence you're about to create.

Create a new layer for the still images; name this new layer **Stills**. Insert a keyframe into frame 2 (press F6), and then import a photograph or create a graphic to support the phrase *circumscribed clientele*, such as a circle around a drawing of a student from the '60s. Click frame 3 and then select Insert, Timeline, Blank Keyframe (or press F7). Insert a graphic to support the word *cool*. In frame 4, insert a blank keyframe and place the following text: **Derogatorily**. To animate the international "no" sign on top of it, select Insert, Timeline, Layer (name the layer **No sign**). In the No sign layer, click frame 5 and insert a blank keyframe (press F7). Draw a circle with a line through it, convert the circle to a movie clip by selecting it and pressing F8, and name it **no**. In frame 10 of the No sign layer, insert a keyframe. Open the Actions panel and type **stop();**, and in frame 11 of the No sign layer, insert a blank keyframe (F7). Return to frame 5 and, using the Properties panel, select Motion Tween. Then, select the no symbol onstage in frame 5 and use the Properties panel to set a Color style of Alpha to 1%. (The no sign will fade on from frame 5 to frame 10.)

For the two mentions of the word *swinging*, we'll show a graphic of a swing and then show that swing in motion. In frame 11, draw the swing. Next, in frame 12, start an animation of that swing that continues to

frame 20, where you'll place a keyframe and a `stop()` action.

For the last two phrases (*coffee house* and *place to be and the place to be seen*), just place a photo or logo from your favorite coffee shop (in frame 21) and the text **be and be seen** in frame 22.

> ### 📌 NOTE
>
> You really can do anything you want, but I wanted some of the phrases to be supported with an animation and some with a still frame. In fact, there are a million other ways to do this, such as putting everything in single frames and on some frames placing a movie clip that contains multiple frames and a `stop()` on its last frame.

STEP 4 ▼
Gathering the Cue Points

Open `gathering_tool.swf` and enter the path to `coffee_house_1969.flv` into the Media field—don't worry about loading captions this time. Play the video and click the Add button each time the man says one of the previous phrases. You can remove cue points you added by mistake by clicking their triangles and then clicking the Remove button. Each cue point's name defaults to New Cue Point. Go through the added cue points by clicking each triangle or clicking the Prev or Next button; then enter a simple name for each one, such as **Circumscribed**, **Cool**, and so on. The user won't ever see this text the way we're building this project, but it helps to confirm that the cue points are in the right place.

When the cue points are in place, we'll add parameters to each one, such as a frame number and an option of whether the animation should stop there or play. I came up with the idea that each cue point will have parameters for frame (the frame number to jump to in the Content symbol) and option (either play or stop meaning that when the user jumps to the frame, it will begin to play or simply stop there). Click the first cue point and click the plus button to add a parameter. Set the name to **frame** and the value to **2**. This means when this cue point is reached, we'll jump to frame 2 in the Content symbol, where the "Circumscribed Clientele" graphic appears. Click the plus button again and name the second parameter **option**; then set the value to **stop** (see Figure 3.22). The plan is that, when the user jumps to that frame, it will stop there.

Go through all the cue points so each one has parameters for name and option, as shown in the following table:

Name	Parameters	
Circumscribed	frame	2
	option	stop
Cool	frame	3
	option	stop
Derogatorily	frame	4
	option	play
Swinging (1)	frame	11
	option	stop
Swinging (2)	frame	12
	option	play
Coffeehouse	frame	21
	option	stop
Place to be	frame	22
	option	stop

After you have all the cue points and parameters set, click the Export XML button. Copy the XML string that appears and create a new text document with Notepad or a similar program. Next, paste in the XML text you copied and save the file as **coffee_house.xml** in your working directory.

FIGURE 3.22 **This cue point has two parameters:** frame (2) **and** cption (stop).

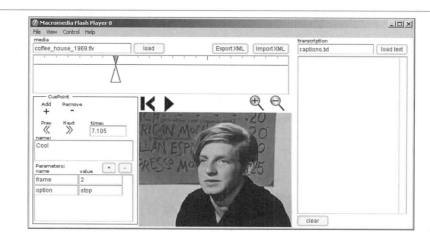

STEP 5 ▼

Implementing the ActionScript in imagesTemplate.fla

Go to the main timeline of `imagesTemplate.fla`. Drag an instance of the Content symbol onto the stage if you haven't done so already. (It might be a bit tricky considering nothing is in the first frame of the Content symbol.) Use the Properties panel to set the instance name to **content** and the upper-left corner to **0,0**.

Select the first keyframe, open the Actions panel, and type the code in Listing 3.6.

Notice that we completely ignore the first parameter received in `showText()` (that is, name). Instead, the code digs into `wholeObject`, which includes all the same properties that would be received from a standard `cuePoint` event. In this case, these properties are `type`, `target`, and `info`—inside of which are properties for `name`, `time`, and `parameters` (which itself contains whatever properties you injected into the `.flv` file or specified in the XML file). Here the code just grabs `info.parameters.frame` and `info.parameters.option`.

STEP 6 ▼

Entering the ActionScript in main_coffee.fla

Inside `main_coffee.fla`, be sure you have an `FLVPlayback` component onstage; if not, drag one from the Components panel. Give it an instance name of **playback**.

LISTING 3.6 **This Code Handles New Captions by Jumping to the Appropriate Frame in the** content **Instance**

```
function clear(){
    content.gotoAndStop(1);
}
clear();

function showText(name:String, wholeObject:Object, speed:String){
    content.gotoAndStop(wholeObject.info.parameters.frame);

    if( wholeObject.info.parameters.option == "play" ){
        content.play();
    }
}

function getSize():Object{
    return { width:250, height:250 };
}
```

Copy a CaptionHolder symbol from one of the other main files you've created (main.fla or main_audio.fla). Or simply select Insert, New Symbol and set the Create New Symbol dialog box as was shown previously in Figure 3.13 (step 2 of the fourth project). Place an instance of the CaptionHolder symbol onstage and give it an instance name of **captions_clip**. Arrange the screen so captions_clip is next to the video and not on top of it. The 320 × 50 rectangle shape in the CaptionHolder symbol is not an accurate representation of where the imagesTemplate.swf will appear because that

file is actually 250 × 250. You can double-click the CaptionHolder and double-click again so you're inside the Rectangle symbol and then resize that shape to make it 250 × 250. Back in the main timeline, you should select Modify, Document and increase the main_coffee.fla file's width to at least 600 so the FLVPlayback component (instance name playback) and the CaptionHolder symbol (instance name captions_clip) fit side-by-side, as shown in Figure 3.23.

Finally, select the first keyframe, open the Actions panel, and type in the code in Listing 3.7.

FIGURE 3.23 The FLVPlayback **(left) and** CaptionHolder **(right) are arranged side-by-side.**

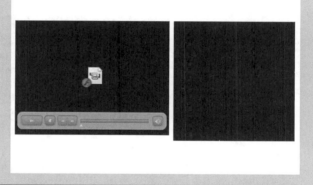

LISTING 3.7 **This Code Associates an Instance of the** EventChannel **Class with the** imagesTemplate.swf **File**

```
var playback:mx.video.FLVPlayback;
playback.autoPlay = false;
playback.contentPath = "coffee_house_1969.flv";

var myEventChannel:EventChannel = new EventChannel();

//send init() function to the CaptionHolder instance
//on stage (captions_clip)

var url = "imagesTemplate.swf";
var eventList = ["actionscript"];
captions_clip.init( url, myEventChannel, eventList );
```

continues

LISTING 3.7 **Continued**

```
//alternative code to effectively turn the FLVPlayback
//into autoPlay=true
function ready(){
   playback.play();
}
myEventChannel.addEventListener( "ready", this );
myEventChannel.init( playback, "coffee_house.xml" );
```

This code should look very familiar—the only changes are the filenames for the .flv, imagesTemplate.swf, and .xml files.

STEP 7▼
Testing main_coffee.fla

Make sure all the following support files are present in the same folder where your main_coffee.fla file is:

- ▶ coffee_house_1969.flv

- ▶ coffee_house.xml

- ▶ imagesTemplate.swf

- ▶ CaptionHolder.as

- ▶ EventChannel.as

That folder should also contain the FLVPlayback skin you selected, such as MojaveOverNoVol.swf.

In main_coffee.fla select Control, Test Movie.

I hope that this template shows you another way to use cue points for more than just captions and also gives you the ability to design and build additional template types. Like many projects in this book, extra templates are available for download; plus, I expect readers to share their templates.

Exploring the Support Classes

In each chapter in this book, I include this "Exploring the Support Classes" section as a behind-the-scenes look at the support files. You certainly don't have to study how everything was built, but I feel responsible to at least provide an architectural overview of all the code. If you're interested in adding features to this project or just want to learn more about how I chose to program this project, this section should be interesting.

I've produced the class diagram in Figure 3.24. Keep this figure handy as you read the following overview.

The two pieces we've built for the project in this chapter are the main.swf (far left) and the various captionType.swf templates (far right). We also created the external .flv and .xml files that get loaded at runtime. Notice that all captionType.swf templates *implement* the interface file named ICaption.as. There you'll see the three required methods each captionType.swf must implement. Recall, too, that inside our main.swf we created a symbol called `CaptionHolder`, which was associated with the `CaptionHolder` class (center). The main thing the `CaptionHolder` class does is load the particular `captionType.swf` filename specified when the `main.swf` triggers the `init()` method on its instance of the `CaptionHolder` class (shown as `captions_clip`).

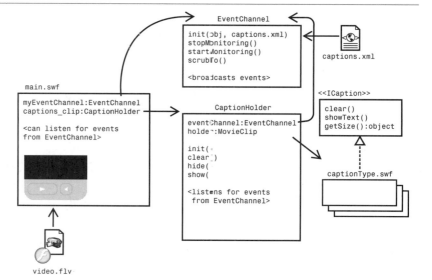

FIGURE 3.24 This diagram shows where your main file and `captionType` templates fit and how they relate to the `EventChannel` and `CaptionHolder` class files.

Before you call `init()` on the `CaptionHolder` instance, you must first create an instance of the `EventChannel` class. You'll see that the `CaptionHolder` class has an `EventChannel` instance (shown as a variable named `eventChannel` in the `CaptionHolder` class). In addition to loading the appropriate `captionType.swf`, the `CaptionHolder` also sets up listeners for events broadcast from the `EventChannel`. When the `EventChannel` broadcasts that a new caption should appear, `CaptionHolder` triggers the `showText()` method in the `captionType.swf` template.

The `EventChannel` does several things. First, it first loads an optional `.xml` file full of captions (if specified in `main.swf`). The `EventChannel` then sets up listeners for every event that can be broadcast from the media type you're using; this is because it supports

the `FLVPlayback` or `MediaPlayback` components plus plain `Sound` objects. If you send a reference to an `FLVPlayback` component when you first call the `EventChannel`'s `init()` method, all the events for `FLVPlayback` components are listened for. If you pass a reference to the `MediaPlayback` component, a different set of events are listened for. This means you can use the `EventChannel` as a proxy for any media type. Normally, you'd use `addEventListener()` on an instance of the `FLVPlayback` component, but this way you can use `addEventListener()` on the `EventChannel` instance. This has several advantages: The `EventChannel` hijacks the ready event and fires that event only after the `.xml` is fully loaded (and therefore is *really* ready). The `EventChannel` also merges the cue points in the `.xml` into ActionScript cue points. Finally, the `EventChannel` broadcasts a `cuePoint` event for regular Sound instances—something that's not built in to Flash's Sound class.

So, the `EventChannel` class *channels* all the event types that the different media types broadcast. Therefore, you can set up listeners if you want. In addition, the `CaptionHolder` instance is listening for all the possible events that should trigger the `showText()`—that is, so the text changes in your `captionType.swf` template.

The thinking behind the `EventChannel` class was that I wanted a unified way to listen for all the types of events related to captions. `FLVPlayback` components have a `cuePoint` event, but they're not the same as a `cuePoint` events broadcast from the `MediaPlayback` component. In addition, `.flv` files generated by Captionate broadcast events for `onCaption` and `onMarker`. Using the `EventChannel` means you don't have to think about how these syntaxes vary: You just channel them all to the `CaptionHolder` and the events you want to listen for are channeled to your `captionType.swf` display.

Final Thoughts

Now that you understand several kinds of cue points, you can select whichever one works best for your project. The framework built in this chapter lets you easily create new templates for displaying captions or responding to cue points by displaying graphics or animations. All you have to do is synchronize and design.

Let me give you a few more ideas of ways I've added synchronization beyond simply text captions. I built a kiosk for a history museum that included traditional captions of the narrator's script but that also had graphic highlights that appeared on a detailed map to supplement the audio discussion. In another project, I temporarily hid the video clip when the actor asked the user to interact with a survey question (built in Flash) that would appear in place of the video. There are so many more uses for captions and synchronization. As you can do for all the projects in this book, you can send me your ideas or any templates you build, and I can then share them with other readers on my website (www.phillipkerman.com/at-work/).

CHAPTER 4: Creating a Portfolio

About the Project

In this project, you'll build a vehicle to display images, Flash animations, or videos as a portfolio. Naturally, this involves adding as many of your personal images as you want to include. In addition, you have full control of the layout and exact functionality of the project. There are three content areas from which you can assemble your own portfolio using all or some of the following elements: a display area where the selected content loads, a list of thumbnail images, and a chapter listing (that is, thumbnails grouped into categories).

Prerequisites

There are almost no prerequisites for this project. I'm supplying sample images, but if you have your own content, such as a few JPG files, the project will be much more interesting. Also, experience in creating XML will enable you to externalize the list of images, but it is not required.

@work resources

Planning the Projects

The focus of this chapter is on organizing and tagging your images, creating a selection of templates for the three areas and learning how to extend these later, and learning how to implement the "engine" that I built to support this project. This engine is a code framework that insulates you from much of the grunt work, such as managing how the images download. You'll build several useful templates for the three content areas that conform to the engine's requirements. The cool part is that you can customize the look and feel of the templates and build additional templates if you wish. I added every common feature you might expect from a portfolio, but I also left room for you to add any features you want.

When you prepare a portfolio, you have the content (your images) and the display. The display is the Flash framework that gives the user a way to access and view your content; this is the engine I've provided for you along with the templates you create. There's a little bit to say about the content but much more about the framework. Just like how a house with a good foundation can be decorated, painted, or remodeled, our portfolio should work well regardless of the nature of the content you use with it.

Media Selection

Flash can import and display at runtime the following media types:

- Static images (.jpg, .gif, .png, .swf)

- Animated images (.swf, .flv)

- Audio (.mp3)

While authoring, you will discover that Flash supports countless other media types. But these are the types that can remain external from your Flash file and be loaded at runtime. Keeping the media files external and in their native file formats gives you two great advantages. First, you have the flexibility to swap out the media files at any time—even after the project is delivered. Second, you break up into smaller pieces an otherwise interminable download (where everything downloads at once). That is, users download only the elements they request, when they request them.

You might not have put the .swf file format into the static image category, but a one-frame .swf makes sense, especially for vector graphics. Also, I realize that video (.flv) and Flash animations (.swf) aren't really the same (and, for that matter, the code to load .swf and .flv files is completely different), but I think they belong together.

The point of this list is to point out the three standard image formats Flash supports: .jpg, .gif, and .png. At the end of the chapter I'll show you how to create a display template so you can include video files in your portfolio. First, though, let's cover the considerations for the image formats. The .gif file format supports a maximum of only 256 colors, so I'd avoid these files unless that's the only content you have. The main difference between .jpg and .png is simple: Only .png files can include an *alpha channel*. Both .png and .jpg files have 8 bits (256 gradations) of red, green, and blue, but .png adds an additional 8 bits of transparency. Also, even when your image doesn't contain transparency, .png files still might be better because .jpg files are always compressed (if only a tiny bit) and that compression can lead to subtle image artifacts. The quality issue can be really subtle, so be sure you're willing to force users to endure a longer download time if you choose to use .png because .png files are often larger than .jpg files.

Internal Versus External

Following the preceding praise for keeping media external, it might sound odd to hear what I am about to say: Some situations warrant importing the media files so that they're embedded in your Flash file. I'm thinking about the thumbnails, not the primary display files, which we will keep external in all the display templates that follow. We'll build thumbnail templates that support both internal and external images. Understanding the relative considerations is important.

Normally, the main issue affecting how quickly something downloads is the total file size. If your entire portfolio contains a few dozen images, the corresponding thumbnails, which might measure, say, 40 × 40 pixels, are only a few additional KB. However, if each thumbnail must be requested and downloaded separately, the total download time will be greater than if you downloaded all the thumbnails at the same time because each server request takes additional time. That is, 50 separate 1KB thumbnail images download much more slowly than a single 50KB .swf file that contains all 50 thumbnail images. So, there's a good case for storing the thumbnail images inside a single thumbnail .swf file—the download time will likely be shorter.

Storing thumbnails internally is also much less complex than storing the thumbnail files externally. Say you have 50 external .jpg files for thumbnails, one for each of your 50 portfolio items. Not only do you have to manage all those external files, but you also have to write code to load them sequentially. Flash will fail—as will any HTTP-based tool—if you tell it to request 50 external images all at once. There's no code whatsoever if you embed the images into your Flash file.

Another nice thing about embedding the thumbnails is that you can do anything you want with them once they're inside Flash. One way we'll use thumbnails inside Flash is to place each thumbnail file on its own separate frame of a movie clip. With this approach, you can easily add animation; for example, you could add a sparkle animation when the user rolls the mouse pointer over the thumbnail. Naturally, you can also crop the image however you want. Simply resizing an image will lose detail, but you might want to include only an excerpt of the full image in its thumbnail instead. Be sure to crop or *resize* images outside of Flash because importing content you don't need adds to the file size.

📌 NOTE

There are probably a million ways to embed into a .swf file images that are used for thumbnails, but we'll do it in only two ways. One way is to set the linkage identifier uniquely for each imported image and then use those IDs in your ActionScript to place the image onstage. The other way is to place each thumbnail into its own frame of a movie clip and jump to that frame using the `gotoAndStop()` method. You can pick the approach that best fits your project, but realize that, when you decide to embed, you have these additional questions to answer.

In case you think I'm trying to force you to internalize your thumbnails, realize that we're still going to build one template that loads the images externally—mainly to demonstrate the benefit of keeping content separated from the engine. This way, if you want to update thumbnails without returning to the Flash file, you can.

Stage Layout

As mentioned earlier, there are three engine elements from which you can choose: display, thumbnails, and chapters. We'll be building a .swf template for each of these areas; in fact, we'll build a variety of templates for each to support different behaviors. The figure on the opening page of the chapter shows a layout that uses all three elements. The most common variation of the portfolio project is to forgo the chapter categories. So, if you don't want to categorize your images and instead want to display all the thumbnails in one group, you don't need a chapter listing. To accomplish this, you just put all your images in a single chapter and choose not to include a chapters element in the layout. Figure 4.1 shows how the finished project would appear with no chapter listings.

Another variation is to simply have a display of the larger images with no chapters and no thumbnails. For this display option, you'll have to give users a way to go to the next image because they won't have thumbnails from which to choose. But the point is that you can select the elements of the engine you want to work with and use in the final portfolio project. Figure 4.2 shows how this variation focuses on the content and nothing else.

FIGURE 4.1 You don't need to include a selection area for chapters if you don't want any chapters.

FIGURE 4.2 You can build a layout with only a display, although you should give the user a way to advance to the next image.

Just as important as which of the three elements you're using in your final portfolio project is the position of these elements on the stage. When you specify the elements you want to include, you also specify the rectangle coordinates in which you want them to appear (that is, their x, y, width, and height). Figure 4.3 shows the layout tool I created to help you visualize the rectangles for each element.

For example, you can make the thumbnails appear horizontally along the bottom of the stage or vertically on the left side (really anywhere you want). I said you'll be specifying the entire rectangle for an element, not just the x and y location. The engine won't scale the different elements to fit the rectangle you choose because doing so would likely distort the content. Instead, the upper-left corner of each element aligns with the rectangle's upper-left corner and then the engine tells each element what its dimensions are. You'll have to write the code to accommodate those dimensions. For example, you'll have to widen the scrollbar of the thumbnails element to fill the full width if you choose to place that element in the rectangle across the bottom of the stage. If you choose to ignore the dimensions of the rectangle, the element will appear as is, bleeding down and to the right. The engine, however, masks each element so it doesn't appear outside the rectangle you specify.

FIGURE 4.3   In this layout, the display area's rectangle is 200 pixels wide and 200 pixels tall, and its upper-left corner is at 40 x and 40 y. Specify each element's rectangle in this manner.

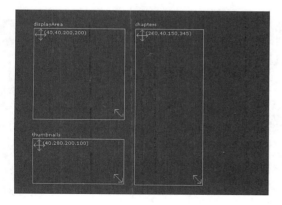

Communication Gateways

You'll find a detailed class diagram at the end of the chapter, but I think it's worth seeing an overview of the directory structure now so you'll better understand where, within the big picture, we'll be working.

Each .swf template is designed to be one of the element types: display, thumbnails, or chapter. You can make several templates for each element type so that you'll have a selection from which to choose. For example, you'll make a thumbnailsH.swf and a thumbnailsV.swf—one for when you want thumbnails to appear horizontally and one for when you want to display thumbnails vertically. When you're ready to assemble a portfolio, you create a main file that acts as the controller; in fact, it creates an instance of the PhotoController.as class. The PhotoController class handles loading all the element types you specify in the main file. The main file is responsible for two tasks. First, the main file lists the data for every image you want to include, such as its filename, a caption, and the chapter to which it belongs. Second, the main file specifies the elements—not just which ones to include, but also their respective rectangles and which template version to use (for example, thumbnailsV.swf or thumbnailsH.swf). This way you can easily change the layout or behavior to make new portfolios for different purposes.

When everything is running, the main PhotoController class instance handles all information exchange. That is, if the user clicks a thumbnail, the thumbnail element tells the controller and the controller in turn tells the display to show a new image. Elements never talk to each other; they talk only to the controller. This structure makes some cool things possible. For example, if the controller says, "display, show this image," then the display can handle that task however it wants. One display template we'll build will fade out the old image and fade in a new one. Another display template will slide the old image out and slide a new one in. The controller doesn't care how the display handles it; the controller always gives the display the same message (to show an image). By varying how the display (or any element) handles the various messages it receives from the controller, you can make very different templates that behave very differently.

Project:
Media Preparation

This optional project covers the basics of preparing media to appear in the portfolio project. It's optional because you can just use the sample media in the downloaded files if you prefer.

STEPS▼

1. **Resizing images**
2. **Preparing the thumbnails**
3. **Tagging the images**

STEP 1▼
Resizing Images

You need to make sure that the images that appear in the display area are resized properly. You don't have to resize all your content to the same dimensions (for example 200 ×

200 pixels). However, the images should all fit within a given size. For example, if you plan to have a display area 400 pixels wide by 300 pixels tall, images can be any size as long as they're not wider than 400 pixels and not taller than 300 pixels. Many image editing tools have best-fit algorithms for this purpose. Basically, you want the larger dimension to match the maximum (width or height); you can let the other dimension fall wherever it may (without distortion).

STEP 2▼
Preparing the Thumbnails

Regardless of whether you're planning to embed the thumbnails into the Flash movie or not (as discussed earlier), you must prepare the thumbnails. Prepare them by cropping, adjusting their contrast, and resizing their dimensions. Then either save the files in a known location or import them into your Flash file. At a minimum, you must resize the thumbnails using an image editing tool such as Photoshop. The thumbnails I supply are all 40 × 40, but you can use any size you want. You shouldn't import the full-sized images and scale them inside Flash because not only will they look bad, but the file size of the final .swf file will be much bigger than is necessary.

By the way, it's often better to *crop* the thumbnail instead of simply resizing the full image to a mini version. Consider that when you reduce only a portion of the original image to the size of a thumbnail, the cropped image isn't scaled as much as the full version. For example, if you have a photograph of a person standing up that is 400 pixels tall and scale it down to 40 pixels, that's a 90% reduction. However, if you first

crop the image to just the person's head—
say, to include just 80 pixels of the original
400 pixels in height—scaling that cropped
version down to 40 pixels is only a 50%
reduction. Figure 4.4 shows how cropping
might be more appropriate than just resizing.

FIGURE 4.4   When the original image (top) is simply
resized to 10% (bottom left) you can't see any detail. By cropping it first, however, you can select which portion to highlight (bottom right).

Original

—Resized only   —Cropped and resized

Finally, consider making all your thumbnails
the same size—such as a 40 × 40 pixels
square. This is a subjective size, but be sure to
think about how the thumbnails will appear
when spread out horizontally or vertically.

✎ NOTE

I think horizontally presented thumbnails look best if
they're all the same height (or the same height and
width). Vertically presented thumbnails look best
when at least their widths are the same. This comment
is subjective, but you should at least think about how
the thumbnails are to appear when deciding how you
want to size the thumbnail images.

STEP 3 ▼
Tagging the Images

You won't actually physically tag the image
files, such as by renaming the files with a
specific convention or injecting information
into the EXIF metadata that all .jpg files
support for tracking camera information
such as shutter speed, time, and date. Rather,
you must categorize and identify each image.
You need to enter data for your portfolio into
the main file (or, in the case of the
"Externalized Image Information" project,
into an XML file). Each image in this
project's design supports the attributes, which
are all strings, listed in Table 4.1.

✎ NOTE

If you look in the ImageInfo.as class file, you'll find
formal definitions for the properties listed in Table 4.1.

TABLE 4.1   Properties for Each Image in the imageData
Array

Property	Description
ID	A unique identifier. Every image should have a different ID.
name	A short description of the image, suitable for the text that appears when the viewer rolls over the thumbnail.

TABLE 4.1   Continued

Property	Description
url	The path to and filename of the image. This can be *relative* or *explicit*. However, explicit paths might require additional Flash Player security adjustments. You can name your files anything you want. You don't have to come up with a potentially cryptic naming convention such as img1_ch1.jpg, img2_ch1.jpg, and so on. Such conventions collapse when you need to add, remove, or change the image sequence.
thumbnail	An identifier for the thumbnail that contains one of the following three values, depending on whether you're embedding the thumbnails or linking to external files: the URL for the external image file (that is, the path to the thumbnail image), the linkage identifier for the imported image, or the frame label where the image resides inside a movie clip.
chapterID	The identifier for the chapter in which this thumbnail should appear. Each chapter also has a name and an ID attribute as you'll see in Listing 4.1.
caption	A longer description that's appropriate for appearing with the full image.

> 📌 **NOTE**
>
> If you do type an explicit path for the url property, you might find that the project works only after it's posted on a web server. The new local file security restrictions with Flash Player 8 might require you to specifically authorize connections to the Internet when you test the project on your desktop. See Appendix A, "Resources," for details about granting such access.

As I said, you won't be tagging the images. In this step, you are preparing to list the images either in an XML file or in an array specified in Flash's Actions panel. Basically, just gather all the images you'll be using and think about how you're going to identify them (by name, caption, and to which chapter they belong). Because there are different ways to identify the thumbnails—either with XML or in the Actions panel—I suggest you start with just a few images. At this point, you're really just familiarizing yourself with your content so it's easy to enter data later when you do so using different techniques.

Project:
Main Framework and Minimum Support Templates

This project is the bare-bones framework of the entire portfolio project. You'll use the main file you build here in the subsequent projects in this chapter, each time adding features you choose. The templates for the display, thumbnails, and chapters elements are so simple that you will likely replace them with more advanced versions you create later. They're still useful in showing the minimum requirements for each one, though. Do this project even though it doesn't have as many features as the subsequent projects.

At the end of this project, you'll have three .swf files for the three elements (display, thumbnails, and chapters) plus a main .swf that loads the three elements into specific locations on the stage.

STEPS ▼

1. **Creating the main file**
2. **Creating a holder for the** ProgressBar **clip**
3. **Entering image information**
4. **Entering template information**

5. Instantiating the `PhotoController`
6. Creating a simple display template
7. Creating a simple thumbnails template
8. Coding the thumbnails template
9. Testing it
10. Creating the simple chapters template
11. Including the chapters template and testing

Creating the Main File

Create a working folder and copy all the .as files from the `starter_files` folder you downloaded for this chapter into that working folder. Create a new Flash file and immediately save it as **main_simple.fla** in your working folder. Select Modify, Document and set the background color to black and the frame rate to 31 fps so the transitions will look smooth.

There are only three things you need to do with `main_simple.fla`, the file that will become your main controller: You must create a `ProgressBar` movie clip, specify all the image and chapter information, and specify which templates to use and where they should appear on the stage. (Of course, you'll have to make the templates, too, but we'll do that in the following projects in this chapter.)

Creating a Holder for the ProgressBar Clip

Select Insert, New Symbol. In the Create New Symbol dialog box shown in Figure 4.5, name the symbol **ProgressBar** and select the

Movie Clip option. Click the Advanced button to expand the dialog box if it isn't already and enable the Export for ActionScript option. This reveals the Identifier and AS 2.0 Class fields. Enter **ProgressBar** into each field (as shown in Figure 4.5) and click OK.

Now the `ProgressBar` symbol holds a place for the `ProgressBar.as` class file that defines its behavior.

FIGURE 4.5 This empty symbol points to the `ProgressBar.as` class file.

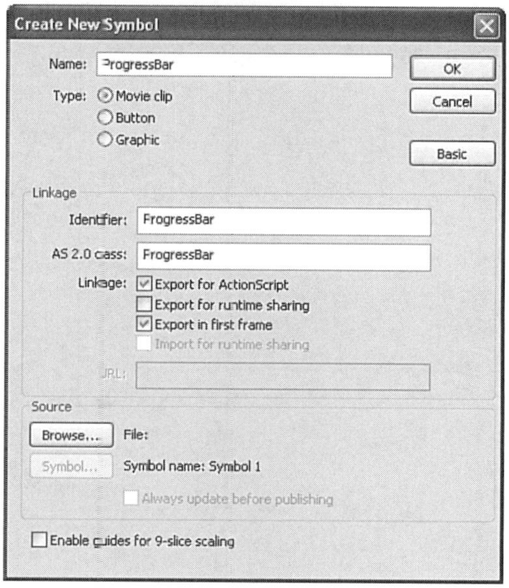

You'll be taken inside the `ProgressBar` clip. Be sure to return to the main timeline before going on to the next step.

Entering Image Information

Create a new folder in your working directory called **images**. Copy all the files from the images_full folder you downloaded for this chapter into your images folder, or place your own images there.

Return to main_simple.fla, select the first keyframe, and open the Actions panel. Enter the code shown in Listing 4.1 (and available from the main_simple.fla in the finished_source folder).

Basically, this code creates two arrays: the chapterData array that contains two chapter objects (each with ID and name properties)

and the imageData array with four image objects (each with ID, name, url, thumbnail, chapterID, and caption properties). Remember that your images don't have to be named with a particular convention, even though I used a url that includes sequentially numbered image filenames— image1.jpg, image2.jpg, and so on. When we add the code to load the templates, we'll just pass the two chapterData and imageData arrays to the PhotoController class.

LISTING 4.1 This Code Specifies All the Image Information

```
var chapterData:Array = new Array();
chapterData.push ( { ID:"ch1",  name:"chapter one"} );
chapterData.push ( { ID:"ch2",  name:"chapter two"} );

var imageData:Array = new Array();

imageData.push ( {  ID: "i1",
                  name: "image one",
                   url: "images/image1.jpg",
             thumbnail: "thumbnail1",
             chapterID: "ch1",
               caption: "this is my first image"  } ) ;

imageData.push ( {  ID: "i2",
                  name: "image two",
                   url: "images/image2.jpg",
             thumbnail: "thumbnail2",
             chapterID: "ch1",
               caption: "this is my second image"  } ) ;

imageData.push ( {  ID: "i3",
                  name: "image three",
                   url: "images/image3.jpg",
             thumbnail: "thumbnail3",
             chapterID: "ch1",
               caption: "this is my third image"  } ) ;

imageData.push ( {  ID: "i4",
                  name: "image four",
                   url: "images/image4.jpg",
             thumbnail: "thumbnail4",
             chapterID: "ch2",
               caption: "this is my first in chapter 2"  } ) ;
```

CHAPTER 4: Creating a Portfolio

STEP 4▼
Entering Template Information

Add the code in Listing 4.2 *above* what you added in step 3. (I suggest putting it above the existing code only because you'll modify it later, so it's handy to have this part at the top.)

This code creates the clipsToLoadArray array that we will pass to the PhotoController. Specifically, this array lists the templates you want the PhotoController to use. The three available types are "displayArea", "thumbnails", and "chapters" (this code does not yet define the "chapters" type). The url property defines the path and filename of the templates, both of which we'll create next. Finally, the rect property is a

Rectangle instance that defines the space on the stage in which you want the templates to appear. Note that the parameters for the Rectangle constructor are top (Y), left (X), width (in pixels), and height (in pixels)—not top, left right, bottom. Figure 4.6 shows how the two rectangles defined in Listing 4.2 will appear on the stage.

STEP 5▼
Instantiating the PhotoController

Here's one more line of code. It must be added below all the code you added in the last two steps:

```
photoController =
new PhotoController( this,
                     clipsToLoad,
                     imageData,
                     chapterData );
```

This code simply creates a PhotoController by passing a reference to the current timeline (using the this keyword), plus the three arrays you created in steps 3 and 4.

LISTING 4.2 This Code Defines the Types, Positions, and Filenames for the Elements That Will Appear on the Stage

```
import flash.geom.Rectangle;

var clipsToLoad:Array = new Array();

clipsToLoad.push( {type: "displayArea",
                   url: "display_simple.swf",
                   rect: new Rectangle(10,10,200,200) } );

clipsToLoad.push( {type:"thumbnails",
                   url:"thumbnails_simple.swf",
                   rect: new Rectangle(10,220,500,150) } );
```

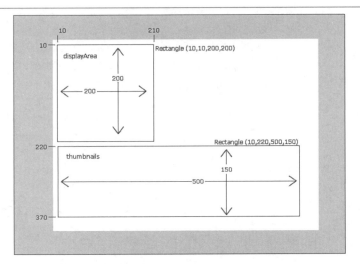

You can save the `main_simple.fla` now, but
we won't publish until after we create the
two `.swf` files: `display_simple.swf` and
`thumbnails_simple.swf`.

Select Modify, Document and set the movie
dimensions to 200 × 200. Select the first
keyframe, open the Actions panel, and enter
the code shown in Listing 4.3. This code is
also available in the `display_simple.fla` file
in the `finished_source` folder you downloaded for this chapter.

STEP 6▼
Creating a Simple Display Template

Create a new Flash file and immediately save
it in your working folder as **display_simple.fla**.

LISTING 4.3 This Code
Loads Images into a Movie
Clip

```
1    //reference back to controller
2    var controller:PhotoController;
3    //holder for loaded images
4    var imageHolder:MovieClip =
     createEmptyMovieClip( "imageHolder", 0 );
5
6    //required:
7    function setController( p_controller ){
8        controller = p_controller;
9    }
10   //required
11   function showImage( imageInfo:ImageInfo ){
```

LISTING 4.3   Continued

```
12      if( imageInfo == undefined ){
13          imageHolder.unloadMovie();
14          return;
15      }
16      imageHolder.loadMovie( imageInfo.url );
17  }
```

The `controller` variable gives this display template a reference back to the `PhotoController` instance in case it wants to get any information or invoke an event. We're not doing that here, but later you'll see how to add a feature that automatically advances to the next image when the user clicks. That action involves telling the controller to go to the next image. Notice that I indicated `setController()` and `showImage()` were required. The idea is that any template you design to behave as the `displayArea` type must include both methods (`setController()` and `showImage()`). The `setController()` method is how this template is given a reference to the `PhotoController` class and the `showImage()` method is how the `PhotoController` class can tell the template to display an image. If you're familiar with object-oriented programming, you can say a `displayArea` implements the interface `IDisplayArea.as`, meaning it includes all the methods listed in the `IDisplayArea.as` file. However, because we haven't actually created a `displayArea` class and formally stated that it will implement `IDisplayArea`, you won't receive any script errors if you failed to include the two required methods.

The core of this code is line 16. It loads the `url` property found in the `imageInfo`

parameter. When `showImage()` is invoked, all the information about the requested image is sent (captions, url, and so on), even though we need just the `url` property to load that file.

Before we move to the next step, save `display_simple.fla` and then select Control, Test Movie to generate the `display_simple.swf` file. You'll only see a plain white screen because no photos are loading yet.

STEP 7 ▼
Creating a Simple Thumbnails Template

Create a new Flash file and immediately save it in your working directory as **thumbnails_simple.fla**. Select Modify, Document and set the Movie Dimensions to 500×150. Use the Text tool to place a text field in the middle of the stage. Adjust the margins so the text field is wide enough to accommodate the longest string you expect to use the `name` property (or, in the case of the values provided in step 3, "image one"). Use the Properties panel to set the text type to Dynamic Text and the instance name to **rollover_txt**.

NOTE

To make a text field's margins accommodate any width, you can use ActionScript to set the field's `autoSize` property to `true`, as in `rollover_txt.autoSize = true;`.

Select Insert, New Symbol. Name the symbol **allThumbs**, select the Export for ActionScript option, and ensure that the Linkage field also reads `allThumbs`. (Don't enter anything into the AS 2.0 Class field.) Click OK to be taken inside the `allThumbs` clip. While inside `allThumbs`, select File, Import, Import to Stage. Browse to the file `thumbnail1.jpg`, which you can find inside the folder `images_thumb`, and click Open. Flash should display a dialog box asking whether you want to import a series of images (see Figure 4.7). Click Yes; all the thumbnails will appear on their own keyframes.

FIGURE 4.7 **One convenient result of naming the thumbnails sequentially is that we can import them all at once.**

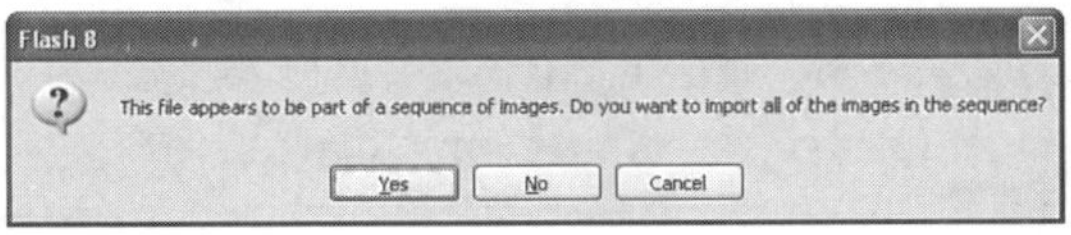

Ensure that each image is positioned so its upper-left corner is aligned with the clip's registration point (the plus sign).

NOTE

If your images are named in such a way that they fail to trigger Flash's automatic import feature (shown in Figure 4.7), you'll have to import each images into its own keyframe. There are several ways to do this. Personally, I'd first import all the images into one frame. After selecting File, Import, Import to Stage, select all the images (either hold down Shift to select all the images or hold down Ctrl to selectively pick the images you want to import). With all the images on a single keyframe, you can select an image; cut it (press Ctrl+X); insert a blank keyframe (press F7); and then select Edit, Paste in Place (press Ctrl+Shift+V). If you have a lot of images, return to my original suggestion that you start with just a few and then, after you see the different ways to either embed or link to thumbnails, you can select the approach you like best.

TIP

Here's a great tip that's not readily obvious. Say you want to align all the thumbnails but they appear in separate keyframes. Simply enable the Edit Multiple Frames onion skin option and then select the Onion All option from the Modify Onion Markers menu. Choose Edit, Select All and use either the Properties panel or the Align panel to set each image's X and Y position to `0`. Remember to turn off the Edit Multiple Frames option when you're done.

Finally, there is a bit of a chore: Click the first keyframe and use the Properties panel to set the frame label for that keyframe to **thumbnail1**. Click the keyframe in frame 2 and label this frame **thumbnail2**. Repeat this pattern for all the thumbnails. (If you need to import 10,000 personal thumbnail images, I suggest that you do only the first 4 here because you might prefer one of the alternative import methods that appear later in this chapter.)

STEP 8 ▼
Coding the Thumbnails Template

Be sure to return to the main timeline of the thumbnails_simple.fla file. Select the first

keyframe, open the Actions panel, and type the code in Listing 4.4. This code is also available in the thumbnails_simple.fla file in the finished_source folder you downloaded with this chapter.

LISTING 4.4 This Code Both Displays the Thumbnails and Lets the User Click to Select One

```
1    rollover_txt.text = "";
2
3    //required:
4    function setController( p_controller:PhotoController ){
5        controller = p_controller;
6        displayThumbs();
7    }
8
9    //required
10   function displayThumbs(){
11       var allImages = controller.getImageData();
12
13       var total = allImages.length;
14       var leftEdge = 0;
15       var SPACE:Number = 10;
16
17       var thumbHolder:MovieClip =
         createEmptyMovieClip( "thumbHolder", 0 );
18
19       for(var i = 0; i<total; i++){
20           var thisImage = allImages[i];
21           var thisThumb:MovieClip =
             thumbHolder.attachMovie( "allThumbs", "thumb"+i, i );
22
23           //go to correct frame
24           thisThumb.gotoAndStop( thisImage.thumbnail );
25           thisThumb._x = leftEdge;
26
27           //stuff the info into the thumbnail clip
28           thisThumb.imageInfo = thisImage;
29
30           //adjust spacing
31           leftEdge += ( thisThumb._width + SPACE );
32
33           //set some callbacks
34           thisThumb.onPress = clickThumb;
35           thisThumb.onRollOver = rollThumb;
36       }
```

continues

LISTING 4.4   **Continued**

```
37    }
38    function clickThumb(){
39        controller.clickThumb( this.imageInfo );
40    }
41    function rollThumb(){
42        rollover_txt.text = this.imageInfo.name;
43    }
```

Like the `displayArea` type, I designed the thumbnails template type to require a `setController()` method. This template type also requires a `displayThumbs()` method. Basically, any time the chapter changes, the thumbnails have to update. Here you can see that, inside `setController()`, on line 6 we immediately call our own `displayThumbs()` method to display the first set of thumbnails. Just note that `displayThumbs()` is publicly available to the controller, meaning that the `PhotoController` class can trigger it too.

Let's walk through the `displayThumbs()` method. Line 11 goes back to the controller to get all the image data and *stuffs* it into `allImages`. In fact, `getImageData()` retrieves the images in only the current chapter. On line 25, the `leftEdge` variable tracks where to position each new thumbnail. After each thumbnail is created, `leftEdge` is increased by that thumbnail's width plus `SPACE` (the space between each image, whose value you can modify in line 15). All the movie clips are going to get attached inside `thumbHolder`. This approach makes it easier when we want to clear all the current thumbnails and make new ones—we just start over by creating a new `thumbHolder` instead of explicitly removing every movie clip we attached.

Notice that line 24 jumps to the frame label we entered at the end of step 7, based on the `thumbnail` property. Line 28 is a bit tricky because the code stores image information in a homemade property called `imageInfo` for each thumbnail movie clip instance. Then, both lines 39 and 42 grab the `imageInfo` property of whichever thumbnail is clicked or rolled over. Notice that we invoke the controller's `clickThumb()` method by passing the entire ActionScript object (contained in the thumbnail's `imageInfo` property) which includes those properties for ID, name, url, and so on that we specified way back in step 3. This way, when the thumbnail is selected, we can send all the image details. Even though our simple display template cares only about the url property (to load the image), you might want the display to show more information, such as the image's caption.

This code shows that the `PhotoController` class supports at least two *public methods*: `getImageData()` and `clickThumb()`. All public methods are defined in the `IPhotoController.as` interface file that the `PhotoController.as` class implements.

Because it was such a chore to label all the frames, you might think it would be easier to jump to a frame number instead of to a label (I know I did). To do that, we could change line 24 to read

thisThumb.gotoAndStop(i+1). Naturally, this approach requires that all the thumbnails are placed in keyframes in the order you'd like them to appear, which is still easier than labeling each frame. However, this approach falls short if you intended to support multiple chapters. Because the thumbnails for all the chapters reside in the thumbnails.swf template, chapter 2's first image might not appear until frame 4, but the i variable starts back at 0 every time.

Before you go to the next step, save thumbnails_simple.fla and then select Control, Test Movie to generate the thumbnails_simple.swf file.

STEP 9▼
Testing It

Return to the main_simple.fla file and select Control, Test Movie. You should see the thumbnails appear and, when you click one, the larger version of the image should appear in the display area, as shown in Figure 4.8.

If, when you test the movie, the Output panel displays a message starting Error opening URL, go back to ensure that you've generated both display_simple.swf and thumbnails_simple.swf (not the .fla versions of those files) and that you've specified their filenames correctly in the clipsToLoad array declaration in the main_simple.fla file. Similarly, if you get

that message when you click a thumbnail, make sure that the images folder has the .jpg files specified in the imageData array.

When it works, it should work pretty well.

FIGURE 4.8   A simple but functional portfolio is born.

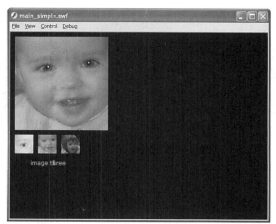

STEP 10▼
Creating the Simple Chapters Template

You probably noticed that there's no way to see the fourth image specified in the imageData array. That's because it's in the second chapter. Check out how easy you can make a chapters template using the List component.

Create a new Flash file and immediately save it in your working directory as **chapters_components.fla**. Open the Components panel by pressing Ctrl+F7 and drag an instance of the List component onto the stage. Use the Properties panel to give the list an instance name of **chapterList** and set the upper-left corner to 0 x, 0 y. If the list doesn't align correctly, open the Info panel and click the upper-left square; then try setting 0 x and 0 y in the Properties panel again.

Select the first keyframe, open the Actions panel, and type the code in Listing 4.5. This code is also available in the chapters_components.fla in the finished_source folder you downloaded with this chapter.

LISTING 4.5 This Code Populates and Defines the Behavior for the Chapters List

```
1   import mx.controls.List;
2   //reference back to controller
3   var controller:PhotoController;
4   //component on stage
5   var chapterList:List;
6   chapterList.addEventListener( "change", this );
7
8   //required
9   function setController( p_controller:PhotoController ){
10      controller = p_controller;
11
12      var allChapters:Array = controller.getChapterData();
13      var total = allChapters.length;
14      //clear list and populate
15      chapterList.removeAll();
16      for ( var i = 0; i<total; i++ ){
17          chapterList.addItem( {label:allChapters[i].name,
18                                  data:allChapters[i]} );
19      }
20      //select first chapter
21      chapterList.selectedIndex = 0;
22  }
23
24  function change(evt){
25      controller.pickChapter( evt.target.selectedItem.data );
26  }
27
28  //demonstrates using the sizeToRect() method
    // (called by controller)
29  function sizeToRect( rect:flash.geom.Rectangle ){
30      chapterList.setSize( rect.width, rect.height );
31  }
```

You might have guessed that, like the other two template types we've created (displayArea and thumbnails), the chapters template type also needs a setController() method. In this case, the code inside the setController() method immediately populates the chapterList component with the chapter names. Line 12 gets all the chapter data by calling the PhotoController's public method getChapterData(). The rest is pretty basic component work: Clear the list, populate it, and define how the change event is handled. Whenever the user changes the chapter, the change() method on line 24 is triggered. Note that each item in the chapterList has a label property and a data property (assigned on lines 17 and 18). The label property (what the user sees) contains the chapter's name property; a data property is assigned the value of the entire chapter info object as defined in ChapterInfo.as with the ID and name properties and originally set in the chapterData array in your main file way back in step 3. When the user changes the selected item in the list, we grab the data and send that to the controller's public method pickChapter() (line 25).

The biggest new thing here is the sizeToRect() method. The controller invokes this method and passes the size of the rectangle that was first passed in the clipsToLoad array of the main file back in step 4. In fact, all template types can include the sizeToRect() method. I added it now because it's so easy to resize a component using setSize() on line 30. The advanced templates in the projects that follow also support this method, but it can take a lot of work if you're not using components. Keep in mind that if you are just creating a single portfolio, you can decide on the size for each element (display, thumbnails, and chapters) and never worry about resizing. If, however, you want to build a template and have it automatically adjust to any given size, you'll have to write code to reposition all the user interface elements and place that code inside the sizeToRect() method.

Before you go to the next step, save chapters_components.fla and then select Control, Test Movie to generate the

chapters_components.swf file. That's the filename you'll specify next.

STEP 11▼
Including the Chapters Template and Testing

Return to the main_simple.fla file. We need to push() more ClipInfo objects to the clipsToLoad array. So, find the two push() methods you inserted in step 4 and add the following code on a new line following the second push() method:

```
clipsToLoad.push( {type:"chapters",
    url:"chapters_components.swf",
    rect new Rectangle(220,10,100,200) } );
```

This code loads a third element, so in all you'll have the elements display_simple.swf, thumbnails_simple.swf, and chapters_components.swf.

Select Control, Test Movie. You should be able to navigate to the second chapter now, as Figure 4.9 shows. The coolest part is that you can tweak the rectangle and the List component adjusts automatically.

This project was a bit arduous considering that the results are so basic. But now that you have the framework in place and you understand the basics, you can create advanced templates to replace the simple ones (display_simple.swf, thumbnails_simple.swf, and chapters_components.swf). In fact, you won't do anything to main_simple.fla except to change the template filenames it loads. In the last project in this chapter, you'll make the main file load image information from an XML file. In the next several projects, you'll build replacement templates that are displayed inside your main file.

FIGURE 4.9   The finished, basic project now includes the chapter selection element.

STEPS▼

1. Creating the `display_slide.fla` **file**
2. Writing the code for `display_slide.fla`
3. Modifying the main file to run `display_slide.swf`
4. Creating the `display_fade.fla` **file**
5. Writing the code for `display_fade.fla`
6. Modifying the main file to run `display_fade.swf`

Project:
Advanced Display Templates

The features you'll add to the basic templates you developed in the first part of this chapter will focus on improving the functionality or effectiveness for the user. You can also consider ways to reduce your production work, but that's secondary to improving the user experience. You'll create two variations of the display template in this project: one that performs an *alpha transition* to fade between images and another that slides the old image off and the new image on. In addition, the fade variation will include an automatic centering feature so your images always appear in the center of the display's rectangle regardless of the size of the rectangle or the image itself.

STEP 1▼
Creating the display_slide.fla File

Create a new Flash movie and save it in your working folder as **diplay_slide.fla**. Select Modify, Document and set the movie dimensions to 200 × 200. By the way, the slide effect appears correctly only when all your images are the same size (in the case of my examples, it's 200 × 200 pixels).

STEP 2▼
Writing the Code for display_slide.fla

Select the first keyframe, open the Actions panel, and type the code in Listing 4.6.

Remember that you can copy and paste the code from the file display_slide.fla that's in the finished_source folder you downloaded for this chapter.

LISTING 4.6   This Code Slides the Images onto the Stage

```
1    import flash.display.BitmapData;
2    //reference back to controller
3    var controller:PhotoController;
4    //constants:
5    var SLIDE_DURATION:Number = 0.5;//in seconds
6
7    //destinations for tweens:
8    var left = -200;
9    var middle = 0;
10   var right = 200;
11
12   //track whether we need to animate two clips or just one
13   var imageVisible:Boolean = false;
14
15   //need two clip holders
16   var lowerImage:MovieClip = createEmptyMovieClip("lowerImage",
                                                      0);
17   var upperImage:MovieClip = createEmptyMovieClip("upperImage",
                                                      1);
18
19   //manages loading images
20   var mcl:MovieClipLoader = new MovieClipLoader();
21   var listener = new Object();
22   listener.onLoadInit = function( target ){
23    //with the new image loaded into upper, tween both clips
24    new mx.transitions.Tween( target,
                               "_x",
                               mx.transitions.easing.Regular.easeOut,
                               left,
                               middle,
                               SLIDE_DURATION,
                               true );
25    new mx.transitions.Tween( lowerImage,
                               "_x",
                               mx.transitions.easing.Regular.easeOut,
                               (imageVisible ? middle : right),
                               right,
```

continues

Project: **Advanced Display Templates**   117

LISTING 4.6   Continued

```
                                                    SLIDE_DURATION,
                                                    true );
26    imageVisible = true;
27  }
28  mcl.addListener( listener );
29
30  //required:
31  function setController( p_controller ){
32    controller = p_controller;
33  }
34
35  //required
36  function showImage( imageInfo:ImageInfo ){
37    if( imageInfo == undefined ){
38      //just move the current image off
39      new mx.transitions.Tween( upperImage,
                                  "_x",
                                  mx.transitions.easing.Regular.easeOut,
                                  (imageVisible ? middle : right),
                                  right,
                                  SLIDE_DURATION,
                                  true );
40      imageVisible = false;
41      return;
42    }
43
44    var w = upperImage._width;
45    var h = upperImage._height;
46    var bitmapData:BitmapData =
      new BitmapData( w, h, true, 0x00FFFFFF );
47
48    //draw whatever is in upper, into lower
49    bitmapData.draw( upperImage );
50    lowerImage.attachBitmap( bitmapData, 0 );
51
52    //put lower where upper is, and move upper off to the left
53    lowerImage._x = upperImage._x;
54    upperImage._x = left;
55
56    //load new image into upper
57    mcl.loadClip( imageInfo.url, upperImage );
58  }
```

The normal sequence is to first copy the contents of the upperImage clip (the currently loaded image) into the lowerImage clip using the BitmapData.draw() method (lines 44–50).

CHAPTER 4: Creating a Portfolio

This way, we can begin loading a new image into upperImage (line 57) and the old image looks like it's still present. Compare this sequence to how the captions appear in the captionType2 template from Chapter 3, "Creating a Video with Synchronized Captions."

After the new image completely loads (that is, inside the onLoadInit() method), the two images *tween*: The new one moves from the left to the middle, and the old one goes from the middle to the right (line 25). Notice that I use the imageVisible variable to track whether an image is currently showing. The start _x property of the lowerImage clip's tween includes a condition (line 25). Basically, the image goes from the middle to the right only when there's currently an image present; otherwise, it goes from the right to the right (which has no visual effect). If the user selects a new chapter, the showImage() method is invoked with undefined as the parameter, which is how lines 37–42 know to simply move the current image offstage and reset imageVisible to false.

One last tidbit: You can change the SLIDE_DURATION variable to make the tween go faster or slower.

Before you go to the next step, save display_slide.fla and then select Control, Test Movie to generate the display_slide.swf file. That's the filename you'll specify next.

STEP 3 ▼
Modifying the Main File to Run display_slide.swf

Return to the main_simple.fla file and select File, Save As. Save the new file in your working directory with the name **main_with_slide.fla**. If you don't have main_simple.fla, use the one from the finished_source folder you downloaded for this chapter because the file must include the ProgressBar symbol we created in step 2 of the previous project. Select the first keyframe and, in the Actions panel, modify just the part of the code where you populate the clipsToLoad array. Edit that portion of the code to read as follows:

```
import flash.geom.Rectangle;
var clipsToLoad:Array = new Array();
clipsToLoad.push( {type:"displayArea",
    url:'display_slide.swf',
    rect:new Rectangle(10,10,200,200) } );
clipsToLoad.push( {type:"thumbnails",
    url:"thumbnails_simple.swf",
    rect:new Rectangle(10,220,500,150) } );
clipsToLoad.push( {type:"chapters",
    url:"chapters_components.swf",
    rect:new Rectangle(220,10,100,200) } );
```

The main change is that we're pointing to display_slide.swf. But I want to be sure to also include the chapters template.

Select Control, Test Movie. The images will slide in from the left and slide off to the right, as Figure 4.10 shows. Notice, too, that when you change chapters, the current image zooms off. Now we can make another variation of the display template.

FIGURE 4.10 The new image slides in and the old image slides out.

FIGURE 4.10 The new image slides in and the old image slides out.

sizeToRect() method. To display any captions images might have, use the Text tool and create a text field anywhere on the stage (we'll also center it with code). Use the Properties panel to set its type to Dynamic Text and its instance name to **caption_txt**. Also set its color to something bright (such as white) because the main file has a black background.

STEP 5▼
Writing the Code for display_fade.fla

Select the first keyframe, open the Actions panel, and type the code in Listing 4.7. This code is also available in the display_fade.fla file in the finished_source folder you downloaded with this chapter.

STEP 4▼
Creating the display_fade.fla File

Create a new Flash movie and save it in your working folder as **display_fade.fla**. This time we don't even need to modify the movie's dimensions because we'll add code to support the

---

LISTING 4.7 This Code Fades the New Image on Top of the Old Image

```
1   import flash.display.BitmapData;
2   //reference back to controller
3   var controller:PhotoController;
4   //constants:
5   var FADE_DURATION:Number = 0.5;
6   //in seconds
7   //stuff for caption and centering:
8   caption_txt.text = "";
9   caption_txt.autoSize = true;
10  var stageWidth:Number;
11  var stageHeight:Number;
12  //track whether we need to fade on/off, just off, or just on
13  var imageVisible:Boolean = false;
14  //make the holders
15  var lowerImage:MovieClip = createEmptyMovieClip("lowerImage",
                                                     0);
16  var upperImage:MovieClip = createEmptyMovieClip("upperImage",
                                                     1);
17  //manages loading images
18  var mcl:MovieClipLoader = new MovieClipLoader();
```

LISTING 4.7   Continued

```
19   var listener = new Object();
20   listener.onLoadInit = function( target ) {
21     //in case the clip contains a .swf:
22     lowerImage.blendMode = "layer";
23     upperImage.blendMode = "layer";
24     centerEverything();
25     caption_txt._visible = true;
26     new mx.transitions.Tween(    target,
                                    "_alpha",
        mx.transitions.easing.Regular.easeOut,
                                        0,
                                        100,
                                  FADE_DURATION,
                                        true );
27     new mx.transitions.Tween( lowerImage,
                                    "_alpha",
        mx.transitions.easing.Regular.easeOut,
                    (imageVisible ? 100 : 0),
                                        0,
                                  FADE_DURATION,
                                        true );
28     imageVisible = true;
29   };
30   mcl.addListener(listener);
31   //required:
32   function setController(p_controller) {
33     controller = p_controller;
34   }
35   //required
36   function showImage( imageInfo ImageInfo ) {
37     //fill caption (but make invisible until after image loads)
38     caption_txt._visible = false;
39     caption_txt.text = imageInfo.caption;
40     if ( imageInfo == undefined ) {
41       //just fade out current image
42       new mx.transitions.Tween( upperImage,
                                    "_alpha",
          mx.transitions.easing.Regular.easeOut,
                    (imageVisible ? 100 : 0),
                                        0,
                                  FADE_DURATION,
                                        true );
43       imageVisible = false;
44       return;
45     }
46     var w = upperImage._width;
47     var h = upperImage._height;
```

continues

LISTING 4.7   Continued

```
48    var bitmapData:BitmapData =
      new BitmapData( w, h, true, 0x00FFFFFF );
49    //draw whatever is in upper, into lower
50    bitmapData.draw( upperImage );
51    lowerImage.attachBitmap( bitmapData, 0 );
52    //synch lower with upper in case they're not the same size
53    lowerImage._x = upperImage._x;
54    lowerImage._y = upperImage._y;
55    lowerImage._alpha = ( imageVisible ? 100 : 0 );
56    //make upper alpha 0, and load image into it
57    upperImage._alpha = 0;
58    mcl.loadClip( imageInfo.url, upperImage );
59  }
60  //when controller tells us our size
61  function sizeToRect( rect:flash.geom.Rectangle ) {
62    //save the intended dimensions
63    stageWidth = rect.width;
64    stageHeight = rect.height;
65  }
66  function centerEverything() {
67    upperImage._x = stageWidth/2-upperImage._width/2;
68    upperImage._y = stageHeight/2-upperImage._height/2;
69    caption_txt._x = stageWidth/2-caption_txt._width/2;
70    caption_txt._y = upperImage._y+upperImage._height;
71  }
```

Much of this code is similar to the display_slide.fla file, but let me point out the new stuff. Notice when the controller invokes sizeToRect() that the intended dimensions are saved in the homemade variables stageWidth and stageHeight. The centerEverything() method is called inside the onLoadInit handler when a new image completely loads (line 24). Inside centerEverything(), we simply move the upperImage clip and caption_txt field. The lowerImage clip is effectively centered because it's set to match the upperImage clip at the same time it copies upperImage's contents on lines 48–54. In line 39, the caption_txt field is populated with the image's caption property.

One other interesting thing to note is lines 22–23. The layer blend mode is very subtle. In fact, you won't notice any difference unless your images are actually .swf files. To see the effect of not having the layer blend, *comment out* lines 22 and 23 by typing // at the beginning of each line, which makes Flash ignore those lines. Then create a .fla file containing two overlapping movie clips that contain a filled oval with a thick stroke, export a .swf, and in your main.fla file point to a .swf file instead of image1.jpg when you define the imageData array. Basically, when you do an alpha tween on clips containing vector images, the transparency varies unless you set the blend mode to layer, as shown in Figure 4.11.

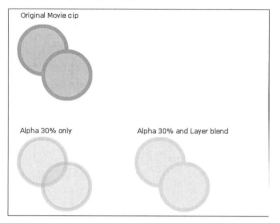

Before you go to the next step, save `display_fade.fla` and then select Control, Test Movie to generate the `display_fade.swf` file. That's the filename you'll specify next.

STEP 6▼
Modifying the Main File to Run display_fade.swf

Return to one of the main files you have created in this chapter—`main_simple.fla` or `main_with_slide.fla`—and select File, Save As. Save the new file in your working directory, but name it **main_with_fade.fla**. Select the first keyframe, and in the Actions panel modify just the part of the code where you populate the `clipsToLoad` array. Edit that portion of the code to read as follows:

```
import flash.geom.Rectangle;
var clipsToLoad:Array = new Array();
```

```
clipsToLoad.push( {type:"displayArea",
    url:"display_fade.swf",
    rect:new Rectangle(10,10,300,300) } );
clipsToLoad.push( {type:"thumbnails",
    url:"thumbnails_simple.swf",
    rect:new Rectangle(10,320,500,150) } );
clipsToLoad.push( {type:"chapters",
    url:"chapters_components.swf",
    rect:new Rectangle(320,10,100,200) } );
```

There are actually several changes to the code this time. The `displayArea` rectangle is enlarged to 300 × 300 pixels because my images are all 200 × 200 pixels and we're also including the caption this time. Recall that the previous display templates left the `sizeToRect()` method blank so everything was top-left justified. The other rectangles are also moved to accommodate the larger display area. (By the way, there's no reason why you can't have your templates overlap—it depends how you design them and how you want them to appear.)

Select Control, Test Movie. The images do not cross fade but they're always centered. Replace one or more of the sample images with an image that's smaller than 200 × 200 to see the centering feature in action. In addition the caption from the `imageData` array appears under the image.

With these two alternative `display` templates in your toolkit, we'll move on to making alternative templates for the `chapters` and `thumbnails` templates. The question I usually ask myself at this point is, "What other cool display templates can I make?" Feel free to try creating your own templates and then email your successes to me; I'll upload to my website (www.phillipkerman.com/at-work/) templates readers send me and that I build.

Project:
Alternative Chapter Templates

As much as I like Flash components, the `chapters_components.fla` file we built earlier makes the portfolio look too generic. In this project, you'll build two alternative `chapters` templates. One is hardwired because you will make one button for each chapter. It's appropriate for when your chapter list is fixed (that is, when you don't plan on changing the chapter categories without remaking the `chapters` template). The other template we'll make in this project is dynamic because the code attaches movie clips containing buttons as needed and can accommodate any number of chapters.

STEPS▼

1. Creating the `chapters_hardwired.fla` **file**
2. Writing the code for `chapters_hardwired.fla`
3. **Modifying the main file to run** `chapters_hardwired.swf`
4. Creating the `chapters_homemade.fla` **file**
5. **Writing the code for** `chapters_homemade.fla`
6. **Modifying the main file to run** `chapters_homemade.swf`

STEP 1▼
Creating the chapters_hardwired.fla File

Create a new Flash file and save it in your working directory as **chapters_hardwired.fla**. Select Modify, Document and set the movie dimensions to 150×200. We're not going to

support the `sizeToRect()` method that lets us change the layout based on the `Rectangle` dimensions specified in the main file. In this project, we'll just pick a size (in this case, 150 200) and stick with it.

Draw three shapes that will become chapter buttons (such as the shapes shown in Figure 4.12). One by one, click to select each shape and then select Modify, Convert to Symbol (or press F8); in the Create New Symbol dialog box for each symbol, make sure the Movie Clip option is selected. Use the Properties panel to give the three buttons the respective instance names **b1**, **b2**, and **b3**.

FIGURE 4.12   Hardwired buttons don't have to be pretty. The shapes 1, 2, and 3 will become separate buttons in this chapters template.

STEP 2▼
Writing the Code for chapters_hardwired.fla

Select the first keyframe, open the Actions panel, and type the code in Listing 4.8. You can also copy this code from the file `chapters_hardwired.fla` in the `finished_source` folder.

LISTING 4.8 The Complete Code for the Hardwired chapters Template	1	`import flash.filters.GlowFilter;`
	2	`var glowFilter:GlowFilter = new GlowFilter();`
	3	
	4	`//reference back to controller`
	5	`var controller:PhotoController;`
	6	
	7	`//required`
	8	`function setController( p_controller:PhotoController ){`
	9	`  controller = p_controller;`
	10	`  //highlilght first button`
	11	`  b1.filters = [glowFilter];`
	12	`}`
	13	`function clearFilters(){`
	14	`  b1.filters = [];`
	15	`  b2.filters = [];`
	16	`  b3.filters = [];`
	17	`}`
	18	`b1.onPress = function(){`
	19	`  clearFilters();`
	20	`  this.filters = [glowFilter];`
	21	`  controller.pickChapter(0);`
	22	`}`
	23	`b2.onPress = function(){`
	24	`  clearFilters();`
	25	`  this.filters = [glowFilter];`
	26	`  controller.pickChapter(1);`
	27	`}`
	28	`b3.onPress = function(){`
	29	`  clearFilters();`
	30	`  this.filters = [glowFilter];`
	31	`  controller.pickChapter(2)`
	32	`}`

You have to admit that hardwired solutions are often elegant because they take so little code. Anyway, when the user clicks one of these three buttons, we do three things: We clear the `filters` property from each button (those filters could have been applied the last time a button was clicked), apply a `GlowFilter` to the selected button (b1, b2, or b3), and then trigger the controller's `pickChapter()` method. Perhaps the most important difference in this

`chapters_hardwired.fla` template from the `chapters_components.fla` template we created earlier is the way `pickChapter()` is invoked. This time we're simply passing the index (0, 1, or 2 on line 21, 26, or 31, respectively), where back in step 10 in the "Main Framework and Minimum Support Templates" project earlier in the chapter, we passed an entire `ChapterInfo` object—that is, an ActionScript object with properties for ID and name. Note that this works only because the `PhotoController` class's `pickChapter()` method accepts either the `Object` or the `Number` data type.

Before you go to the next step, save the `chapters_hardwired.fla` file and then select Control, Test Movie to generate the `chapters_hardwired.swf` file. That's the filename you'll specify next.

STEP 3▼
Modifying the Main File to Run chapters_hardwired.swf

Return to one of the main files you have created in this chapter (`main_simple.fla`, `main_with_slide.fla`, or `main_with_fade.fla`) and select File, Save As. Save the new file in your working directory, but name it **main_with_hardwired.fla**. Select the first keyframe, and in the Actions panel modify just the part of the code where you populate the `clipsToLoad` array. Edit that portion of the code to read as follows:

```
import flash.geom.Rectangle;

var clipsToLoad:Array = new Array();
clipsToLoad.push( {type:"displayArea",
    url:"display_simple.swf",
    rect:new Rectangle(10,10,200,200) } );
clipsToLoad.push( {type:"thumbnails",
    url:"thumbnails_simple.swf",
    rect:new Rectangle(10,220,500,150) } );
clipsToLoad.push( {type:"chapters",
    url:"chapters_hardwired.swf",
    rect:new Rectangle(220,10,150,200) } );
```

You're welcome to point to one of your advanced `display` templates instead of to `display_simple.swf` if you prefer. Test the movie. As sloppy as the graphics in my new

chapter buttons are, I feel that the portfolio better represents me than when the portfolio uses the standard `List` component. You can certainly improve upon these graphics to match your style.

You'll probably notice that because the `chapters_hardwired.swf` file has buttons for three chapters, you need to update both the `chapterData` and `imageData` arrays (or live with the fact that the 3 button doesn't do anything). So, you change how the `chapterData` array is populated to read as follows:

```
var chapterData:Array = new Array();
chapterData.push ({ID:"ch1",
                name:"chapter one"});
chapterData.push ({ID:"ch2",
                name:"chapter two"});
chapterData.push ({ID:"ch3",
                name:"chapter three"});
```

In addition, you'll want at least one of the images to have its `chapterID` match this added chapter's ID (ch3). For example, still in the `main_with_hardwired.fla` file, add another `imageData.push()` statement just before the `photoController` instance is created (before the line that begins `photoController = new PhotoController(this,      )`, like so:

```
imageData.push ( {          ID:"i5",
            name: "image five",
         url:"images/image5.jpg",
            thumbnail:"thumbnail5",
                chapterID:"ch3",
        caption:"I'm in chapter 3"  } );
```

Naturally, you'll also need both an `image5.jpg` file in the `images` folder and a frame in the `thumbnails_simple.fla` allThumbs symbol. And don't forget to select Control, Test Movie to create the `thumbnails_simple.swf` file if you make an edit.

STEP 4▼
Creating the chapters_ homemade.fla File

Create a new Flash file and save it in your working directory as **chapters_homemade.fla**.

Select the Rectangle tool and draw a filled rectangle shape that will become a button. Use the Properties panel to set the shape's width to 140 and its height to 20. Use the Text tool to create a text field, and set the text field's size, position, and margins to fit within the rectangle. Use the Properties panel to set the text's type to Dynamic Text, ensure the Selectable button is disabled (that is, not pressed in), and give the text an instance name of **_txt**. Finally—because of some limits when using filters with text—click the Embed button and select Basic Latin. Not only does this action resolve the bugs with filters, it ensures that your selected font will appear correctly on all computers.

Finally, select everything (both the rectangle shape and the text field) and select Modify, Convert to Symbol. In the Convert to Symbol dialog box, make sure the Movie Clip option is selected, name the symbol **buttonClip**, and select the upper-left Registration square. Also, select the Export for ActionScript check box (click the Advanced button first if you don't see the Linkage area of the dialog box).

Make sure the Identifier text box reads `buttonClip`, as shown in Figure 4.13; then click OK.

Remove the instance now on stage (it's safe in your Library).

FIGURE 4.13 The button should be upper-left registered and have a linkage identifier (but no AS 2.0 class name, however).

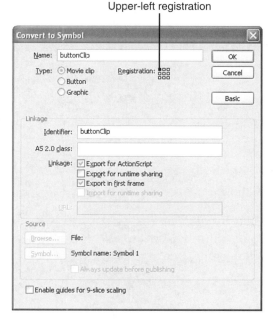

STEP 5▼
Writing the Code for chapters_homemade.fla

Select the first keyframe, open the Actions panel, and type the code in Listing 4.9. You can copy this code from the chapter_homemade.fla in the finished_source folder.

LISTING 4.9 **This Code Creates a Custom Button for Each Chapter**

```
1   import flash.geom.Rectangle;
2   import flash.filters.GlowFilter;
3   glowFilter = new GlowFilter();
4
5   //reference back to controller
6   var controller:PhotoController;
7   var owner:MovieClip = this;
8   var totalChapters:Number;
9
10  //required
11  function setController(p_controller:PhotoController){
12    controller = p_controller;
13
14    var allChapters:Array = controller.getChapterData();
15    //totalChapters is not a local var because highlightOnly()
      // needs to know how many buttons to affect
16    totalChapters = allChapters.length;
17
18    var SPACE = 10;
19
20    for ( var i = 0; i<totalChapters; i++ ){
21      var  thisButton:MovieClip =
          attachMovie( "buttonClip", "b"+i, i );
22      thisButton._txt.autoSize = true;
23      thisButton._txt.text = allChapters[i].name;
24      thisButton.chapterData = allChapters[i];
25      thisButton._y = i * ( thisButton._height + SPACE );
26      thisButton.onPress = pickChapter;
27    }
28    //highlight first button
29    highlightOnly( b0 );
30  }
31
32  function pickChapter(){
33    highlightOnly( this );
34    controller.pickChapter( this.chapterData );
35  }
36
37  function highlightOnly( clip:MovieClip ){
38    //turn off filter on all others
39    for ( var i = 0; i<totalChapters; i++ ){
40      owner["b"+i].filters = [];
41    }
42    clip.filters = [glowFilter];
43  }
44  function sizeToRect( rect:flash.geom.Rectangle ){
45    //only centering horizontally (ignoring height)
```

LISTING 4.9   **Continued**

```
46    stageWidth = rect.width;
47    for ( var i = 0; i<totalChapters; i++ ){
48        owner['b'+i]._x =  stageWidth/2 - owner['b'+i]._width/2;
49    }
50 }
```

This code attaches a new buttonClip symbol for as many chapters as needed; it grabs it via the getChapterData() method on line 14. All button instances that are created have the same onPress behavior—namely, to trigger the local pickChapter() method, which in turn highlights only the selected button and calls the controller's pickChapter() method. Notice this time we're passing the whole chapterInfo object, which was stored inside a homemade chapterData property for each button on line 24. We could have saved the value of i in a different custom property on line 24 because pickChapter() accepts an index or the whole chapterInfo object.

Finally, notice that we're doing some centering, but just horizontally. Each button is 10 pixels lower than the next based on the value of the SPACE variable. If you have more chapters than will fit in the space allotted (by the value set in the main file), the extra buttons appear below the bottom of the rectangle. However, when sizeToRect() is called, the buttons' _x values are adjusted so they're centered horizontally.

Before we go to the next step, save the chapters_homemade.fla file and then select Control, Test Movie to generate the chapters_ homemade.swf file. That's the filename you'll specify next.

STEP 6▼
Modifying the Main File to Run chapters_homemade.swf

Return to one of the many main files you have created in this chapter and select File, Save As. Save the new file in your working directory with the name **main_with_homemade.fla**. Select the first keyframe and open the Actions panel so we can modify just the part where we populate the clipsToLoad array. Edit that portion of the code to read as follows:

```
import flash.geom.Rectangle;

var clipsToLoad:Array = new Array();
clipsToLoad.push( {type:"displayArea",
    url:"display_simple.swf",
    rect:new Rectangle(10,10,200,200) } );
clipsToLoad.push( {type:"thumbnails",
    url:"thumbnails_simple.swf",
    rect:new Rectangle(10,220,500,150) } );
clipsToLoad.push( {type:"chapters",
    url:"chapters_homemade.swf",
    rect:new Rectangle(210,10,200,200) } );
```

Again you're welcome to use a different displayArea template in place of the display_simple.swf template if you want. You don't have to tinker with the chapterData or imageData arrays because the chapters_homemade.swf you just created is dynamic. Select Control, Test Movie. You'll see the screen layout, as shown in Figure 4.14.

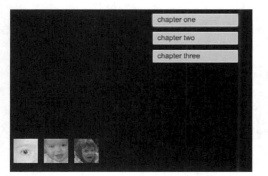

Project:
Advanced Thumbnail Templates

There are plenty of features worth adding to the thumbnails_simple.fla file you created earlier in this chapter. First, it's critical that we provide some sort of scrolling mechanism. When the width of all the thumbnails exceeds the width of the rectangle specified in the main file, the user needs a way to scroll to view all the thumbnails. Second, it would be nice to highlight the currently selected thumbnail and provide a visual indicator, such as changing the brightness of the thumbnail, so the user knows the thumbnail is clickable. Finally, to make the portfolio more customizable, we'll make an option to scroll through the thumbnails vertically as well as horizontally. In addition to these features, I'll show you another way to embed images (besides importing them into a movie clip) as well as how you can import all the thumbnails at *runtime*.

Of these features, scrolling is the hardest part to build. The feature gets pretty complex

when you support such things as click-and-hold, where it scrolls a little bit on the first click and then starts scrolling continuously, and a *scrubber* the user can drag back and forth. Also remember that we want the portfolio layout to adapt to any size rectangle specified in the main file.

At the end of this project, you'll have the following thumbnail templates:

- ▶ thumbnailsH_clip.fla
- ▶ thumbnailsH_import.fla
- ▶ thumbnailsH_linkage.fla
- ▶ thumbnailsV_clip.fla
- ▶ thumbnailsV_import.fla
- ▶ thumbnailsV_linkage.fla

That's three vertical and three horizontal thumbnail template arrangements. I used the three suffixes to mean the following: clip is for clip-based thumbnails (that's the same as how you imported images into keyframes of a movie clip inside the thumbnails_simple.fla); import looks for external .jpg files to import, and linkage requires the imported thumbnail images to have linkage identifiers (for each image in the Library). Luckily, the bulk of the code is the same for all these variations. That shared code is stored in the file thumbnails_core.as, which is included in all six template files.

STEPS▼

1. **Creating the clip-based horizontal thumbnail template**
2. **Entering the code for** thumbnailsH_clip.fla
3. **Using** main_tester_app.swf **to test your template**

4. Creating the `thumbnailsH_linkage.fla` template

5. Modifying the code for the `thumbnailsH_linkage.fla` **file**

6. Creating the `thumbnailsH_import.fla` template

7. Entering the code for `thumbnailsH_import.fla`

8. Creating vertical thumbnail templates

STEP 1▼
Creating the Clip-based Horizontal Thumbnail Template

Create a new Flash file and save it in your working directory as **thumbnailsH_clip.fla**. Because this template is clip-based, you need all the thumbnail images stored in labeled keyframes of a movie clip symbol with the linkage identifier of `allThumbs`. This is identical to what you did in step 7 of the first project, "Main Framework and Minimum Support Templates," when you created `thumbnails_simple.fla`. In fact, it's easiest to simply copy the `allThumbs` symbol from `thumbnails_simple.fla` and paste it into this movie. The `allThumbs` symbol should be in the Library, not on the stage (so delete it from the stage if you pasted it there).

Before we move onto the new stuff—scroller controls and code—add an animation to one of the frames in the `allThumbs` symbol. After all, one of the key advantages to this clip-based approach to thumbnails, as opposed to linkage or runtime import of thumbnails, is that you can do anything you want in the frame where the thumbnail exists. For example, in the version of this file found in

the `finished_source` folder, in the second keyframe of `allThumbs` there's a little sparkle animation on top of the thumbnail (see Figure 4.15).

FIGURE 4.15   You can easily add an animated movie clip on top of an individual thumbnail.

I created an animated movie clip and placed it on top of the thumbnail. There's really no limit to what you can do in the thumbnail's frame. You can even make a custom animation for each thumbnail if you want. However, if you create something that's larger than the thumbnail, the spacing of the thumbnails in the portfolio will be affected.

The onstage elements include buttons for scrolling right and left, a scrubber bar, and a background to the scrubber. You can use button symbols instead of movie clip symbols as I did if you want to take advantage of Over and Down states; otherwise, you can use movie clips to accomplish the same goal. Specifically, you need to create the following four instances on stage (either buttons or movie clips):

- ▶ `left_btn`
- ▶ `scrubber`
- ▶ `scrubber_back`
- ▶ `right_btn`

Figure 4.16 shows the layout of these elements.

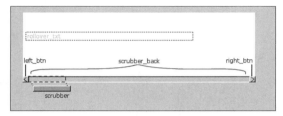

Although most of the layout is handled automatically, there are some critical requirements. All these instances should use the upper-left Registration option when you convert them to symbols. The contents of each clip should appear with its upper-left corner at the registration point. The x position for the left_btn instance should be 0 unless you want it to appear differently (that is, not flush left). The scrubber_back should be underneath the scrubber. In addition, scrubber_back should be aligned to the left, and you should adjust the location of the left_btn instance so its right edge touches the right edge of the scrubber_back instance (again, unless you want these elements spaced differently). Finally, because scrubber_back will be stretched, any strokes you use should be set to Scale: None in the Properties panel (as shown in Figure 4.17) so the strokes don't become too thick or thin as the scrubber_back is scaled. Alternatively, you can use 9-slice guides to define which portion should stretch, but I think non-scaling strokes is all you need. The 9-slice feature is a new feature in Flash 8 and was covered in more detail in Chapter 1, "Exploring Flash 8."

FIGURE 4.17 By setting the stroke's Scale option to None, you won't see the thickness change when the scrubber_back symbol is scaled.

Scale option set to None

You can also place a dynamic text field in the middle of the stage with the instance name rollover_txt. Don't forget to give all the buttons and scrubber parts instance names, too!

STEP 2▼
Entering the Code for thumbnailsH_clip.fla

In the main timeline of the thumbnailsH_clip.fla file, select the first keyframe, open the Actions panel, and paste the code shown in Listing 4.10 (which you can find in the thumbnailsH_clip.fla file in the finished_source folder you downloaded for this chapter).

LISTING 4.10 This Code Displays the Thumbnails Horizontally and Supports Scrolling

```
1    #include "thumbnails_core.as"
2
3    //init buttons
4    left_btn._visible = false;
5    right_btn._visible = false;
6    scrubber._visible = false;
7    scrubber_back._visible = false;
8    scrubber.useHandCursor = false;
9
10   //required
11   function displayThumbs(){
12
13     var allImages = controller.getImageData();
14     var total = allImages.length;
15
16     //make a holder so it's easy to dispose of / mask etc.
17     var thumbHolder:MovieClip =
         createEmptyMovieClip( "thumbHolder", 0 );
18     maskRect = new Rectangle( 0, 0, myWidth, myHeight );
19     thumbHolder.scrollRect = maskRect;
20
21     //starter lefter edge (gets moved as images load)
22     leftEdge = 0;
23
24     for( var i = 0; i<total; i++ ){
25       var thisImage = allImages[i];
26
27       var thisThumb:MovieClip =
           thumbHolder.attachMovie( "allThumbs", "thumb"+i, i );
28       thisThumb.gotoAndStop( thisImage.thumbnail );
29
30       //adjust loc and alpha
31       thisThumb._x = leftEdge
32       thisThumb._alpha = DIM_VALUE;
33
34       //stuff the info in the image
35       thisThumb.imageInfo = thisImage;
36       thisThumb.selected = false;
37
38       leftEdge += ( thisThumb._width + SPACE );
39
40       thisThumb.onPress = clickThumb;
41       thisThumb.onRollOver = rollThumb;
```

continues

LISTING 4.10   **Continued**

```
42        thisThumb.onRollOut = rollOffThumb;
43      }
44      scrollPosition = 0;
45      calculateScrubberSettings();
46    }
47
48    scrubber.onPress = function(){
49      var  min = scrubber_back._x;
50      var max =  min + scrubber_back._width - scrubber._width;
51      var offsetX = scrubber._x - _xmouse;
52      onMouseMove = function(){
53        var destination = _xmouse + offsetX;
54        if( destination > max ) destination = max;
55        if( destination < min ) destination = min;
56        var p = ( destination - min ) / ( max - min );
57        scrollPosition = maxScroll * p;
58        updateScrollPosition();
59        updateScrubberPosition();
60        updateAfterEvent();
61      }
62    }
63
64    function calculateScrubberSettings(){
65      maxScroll = leftEdge  - myWidth - SPACE;
66      updateScrubberPosition();
67      var showScrubber = ( leftEdge > myWidth );
68      left_btn._visible = showScrubber;
69      right_btn._visible = showScrubber;
70      scrubber._visible = showScrubber;
71      scrubber_back._visible = showScrubber;
72    }
73
74    function updateScrollPosition(){
75      if ( scrollPosition < 0 ) scrollPosition = 0;
76      if ( scrollPosition > maxScroll ) scrollPosition =
                                          maxScroll;
77      maskRect = new Rectangle( scrollPosition,
                                  0,
                                  myWidth,
                                  myHeight );
78      thumbHolder.scrollRect = maskRect;
79    }
80
81    function updateScrubberPosition(){
82      var  min = scrubber_back._x;
83      var max =  min + scrubber_back._width - scrubber._width;
84      var p = scrollPosition/maxScroll;
85      scrubber._x = min + p * ( max - min );
```

LISTING 4.10   Continued

```
86     }
87
88     function sizeToRect( rect:flash.geom.Rectangle ){
89       var h = rect.height;
90       var w = rect.width;
91
92       myWidth = w;
93       myHeight = h;
94
95       left_btn._y = h - left_btn._height;
96       right_btn._y = h - right_btn._height;
97       scrubber._y = h - scrubber._height;
98       scrubber_back._y = h - scrubber_back._height;
99
100      right_btn._x = w - right_btn._width;
101      scrubber_back._width = w -
                              left_btn._width -
                              right_btn._width;
102      if( scrubber_back._width < scrubber._width * 2 ){
103        scrubber._width = Math.max(15, scrubber_back._width/3 );
104      }
105
106      updateScrollPosition();
107      calculateScrubberSettings();
108    }
```

The first line directs Flash to include all the code from the thumbnails_core.as file. Therefore, be sure to copy that file from the finished_source folder that you downloaded and place a copy in your working folder.

Lines 4–7 initially make all the buttons invisible because we won't need them unless the combined width of all the thumbnails exceeds the width of the rectangle given for the thumbnails area. The displayThumbs() function is nearly identical to the one we made for thumbnails_simple.fla (step 7 of the first project, "Main Framework and Minimum Support Templates"). Notice that line 32 sets the _alpha property of each thumbnail to the value of DIM_VALUE (50%), which is a constant found in

thumbnails_core.as. Also, line 38 uses the SPACE constant, which you can also change in the core file. Finally, lines 40–42 define what happens when the user clicks or rolls over the thumbnails—namely, one of three homemade methods (clickThumb, rollThumb, and rollOffThumb) is triggered. I'll focus on those methods when I cover excerpts from the thumbnail_core.as file in a minute.

The calculateScrubberSettings() function (line 64) is called after the thumbnails have all been instantiated on line 45. At that point, we know how wide all the thumbnails are so this code calculates both the home-made variable maxScroll (how much extra you can scroll) and whether the scrubber should appear at all. These calculations are based on the rectangle in which this whole thumbnails element is presented, which is set in sizeToRect(). In sizeToRect(), we also align all the buttons to the bottom of the rectangle and space them out horizontally so that left_btn is flush left, right_btn is flush right, and scrubber_back is stretched to fill the gap between those two buttons.

The only other highlight I want to mention here is that the way we're making the thumbnails appear to scroll is by using the new scrollRect movie clip property from Flash 8. You can see in lines 77 and 78 that we first make a rectangle (with its x value shifted by the amount of the homemade variable scrollPosition) and then set the scrollRect property to that rectangle. This technique is effectively the same as moving a clip that's under a mask, but it's more elegant and performs much faster.

All the thumbnail variations we will make share a core set of functionality that's defined in the file thumnails_core.as. Here is an interesting excerpt from thumbnails_core.as:

```
function clickThumb(){
    controller.clickThumb( this.imageInfo );
    highlightOnly( this );
}

function rollThumb(){
    rollover_txt.text = this.imageInfo.name;
    this._alpha = BRIGHT_VALUE;
}

function rollOffThumb(){
    rollover_txt.text = "";
    this._alpha = this.selected ?
                BRIGHT_VALUE :
                DIM_VALUE;
}
```

Clicking a thumbnail triggers the clickThumb() method in the controller and highlights—or bumps up the alpha from 50 to 100—just that thumbnail. Rolling over a thumbnail highlights the thumbnail (also by changing its alpha) and displays the *rollover* text. Rolling off the thumbnail un-highlights the thumbnail, unless it's currently selected, in which case it leaves it highlighted. In every case, rolling off also clears the text.

Before we move on to the next step, save the thumbnailsH_clip.fla file and then select Control, Test Movie to generate the thumbnailsH_clip.swf file. The .swf you generate is completely blank. But if you see an error that reads File not found. #include "thumbnails_core.as", be sure you place a copy of the file thumbnails_core.as (found in the finished_source folder you downloaded for this chapter) next to your thumbnailsH_clip.fla and select Test Movie again.

STEP 3 ▼
Using main_tester_app.swf to Test Your Template

At this point, you should be familiar with creating a main file with a ProgressBar symbol and modifying the clipsToLoad array; in this case, just change thumbnails_simple.swf to read thumbnailsH_clip.swf. You just open an old main file you've created or take one from the finished_source folder, select Save As, and change the clipsToLoad array to establish the layout and filenames for the elements (display, thumbnail, and chapters) you want to include. Instead of doing that again, copy into your working directory the handy application I built for quick testing, called `main_tester_app.swf`. This tool lets you visually lay out the elements and select which templates to load (as shown in Figure 4.18). Here's how you use it: Drag each element (display, chapters, and thumbnails) to position them where you want, resize them by dragging their bottom-right corners, and then select the `.swf` template you want from the `ComboBox` components. Realize that the final project stage is shown in black so that you can easily position the elements right on the edge if you want. The best feature is that, when you click the Generate AS button, it generates the ActionScript to declare a `clipsToLoad` array matching what you laid out. All you do is copy the text that appears and paste it into your own main file. You can also click the Test button to load the templates in position.

FIGURE 4.18 The `main_tester_app` application file lets you quickly check your templates and generates the code for the rectangles.

One problem at this point is that you probably won't see the `thumbnailsH_clip.fla` template you just created scroll because there aren't enough images to necessitate scrolling. There are two ways to trick the scrolling thumbnail templates to actually scroll that don't involve manually adding more images. First, you can make the rectangle specified in the `clipsToLoad` array very narrow—say 100 pixels wide, as this code from the main file uses:

```
clipsToLoad.push( {type:"thumbnails",
        url:"thumbnailsH_clip.swf",
    rect:new Rectangle(10,220,100,150) } );
```

Second, you can change the value for the `SPACE` constant in the `thumbnails_core.as` file to a large number, such as `200`, to increase the space between each thumbnail to 200 pixels. If you change the `SPACE` variable (or anything in the `thumbnails_core.as` file), realize that you'll have to reexport the `thumbnailsH_clip.swf` file and then run the main file to see the results.

STEP 4▼
Creating the thumbnailsH_linkage.fla Template

This template uses each imported thumbnail's linkage identifier to create a strip of thumbnails from which the user can select. The benefit over the clip-based templates we've created so far is that here we won't have to manually place each thumbnail on its own manually labeled keyframe. In fact, we don't have to place any thumbnails—just set their linkage identifiers.

This version of horizontally scrolling thumbnails uses the same onscreen clips or buttons we created for thumbnailsH_clip.fla (assembled back in step 1): left_btn, right_btn, scrubber_back, and scrubber. It also uses almost all the same code. Instead of extracting the parts you need, simply open the old thumbnailsH_clip.fla file (or the thumbnailsH_clip.fla file in the finished_source folder you downloaded for this chapter) and select File, Save As; save the file into your working directory with the filename **thumbnailsH_linkage.fla**.

The main difference between this template and the other thumbnails templates we've made so far is that we don't need the allThumbs symbol; therefore, delete it from the Library panel. All the bitmap items (the imported .jpg files) are still safe in the Library. Next, select each bitmap item in the Library and set its linkage to the same name used in the imageData array for the thumbnail property: thumbnail1, thumbnail2, thumbnail3, and so on. To do this, select the first image in the Library, right-click (or use the Library's options menu), and select Linkage. Select the Export for ActionScript check box; this, in turn, automatically selects the Export in First Frame option. Set the Identifier to read thumbnail1 (not thumbnail1.jpg), as shown in Figure 4.19. Repeat this process for each thumbnail.

FIGURE 4.19 For each imported .jpg file, set a linkage identifier.

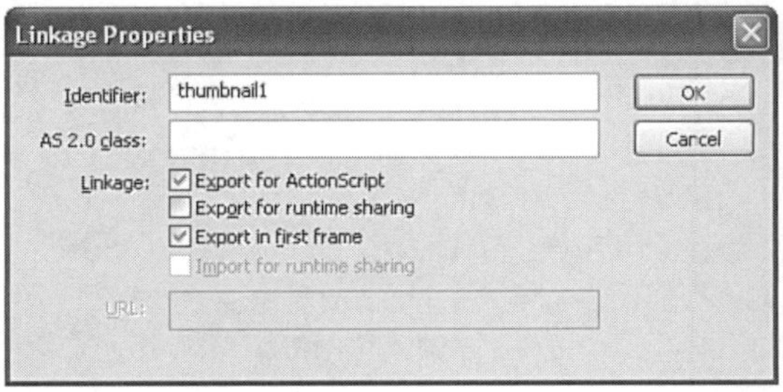

STEP 5 ▼
Modifying the Code for the thumbnailsH_linkage.fla File

It turns out there are only a few lines of code to change from the clip-based template to make this template use linkage identifiers instead.

While still inside thumbnailsH_linkage.fla file, select the first keyframe and open the Actions panel. You'll see the code from the clip-based template. Find the part in the for loop (which starts on line 24) where each thumbnail is attached to thumbHolder, and comment out lines 27 and 28 to make them read as shown in Listing 4.11.

LISTING 4.11 These Are the Lines You Comment Out from the Clip-based Thumbnails Template

```
27  //var thisThumb:MovieClip =
        thumbHolder.attachMovie( "allThumbs", "thumb"+i, i );
28  //thisThumb.gotoAndStop( thisImage.thumbnail );
```

CHAPTER 4: Creating a Portfolio

Enter the following replacement code below what you just commented out:

```
var bd:BitmapData =
BitmapData.loadBitmap(thisImage.thumbnail);
var thisThumb:MovieClip =
thumbHolder.createEmptyMovieClip("thumb"+i,
                                  i);
thisThumb.attachBitmap( bd, 0 );
```

This code uses the static loadBitmap() method to effectively copy a bitmap item's pixels into a BitmapData instance (bd). That BitmapData instance is attached to level 0 in the empty thisThumb clip using the attachBitmap() method.

> **NOTE**
>
> The only reason it works to reference BitmapData instead of using the full path flash.display.BitmapData is because the thumbnails_core.as file includes this line:
>
> import flash.display.BitmapData;

Save the thumbnailsH_linkage.fla file and select Control, Test Movie to generate thumbnailsH_linkage.swf. Test this .swf file using the main_tester_app.swf file, located in the main_tester_app folder. You won't see much difference except that none of the thumbnails are animating now.

STEP 6 ▼
Creating the thumbnailsH_import.fla Template

This template looks the same as the other two horizontal thumbnails templates we just created, but it behaves much differently. In this template, every thumbnail is loaded in sequence at runtime. Start by first opening either the thumbnailsH_clip.fla or thumbnailsH_linkage.fla file; then copy all the elements on the stage; including the buttons, scrubber, and text. Create a new Flash document, paste the onscreen elements you just copied, and then save the new file as **thumbnailsH_import.fla**. (Don't simply open the old file and save it with a new filename because you'll have all those embedded images, which aren't needed for this version of the template.)

> **NOTE**
>
> You'll see that importing thumbnails at runtime (as you do with the template we'll create next) is definitely easier than either embed option—linkage or clip-based. However, it's worth reviewing the relative considerations. Labeling keyframes as we did in the clip-based solution and giving the images linkage identifiers as we did in this step are both a pain. I like the clip-based approach because you can fine-tune the exact placement of each thumbnail and add animations. Ultimately, however, I think the clip-based approach is a tiny bit more work.

STEP 7 ▼
Entering the Code for thumbnailsH_import.fla

Open the finished version of thumbnailsH_import.fla—it's located in the finished_source folder you downloaded for this chapter—select the first keyframe, open the Actions panel, and copy the code from the first keyframe. Go to your thumbnailsH_import.fla file and paste the code into the Actions panel.

Let's walk through the differences between the code you just added to `thumbnailsH_import.fla` and the code in the two templates that embed the thumbnails (`thumbnailsH_linkage.fla` and `thumbnailsH_clip.fla`). Here are the highlights of the code in `thumbnailsH_import.fla`, which you should have open while you read the following paragraph. The main difference is that, instead of laying out the thumbnails while looping through the `allImages` array in the `displayThumbs()` method, the `imageInfo` objects are stuffed into an array called `thumbsRemaining` (line 31). Then, we start loading the images in line 36. The `loadNextImage()` function (lines 81–97) pulls off the first image in the array and issues the `loadClip()` method on a `MovieClipLoader` instance. Then, after the image finally loads in the `MovieClipLoader`'s `onLoadInit()` (lines 59–78), the layout is adjusted and `loadNextImage()` is called again. Basically, we create an array of images to load; begin loading one; and, when it loads, strip the image off the array (using `shift()`) and do the layout; then we load the next image.

You can make a couple important adjustments to the `loadNextImage()` function. Notice the variable `path` on line 86 (currently `""`). You can change that to load images from any path, such as a subfolder or my domain (to see how it might behave when posted online). The `randomStr` variable on line 90 is needed only if you want to ensure that the images aren't getting cached and therefore loading immediately. Finally, the `suffix` variable (line 93) is there only because—as you may recall—our current `imageData` array specifies `thumbnail1` and not `thumbnail1.jpg`. You can change the suffix to `""` if you plan to include the full filename

in your data source. (It's just easier to add it here because our other templates use keyframe labels, which can't have periods in their names.)

Save the `thumbnailsH_import.fla` file and select Control, Test Movie to generate `thumbnailsH_import.swf`. Test this new `.swf` file using the `main_tester_app.swf`. The main difference you'll see is that the images load in sequence. In fact, unless the thumbnails are stored online, all the thumbnails will load immediately. (It's cooler to watch them load in sequence if each one takes a second to load.)

STEP 8 ▼
Creating Vertical Thumbnail Templates

At this point, it's probably nothing more than a chore to physically create a vertical equivalent for each of the three horizontal thumbnail types: clip-based, linkage, and import. Besides a few significant visual differences, which I'll describe next, creating the vertical templates really just involves modifying the horizontal template you want to use. You can use any of the three vertical thumbnail templates (`thumbnailsV_clip.fla`, `thumbnailsV_linkage.fla`, or `thumbnailsV_import.fla`) in the `finished_source` folder you downloaded for this chapter.

The primary difference between the vertical and horizontal versions of the thumbnail templates is how the scrolling behaves. There's no scrubber in the vertical templates. Instead, we just widen the two arrow buttons to the width of the given rectangle (see Figure 4.20).

All three vertically based templates need only a clip or a button for the up_btn and down_btn elements. Because these two instances are stretched to the width of the given rectangle, you should use strokes with their Scale values set to None (as shown in Figure 4.17, earlier in the chapter) to ensure that the stroke line doesn't become too thick or thin when the arrow button is scaled. The only tricky thing to realize is that the thumbnails will appear *between* the up_btn and down_btn.

I considered making the scrolling templates automatically covert to vertical or horizontal depending on whether the rectangle was tall or wide. But it seemed like you might want a tall rectangle to do horizontal scrolling or even define a rectangle with equal height and width (also known as a square). In any event, be sure to play with all six versions of the thumbnails templates using the main_tester_app.swf I built.

Project:
Externalized Image Information

The hardwired approach of defining image information is not always ideal. That is, way back in step 3 of the first project, "Main Framework and Minimum Support Templates," we created an imageData array full of imageInfo objects with properties for ID, name, caption, url, thumbnail, and chapterID. Placing this information in an external XML file, or generating the XML data from a database, has definite productivity advantages. You don't have to tinker around inside Flash, populating the array. If you need to make a change, you just make a change to the external source.

This project puts all the image data into an intuitive XML format.

STEPS▼

1. Creating and populating the images.xml file
2. Creating the main_external.fla file
3. Coding the main_external.fla file

STEP 1▼
Creating and Populating the images.xml File

Open a text editor such as Notepad and select File, Open. Make sure that you select All Files from the Files of Type drop-down menu and open the images.xml file in the finished_source folder you downloaded for this chapter. Inside the main <portfolio> node, you'll find the following XML equivalent to the imageData array we created in the original main_simple.fla file:

```
<chapter ID="ch1" name="chapter one">

  <image ID="i1" name="image one"
      url="images/image1.jpg"
  thumbnail="thumbnail1"
    caption="this is my first image" />

  <image ID="i2" name="image two"
      url="images/image2.jpg"
  thumbnail="thumbnail2"
    caption="this is my second image" />

  <image ID="i3" name="image three"
      url="images/image3.jpg"
  thumbnail="thumbnail3"
    caption="this is my third image" />

</chapter>

<chapter ID="ch2" name="chapter two">

  <image ID="i4"
      name="image four"
      url="images/image4.jpg"
  thumbnail="thumbnail4"
    caption="this is the first in ch2" />

</chapter>
```

In the actual file, you'll see a third <chapter> node (its code is located below the code excerpt I included here) stocked with tons of images. That <chapter> node is simply another way of testing the scrolling thumbnail templates. This code uses the same sample image data as the other templates we created in this chapter. However, notice two differences: None of the images have an explicit chapterID attribute. You can tell which images go in which chapter because they're nested inside a <chapter> node and that node has an ID attribute. The second difference is really more of a bonus: All the chapter information (name and ID) are listed as *attributes* in the <chapter> nodes. This XML combines information from both the chapterData and imageData arrays and is all taken care of when parsing the XML. Basically, we build the chapterData array while extracting the image information. Plus, each image is injected with a chapterID that matches the ID for the node in which it resides.

Before you proceed to the next step, copy the images.xml file into your working directory. You're welcome to edit this file to refer to your personal image files.

STEP 2▼
Creating the main_external.fla File

Create a new Flash movie and save it as **main_external.fla** in your working directory. Select Modify, Document and set the frame rate to 31fps and the background color to black. You'll also need a ProgressBar clip like we made in step 2 of the "Main Framework and Minimum Support Templates" project. Select Insert, New Symbol. In the Create New Symbol dialog box (refer to Figure 4.5), name the symbol **ProgressBar** and select the Movie Clip option. Click the Advanced button to expand the dialog box if it isn't already expanded and enable the Export for ActionScript option. That reveals the Identifier and AS 2.0 Class fields. Enter **ProgresBar** into each field (as shown previously in Figure 4.5) and click OK. Because you'll be taken inside your new ProgressBar clip, be sure to return to the main timeline by clicking Scene 1 or by pressing Ctrl+E.

To support the *parsing* code that follows in the next step, you need to include the DataBindingClasses. First, make sure that your Library panel is open—select Window, Library if it is not. Next, select Window, Common Libraries, Classes. Drag the DataBindingClasses item into your Library panel, as shown in Figure 4.21. Now we can use XPath expressions to parse the XML.

the code in Listing 4.11 (which you can grab from the file main_external.fla in the finished_source folder).

FIGURE 4.21 Drag the DataBindingClasses into your file's Library to support XPath parsing.

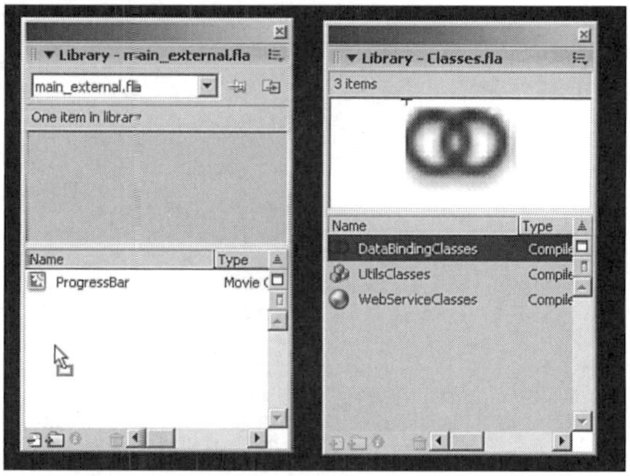

STEP 3 ▼
Coding the main_external.fla File

In the main_external.fla, select the first keyframe, open the Actions panel, and paste

LISTING 4.11 This Code Reads Image Data from an XML File	

```
1   import flash.geom.Rectangle;
2   import mx.xpath.*;
3
4   var clipsToLoad:Array = new Array();
5   clipsToLoad.push( {type: "displayArea",
6                      url: "display_simple.swf",
7                      rect: new Rectangle(10,10,200,200) } );
8
9   clipsToLoad.push( {type:"thumbnails",
10                      url:"thumbnailsH_clip.swf",
11                      rect:new Rectangle(10,220,500,150) } );
12
13  clipsToLoad.push( {type:"chapters",
14                      url:"chapters_components.swf",
15                      rect:new Rectangle(220,10,100,200) } );
16
17  var chapterData:Array = new Array();
18  var imageData:Array = new Array();
```

continues

LISTING 4.11   Continued

```
19
20   var xmlData:XML = new XML();
21   xmlData.ignoreWhite = true;
22   xmlData.onLoad = function(){
23     var allChapters:Array =
       XPathAPI.selectNodeList( this.firstChild,
                                 "/portfolio/chapter" );
24     var totalChapters = allChapters.length;
25
26     for(var i = 0; i<totalChapters; i++){
27
28       var thisChapter:XMLNode = allChapters[i];
29       chapterData.push ( new ChapterInfo( thisChapter ) );
30       var chapterID = thisChapter.attributes.ID;
31
32       var imagesInThisChapter:Array =
         XPathAPI.selectNodeList( thisChapter,
                                   "/chapter/image" );
33       var totalImages = imagesInThisChapter.length;
34
35         for( var j = 0; j<totalImages; j++ ){
36           var thisImage =
             new ImageInfo( imagesInThisChapter[j] );
37           thisImage.chapterID = chapterID;
38           imageData.push( thisImage );
39         }
40     }
41     proceed();
42   }
43
44   xmlData.load("images.xml");
45
46   function proceed(){
47     photoController = new PhotoController( this,
48                                            clipsToLoad,
49                                            imageData,
50                                            chapterData );
51   }
```

We'll focus on lines 20–44 because the rest should look familiar. Line 44 begins to load the XML, but we can't instantiate the PhotoController until the data is fully loaded. When the XML finally loads, line 23 gets an array of the chapter nodes; then line 26 loops through all the <chapter> nodes. For each chapter, we stuff a ChapterInfo object into the chapterData array. Not only does the ChapterInfo.as class define the properties for the chapters—ID and name—but you can also pass an XMLNode to its *constructor*, as in line 29.) Line 32 grabs an array of all the image nodes in the chapter, and then line 35 loops through each image. Line 36 makes an instance of the homemade `ImageInfo` class by passing an `XMLNode`; however, because there's no `chapterID` in the XML, line 37 adds it before finally pushing the information into the `imageData` array on line 38.

You can test this code with any `images.xml` file you created. Also, I have provided an alternative version of the `_main_tester_app_external.swf` application, which draws the image information from an `images.xml` file. You can find this version of the testing application in the `finished_source` folder you downloaded for this chapter.

Exploring the Class Structure

Check out Figure 4.22 while I provide the following overview of the code behind the scenes.

The parts we create are `main.swf` (on the left) and the three template types: `display.swf`, `chapters.swf`, and `thumbnails.swf` (on the right). Our `main.swf` needs to create three arrays when it creates its `photoController` instance (of the `PhotoController` class): `clipsToLoad`, `imageData`, and `chapterData`. Those three arrays contain objects based on the data types `ClipInfo`, `ImageInfo`, and `ChapterInfo`, respectively. (Really, these are simply ActionScript objects with specific properties.) The `main.swf` also has the `ProgessBar` symbol associated with the `ProgressBar` class (bottom left).

The bulk of the work is handled by the `PhotoController` class. Depending on which template types you specify in the `clipsToLoad` array, the `PhotoController` loads up to three `.swf` files (display, chapters, and thumbnails). Each of those template types maintains a reference back to the `PhotoController` shown as the variable name `controller`. In addition, each template type has an interface it should implement: `IDisplayArea`, `IChapters`, and `IThumbnails`. The `PhotoController` formally implements the `IPhotoController` interface, which provides a list of public methods.

In summary, the `main.swf` file defines the elements you want and where you want them; your templates for the various element types (display, chapters, and thumbnails) define how to present the display, chapters, or thumbnails; and the `PhotoController` handles all the technical details of parsing data and loading clips. Maybe that's a simplification, but like all the projects in this book, the model here is that you must define how everything appears but the support files do as much of the grunt work as possible.

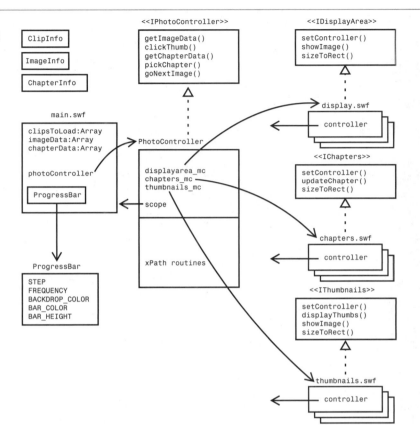

Final Thoughts

I promised to show you how to make a display template that plays videos instead of simply displaying images. You can find the finished file, `display_video.fla`, in the `finished_source` folder, but it's really easy! Take the code from the `display_simple.fla` and locate the following line:

```
imageHolder.loadMovie(imageInfo.url);
```

Change this line to the following:

```
myVideo.contentPath = imageInfo.url;
```

Then open the Components panel and drag an `FLVPlayback` component onto the stage. Give it an instance name of **myVideo**. That's it! Remember to make sure that the objects in the `imageData` array you send to the `PhotoController` class have `url` properties that point to `.flv` files (and not to `.jpg` files).

> 📌 **NOTE**
>
> You'll also find in the `finished source` folder a set of files that let you "display" MP3 audio files (`main_audio.fla`, `thumbnailsV_audio.fla`, and `display_audio.fla`).

Although a lot of the structure for this portfolio project is already built, there's a lot of opportunity for you to both customize the user features and extend the project by creating your own templates. Not only can you change the look (such as the look of the navigation buttons), you can easily change the behavior of the elements. For example, you can easily display each image's caption instead of its name when rolling over thumbnails. Or something more advanced, such as displaying the actual thumbnail only when the user rolls over an image number. Like many other projects in this book, I suspect readers will think up—and build—additional templates that work within the framework described in this chapter. And as usual, if you email them to me, I can share them on my site (www.phillipkerman.com/at-work/).

I should note that there are some additional features in the framework that we didn't explore in this chapter. It turned out that after I built the framework, I began to think about all the wild features you might ever want in a portfolio. The main thing came up is the possibility that you might want another way to jump to the next image besides clicking a thumbnail. For example, maybe you want only a display (no thumbnails and no chapters—after all, I did say that you could use any combination of these elements). Maybe you want to automatically advance to the next image every 5 seconds or let the user click the display to jump to the next image. In fact, I added such a feature to the version of `display_simple.fla` in the `finished_source` folder. It calls the public method `PhotoController.goNextImage()`. The only catch is that you'll probably want to add support for `updateChapter()` and

`showImage()` to your thumbnails and chapters elements so that they keep in synch. (For example you want a highlight on the current thumbnail to update if the display image changes.) I added this support to all the templates in the `finished_source` folder.

Another thing that I suspect many people will want to change is the color and size of the progress bar. Open `ProgressBar.as`, and you'll find several *constants* (variables spelled in all uppercase) that you can change. Most are very intuitive (such as `BAR_COLOR` and `BAR_HEIGHT`). `BACKDROP_COLOR` is the color of the rectangle that covers your content during the load. If your main background is black, you'll probably want to leave `BACKDROP_COLOR` as is (black). Otherwise, feel free to change it.

Put these steps in order on the right side
of the screen

Publish		Create a new file
Create the content	
Upload the .swf and .html	

About the Project

The quiz you build in this chapter uses a template approach. That is, each question is based on a particular template. For example, there's a template for a multiple-choice question and one for a drag-and-drop kind of question. I built an engine that will display any template you build. The engine handles all the work that's common throughout a quiz, such as programming the Previous and Next buttons and keeping track of the score. The template approach not only means that you can have as many questions as you want, but you can also design and build additional templates for question types I haven't considered.

Prerequisites

It's important that you understand *Extensible Markup Language (XML)*, and it's a plus if you know *XPath*. In addition, you'll need to know the basics of using *V2 Components* to follow how I created the templates (see Appendix B, "Components," for more information).

@work resources

Download the `chapter_5_downloads.zip` file for this chapter from the accompanying CD-ROM.

Planning the Projects

In this chapter, you'll build a dynamic and reusable quiz suitable for assessing a user's knowledge and experience in any number of areas. Of course, the reliability of the results is only as good as the content of the questions. However, by selecting a variety of appropriate question types and modifying the phrasing of the questions, you can use this project for many situations—anything from orienting new employees to your company policies to certifying safety knowledge to surveying customer satisfaction.

I should also note that you won't rebuild the quiz engine I created for this chapter; rather you'll learn how to use it to display question-type templates that you build. If you want a quiz that uses only multiple-choice questions, you need only one template—the multiple-choice template you build in this chapter. Regardless of how many questions in your quiz use that template, the same template is recycled for each new question. The content for the questions arrives in the quiz engine as XML, either from a text file or from a database. In addition to building the templates, this chapter covers how to organize the question contents in the XML format.

This chapter covers how to build the quiz and collect user results. Those results can be sent to a centralized database using your choice of application server. The second part of this quiz-management process appears in Chapter 6, "Saving and Evaluating Quiz Results," where you'll see how to collect and analyze results for the boss or teacher to review.

Similar to projects such as the portfolio/slideshow presentation from Chapter 4, a good quiz depends on good content. Most of the planning tips I provide here have to do with writing quality questions and designing the most effective vehicle for presenting and gathering user answers to those questions.

Writing Effective Questions

Building an effective quiz goes much deeper than the technical details you'll learn in the projects in this chapter. Writing good questions is an art form. It's not easy coming up with distractors (wrong answers) that are both plausible and not deceptive (that is, "trick answers"). For example, if you asked, "Who was the first person to walk on the moon?" the option "Lance Armstrong" is obviously incorrect while "Neil-don't call me Buzz-Armstrong" is deceptive. A good set of options for this question is "John Glenn, Buzz Aldrin, Neil Armstrong, or Yuri Gagarin".

Here are a few more qualities of good questions:

- **A question should test only a single concept or skill**—For example, don't ask a question about geography that also tests a person's spelling.

- **Be conscious of *accessibility issues***— You don't want the process of simply answering your question to be a test of the user's physical dexterity or vision.

- **Use clear and simple language**— Avoid complex language and jargon unless it's warranted by the question's objective. For example, if you asked, "What did the legislature receive as a *quid pro quo* for changing the law?"

realize that you're effectively testing for both a specific answer (what the legislature received) as well as trying to test Latin (*quid pro quo*).

▶ **Pick the right tool for the job**—Select the appropriate question format and question phrasing for the skill being tested. If it's important that a user knows both what is and isn't the case, you can write a multiple-choice question such as "choose all that apply" (or make it easier by saying "select the two that apply"). A drag-and-drop question can test that the user knows the correct sequence of events.

Despite a common opinion that quizzes can't really test anything, quizzes *can* both teach and determine whether a person has specific experiences. Regardless, it always depends on you writing a good question.

📌 TIP

Now that I'm done with this mini-lecture about the value of quality questions, I'll add that my opinion is far from the last word. For more information, I recommend checking out the writings of experts in this area, including Benjamin S. Bloom and Thomas M. Haladyna.

Designing Question Templates

After you build templates for three question types (multiple-choice, hot-spot, and drag-and-drop), you'll know the technical requirements to build many more that you might want to design. Writing the ActionScript to create the template is the easy part. Designing an effective question type that works well as a template—that is, without the question type getting stale—is much more work than the Flash programming necessary to implement it.

A good template should work for a variety of situations and questions. Remember that the same template will likely appear in a series of questions; only the content changes. The core task should be clear and sensible. You don't want the template to become a chore. For example, it's clear what the user is supposed to do if you have four options and the instructions say, "Pick the animal that can run fastest." Compare that to saying, "Drag the name of the animal that runs fastest to the right of the screen."

Although a pure template is free from specific content, you should exercise your templates with real content. It's amazing what you find out when you begin to populate a quiz with actual questions (or, in the case of this chapter, when you create an XML file with the question content). For example, you might design a multiple-choice template with one long question and multiple, very short answers. When you begin to write the questions, however, you might find that some questions are short but the possible answers are very long. Here's an example where the answers are very short:

What was the last name of the host of *Jeopardy*?

a) Smith

b) Trebek

c) Tribeca

d) Feldman

Here's another example that would require a totally different layout, which might not be apparent until you wrote the question:

How do you make French toast?

a) Toast the bread, mix water and milk, dip the toast in the water mixture, re-toast, serve with garnish of olives.

b) Mix eggs with milk, dip bread into the egg mixture, fry, serve with syrup, butter, and powdered sugar.

c) Slice a loaf of French bread into cubes, place on a cookie sheet and bake for 20 minutes at 300°, serve with French press coffee.

Finally, the hardest task in designing a question type is to identify, early in the design, the range of questions the template will need to accommodate. It's hard because you can't predict the future. For example, I designed several question types with the idea that each would have a "correct answer." I could foresee that some questions had one "correct answer" where others (namely the multiple-choice questions with multiple correct answers) would need to support multiple correct answers. That was easy enough because I had it in mind early on.

Short of becoming clairvoyant, the specific tip I can give you is to try to plan and design all your templates before building the first one, although I realize that this isn't always practical. For the projects in this chapter, I've set up the following parameters:

- ▶ Each question uses one of the template types you build.

- ▶ If you plan to display the quiz results without connecting to a database, the data for each question must include an array of correct answers. If you don't include the answers (which end up in the .swf file that downloads to the user's machine), those questions aren't graded on the user's computer. You'll still be able to have the server grade those questions, however. Grading the questions on the user's computer is a

security problem because a user can hack into those answers to figure out which one is correct. In addition, if you want to save the scores for the teacher or boss to review, you must send the answers to a centralized server.

- ▶ Each question will support the concept of "can proceed." Normally, only after the user has fully answered the question does the Next Question button appear. Depending on how you design the feature, you can control when the user is allowed to proceed to the next question.

- ▶ Because users can return to previously answered questions, each template needs code that can restore the display to how the user left it, with their previously selected answers marked as selected.

✎ NOTE

The code I built for the quiz engine in this chapter adheres to a few principles: First, the quiz is not timed. Second, users decide when they've fully answered a question, meaning the quiz doesn't advance to the next question until users click the Next Question button. Finally, users are allowed to review their answers at any time. I think these features make for a good quiz-taking experience, although I can see cases where they might not be appropriate. For example, you might want to disclose the answer to an earlier question to ask the user a deeper question about the content. In that case, you'd want to disable the Previous Question button. In any event, I made it easy for you to turn off these settings, but remember one important thing: The goal for most assessment quizzes is *not* to successfully trick as many users as possible. You want to give the qualified users a fighting chance to pass the quiz.

CHAPTER 5: Creating an Assessment Quiz

Client-side Versus Server-side

It is easy to decide whether some tasks should be handled in the client-side Flash movie or on the server. However, other tasks aren't so clear-cut and, in fact, can be handled equally well on either end. It might seem silly, but don't do the work twice! For example, if you're planning on having the server person calculate the user's score (for the statistical analysis), there's no need to make the Flash person also write code that calculates the score. Obviously, this double-work issue probably won't occur if you are the "Flash person" *and* the "server person," but I've seen it happen many times. Not only does it mean more work for everyone, but it also makes maintenance and troubleshooting more difficult.

You should perform tasks on the client side when you need speed or when it's simply more convenient. Sending a request back to the server takes time; so, for example, we'll download the content for the entire quiz instead of making requests for each question. Sometimes seemingly excessive round-trips to the server *are* warranted. For example, you might want to send data back to the server for each question as the user answers it. If the user quits in the middle of the quiz, she'll be able to pick up where she left off when she returns if you set up the server to remember the last question she requested.

It turns out that in this chapter there are only two server-side calls: one to retrieve the quiz and one to send the user's answers back. And, in fact, you can make zero server-side calls if you simply load the quiz from a text file. (In the next chapter, you'll see more server-side work to aggregate statistical information about several users or several

quizzes.) After the quiz is downloaded from the server, all the work displaying questions, gathering the user's answers, and tracking the current question is handled on the client side.

The sorts of tasks that make sense for the server side include any kind of centralized database access, such as storing all the user's answers, and anything that involves security. For example, I built my engine to allow for the correct answers to be downloaded along with the rest of the quiz information. This way, I can give users immediate feedback or at least display their scores without any server-side work. However, you should opt to leave this information out of the original download if you're at all concerned with a user hacking into the data. You don't want to send the quiz *and* the correct answers if you think a sophisticated user will attempt to capture this data traveling over the wire.

Planning for Extensibility

When you get started with the projects in this chapter, you'll notice that the starter files contain what might appear to be excessive additional support files. These support files primarily support extensibility. For example, the quiz content is drawn from a file called quiz.xml in a folder called schemas. Not only does keeping the content external mean you can change the content without editing the source Flash files, but you'll see in Chapter 6 that you can also change the name and location of the quiz.xml file by updating the urls.xml lookup table. You can even change the name and location of that urls.xml file. In addition, Chapter 6 shows you how to connect to an application server to dynamically supply the quiz content to support multiple quizzes and even track which quizzes each user has taken. The point is that there's a lot of functionality you might or might not use.

The reason I mention these features is partially because I want you to know about the available features. However, a key planning step is to consider and plan for all the optional features you might want. Here are the objectives I established early when building this quiz engine:

▶ Each question type could be reused by simply swapping the specific question content.

▶ You can add as many additional templates types as you want.

▶ The quiz works with static content by drawing content from the `quiz.xml` text file, as you do in this chapter, or with dynamic content from a server, as you do in Chapter 6.

▶ Sending correct answers to the client along with the original quiz (a slight security flaw) remains optional.

▶ Users will send a user ID and quiz ID when requesting the quiz content so the server knows which quiz to supply and which user is requesting it.

▶ Most details, such as quiz content and all other support files, are kept external. However, three parameters are passed in from the HTML file that hosts your `.swf` file using the *FlashVars* feature: `userID`, `quizID`, and `urlList` (the location of the `urls.xml` lookup file containing the addresses of all the other support files). The FlashVars feature lets you pass variables from

your `.html` document to the `.swf` embedded in that `.html` document.

Although I doubt that these features will satisfy the needs of every quiz from now to eternity, they do demonstrate a good plan for extensibility.

> **📌 TIP**
>
> Although we'll work with files in the `starter_files` folder that you downloaded for this chapter, you can copy and paste code from the files in the `finished_source` folder to save yourself some typing.

Project: Quiz Content

In this project, you will create an XML file that stores the questions for a quiz. That XML file will store an unlimited number of `<question>` nodes. Each `<question>` node will contain the content for a different question, and the exact form of the `<question>` node will vary depending on the question type. For example, the content for a multiple-choice question will differ from the content for a drag-and-drop question. In later projects in this chapter, you'll build a separate template `.swf` for each question type, but here you'll create the XML document.

The quiz content is made up of questions stored in an XML file that, while testing, is kept external to the `quiz.swf` file. That will work fine as is for many people. But later, if you want, you can move the XML file to a web server or have an application server generate the XML on request. It's perfectly workable to begin with a static XML document and later build a server-side application (say, in PHP) that draws the questions from an online database so you can easily manage the quiz content.

STEPS▼

1. **Studying the XML format**
2. **Writing sample content for** `multipleChoiceSingle`
3. **Writing sample content for** `multipleChoiceMultiple`
4. **Writing sample content for** `hotSpot`
5. **Writing sample content for** `dragAndDrop`

STEP 1▼
Studying the XML Format

Inside the `schemas` folder, which is in the `starter_files` folder you downloaded for this chapter, find the `quiz.xml` text file. Copy that file into a working folder. Use a text editor such as Notepad to open your copy of the `quiz.xml` file. Within the main `<quiz>` *node*, you'll see one sample question node:

```
<question type="minimumType"
        questionID="minimumID"
        correctAnswers="0,1,2">

</question>
```

Every question in the quiz must have, at a minimum, a `type` and a unique `questionID` attribute. The `type` attribute determines which template `.swf` to use (if you left `type` set to `"minimumType"`, the engine looks for `minimumType.swf`). The `questionID` attribute

offers a way to ensure that each question has a unique identifier, provided that you end up storing the questions in an online database. Like all attributes, the `questionID` attribute can be any string of characters. Finally, the `correctAnswers` attribute is an optional way to immediately show the user his results at the end of a quiz without using the server to do that work—which is still another way to do it. This attribute is optional and, in fact, something you should leave out if you're concerned that users will attempt to cheat.

STEP 2▼
Writing Sample Content for multipleChoiceSingle

For every new question type, you will add attributes or child nodes to the `<question>` node where additional information for the particular question template can be stored. You'll build four templates in this chapter: multiple-choice, multiple-choice with multiple correct, click-a-picture, and drag-and-drop.

Next, you'll create sample questions for each template type. If you don't want to type, you can copy text from the `quiz.xml` file located in the `finished_source/schemas` folder that you downloaded for this chapter. Replace the sole `<question>` node in the `quiz.xml` file with the `<question>` node shown in Listing 5.1. Notice that the listing shows a complete `quiz.xml` file, not just the `<question>` node.

```xml
<?xml version="1.0"?>
<quiz quizID="123">

<question type="multipleChoiceSingle"
          questionID="oregonCapital"
          questionText="What is the capital of Oregon?"
          correctAnswers="0">
   <possible label="Salem"/>
   <possible label="Portland"/>
   <possible label="Eugene"/>
</question>

</quiz>
```

The `type` attribute (in this case, `multipleChoiceSingle`) will match the filename of the first template we build (namely, `multipleChoiceSingle.swf`). Because we know that a multiple-choice question always has a single question, it was logical to put it into an attribute (`questionText`). To accommodate as many options as needed, I created the `<possible>` children nodes each with a `label` attribute that will appear on the button on the quiz screen. Notice the optional `correctAnswers` attribute has a value of 0 because Salem (the first answer, with an index value of 0) is the capital of Oregon.

You'll add `<question>` nodes directly above the last line (`</quiz>`). You can keep the `quiz.xml` file open.

STEP 3▼
Writing Sample Content for multipleChoiceMultiple

Add the `<question>` node shown in Listing 5.2 directly above the last line in the `quiz.xml` file to create a multiple-choice question that has more than one correct answer.

```xml
<question type="multipleChoiceMultiple"
          questionID="fruits1"
          questionText="Which are fruits?"
          correctAnswers="1,2">
   <possible label="Hamburger"/>
   <possible label="Banana"/>
   <possible label="Peach"/>
   <possible label="Cinnamon Roll"/>
</question>
```

The template that draws on this data is nearly identical to the `multipleChoiceSingle` `<question>` node shown in step 2. However, the `multipleChoiceMultiple` template uses a comma-delimited string for the `correctAnswers` attribute. Even if you don't plan to use the `correctAnswers` attribute (it's optional, after all), you'll see later that this template also differs from the regular `multipleChoiceSingle` template in that check box buttons appear instead of the radio buttons that appear for exclusive choice questions.

STEP 4▼
Writing Sample Content for hotSpot

The `hotSpot` question type is probably not as familiar as the two multiple-choice variations covered so far. In this template, the user sees a photograph and is asked to click a particular object in the image. The user sees a circle where he clicks.

Add the code shown in Listing 5.3 to the `quiz.xml` file as you have in the last two steps.

I decided to put the required information into the attributes of a child node named

`<details>`. The `image` attribute is the URL where the photograph resides, the `diameter` attribute specifies the diameter for the circle that is drawn where the user clicks, and `tolerance` is the distance in pixels away from the correct location where a user's guess is still considered correct. The `correctAnswers` attribute contains the x and y position (measured from the upper-left corner of the photo) where the user is supposed to click. Later, when you build this template you'll see that accepting a guess that's "close enough," such as a click that's within the specified `tolerance` attribute, becomes problematic. Ultimately, if you want to judge the user's guess on the server side, you can simply leave out the `correctAnswers` attribute altogether. Any `<question>` nodes in your quiz for which there are no `correctAnswers` attributes are not included in the client-side grading code.

STEP 5▼
Writing Sample Content for dragAndDrop

Add the code in Listing 5.4 to the `quiz.xml` file, just above the last line of the growing file. This code defines the content for a basic drag-and-drop type of question.

LISTING 5.3 **This** `<question>` **Node Defines the Content for a** `hotSpot` **Template Type**

```
<question type="hotSpot"
          questionID="pickSafetySwitch"
          questionText="Click on the man's left ear"
          correctAnswers="260,125">
    <details image="http://www.phillipkerman.com/at-work/phillip.jpg"
             diameter="100"
             tolerance="100" />
</question>
```

LISTING 5.4 This `<question>` Node Defines the Content for a dragAndDrop Template Type

```
<question type="dragAndDrop"
          questionID="flash101"
          questionText="Put these steps in order on the right"
          correctAnswers="1,2,0,3">
    <possible label="Publish"/>
    <possible label="Create a new file"/>
    <possible label="Create the content"/>
    <possible label="Upload the .swf and .html"/>
</question>
```

This format should be easy to understand. The `label` attributes for the `<possible>` nodes appear on tiles the user must arrange in the correct order. Notice that the `correctAnswers` attribute is really a comma-separated string of the tile numbers when placed in the correct order, starting with "Create a new file" and ending with "Upload the .swf and .html". Notice also that the `correctAnswers` attribute specifies the correct order by starting with zero. So, `"Publish"` (the `<possible>` node in the zero index) is the third step because the value of `correctAnswers` is `"1,2,0,3"` (a zero in the third slot).

You'll see that this template is hardest to program, but it is very effective for testing whether users know the correct order or sequence of events.

Be sure to save the `quiz.xml` file, or simply copy the version from inside the `finished_source/schemas` folder you downloaded for this chapter.

Project:
Starter Template

The quiz engine reads the `quiz.xml` file and then loads the `.swf` file matching the current question node's `type` attribute. We're going to build a `.swf` template for each type of question. Later you'll be able to recycle the same template with different question content—just add more `<question>` nodes to the `quiz.xml` file. Each template must support the same minimum set of functions, defined formally as the interface `IQuestion.as` that each template must implement.

In this case, there are only two:

- ▶ function init(owner:MovieClip, questionData:XMLNode)—This is called by the quiz engine after the template loads. The first parameter (owner) is a reference to the `QuizHolder.as` class to provide handy utilities such as XPath parsing and, more importantly, to report when the user has finished answering (see the following `canProceed()` method). The second parameter is the entire `<question>` node. That is, when `init()` is called, the template receives the `<question>` node for the given question in your `quiz.xml` file.

- ▶ function getAnswers()—This returns an array of user selections to the quiz engine so it can keep track of and eventually send answers back to the server.

There's one last requirement for each template: It must report back to its owner (the reference to the QuizHolder class) when the user is allowed to or not allowed to proceed. Namely, the template must call owner.canProceed(true) so the quiz engine knows to enable the Next Question button. For example, if the user hasn't dragged any tiles in the dragAndDrop template, you might not want the user to advance. When all tiles are in position, the template calls owner.canProceed(true) so the Next Question button activates. Perhaps not as obvious is the fact that the template also needs to call owner.canProceed(false) if the user removes one of the tiles because he isn't allowed to proceed until all tiles are in place.

The first template you build is just a starter file that supports all these requirements. That way, you can create additional templates by simply opening the starter file; selecting File, Save As; and then making customizations.

STEPS▼

1. Creating the starter file
2. Placing text on the stage
3. Entering skeleton code
4. Publishing
5. Modifying the quiz.xml file
6. Testing the quiz engine

STEP 1▼
Creating the Starter File

Open a new file in Flash and select File, Save As. Name the file **starterTemplate.fla** and save it in your working folder (not in the schemas folder where the quiz.xml file resides).

STEP 2▼
Placing Text on the Stage

Use the Text tool to create a block of text on the stage. Use the Properties panel to set it to Dynamic Text and give it the instance name **question_txt**.

STEP 3▼
Entering Skeleton Code

Select the first keyframe and open the Actions panel. Type the code in Listing 5.5— you can block and copy it from the starterTemplate.fla file in the finished_source folder you downloaded for this chapter if you don't feel like typing.

LISTING 5.5 The Code for a Starter Template on Which All Templates Are Based		

```
1    var questionData:XMLNode
2    var owner:MovieClip;//really QuizHolder
3
4    var existingAnswers:Array;
5
6    //initialize the question text
7    question_txt.multiline = true;
8    question_txt.wordWrap = true;
```

continues

LISTING 5.5   Continued

```
9     question_txt.autoSize = true;
10    question_txt.selectable = false;
11    question_txt.text = "";
12
13    //required by interface:
14    function init( p_owner:MovieClip, p_questionData:XMLNode ){
15      //save two parameters
16      owner = p_owner;
17      questionData = p_questionData;
18
19      question_txt.text =
         "whole question node " + questionData;
20
21      //get existingAnswers
22      existingAnswers = questionData.attributes.theirAnswers;
23      if ( existingAnswers == undefined ){
24         question_txt.text += newline + "no answers yet";
25      }else{
26         question_txt.text +=
            newline + "existingAnswers: " + existingAnswers;
27      }
28
29      //dummy way to set existingAnswers
30      onMouseDown=function(){
31         existingAnswers = [ _xmouse, _ymouse ];
32         updateState();
33      }
34      updateState();
35    }
36
37    //required by interface:
38    function getAnswers():Array{
39       return existingAnswers;
40    }
41
42    //handy way to keep owner in the loop
43    function updateState(){
44       var canProceed = (existingAnswers != undefined);
45       owner.canProceed(canProceed);
46    }
```

To make additional templates, you replace the contents of the init() and getAnswers() functions and can change the way canProceed() is called in line 45. But you'll always have those three functions. Naturally, you'll also have to change the core business of the question type, but that varies for each question. This starter template simply displays the entire <question> node plus the existingAnswers attribute that is sent by the quiz engine only after the user finishes a question. The user answers this dummy question by clicking anywhere on the stage, at which time her answer—really just the x and y location she clicked—is collected and she's allowed to advance to the next question.

Lines 1 and 2 identify the global variables you receive as parameters in the init() function (in lines 16 and 17). The existingAnswers variable that first appears in line 4 is undefined at first. The questionData variable (that is, the whole <question> node) has a value for existingAnswers only after the user visits this question; you don't set this in the XML file. For example, say the user answers a question, leaves, and then comes back; the existingAnswers will have a value because the quiz engine takes care of setting it upon calling the getAnswers() method on line 38, right before the user advances to the next question.

Lines 19–27 simply display what was received in the init() function. In the complete question templates, the content of the questionData variable is parsed to create the visual display. Lines 29–33 define what happens anytime the user clicks. Namely, the existingAnswers variable is set to intentionally unimportant values and then the handy updateState() function is triggered. You can see that updateState() is also called at the bottom of the init() function (line 34). Basically, anytime the user interacts with your template, you'll need to tell the owner that it's okay or not okay to proceed by calling canProceed() (as line 45 does).

STEP 4▼
Publishing

Save the starterTemplate.fla file and then select Control, Test Movie to generate the starterTemplate.swf file. Nothing will appear because the init() function is called from the quiz engine. Close the starterTemplate.swf file.

STEP 5▼
Modifying the quiz.xml File

To test the starter template, you must edit the quiz.xml file you created in the preceding project to look for a template called starterTemplate. Simply back up the quiz.xml file (in the schemas folder) and make a copy of the file. Then edit the original so that each question node's type attribute is starterTemplate. The starter template is so simple that it will work in place of any template you come up with. Listing 5.6 shows an abbreviated quiz.xml you can use.

LISTING 5.6 This `quiz.xml` **File Points to the** `starterTemplate`

```xml
<?xml version="1.0"?>
<quiz quizID="123">
<question type="starterTemplate"
          questionID="oregonCapital"
          questionText="What is the capital of Oregon?"
          correctAnswers="0">
    <possible label="Salem"/>
    <possible label="Portland"/>
    <possible label="Eugene"/>
</question>

<question type="starterTemplate"
          questionID="test"
          questionText="test...">
    <test/>
</question>

</quiz>
```

Save the `quiz.xml` file. The important parts in this `quiz.xml` file are the two `type` attributes in the two `<question>` nodes because they point to the `starterTemplate.swf` you just built.

STEP 6 ▼
Testing the Quiz Engine

Open the `quiz.fla` and select Control, Test Movie. Figure 5.1 shows you what you'll see: the question node's contents in a text field and the Next button, which is disabled until the user clicks anywhere on the stage. Notice, too, that after the user clicks, he can go to the next question and come back to see the value of his `existingAnswers` in the text field.

The starter template isn't terribly impressive, but it's a skeleton you can use to quickly

crank out as many new templates as you want—as you're about to see. Not only is the `starterTemplate.fla` the basis of the rest of our templates, it also proves that the `quiz.swf` engine and `quiz.xml` files are working properly.

FIGURE 5.1 The starter template displays the question node to prove that the quiz engine is working properly.

```
whole question node <question
type="starterTemplate"
questionID="oregonCapital"
questionText="What is the capital
of Oregon?"
correctAnswers="0"><possible
label="Salem" /><possible
label="Portland" /><possible
label="Eugene" /></question>
no answers yet
```

Previous   Next

Project:
Multiple-Choice/Single Answer Template

This template is appropriate for multiple-choice questions that have one correct answer. Users will see the question and a radio button for each possible answer. Radio buttons are appropriate for exclusive choices, whereas check box buttons are appropriate for when there may be more than one correct answer. After the user makes a selection, he'll be able to move on to the next question by clicking the Next button. If he returns to the question by clicking the Previous button, his previously selected answer appears selected.

STEPS▼

1. **Creating the** `multipleChoiceSingle.fla` **file**
2. **Laying out the stage**
3. **Adding the** `RadioButton` **component**
4. **Changing the ActionScript**
5. **Testing the** `multipleChoiceSingle` **template**

STEP 1▼
Creating the multipleChoiceSingle.fla File

Open the `starterTemplate.fla` file you created in the previous project, or open the one in the `finished_source` folder you downloaded for this chapter, and select File, Save As. Save the file as **multipleChoiceSingle.fla** in your working folder.

STEP 2▼
Laying Out the Stage

Set the position, font, and margins for the `question_txt` text field however you want the question to appear. For example, I set my text very large, as shown in Figure 5.2.

FIGURE 5.2 The `question_txt` field can be positioned and styled however you like.

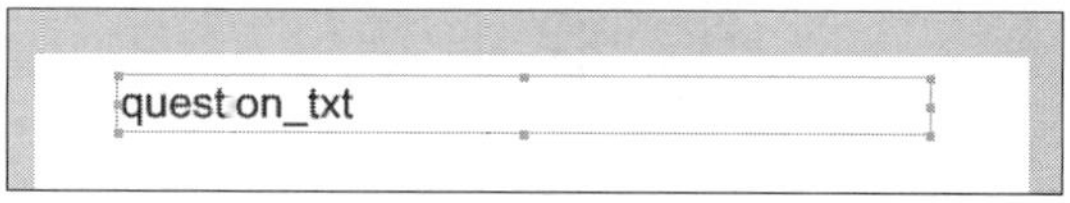

quest on_txt

STEP 3▼
Adding the RadioButton Component

Because this template places radio buttons on the stage, you must make sure that a `RadioButton` component exists in the Library. Select Window, Components and expand the User Interface folder in the Components panel. Select Window, Library to open your file's Library; then drag an instance of `RadioButton` into your Library, as shown in Figure 5.3. Even if you drag the `RadioButton` onto the stage, you can delete that instance because the component is safely stored in the file's Library.

STEP 4▼
Changing the ActionScript

Select the first keyframe and open the Actions panel. Completely replace the ActionScript from the `starterTemplate.fla` file with the code in Listing 5.7 (which is also available in the `multipleChoiceSingle.fla` file in the finished_source folder you downloaded for this chapter).

You can see the bulk of code is in the init() function. I grab the questionText attribute (line 16) and the existingAnswers attribute (if any) in line 19. Notice that although the quiz engine treats existingAnswers as an array, this template has a maximum of one answer. So, it's simply an array with one value. Initially, the value is -1 (line 21), but it changes to the answer's index (on line 49).

FIGURE 5.3   Drag the RadioButton **component into your file's Library.**

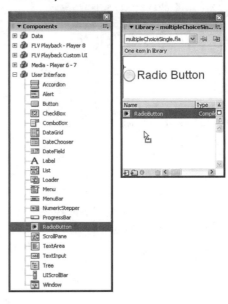

LISTING 5.7   This Code Assembles the multipleChoiceSingle **Layout**

```
1    import mx.controls.RadioButton;
2
3    var questionData:XMLNode;
4    var owner:MovieClip;//really QuizHolder
5    var existingAnswers:Array;
6
7    question_txt.multiline = true;
8    question_txt.wordWrap = true;
9    question_txt.autoSize = true;
10   question_txt.text = "";
11
12   function init( p_owner:MovieClip, p_questionData:XMLNode ){
13      owner = p_owner;
14      questionData = p_questionData;
15      //set the question text
16      question_txt.text = questionData.attributes.questionText;
17
18      //get their old answers (or set it to -1)
19      existingAnswers = questionData.attributes.theirAnswers;
20      if ( existingAnswers == undefined ){
21         existingAnswers = [-1];
22      }
23
24      //spacing and top left for buttons
```

LISTING 5.7 **Continued**

```
25      var padding = 20;//between possible answers
26      var topY = question_txt._y +
                    question_txt._height +
                    padding;
27      var topX = question_txt._x;
28
29      //make all the buttons:
30      var possible:Array =
        owner.selectNodeList(questionData, "/question/possible");
31      var total = possible.length;
32      for(var i = 0; i<total; i++){
33          var obj = { label:possible[i].attributes.label,
                        data:i,
                        groupName:"radioGroup",
                        tabIndex:i+1};
34
35          var thisRB:RadioButton =
            createClassObject( RadioButton, "rb_"+i, i, obj );
36          thisRB.move( topX, topY + padding );
37          thisRB.addEventListener( "click", this );
38
39          thisRB.setSize( Stage.width, 20, false );
40
41          topY += padding;
42          //see if it's already selected:
43          thisRB.selected = ( existingAnswers[0] == i );
44      }
45      rb_0.getFocusManager().setFocus(rb_0);
46      updateState();
47  }
48  function click(evt){
49      existingAnswers[0] = evt.target.data;
50      updateState();
51  }
52  function getAnswers():Array{
53      return existingAnswers;
54  }
55  function updateState(){
56      var canProceed = ( existingAnswers[0] != -1 );
57      owner.canProceed( canProceed );
58  }
```

Line 30 is quite fancy because it creates an array of all the possible nodes by calling the XPath utility selectNodeList() on the owner (the QuizHolder.as class). I've created a few similar such functions in the QuizHolder class that provide all the question templates easy access to XPath commands. You *could* add the necessary `DataBindingClasses` and do XPath parsing within this question template, but this way each question type doesn't need to include the overhead that comes with the `DataBindingClasses`. (In addition to `selectNodeList()`, there's `selectSingleNode()` and `selectSingleNodeValue()`—detailed in the interface `IQuizHolder.as` and the `QuizHolder.as` class itself. All three functions also appear in Chapter 7, "Creating a PowerPoint-style Slide Presentation" and Chapter 10, "Building a Photo Share Application.") For now, just realize that those functions make parsing XML much easier.

In case you're not familiar with the `createClassObject()` function (line 35), it's effectively the same as the `attachMovie()` method, but for components only. Here it creates an instance of the `RadioButton` class. After each radio button is created and moved into position, I add an event listener (line 37) so that clicks are directed to the `click()` function on line 48. Also notice that line 45 gives focus to the first radio button instance (`rb_0`).

The rest of the code is fairly simple: `click()` sets the `existingAnswers` variable (well, the 0 index because there's always just one answer) to the selected button's data and calls `updateState()`, which simply tells the owner we can proceed. The `getAnswers()` function remains unchanged but is needed so the quiz engine (`owner`) can ask for and receive the selected answer.

STEP 5 ▼
Testing the multipleChoiceSingle Template

Save the `multipleChoiceSingle.fla` file and select Control, Test Movie to generate a `.swf` file. Go back to the `quiz.xml` file and make sure the first question node's type attribute is set to `"multipleChoiceSingle"`. Finally, open the `quiz.fla` and select Control, Test Movie. You should see the first question as shown in Figure 5.4.

FIGURE 5.4 Our first template: the classic multiple-choice question with a single correct answer.

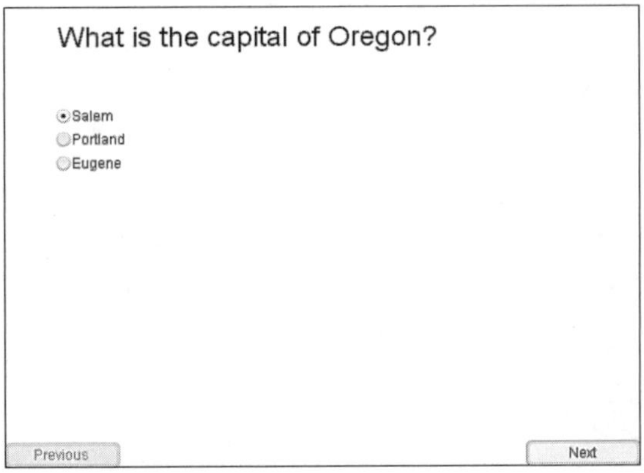

What is the capital of Oregon?

- ⦿ Salem
- ◯ Portland
- ◯ Eugene

Previous   Next

Project:
Multiple-Choice/Multiple Answer Template

This template is appropriate for questions that have one or more correct answers. (By the way, you can easily vary the difficulty of this sort of question by revealing how many correct answers there are. For example, you can say, "Select the two options that…" or you can phrase the question as, "Select all the options that….") Users will see the question and a check box for each possible answer. After the user makes a selection, she'll be able to move on to the next question. However, you'll see that the `multipleChoiceMultiple` template has a few more lines of code than the `multipleChoiceSingle` template because it's possible for the user to deselect all options, in which case you don't want to let her advance.

STEPS▼

1. Creating the `multipleChoiceMultiple.fla` file
2. Laying out the stage
3. Adding the `CheckBox` component
4. Changing the ActionScript
5. Testing the `multipleChoiceMultiple` template

STEP 1▼
Creating the multipleChoiceMultiple.fla File

Open the `starterTemplate.fla` you created in the first project, or open the one in the `finished_source` folder you downloaded for this chapter, and select File, Save As. Save the file as **multipleChoiceMultiple.fla** in the `starter_files` folder where you've been working.

STEP 2▼
Laying Out the Stage

Just as you did in the `multipleChoiceSingle` template, set the position, font, and margins for the `question_txt` field however you want the question to appear. In fact, you can simply copy the `question_txt` design from the `multipleChoiceSingle` template for consistency.

STEP 3▼
Adding the CheckBox Component

Because this template places `CheckBox` buttons on the stage, you must make sure that a `CheckBox` component exists in the Library. Select Window, Components and expand the User Interface folder in the Components panel. Open your file's Library by selecting Window, Library, and then drag a `CheckBox` component from the Components panel to the Library panel.

STEP 4▼
Changing the ActionScript

Select the first keyframe and open the Actions panel. Completely replace the ActionScript from the `starterTemplate.fla` file that appears there with the code shown in Listing 5.8, which you can copy from the `multipleChoiceMultiple.fla` file, located in the `finished_source` folder you downloaded for this chapter.

LISTING 5.8 This Code Assembles the `multipleChoiceMultiple` Layout

```
1    import mx.controls.CheckBox;
2
3    var questionData:XMLNode
4    var owner:MovieClip;//really QuizHolder
5    var existingAnswers:Array;
6
7    //initialize the question text
8    question_txt.multiline = true;
9    question_txt.wordWrap = true;
10   question_txt.autoSize = true;
11   question_txt.text = "";
12
13   function init( p_owner:MovieClip, p_questionData:XMLNode ){
14      owner = p_owner;
15      questionData = p_questionData;
16      //set the question text
17      question_txt.text = questionData.attributes.questionText;
18
19      //get their old answers (or create a new array)
20      existingAnswers = questionData.attributes.theirAnswers;
21      if ( existingAnswers == undefined ){
22         existingAnswers = new Array();
23      }
24
25      //spacing and top left for buttons
26      var padding = 20;//between possible answers
27      var topY = question_txt._y +
                       question_txt._height +
                       padding;
28      var topX = question_txt._x;
29
```

LISTING 5.8 **Continued**

```
30    //make all the buttons:
31    var possible:Array =
      owner.selectNodeList(questionData, "/question/possible");
32    var total = possible.length;
33    for( var i = 0; i<total; i++ ){
34        var obj = { label:possible[i].attributes.label,
                        data:i };
35        var thisCB:CheckBox =
          createClassObject( CheckBox, "cb_"+i, i, obj );
36        thisCB.move( topX, topY + padding );
37        thisCB.addEventListener( "click", this );
38
39        thisRB.setSize( Stage.width, 20, false );
40
41      topY += padding;
42
43        //see if it's already selected:
44        if( utils.findInArray( i, existingAnswers ) != -1 ){
45            thisCB.selected = true;
46        }else{
47            thisCB.selected = false;
48        }
49    }
50    cb_0.getFocusManager().setFocus( cb_0 );
51    updateState();
52  }
53  function click( evt ){
54      if( evt.target.selected == true ){
55          existingAnswers.push( evt.target.data );
56      }else{
57          var index =
            utils.findInArray( evt.target.data, existingAnswers );
58          existingAnswers.splice( index, 1 );
59      }
60      updateState();
61  }
62  function getAnswers():Array{
63      return existingAnswers;
64  }
65  function updateState(){
66      var canProceed = ( existingAnswers.length > 0 );
67      owner.canProceed( canProceed );
68  }
```

This code is similar to the code in Listing 5.7 in the previous project, so rather than going over the code line by line, I will instead point out the differences. The existingAnswers array stores the indexes of all the selected CheckBoxes—for example, the value [2, 3] means that the third and fourth items in the list are selected. You can see that the initial value of `existingAnswers` is set to a plain array on line 22. The `if` statement on line 44 checks whether a `CheckBox`'s index appears anywhere in the `existingAnswers` array. I'm using a static function I wrote called `findInArray()` (in the `utils.as` class file). This function accepts a value and an array and returns either the index where the value is found or `-1` if the value isn't in the array. That same function is used inside the `click()` function in line 57. That is, when the user selects an option, we just push the `CheckBox`'s data into the `existingAnswers` array. When the user deselects an option, we first find the index where that item appears in the `existingAnswers` array (line 57) and extract that value from `existingAnswers` (using the `splice()` method on line 58). Finally, the only other difference is how we determine whether the user can proceed. Specifically, she can proceed only when the `length` of `existingAnswers` is greater than 0 (see line 66).

STEP 5 ▼
Testing the multipleChoiceMultiple Template

Save the `multipleChoiceMultiple.fla` file and select Control, Test Movie to generate a `.swf` file. Go back to the `quiz.xml` file and make sure you have at least one `question` node whose `type` attribute is set to `"multipleChoiceMultiple"` (and that the node's format matches what you built in step 3 of the first project). Finally, open the

quiz.fla file and select Control, Test Movie. The first question appears, as shown in Figure 5.5.

FIGURE 5.5 This multiple-choice template uses the `CheckBox` component because there can be more than one correct answer.

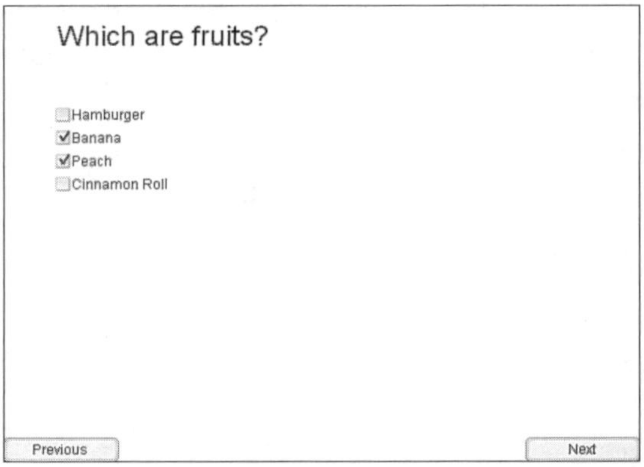

Which are fruits?

☐ Hamburger
☑ Banana
☑ Peach
☐ Cinnamon Roll

Previous   Next

Project:
A Hotspot Template

In the hotspot question type, the user is asked to click a particular part of a photograph. For example, you can ask the user to click the emergency quick-release button on a cereal-packaging machine. When the user clicks, a circle is drawn on top of the photograph showing his selection. You can adjust the size of that circle by modifying the `diameter` attribute in the `<details>` node inside the `<question>` node that supplies content to this template. Like all the question templates, you can grade the user (that is, see whether he selected the right location) on the client side or the server side. To judge the user's answer on the client side, you include a `correctAnswers` attribute in the `<question>` node that specifies the correct x and y positions (for example, "10,150" means the correct location is at 10x 150y on the photograph—not the main stage). In addition, the `<details>` node includes a `tolerance` attribute specifying how far away from the exact correct location will be accepted as "close enough."

It's a very powerful template, but I should note that it is not suitable for people who have mobility or vision disabilities because it involves detailed use of the mouse. Remember that you're probably not testing people's mouse-moving skills.

STEPS▼

1. Creating the `hotSpot.fla` **file**
2. Laying out the stage
3. Modifying the file's contents
4. Changing the ActionScript
5. Testing the `hotSpot` **template**

STEP 1▼
Creating the hotSpot.fla File

Open the `starterTemplate.fla` file you created in the first project, or open the `starterTemplate.fla` file in the `finished_source` folder you downloaded for this chapter, and select File, Save As. Save the file as **hotSpot.fla** in your working folder.

STEP 2▼
Laying Out the Stage

Set the position, font, and margins for the `question_txt` field as you did in the other question templates. This field will hold the prompt, such as "Click the man's left ear."

📌 NOTE

There's one notable limit to how the hotspot template judges the user's answer when doing the grading on the client side. When the user moves to the next question, his guess—the x and y location where he clicked—is reported to the engine by way of the `getAnswers()` method. At that point, I check whether the user's guess is within the tolerance. If it is, I reset his guess to match exactly the correct answer. That way, when the code that does the grading finally runs, this user's answer, which was close enough, will be exactly correct. I really didn't want the grading code to make exceptions for this template. All user answers are graded as either being exactly the same as the `correctAnswers` attribute or not.

The problem is that this limit can be exploited by a sneaky user to effectively cheat. Such a user can click where he thinks the correct answer appears, then click the Previous button, and then click the Next button to see whether his guess moved at all. If the circle moved, that means the guess was within the tolerance (and my code changed his answer). It's pretty subtle, but I wanted to mention that if you're really concerned about this, you should avoid doing the grading on the client side. You could also set the `tolerance` attribute to a very small number, but that makes the question more challenging for everyone. I'll explain more later, but just know that you shouldn't supply a `correctAnswers` attribute if you want the question to be ungraded on the client side.

STEP 3▼
Modifying the File's Contents

In this template, we'll load an external image into a dynamically generated movie clip. In addition, we'll create an invisible button the size of the image and display a circle where the user clicks. For the circle that appears where he clicks, we'll use `attachMovie()` to effectively drag an instance of the circle that you're about to created from the Library.

Use the Oval tool to draw a circle with the following properties: a black Stroke Color, no Fill, a Stroke Height of 1, and the Scale option set to None (see Figure 5.6). Setting the Scale value to None means that no matter how we scale the clip, the circle will always remain the same thickness.

Select the drawn circle and select Modify, Convert to Symbol. Name it **circle**, make sure that the Movie Clip option is selected, and

select the center Registration position. Click the Advanced button if the dialog box isn't already expanded, and select the Export for ActionScript check box (which should automatically select the Export in First Frame option, which you want selected). The Linkage Identifier text box should also read circle, as shown in Figure 5.7. If you forget to set the linkage identifier, you can open the Symbol Properties dialog box by selecting the symbol in the Library and clicking the Properties button, which is the little blue *i*.

FIGURE 5.6 **The Properties panel controls both how this circle appears and how it scales to different sizes.**

FIGURE 5.7 **The expanded Symbol Properties dialog lets you set the linkage identifier.**

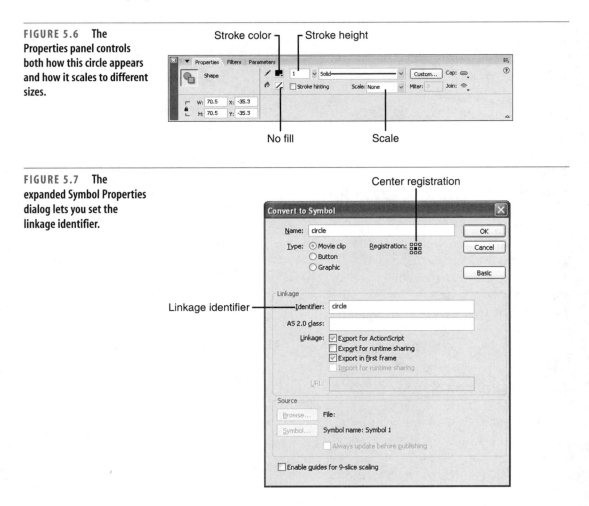

CHAPTER 5: **Creating an Assessment Quiz**

Because that black stroke shows up only on light images, you'll need to draw a thicker white stroke underneath the black stroke to highlight the black stroke. Go inside the circle symbol by double-clicking its Library item, select the entire drawn circle, and copy it. Then select Insert, Timeline, Layer and lock the layer that contains the circle. Click the layer you just created and then select Edit, Paste in Place. With the duplicate circle still selected, use the Properties panel to change the Stroke Color to white and the Stroke Height to 4. Finally, arrange the two layers so the white circle is underneath the black outline. (Feel free to select Modify, Document and change the background color to gray so you can see the white/black circle better, as shown in Figure 5.8.)

FIGURE 5.3 This white and black circle will appear on top of any image when the user clicks the mouse.

STEP 4▼
Changing the ActionScript

Select the first keyframe and open the Actions panel. Completely replace the ActionScript that appears there from the starterTemplate.fla file with the code shown in Listing 5.9 (which you can copy from the hotSpot.fla file in the finished_source folder you downloaded for this chapter).

LISTING 5.9 This Code Assembles the hotSpot Template Layout

```
1   import flash.geom.Point;
2
3   var questionData:XMLNode
4   var owner:MovieClip;//really QuizHolder
5   var existingAnswers:Array;
6   var correctAnswers:Array;
7
8   var imageHolder:MovieClip;//to hold loaded image
9   var circle:MovieClip; //to highlight where they clicked
10  var tolerance:Number; //how close to the correct spot
11
12  //initialize the question text
13  question_txt.multiline = true;
14  question_txt.wordWrap = true;
15  question_txt.autoSize = true;
16  question_txt.text = "";
17
18  function init( p_owner:MovieClip, p_questionData:XMLNode ){
19      owner = p_owner;
20      questionData = p_questionData;
21      question_txt.text = questionData.attributes.questionText;
22
23      correctAnswers =
        questionData.attributes.correctAnswers.split( "," );
```

continues

LISTING 5.9   Continued

```
24
25         existingAnswers = questionData.attributes.theirAnswers;
26
27         var details:XMLNode =
           owner.selectSingleNode(questionData,"/question/details");
28
29         tolerance = Number(details.attributes.tolerance);
30
31         var topY = question_txt._y + question_txt._height + 20;
32         var topX = question_txt._x;
33
34         //create the circle now; move it after they click
35         circle = attachMovie( "circle", "circle", 2 );
36         circle._width = Number( details.attributes.diameter );
37         circle._height = Number( details.attributes.diameter );
38         circle._x = -9000;
39         circle._visible = false; //invisible until image loads
40
41         imageHolder = createEmptyMovieClip( "imageHolder", 0 );
42
43         var mcl:MovieClipLoader = new MovieClipLoader();
44         var listener:Object = new Object();
45         listener.onLoadInit = function( target:MovieClip ){
46            circle._visible = true;
47            //make a 0% alpha rectangle on top of the loaded image
48            var hotSpot = createEmptyMovieClip( "hotSpot", 1 );
49            with ( hotSpot ){
50               beginFill( 0xFF0000, 0 );
51               lineTo( 0, target._height );
52               lineTo( target._width, target._height );
53               lineTo( target._width, 0 );
54               lineTo( 0, 0 );
55               endFill();
56            }
57            hotSpot._x = target._x = topX;
58            hotSpot._y = target._y = topY;
59            hotSpot.onPress = function(){
60               click();
61            }
62            //show old answer if any
63            if( existingAnswers != undefined ){
64               placeCircle();
65            }
66         }
67         mcl.addListener( listener );
68         mcl.loadClip( details.attributes.image, imageHolder );
69
70         owner.canProceed( existingAnswers != undefined );
71      }
```

CHAPTER 5: Creating an Assessment Quiz

LISTING 5.9 **Continued**

```
72    function click(){
73        existingAnswers = [ _xmouse - imageHolder._x ,
                              _ymouse - imageHolder._y ];
74        placeCircle();
75    }
76
77    function getAnswers():Array{
78        if( correctAnswers != undefined ){
79            var userPoint:Point =
              new Point( existingAnswers[0], existingAnswers[1] );
80            var correctPoint:Point =
              new Point( Number( correctAnswers[0] ),
                         Number( correctAnswers[1] ) );
81            if ( Point.distance( userPoint, correctPoint ) <=
                  tolerance ){
82                existingAnswers = [correctPoint.x, correctPoint.y];
83            }
84        }
85        return existingAnswers;
86    }
87
88    function placeCircle(){
89        circle._x =  imageHolder._x + existingAnswers[0];
90        circle._y =  imageHolder._y + existingAnswers[1];
91        owner.canProceed( true );
92    }
```

Hopefully, you're beginning to see the similarities in all the question templates. Because the <question> node for this question type is slightly different from the other questions, Listing 5.10 shows it again for your reference while I discuss Listing 5.9.

Now for the ActionScript in Listing 5.9 (not the XML). In lines 23 and 25, I save both existingAnswers (if any) and the correctAnswers by turning the string version into an array using the split() method. On line 27, I grab the single details node; notice that I'm calling selectSingleNode() and not selectNodeList() as I did to get the <possible> nodes in the other templates because there's just one <details> node. Lines 35–39 attach the circle symbol we created in

step 3 and resize it based on the diameter attribute in the <details> node. The imageHolder clip is created in line 41 and then, way down on line 68 the photograph (specified by the image attribute) is loaded using the MovieClipLoader class. The MovieClipLoader instance (mcl) and listener (lines 43–66) wait for the image to load. When the image finally loads (when onLoadInit() triggers), several things happen: The circle is made visible (line 46); another clip (the instance hotSpot) is created (line 48) into which a rectangle is drawn to cover the photo (lines 49–58); the onPress handler is defined for the hotSpot instance (lines 59–61); and, if the user has any existing answers, the circle is placed on the stage (lines 63–65). In summary, the `init()` function loads the image, defines a clickable area, creates the circle, and optionally positions that circle if the user has already visited this question.

Whenever the user clicks, his click location on the `imageHolder` instance (that is, the photo) is saved in the `existingAnswers` array (on line 73); then the `placeCircle()` method positions the `circle` clip and tells the quiz engine that it's okay to proceed. The `placeCircle()` function is separated from the `click()` method so that I can trigger `placeCircle()` when a returning user arrives and I need to redisplay the circle (line 64).

The `getAnswers()` method (lines 77–86) is called by the quiz engine only when the user moves to the next or previous question. Normally, this method returns the `existingAnswers` array containing where the user clicked. If, however, the `correctAnswers` array exists, I measure the distance between where the user clicked and the correct location. If that distance is less than the `tolerance` attribute, I reset the `existingAnswers` to match the `correctAnswers` (and return that value).

STEP 5▼
Testing the hotSpot Template

Save the `hotSpot.fla` file and select Control, Test Movie to generate a `.swf` file. Go back to the `quiz.xml` file and make sure you have a `<question>` node whose `type` attribute is set to `"hotSpot"`. Finally, open the `quiz.fla` file and select Control, Test Movie.

When you arrive at the first `hotSpot` question, you'll see what's shown in Figure 5.9.

FIGURE 5.9 The `hotSpot` template displays a prompt and image and draws the circle when the user clicks on the image.

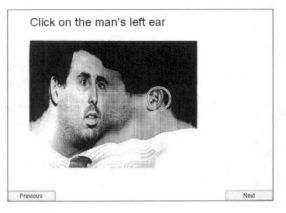

Click on the man's left ear

Previous · Next

LISTING 5.10 The `<question>` **Node**

```
<question type="hotSpot"
          questionID="pickSafetySwitch"
          questionText="Click on the man's left ear"
          correctAnswers="260,125">
<details image="http://www.phillipkerman.com/at-work/phillip.jpg"
          diameter="100"
          tolerance="100" />
</question>
```

Project:
Drag-and-Drop Template

Although this template suffers from the same accessibility flaws that the hotSpot template does (namely, users have to be able to use a mouse), it remains an effective way to test users' knowledge of sequential tasks. Users must arrange out-of-sequence tiles into the correct order by dragging the tiles on the left side of the screen to targets on the right side of the screen. Because the text might get long, depending on how you write the questions, the tiles are drawn dynamically to accommodate any length text. To make the tiles look realistic, we'll add a BevelFilter and a DropShadowFilter effect, which is, in my opinion, a subtle and effective use of a potentially gratuitous special effect.

The code to make tiles dragable is surprisingly simple. You'll see that the code gets much more involved when it has to determine where the user lets go of the tile. That is, when the user lets go of the tile, you need to either snap the tile back to its origin or snap it into a target—but only if the target is close enough and unoccupied.

STEPS▼

1. Creating the dragAndDrop.fla file
2. Laying out the stage
3. Changing the ActionScript
4. Testing the dragAndDrop template

STEP 1▼
Creating the dragAndDrop.fla File

Open the starterTemplate.fla file you created in the first project, or open the file of the same name in the finished_source folder you downloaded for this chapter, and select File, Save As. Save the file as **dragAndDrop.fla** in your working folder.

STEP 2▼
Laying Out the Stage

Just as you did for the previous templates, set the position, font, and margins for the question_txt field, which will contain the text of the question. The tiles and the target locations will appear underneath and left-justified with this text, but you don't have to lay that out by hand (we'll use ActionScript in the next step for that).

STEP 3▼
Changing the ActionScript

This template is nearly all ActionScript—more than 200 lines of it. Open the source dragAndDrop.fla file located in the finished_source folder, select the first keyframe, open the Actions panel, and copy all the ActionScript code located there. Go to the first keyframe of your working version of the dragAndDrop.fla file, which you saved in your working folder in step 1, and completely replace the existing ActionScript with the code you just copied from the final file.

I haven't included the code listing here because it's so long. But it does have verbose comments inline, and I'll walk through a few interesting parts next. (You can follow along with the Flash Actions window open.)

You'll see several important global variables at the top, such as highestClip (line 15), which is used in conjunction with the swapDepths() function (line 130) so the tile the user is currently dragging always appears on top of any other tiles. The scope clip reference (line 13) is simply there so I can dynamically reference tiles or targets using statements such as scope["tile"+n] and scope["target"+n] (lines 109, 110, and 182). Finally, tileBevel, targetBevel, and tileShadow (lines 17–21) define filters (from the flash.filters package) that are applied to the tiles and targets. When the user picks up a tile, I apply both the tileBevel and tileShadow filters (line 134) to make the tile look like it's floating above everything else. Then, when the user lets go of the tile, only the bevel is applied (line 169). The targetBevel filter for the target locations looks "pushed in" because the angle is rotated by 180°. Figure 5.10 shows how a bevel with an angle offset by 180° looks pushed in.

FIGURE 5.10   These two clips have the same bevel filter applied. The angle for the one on the left is 45°; the one on the right has an angle of 205° that's offset by 180°.

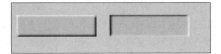

The init() function has several tasks: calculate the required height for tiles (lines 57–61), create the tiles (line 65) that contain a gray rectangle (lines 67–74) and text (lines 92–96) and have events for onPress and onRelease (lines 100–101), create the targets (lines 86–89), and position tiles into their appropriate targets if needed when a user returns to this question (lines 106–112). I should note that you're welcome to change the variables controlling the font and size details (lines 47–54). Be sure that the font you select is installed on the user's machine or that you select a font you've embedded in your file. (If you do select an embedded font, you'll need to uncomment line 97.)

Notice that the existingAnswers array has a slot for each target that contains either –1 (when empty) or the index for the occupying tile. Also notice that the tiles and targets have a homemade index property (lines 83 and 89) plus an initPoint for tiles (line 81).

When the user drags a tile, she invokes the dragMe() function. Three things happen there: The current tile is put into the highest depth above all the other tiles (line 130–131) and a shadow is added (134); if the tile's index is found in the existingAnswers array, that slot is changed to -1 (lines 138–143); and, finally, the onMouseMove() function begins to move the tile where the user drags, provided that it's not offscreen (lines 147–163). Here's the sequence when the user clicks: The appropriate filters are applied (bevel and blur) and the tile is moved above all other tiles; then the current tile is taken out of the existingAnswers array (if the user drops it back on a target, it is added, but while the user drags, the existingAnswers array does not contain that tile's index).

When the user lets go, the onMouseMove() method is removed (line 166) and the plain bevel is applied (line 169). Then there's a fair bit of work to see whether the user dropped the tile on top of an available target. Lines 192–202 simply put the tile back into its initial location or snap it to the target location (and update the existingAnswers array). Preceding that is the gnarly work of lines 175–191, where I basically check each target to see whether the tile's rectangle intersects the target (line 186), in which case I see whether the tile is closest to that target (line 189). Although you can intersect two targets, you should snap the tile only to the target you're closest to. To keep this block of code from getting really ugly, I employed two custom utility functions—getClosestTo() and getClipRect()—that appear in lines 209 and below.

STEP 4▼
Testing the dragAndDrop Template

Save the dragAndDrop.fla file and select Control, Test Movie to generate a .swf file. Go back to the quiz.xml file and make sure you have at least one <question> node whose type attribute is "dragAndDrop". Finally, open the quiz.fla file and select Control, Test Movie. When you arrive at the first drag-and-drop question, you'll see what's shown in Figure 5.11.

FIGURE 5.11   **The finished drag-and-drop template looks pretty sweet with the bevel and drop shadow.**

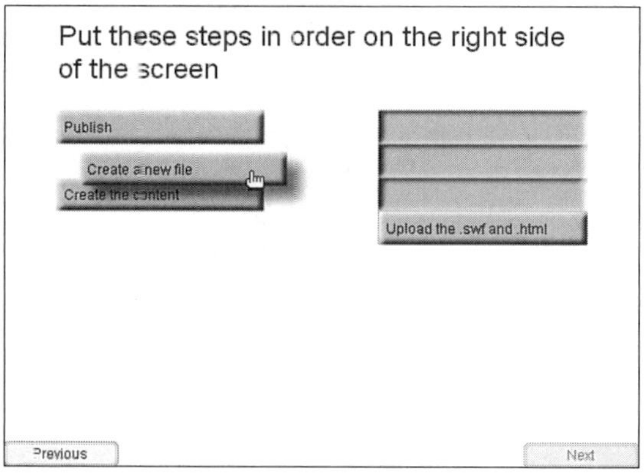

Project: Results Template

When users finish the last question in the quiz, they are given one last chance to make changes before finishing (see Figure 5.12). When they choose to continue, all their answers (basically, an array containing each question's existingAnswers array) can be sent to a server for safe keeping in a database. You'll see how to hook into an application server in Chapter 6. However, we can still build the results page now and display the user's quiz score. So, for the questions that had an attribute for correctAnswers (discussed in the first project in this chapter, "Quiz Content"), you can check the user's answers and determine whether the stated answers and the user's answers match.

In this project, you'll build the results.swf that appears after the user completes the quiz, after he confirms that he has finished answering all the questions. Basically, it's just a way to display the results that are calculated by the quiz engine. In the simple results template you build first, you'll just display the user's score as text. In the advanced results template, you'll create a bar that is filled in as a percentage that matches the user's percentage.

FIGURE 5.12   The quiz engine displays this last-chance warning after the user answers the last question.

STEPS▼

1. Creating the `results.fla` file
2. Laying out the stage
3. Building a simple results template
4. Testing the simple results template
5. Building an advanced results page

STEP 1▼
Creating the results.fla File

Create a new Flash file and select File, Save As. Name the file **results.fla** and save it in your working folder.

STEP 2▼
Laying Out the Stage

Just like all the previous templates, create a block of dynamic text, but this time set its instance name to **results_txt** instead of `question_txt`. This text displays the user's results, so make the margins wide—nearly as wide as the stage. We'll use ActionScript to set the `results_txt` field's `autoSize` property to `true` to make it accommodate any height.

STEP 3▼
Building a Simple Results Template

Select the first keyframe and open the Actions panel. Enter the code in Listing 5.11 (which you can also find in the `results_starter.fla` file in the `finished_source` folder you downloaded for this chapter).

Although this code should look familiar after you've created several templates, it's not the same as the question templates. This code implements the `IResults.as` interface and not the `IQuestion.as` interface as the other templates did. Here the `init()` function receives two pieces of data: the entire XML returned from the server when saving results (the `results` parameter) and a `score` object. The `score` object always has the same three properties: `totalQuestions`, the total number of questions in the quiz; `totalWithScore`, the total number of questions that could be scored, or those that had a `correctAnswers` attribute; and `totalMarkedCorrect`, the number of questions that could be scored *and* that were correct. The score parameter is calculated entirely on the client side in the quiz engine. It can grade only those questions that have a correctAnswers attribute. When you test this locally, you'll see that the results parameter has no value because we're not actually connecting to a server yet. The idea is simply that you can do the grading locally or remotely and, although both the results (well, the results and score parameters) are sent to your results template, you will likely choose to display only one or the other. Here we're displaying both as a test of what's possible.

With the two parameters (results and score) passed to init(), you can do whatever you want. When you do link to an application server, the server can send back literally any XML you want. Naturally, you'll need to know the format of that XML to parse the results. For example, the XML could include scoring for all questions, regardless of whether the correctAnswers attribute was included. The server could send

how the user's results compared to other students' results—whatever you want. You just have to do the legwork on the server, as you'll see in Chapter 6.

STEP 4▼
Testing the Simple Results Template

Before we expand on the results template, as we do in step 5, you should see how this bare-bones version works. Select Control, Test Movie to produce results.swf. Close the .swf file and then open quiz.fla and select Control, Test Movie. Go through the entire quiz, which should now include four scored questions.

The results page should appear as shown in Figure 5.13 (depending on how many questions you correctly answered).

LISTING 5.11 This Code Displays the User's Results in a Text Field

```
results_txt.multiline = true;
results_txt.wordWrap = true;
results_txt.autoSize = true;
results_txt.text = "";

function init( results:XML, score:Object ){
   results_txt.text = results;
   for( var i in score ){
      results_txt.text += newline + i + " = " + score[i];
   }
}
```

FIGURE 5.13   This bare-bones results page will be enhanced later.

```
<?xml version="1.0"?><success>true</success>
totalQuestions = 4
totalWithScore = 4
totalMarkedCorrect = 2
```

STEP 5▼
Building an Advanced Results Page

Replace the code you added in step 3 with the code shown in Listing 5.12, which you can also find in the results_finished.fla file in the finished_source folder.

LISTING 5.12   This Code Displays the User's Results As a Bar Graph

```
1   results_txt.multiline = true;
2   results_txt.wordWrap = true;
3   results_txt.autoSize = true;
4   results_txt.text = "";
5
6   function init( results:XML, score:Object ){
7       results_txt.text = "Congratulations for finishing " +
                                score.totalQuestions +
                                " questions!";
8
9       //if no questions had a score, don't draw the bar graph
10      if ( score.totalWithScore == 0 ) return;
11
12      var barWidth = results_txt._width;
13      var barHeight = 50;
14      var bar:MovieClip = createEmptyMovieClip("bar", 0);
15      bar._y = results_txt._y + 50;
16      bar._x = ( Stage.width - barWidth ) / 2;
17
18      var percentage =
            ( score.totalMarkedCorrect / score.totalWithScore );
19      var correctWidth = barWidth * percentage;
20
21      with( bar ){
22          //outline
23          lineStyle( 2 );
24          moveTo( 0, 0 );
25          lineTo( 0, barHeight );
26          lineTo( barWidth, barHeight );
27          lineTo( barWidth, 0 );
28          lineTo( 0, 0 );
29
30          //filled bar
31          moveTo( 0, 0 );
```

LISTING 5.12 **Continued**

```
32        beginFill( 0x00FF00, 100 );
33        lineTo( 0, barHeight );
34        lineTo( correctWidth, barHeight );
35        lineTo( correctWidth, 0 );
36        lineTo( 0, 0 );
37        endFill();
38      }
39      var _fmt:TextFormat = new TextFormat();
40      _fmt.font = "_sans";
41      _fmt.size = 18;
42      _fmt.color = 0x000000;
43
44      var thisField:TextField =
        createTextField( "percentage_txt", 1, 0, 0, 0, 0 );
45      thisField.selectable = false;
46      thisField.autoSize = true;
47      //thisField.embedFonts = true;
        //only use embedFonts if you're embedding the font
48      thisField.setNewTextFormat( _fmt );
49      thisField.text = Math.floor( percentage * 100 ) + "%";
50
51      //center the text:
52      thisField._x = bar._x +
                        barWidth/2 -
                        thisField._width/2;
53      thisField._y = bar._y +
                        barHeight/2 -
                        thisField._height/2;
54
55      //add a footnote if not every question was scored
56      if ( score.totalWithScore < score.totalQuestions ){
57        //modify the footnote to make it stand out
58        _fmt.size = 12;
59        _fmt.italic = true;
60        var footnote:TextField =
          createTextField( "footnote_txt", 2, 0, 0, 0, 0 );
61        footnote.selectable = false;
62        footnote.autoSize = true;
63        footnote.setNewTextFormat( _fmt );
64        footnote.text = "* only " +
                          score.totalWithScore +
                          " questions were graded";
65        footnote._x = results_txt._x;
66        footnote._y = bar._y + bar._height + 20;
67      }
68    }
```

This code isn't too bad. If the user doesn't have any scored questions, we skip out of the init() function on line 10. If there's something to graph—that is, if the user has at least one question that was scored—the user sees a bar clip (line 14) that is populated with a drawn outline and a filled shape (lines 21–38). The actual percentage is shown on top of the bar in the percentage_txt field (line 44). Finally, if the score is based on fewer than all the questions (lines 56–67), we display how many questions were scored in the footnote_txt field.

Note that the bar graph always shows the percentage of graded questions that were answered correctly.

STEP 6 ▼
Testing the Advanced Results Page

This step is identical to step 4: Select Control, Test Movie to produce results.swf. Close the .swf file, and then open quiz.fla and select Control, Test Movie. You'll see a much improved results page, as shown in Figure 5.14. You'll only get that footnote if at least one of the <question> nodes has no correctAnswers attribute.

FIGURE 5.14 **The completed advanced results page displays a graph showing the user's score.**

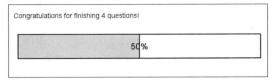

Exploring the Class Structure

To give you some perspective, I've created the class diagram in Figure 5.15 that shows the entire quiz engine.

So far, we haven't ventured far from the bottom-right corner, in which we've made the various question .swf files. These files all implement the IQuestion interface by exposing the functions init() and getAnswers(). Each question is managed by the QuizHolder, which is the owner reference we used to access the XPath routines and trigger canProceed().

You also created a couple of results.swf templates that implement the IResults interface.

The rest of the structure isn't important until Chapter 6. The simple way to think about the rest of the engine is that it's responsible for loading the quiz.xml data, for handling the Next and Previous buttons, and for sending data when it's time to save the answers. As long as your question .swf files (the templates we've been building) abide by a few guidelines, you'll be able to create as many question .swf files as you need to adequately test the user's knowledge.

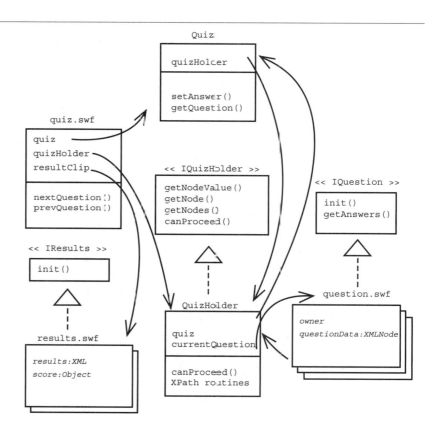

FIGURE 5.15 This class diagram should give you a perspective of where our templates live as well as a map in case you want to modify the source code.

Final Thoughts

With these four question-style templates in hand, you can build quizzes for many occasions. Feel free to make changes to style elements such as typeface and colors. But also realize that you can build more question types—that's the whole idea of building the engine. You'll find additional question templates included in the finished_source folder you downloaded for this chapter.

Here are just a couple ideas for additional question templates:

▶ You can integrate immediate feedback as the users click. For example, each <possible> node could have an

attribute for feedback in addition to the label attribute. This feedback would be appropriate for a non-graded training quiz where the objective is more to teach than to determine a user's existing knowledge.

▶ You could create an agree/disagree opinion-collecting question. For example, one question (that is, one page) could display rows of statements about which the user selects from columns labeled Strongly Disagree, Disagree, Neither Agree Nor Disagree, Agree, and Strongly Agree (such a question template is shown in Figure 5.16 and is available in the finished_source folder). Realize that this sort of question doesn't make sense to grade but rather is a way of collecting user information.

FIGURE 5.16 **Although you don't build this survey-style template** (surveyQuestion.fla) **in this chapter, it works great within the quiz engine.**

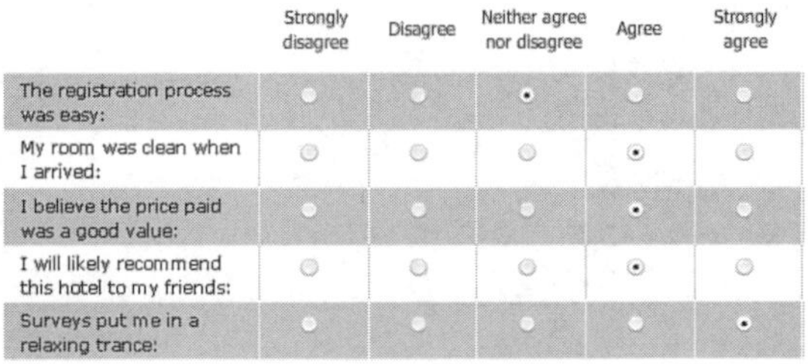

	Strongly disagree	Disagree	Neither agree nor disagree	Agree	Strongly agree
The registration process was easy:	◉	○	◉	○	○
My room was clean when I arrived:	○	○	○	◉	○
I believe the price paid was a good value:	○	○	○	◉	○
I will likely recommend this hotel to my friends:	○	○	○	◉	○
Surveys put me in a relaxing trance:	○	○	○	○	◉

By the way, the grading approach taken in the final project, "Results Page," was simplistic. For one thing, I didn't bother grading questions that didn't include a correctAnswers attribute. Ultimately, grading questions should be handled on the server side because it's not really smart to send the correctAnswers attribute to the user, even if the quiz.swf file normally consumes it. In addition, the dragAndDrop question was graded as either entirely correct or incorrect—with no provision to give partial credit. For example, if the user places the first three items in the correct order but places the fourth item in the first slot, the entire answer is wrong even though three of the items appear in their correct sequence. You can create more sophisticated templates and more sophisticated grading algorithms. But sophisticated grading should be handled on the server because the quiz engine we're working with in this chapter applies the same grading criteria (either all right or all wrong) to every question. However, I was clever enough to design the init() function in the results template to receive both the grading results calculated locally as well as the results from the server. In Chapter 6, you'll see more about integrating the quiz engine we used in this chapter with an application server.

Users	Quizes
Phillip Kerman	Geography
Joe Smith	Safety
Bob Jones	Popular Music 1960

All quiz results for Phillip Kerman

quiz	quizID	percentage
Geography	quizid1	12
Safety	quizid2	34
Popular Music 1960	quizid3	56

About the Projects

The quiz templates you built in Chapter 5, "Creating an Assessment Quiz," draw their content from a static XML text file (quiz.xml). In this chapter, you'll connect the quiz to an *application server* so the questions can be drawn from a database. The quiz still reads the same string data that was in quiz.xml, but in this chapter that file is generated dynamically upon request. Not only will we use an application server to supply the questions, but we'll also create an administrative tool that lets a boss or teacher view all the students' results.

Prerequisites

You should read Chapter 5 first. You need to have access to an application server and online database to run and maintain this quiz. The Flash quiz interfaces with the server application using simple HTTP requests, so you'll use the same code and files whether your server-side application is in ASP.Net, ColdFusion, JSP, or PHP. I've supplied source code that uses PHP and mySQL.

@work resources

Download the chapter_6_downloads.zip file for this chapter from the accompanying CD-ROM.

Planning the Projects

Everything in this chapter is about running the quiz engine from Chapter 5 in a dynamic manner. The fact that you can, quite effectively, deliver the quiz from Chapter 5 on a standard web server might raise the question of why you should even bother with an application server. You should certainly understand the benefits before taking on the additional work involved here.

Benefits of Application Servers

First, I use the term *application server* loosely to refer to any server that can generate varied results based on parameters sent by a request. When you request an HTML page on a standard HTTP web server, you get back a static text string. In the case of application servers, you can send parameters in various forms, but most often as form GET and POST variables). The "page" you get in return is a text string that is generated dynamically. In the case of this project, all the results returned are strings in the form of XML.

Using an application server in conjunction with a database offers several benefits. Most notably, you can save all the user results so the boss or teacher can review all the quiz-takers' results. If you design your quiz to be a survey instead, it's important to be able to analyze the results, so saving them as you learn to do in this chapter is essential.

Although the quiz you built in Chapter 5 is perfectly suitable, the users were basically stuck on an island—questions were hard-wired and results were displayed only if the answers were sent down with the questions. After the user closed the browser, those

results were gone forever. On top of all this, no administrator could track user results. The good news is that everything you built in Chapter 5 will work here and be enhanced by connecting to an application server.

No Live Server?

You can complete this entire chapter without having a live server running. In fact, in the project "API Tester," you'll build a tool that confirms everything is working when your application server is live. Such a testing tool is critical so that both the Flash people and the server-side folks can develop simultaneously instead of waiting for the other team to finish first. (Users' quiz results aren't really saved until you're connected to a live server with a real database.)

Another alternative to having the live server up and running is to develop using a server running locally.

Incidentally, I've provided source code using PHP and MySQL, but you'll still need your own server to run it live. In addition, the table structures were exported from phpMyAdmin to make them easy to integrate into other databases.

Keeping Login Separate

When users complete the quiz, their results will be saved on the server. For the server to know whose results are being received, the client application must send a userID along with the quiz results. In fact, when the user initially requests the quiz.xml file, he must send a quizID so the server knows which questions to send. Perhaps the most critical step you have to address in this chapter is exactly how the users will find their userID and the quizID for the quiz they want to take. (You can use the same code for as many different quizzes as you want.) Basically, you have to get the users logged in first. At that time, the server can send all the appropriate variables (such as a list of available quizzes) to the client, and those variables can be sent back with every subsequent request.

Because there are so many login options, it's best to handle that portion of the operation before users get to the quiz.swf file—which, by the way, remains unchanged from what you created in Chapter 5. That is, users first gather values for userID and quizID using one of several mechanisms that I'll discuss; then they go to the quiz.swf file (well, they go to an HTML page hosting the quiz.swf file, which we'll cleverly call quiz.html). This way, you have the flexibility to use any login approach you want. You can employ an existing secure authentication process you've built using a traditional web page or build something entirely inside Flash where the user provides a username and password. It makes sense to keep the login approach independent so you can easily change it in the future.

Login Options

With the premise that users will arrive at the quiz with, at a minimum, their userID, you can select the best login option for your situation. In this chapter, we build the following three versions: a traditional web login that dynamically generates the quiz.html document, with the variables embedded in the FlashVars tag (a way to send variables from HTML to Flash); a simple Flash login where the user manually enters a userID and quizID that gets tacked onto the end of the quiz.html file's URL as a query string; and an advanced Flash login that retrieves the userID when the user is authenticated by his

username/password, displays a list of available quizzes, and then passes userID and quizID in the *query string*.

> **NOTE**
>
> When I say *query string*, I'm referring to the optional name/value pairs that can appear after the URL. Instead of quiz.html, if the URL is quiz.html?myName=myValue, there's a variable called myName with the value "myValue". Additional pairs can appear if separated by &. Also, all values are strings but don't need quotation marks. Query strings simply provide a way to pass variables from the URL to the HTML page. In our case, we'll then channel the query string from the HTML down to the .swf.

Each of the three login approaches appears as a project in this chapter. The reason I included all three is that your organization might have a preference to handle the login through an existing mechanism. In that case, you can generate the HTML with the userID and quizID in the FlashVars tag.

Ascertaining Variable Values from Inside quiz.swf

The quiz.swf file already includes code to retrieve variables for userID and quizID in either the FlashVars tag or the query string. If the quiz.html document has a FlashVars tag, those are set before the first frame's script runs. If the quiz.swf file finds that any of the expected variables are undefined, it first uses the ExternalInterface class to call a custom JavaScript function (getQueryValue()) that I included in the quiz.html document. The getQueryValue() function returns values found in the query string. Finally, if the variables quiz.swf needs are still undefined (meaning they're not in the query string or the FlashVars tag), it simply reverts to hard-wired defaults ("userID" and "quizID"). That's why the quiz.swf file worked in Chapter 5 without login information—it just used the defaults. The order of priority for looking for login information is FlashVars, ExternalInterface (the query string), and then the default values. The query string is used only if the FlashVars tag is empty, and the defaults are used only as a failsafe. Figure 6.1 shows the sequence.

FIGURE 6.1 Once inside the quiz.swf, if userID or quizID has no value, the FlashVars didn't set them and the quiz.swf checks for a query string using the ExternalInterface class. If that fails to return values for userID or quizID, defaults are used.

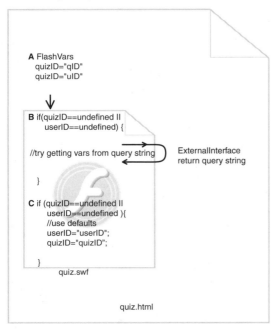

```
A FlashVars
   quizID="qID"
   quizID="uID"
```

```
B if(quizID==undefined ||
     userID==undefined) {

   //try getting vars from query string

   }
```

ExternalInterface
return query string

```
C if (quizID==undefined ||
      userID==undefined ){
    //use defaults
    userID="userID";
    quizID="quizID";

    }
```
quiz.swf

quiz.html

Chapter Projects

At the end of this chapter, you'll have two main projects built: First, you'll be able to hook the quiz into a database to get the questions and save the user results, plus you'll have another Flash application that lets an administrator review all the results. There are several steps you'll need to take to get to that end. As an overview, let me explain the projects you'll work on in this chapter.

Because the quiz and administrator tool makes several method calls to the server, I'll show you a strategy to maintain a list of methods outside the Flash applications (the quiz or administrator tool). This way, you'll be able to make changes to adapt to how the server behaves—say, if you change servers—without needing to return to Flash. This approach also gives you a quick way to switch between testing locally and connecting to a live server. It turns out that the quiz from Chapter 5 already uses this list of methods (urls.xml), but we'll expand on it here.

For your application server to track users' scores, each user needs a unique user ID. Additionally, the server should be able to support multiple quizzes. Therefore, users must supply a quiz ID when they request a quiz. Naturally, you can't expect the users to manually enter a unique user ID and quiz ID themselves. So, much of the work in this chapter covers how to get the users logged in. After the server knows who the user is, it can send a unique user ID and a list of available quizzes. There are a lot of ways a server can authenticate a user and, for maximum flexibility, you don't want the Flash quiz to get hardwired to one particular login mechanism. I explained this topic earlier, so I'll just summarize here by saying I'll show you several ways to handle the necessary login step.

In the end, you should test the entire quiz and reporting system in its final form. However, there's an advantage to building a testing environment that lets you test portions of the project while you're in development. A critical priority is that the quiz and admin tool works just as well in its final online form as it does while testing on local static files. You won't be able to make changes such as saving users' scores with static files, but you should at least be able to simulate everything. Testing locally gives you the opportunity to build the Flash side of things while the server folks are building the server side code. So, one project is to simply run the quiz and admin tool using local files.

It might seem that the hardest part of building a Flash front end that can talk to the server side is doing all the programming in Flash and on the server. However, the real challenge is establishing and agreeing on a working Application Programming Interface (API), the set of methods, their parameters, and the values they return. Part of the reason for including a full project in this chapter where I describe the APIs is so you can use the quiz and admin tool we build here with any server-side technology. I supply the source code in PHP, but your organization might use ColdFusion or API.Net. The API provides a common interchange language that makes the Flash side work with any backend.

After you establish an API, it's much easier to test all the methods using a specially designed miniapplication rather than stepping through the final quiz. I built a simple tool that exercises every method in the API. When you confirm that this portion works correctly with your server, you can be certain

that the quiz and any admin tool you build will work.

The idea of the admin tool is to view and analyze all the quiz results using a nice Flash interface instead of viewing the raw data. Exactly how you assemble and present the results from the quizzes is up to you. You might want to let the admin see the average scores for all users or be able to drill down and see one user's answers. In this chapter, you'll build a simple admin tool. In addition, I'll give you a tour of a more advanced admin tool that I built using the same APIs. You can snoop through the source code for the advanced admin tool, but the reason I built it was to provide a useful tool as well as to give you some ideas for how you can present aggregated data in Flash.

Lastly, I should state what you *won't* do in this chapter. Specifically, you won't learn how to actually build a server-side application. That would involve a fair bit of database design information and implementation using a specific tool (of which there are many to choose from). The basic concept behind this chapter is to provide a practical add-on to the quiz built in Chapter 5. That quiz is great, but it's an island. I'm sure most people will want the data from that quiz to be saved in a server-side application. In this chapter, you'll build everything on the Flash side, including establishing a workable API. When given to a competent server-side person, this system works great. In fact, as a matter of role definition, you should follow this pattern in which the client-side Flash person meets the server-side person in the middle—at the API. Finally, let me remind you that I do provide source code in PHP and MySQL. This is partially as a service to you but mainly to prove that the whole system works. It's just that you won't learn PHP by only reading this chapter.

Project:
External Paths to Server-side Methods

This is a short project, but it's required regardless of which of the subsequent login approaches you take. The basic idea is to maintain a lookup table for all the methods your application supports. Instead of embedding directly into your Flash files the name and address for the server-side methods, you keep all names in an external file. This makes editing the method names easy—say, if the path to your server changes. You won't need a Flash person to open Flash; just find the code to edit and then republish the `.swf` file. Anyone can make edits to the lookup table. Perhaps more important than providing a quick way to change the method names, the lookup table also means we can temporarily point to static XML documents during testing. This way, we'll be able to test everything before the server-side application is up and running.

At the end of this project, you'll have the `urls.xml` file and understand how to add methods to it.

STEPS▼

1. Adding methods to the `urls.xml` file
2. Specifying the location of the `urls.xml` file

STEP 1▼
Adding Methods to the urls.xml File

Start by making a copy of the `starter_files` folder you downloaded for this chapter. This will be your working directory. Go inside the `schemas` folder (now in your working folder) to find `urls.xml`. Open that file in a text editor such as Notepad. The content of the `urls.xml` file is shown in Listing 6.1.

For every method your quiz, login files, or admin tool uses, you'll need to add a `<url>` node within the main `<allPaths>` node of this document. Each `<url>` node has two attributes: `methodName` (the name used inside Flash) and `path` (the actual path to where the method resides). Currently, there are two `<url>` nodes, but we'll add more later. One has the `methodName` attribute of `"getQuiz"` to retrieve the quiz content, and one has a `methodName` of `"saveUserResults"` to save the user results. The `methodName` is hardwired inside Flash, but you can edit the `path`.

LISTING 6.1   The Starter Code for the `urls.xml` **File**

```xml
<?xml version="1.0"?>
<allPaths>
    <url methodName="getQuiz"
        path="schemas/quiz.xml"/>
    <url methodName="saveUserResults"
        path="schemas/saveUserResults.xml"/>
</allPaths>
```

When the `quiz.swf` file needs a quiz, it always looks for the `<url>` node with a `methodName` attribute of `getQuiz`. You can't change the method name because the `quiz.swf` file always looks for `getQuiz`. However, you can change the path to the `getQuiz` method, effectively changing from where Flash requests a quiz. You can use an *absolute path* (also called an *explicit path*) or a *relative path*. Note that paths are relative to the main `.swf` file—not to the `urls.xml` file. That is, the path `schemas/quiz.xml` means `quiz.swf` looks into a `schemas` folder adjacent to wherever `quiz.swf` resides and then looks to a file `quiz.xml`. Although `quiz.xml` currently exists as a static text file, it could just as easily be a server-side method that returns content from a database. For example, when you browse to most files on my home page, you'll receive the content of a static text file, but if you browse to `http://www.google.com/search?q=phillip+kerman` the results are generated dynamically. When testing, we can request the local version of `quiz.xml` in the `schemas` folder. However, when we change the path to `quiz.xml` to, say, `myserver.com/getQuiz.php?quizID=1`, the results can be generated dynamically by the server.

STEP 2 ▼
Specifying the Location of the urls.xml File

Although the `urls.xml` file can list the location of as many methods as we want, you might not like the default location and filename for `urls.xml` itself. Currently, the

`quiz.swf` file gets its list of methods by first looking for the `urls.xml` file in the `schemas` subfolder. There are plenty of reasons you might prefer to keep that file elsewhere or name it differently.

To see how the `urls.xml` file is specified, use a text editor to open the file `quiz_html_minimum.html` in the working directory—a copy of the `starter_files` folder you downloaded for this chapter. Look at lines 30 and 38, where you find `FlashVars`, excerpted here:

```
30  <param name="FlashVars"
         value="urlList=
         http://www.phillipkerman.com/
         macmillan/schemas/urls.xml" />
31
32  <param name="movie" value="quiz.swf"/>
33  <param name="quality" value="high"/>
34  <param name="bgcolor" value="#ffffff"/>
35
36  <embed src="quiz.swf"
37
38  flashVars="urlList=
         http://www.phillipkerman.com/
         macmillan/schemas/urls.xml"
```

Lines 30 is the version part of the object tag for Internet Explorer, and line 38 is the equivalent for Netscape and other browsers. Both statements do the same thing: They set the value for a variable called `urlList`. This variable appears in the `quiz.swf` file immediately and without any extra work. When you see the source `quiz.fla` file, you'll see that it expects this variable to already be set, and it's this value that `quiz.fla` uses to find the lookup table of method names. Let's change both lines to point to the local version of `urls.xml` you just edited.

Change line 30 to read:

```
<param name="FlashVars"
value="urlList=schemas/urls.xml"/>
```

Change line 38 to read:

```
flashVars="urlList=schemas/urls.xml"
```

Again, you can change the value (if you want to change this later), but don't change the variable name (urlList). That's the specific name the Flash file expects.

Save and close the quiz_html_minimum.html file.

Using Just One FlashVars **Variable**

You might be wondering why we're going through the trouble of maintaining a separate list of methods (urls.xml) and the FlashVars variable (urlList) to point to it. We could instead simply list all the methods in the FlashVars, separating pairs of variable names and their values with the & symbol. In fact, we will add a few more values to the FlashVars parameter in the next project, "Traditional Login." However, continually making detailed edits to the FlashVars in the HTML is a bit tedious for us humans. If the server dynamically generates the .html document, it's no big deal. But the whole idea of the urlList variable is to tell Flash, "Hey, go find all the variables you need in this single lookup file." This makes it much more workable when you need to add methods to the url.xml file. You'll see that you can add nodes to the urls.xml file without having to touch anything else.

Project:
Traditional Login

For the quiz.swf file to request a quiz using the value for getQuiz in urls.xml, it needs to know both the userID of the user taking the quiz and the quizID for the quiz the user wants to take. This project creates a structure where you can define the userID and quizID by any means you want. Figure 6.2 shows the flow.

The idea is that your server generates a .html document with FlashVars containing the userID and quizID. Let me note that this is just one of the three login options you'll learn about in this chapter. This one involves the least amount of work inside Flash, but it does require that you have the skills or resources to dynamically generate .html documents. You can build the login.html file (shown on the left side of Figure 6.2) using any approach you want—for example, PHP. After the user is authenticated, your server must generate quiz.html and populate it with FlashVars for the userID and quizID variables (plus the old urlList you already saw). There are a million ways to do the authentication, so this project assumes you can build that using the technology of your choice.

To test whether this approach works, you write a static quiz.html you'll use for testing in which you hard-wire those variables. This is a perfectly legitimate way to simulate how it will work for testing purposes before the server actually generates the quiz.html file.

STEPS ▼

1. **Adding** FlashVars **to** quiz.html
2. **Adding the** debug **switch in** quiz.fla
3. **Testing it**

FIGURE 6.2 **This open-ended traditional approach involves a plain** `login.html` **page (left) that calls out to the server to request a dynamically generated** `quiz.html` **file (on the right) with the necessary variables embedded.**

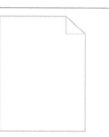

login.html
performs traditional authentication

quiz.html   (dynamic)
FlashVars: userID, quizID, urlList

STEP 1▼
Adding FlashVars to quiz.html

Use a text editor to open the file `quiz_html_minimum.html` in your working directory that you edited in the previous project Select File, Save As and name the file **quiz_html_traditional.html**.

 NOTE

Using verbose filenames serves two purposes. For one thing, long filenames can make clear what the files do. Second, long filenames ensure that the files aren't accidentally overwritten if you ever select Publish from inside Flash. If you created a file named `quiz.html`, all your precious edits would be overwritten if you selected Publish from the `quiz.fla` file. (Because `quiz.html` is the default `.html` filename when editing `quiz.fla`.)

You'll add three additional values to the FlashVars: `userID`, `quizID`, and `debug` (for testing).

Edit line 30 to read as follows (but with no line returns):

```
<param name="FlashVars"
value="debug=true&
      userID=fvUserID&
      quizID=fvQuizID&
      urlList=schemas/urls.xml" />
```

Edit line 38 to read as follows (again, with no line returns):

```
flashVars="debug=true&
      userID=fvUserID&
      quizID=fvQuizID&
      urlList=schemas/urls.xml"
```

In addition to the existing `urlList` discussed in the previous project, these lines of code create dummy values for `userID` and `quizID` (the `"fv"` helps us identify the values that came from `FlashVars`). Notice that multiple `FlashVars` variables are separated with the ampersand (&). In the next step, you'll learn how the `debug` switch lets you see the values for `userID` and `quizID` while you're testing.

STEP 2▼
Adding the debug Switch in quiz.fla

The values for `userID` and `quizID` should be passed as parameters when the `quiz.swf` file requests the quiz content—specifically, when `quiz.swf` calls the `schemas/quiz.xml` because that's the path in the `urls.xml` node containing `getQuiz`. To see that the values exist inside Flash, however, we can add a text field to the quiz.fla and add code so the field displays those values (while testing).

Open quiz.fla, located in your working folder. Place a dynamic text field 20 pixels above the bottom of the stage. Give it the instance name **info_txt**.

Open the Actions panel and click the first keyframe. Read through the first 37 lines of code shown in Listing 6.2.

LISTING 6.2 This Code Looks for External Variables in Several Locations		

```
1    import mx.xpath.*;
2    import flash.external.ExternalInterface;
3
4    //not typed String or Boolean because
         these arrive via ExternalInterface
5    var userID;
6    var quizID;
7    var urlList;
8    var debug;
9
10   //if not in LoadVars, see if vars are in the QueryString
11   if( userID == undefined ){
12       userID =
         ExternalInterface.call( "getQueryValue", "userID" );
13   }
14   if( quizID == undefined ){
15       quizID =
         ExternalInterface.call( "getQueryValue", "quizID" );
16   }
17   if( urlList == undefined ){
18       urlList =
         ExternalInterface.call( "getQueryValue", "urlList" );
19   }
20   if( debug == undefined ){
21       debug =
         ExternalInterface.call( "getQueryValue", "debug" );
22   }
23   //if still no vars, these are the defaults:
24   if( userID == undefined ){
25       userID = "userID";
26   }
27   if( quizID == undefined ){
28       quizID = "quizID";
29   }
30   if( urlList == undefined ){
31       urlList = "schemas/urls.xml";
32   }
33   if( debug == undefined ){
34       debug = false;
35   }
```

Lines 10–22 check all four variables (userID, quizID, urlList, and debug), and if any are undefined—meaning they haven't been set in the FlashVars—this code attempts to find the values in the query string by using the JavaScript function getQueryValue using the ExternalInterface class (more about this homemade function in the next two projects). In this project, none of those variables should be undefined because we set them in the FlashVars. Lines 23–35 assign the default values if those variables are still undefined.

Add the following code after line 36:

```
if( debug == true || debug == "true" ){
    info_txt.autoSize = true;
    info_txt.text = 'userID:   '+
                        userID +
                    ' quizID: '+
                        quizID;
} else {
    info_txt._visible = false;
}
```

This code simply displays the userID and quizID, provided that the debug variable is set to true.

Select File, Save and then select Control, Test Movie to generate the new quiz.swf file.

STEP 3 ▼
Testing It

There are actually three things you can test now. However, it makes sense to test only one thing at a time. First, test that the hand-coded quiz_html_traditional.html file successfully sets and displays values for userID and quizID in the quiz.swf. Second,

you can write a server-side application that dynamically generates a similar HTML document by populating the FlashVars for userID and quizID, and you'll see the values in quiz.swf. Finally, you can write a server-side method for getQuiz, replace the path in the urls.xml file to point to your method, and then test that it receives the userID and quizID as expected. We'll do the first test now. You're welcome to perform the second test with your own application or the provided PHP source files. The third test appears later in the chapter in the project "API Tester."

To test that the FlashVars are arriving in the quiz.swf file, you need to do just one thing: Double-click the quiz_html_traditional.html file you created in step 1 to launch your browser. You should see the string "userID: fvUserID quizID: fvQuizID" in the text field (on top of the first question), as shown in Figure 6.3.

FIGURE 6.3   With the debug variable set to true, your quiz will reveal the userID and quizID, in this case arriving from the FlashVars.

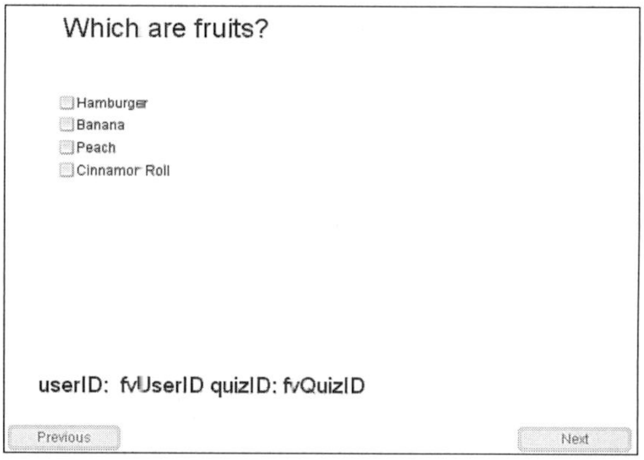

Which are fruits?

☐ Hamburger
☐ Banana
☐ Peach
☐ Cinnamon Roll

userID: fvUserID quizID: fvQuizID

[Previous]   [Next]

Project:
Simple All-Flash Login

Next, you actually build the page that precedes the `quiz.html` file. Figure 6.4 shows the arrangement.

In this project, you'll build the `login_simple.swf` file that lets the user enter her `userID` and `quizID`. I acknowledge that this is not exactly practical because users are not likely to know their `userID` at this point, let alone the `quizID`—but that's why this project is called the simple one! You can think of it as a proof of concept application. When the user clicks Go, a version of the `quiz.html` file loads via `getURL`. Instead of using `FlashVars` for `userID`, `quizID`, and

debug, those values are attached to the end of the query string, which `quiz.swf` retrieves using the `ExternalInterface` class.

STEPS▼
1. **Creating the** `login_simple.fla` **file**
2. **Coding it**
3. **Creating the** `quiz_html_simple.html` **file**
4. **Publishing and testing**

STEP 1▼
Creating the login_simple.fla File

Create a new file in Flash and select File, Save As. Save the file in your working directory as **login_simple.fla**.

Open the Components panel by pressing Ctrl+F7 to do so, and drag onto the stage two `Label` components, two `TextInput` components, one `CheckBox` component, and one `Button` component. Give them instance names as indicated in Figure 6.5.

FIGURE 6.4 The `login_simple.swf` file, on the left, passes collected variables in the query string when launching the `quiz.html` file, on the right.

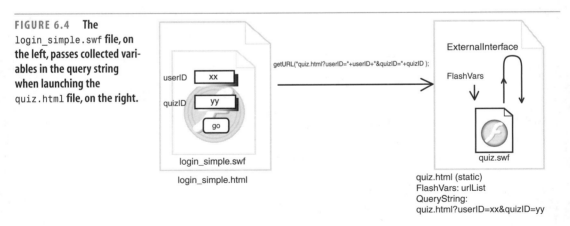

STEP 2 ▼
Coding It

Select the first keyframe, open the Actions panel, and type the code in Listing 6.3. You can also find this code in the login_simple.fla file in the finished_source folder you downloaded for this chapter. Block and copy the code if you don't want to type.

This code lets the user enter a userID and quizID (plus an optional debug flag) and

then open the quiz_html_simple.html file with a query string containing their variables.

FIGURE 6.5   The components you'll need for the simple login are shown with their instance names.

FIGURE 6.5   The components you'll need for the simple login are shown with their instance names.

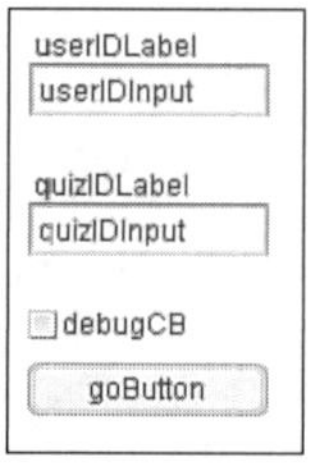

LISTING 6.3   This Code Lets Users Enter a userID and quizID That Is Added to the Query String

```
1    import mx.controls.Label;
2    import mx.controls.TextInput;
3    import mx.controls.Button;
4    import mx.controls.CheckBox;
5
6    var userIDLabel:Label;        userIDLabel.text = "userID";
7    var userIDInput:TextInput;    userIDInput.text = "";
8    var quizIDLabel:Label;        quizIDLabel.text = "quizID";
9    var quizIDInput:TextInput;    quizIDInput.text = "";
10   var debugCB:CheckBox;         debugCB.label = "debug";
11   var goButton:Button;          goButton.label = "Go";
12   goButton.enabled = false;
13
14   goButton.addEventListener( "click", this );
15   userIDInput.addEventListener( "change", this );
16   quizIDInput.addEventListener( "change", this );
17
18   function click(){
19      var url = "quiz_html_simple.html";
20      var str = "userID=" + userIDInput.text +
21              "&quizID=" + quizIDInput.text +
22              "&debug=" + debugCB.selected;
23      //trace( url + "?" + str );
24      getURL( url + "?" + str );
25   }
26   function change(){
27      goButton.enabled =
28      ( userIDInput.text != "" && quizIDInput.text != "" );
   }
```

The key part of this code is the click() function, triggered when the user clicks the Go button. The str variable is generated and tacked onto the end of the url variable. You can uncomment the trace() function in line 23 and comment out line 24 so that, instead of navigating, you'll see the address normally passed to getURL(). Just remember to leave the getURL() uncommented when you finally publish for testing in a browser.

STEP 3▼
Creating the quiz_html_simple.html File

The HTML document that is called from the getURL() in your simple_login.swf file should have FlashVars only for the urlList—but not values for the userID and quizID parameters because those are passed in with the query string. With a text editor, open the quiz_html_minimum.html file, located in the starter_files folder. Ensure that lines 30 and 38 have a single value for urlList as you edited in the first project of this chapter.

Namely, line 30 should read as follows:

```
<param name="FlashVars"
       value="urlList=schemas/urls.xml"/>
```

And line 40 should read as follows:

```
flashVars="urlList=schemas/urls.xml"
```

Select Save As and name the new file quiz_html_simple.html. While you're in the HTML document, feel free to investigate the getQueryValue() function on line 11. This homemade function is called from inside the

.swf file to retrieve values from the query string.

STEP 4▼
Publishing and Testing

Return to the login_simple.fla file and select File, Publish. This command generates both the login_simple.swf file and the HTML file to host it. If you didn't do the preceding project, "Traditional Login," you'll need to add the debug code to the quiz.fla file. (Refer to step 2, "Adding the debug Switch in quiz.fla" in the preceding project and then select File, Test Movie to generate the quiz.swf file.)

Finally, to test this project, you'll need to post the following files on a web server:

- ▶ login_simple.html
- ▶ login_simple.swf
- ▶ quiz_html_simple.html
- ▶ quiz.swf

You'll also have to post a schemas folder and the following files within it:

- ▶ urls.xml
- ▶ quiz.xml
- ▶ saveUserResults.xml

On top of all this, if you want to run the quiz, you'll also need all the template .swf files referred to in the quiz.xml file's <question> nodes. You can grab all these files from the finished_source folder you downloaded for this chapter. Figure 6.6 shows the complete layout.

FIGURE 6.6   To fully test this project, you'll need to post on a web server the two `.html` files and two main `.swf` files (`login_simple.swf` and `cuiz.swf`) in addition to the schemas folder and all the question templates.

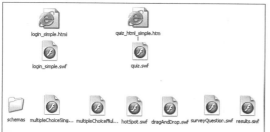

At this point, we've only tested that the values for `userID` and `quizID` entered by the user have successfully arrived in the `quiz.swf`. That's all this project does. We haven't yet connected to the application server. After we do (in a later project), you can run this project and it will send parameters for `userID` and `quizID`, the ones shown on screen while testing, when calling the `getQuiz()` method as specified in the `urls.xml` file.

Launch your web-hosted version of `login_simple.html`, enter a `userID` and `quizID`, click the `debug` option, and then click the Go button to see your variables appear in the debug text field along with the query string in the browser address bar (see Figure 6.7).

FIGURE 6.7   After entering a `userID` and `quizID`, the `quiz_html_simple.html` page loads with additional variables in the query string.

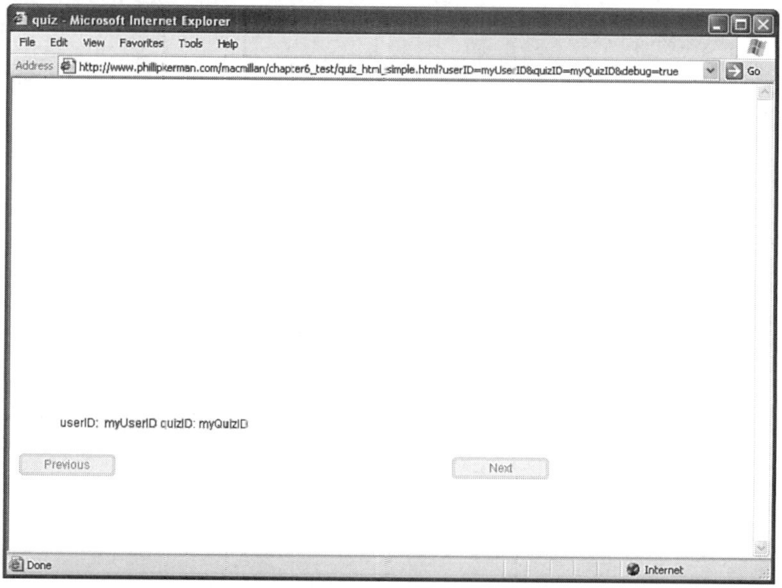

Project:
Advanced All-Flash Login

The previous project was primarily a demonstration of how you can pass variables collected in one `.swf` to a second `.swf` that loads later. In this project, you'll collect the key variables `userID` and `quizID` by connecting the initial login `.swf` to a *server-side script*. This way, we can authenticate users by a username and password instead of asking them to enter a `userID` and `quizID` directly. When the variables arrive from the database, we jump out to the `quiz.html` file in the same manner we did in the last project. However, you'll also see how to use an application server to generate the `quiz.html` page, with embedded `FlashVars` if you prefer to take that route instead of passing the `userID` and `quizID` in the query string.

Figure 6.8 shows the arrangement for this project. You'll build the `login_advanced.swf`

file (on the left in Figure 6.8), which first receives the `urlList` from the `FlashVars`. The user logs in with a `username` and `password` that are sent as parameters to the server-side `requestLogin` method. In addition, a `makeNewUser` method is available to add new users to the roster. When a user is authenticated, his `userID` is returned. The `.swf` file immediately calls another server-side method, `getAllQuizIDs`, that returns a list of quiz names (and, more importantly, their respective `quizIDs`) available to this user. Therefore, you can let users select from a only subset of the quizzes available—perhaps only quizzes they haven't already completed. These added methods (`requestLogin`, `makeNewUser`, and `getAllQuizIDs`) can reside in your application sever named as anything you want, but they appear in the `urls.xml` file with these values for their `methodName` attribute. Finally, the user can select which quiz he wants, and the `userID` and `quizID` are packed up and sent to the `quiz.html` file so the appropriate quiz can begin.

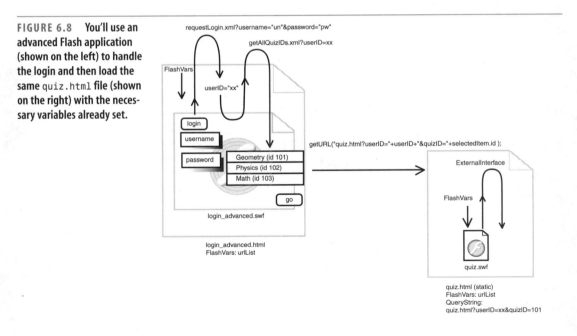

FIGURE 6.8 **You'll use an advanced Flash application (shown on the left) to handle the login and then load the same `quiz.html` file (shown on the right) with the necessary variables already set.**

STEP 1▼
Creating the login_advanced.fla File

Create a new Flash file and select File, Save As. Name the file **login_advanced.fla** and save it in your working folder. Open the Components panel by pressing Ctrl+F7, and drag the following components onstage: three `Label` components, two `TextInput` components, four `Button` components, one `CheckBox` component, and one `List` component. Figure 6.9 shows both the arrangement of these components and their respective instance names. Be sure you give each component an instance name.

FIGURE 6.9 **The components you'll need are shown with their instance names.**

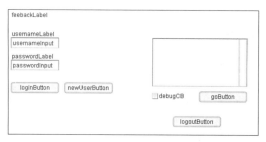

There's one last item you should add to the file besides code: the `DataBindingClasses`, so you can use XPath. The ActionScript you'll add in step 5 uses XPath to conveniently parse the `urls.xml` and the results from the `getAllQuizIDs` method call. Select Window, Common Libraries, Classes. Drag the `DataBindingClasses` from the Classes library to your file's Library. (Alternatively, drag the item on your stage and then delete the instance on the stage—it's safe in your Library.) It turns out that some components automatically include this class, but it doesn't hurt to add it this way.

STEP 2▼
Adding Methods to the urls.xml File

The `login_advanced` file will be calling three additional server-side methods that use the following values for their `methodName` attribute: `requestLogin`, so returning users can retrieve their `userID`s; `makeNewUser`, for new users to acquire a `userID`; and `getAllQuizIDs`, which returns the quiz name and `quizID` for all quizzes available to this user.

Inside the schemas folder (located inside the `starter_files` folder), reopen the `urls.xml` file using a text editor. You should see two `url` nodes for `getQuiz` and `saveUserResults` that you added in the first project in this chapter, "External Paths to Server-side Methods." Add the following three nodes anywhere in the main `allPaths` node (that is, after `<allPaths>` and before `</allPaths>`):

```
<url methodName="requestLogin"
     path="schemas/requestLogin.xml"/>
<url methodName="makeNewUser"
     path="schemas/makeNewUser.xml"/>
<url methodName="getAllQuizIDs"
     path="schemas/getAllQuizIDs.xml"/>
```

For details on how you add methods to the urls.xml file, refer to step 1 in the first project in this chapter. These three lines simply specify where Flash can find the server-side code (or static .xml files) for these three added features.

Now you just need to ensure that those three paths exist, either as a live server-side method or as a static .xml file.

STEP 3▼
Creating Static XML Files in Lieu of Live Server-side Methods

In the project "APIs," later in this chapter, you'll find the details for the three methods added in the preceding step. For now, we just need static XML files in their place that simulate the true server behavior.

The requestLogin and makeNewUser methods are basically the same: They return either success=false and an errorcode or success=true and a userID.

Create a new text file, enter the following code, and save it in the schemas folder as requestLogin.xml:

```
<?xml version="1.0"?>
<success userID="userid1">true</success>
```

Create another new text file, enter the following code, and save it in the schemas folder as makeNewUser.xml:

```
<?xml version="1.0"?>
<success userID="userid2">true</success>
```

Obviously, the responses are hard-wired for success, but based on the userID returned (userid1 or userid2), you will be able to tell which method (requestLogin or makeNewUser) is being called.

Another side effect of simulating a login with static files is that no matter what username and password are sent, the value `<success>true</success>` is always returned. However, we should set up a way to test what happens when the server rejects a user (perhaps her password is wrong or a new user attempts to create an account with a username that's already in use). To set up a simulated rejection, first open the requestLogin.xml file you just created and select File, Save As. Name the copy **requestLogin-fail.xml** and completely replace the contents of this duplicated file with the following code:

```
<?xml version="1.0"?>
<success errorcode="1">false</success>
```

Next, open the makeNewUser.xml file you just created and select File, Save As. Name the copy **makeNewUser-fail.xml** and replace the contents with the following code:

```
<?xml version="1.0"?>
<success errorcode="2">false</success>
```

Now, to simulate failed logins, you can just rename the files by removing -fail from the filenames.

Finally, although the `getAllQuizIDs` method is called last, it's the easiest one to mock up. Create a text file, enter the following code, and save it in the `schemas` folder as **getAllQuizIDs.xml**:

```xml
<?xml version="1.0"?>
<results>
    <quiz quizID="quizid1"
          name="Geography"/>
    <quiz quizID="quizid2"
          name="Safety"/>
    <quiz quizID="quizid3"
          name="Popular Music 1960"/>
</results>
```

STEP 4▼
Creating the login_advanced_html.html File and Adding the FlashVars

Open your working file `login_advanced.fla` and select File, Publish. Open the `login_advanced.html` file with a text editor. Click right before line 11, which begins `<param name="allowScriptAccess...`, and press Enter a few times to insert some new lines. Type the following code:

```
<param name="FlashVars"
       value="urlList=schemas/urls.xml" />
```

Now, search for the statement `<embed src="login_advanced.swf"`. Click right before that string and press Enter a few times. Click after the `.swf` filename and press Enter a few more times. Finally, type the following code:

```
flashVars="urlList=schemas/urls.xml"
```

Figure 6.10 shows the contents of the `login_advanced_html.html` file.

Instead of saving the file with its original filename, select File, Save As and name the file **login_advanced_html.html** so that you won't accidentally overwrite this file by selecting Publish within the `login_advanced.fla` file.

There's also a finished version of this HTML document in the `finished_source` folder you downloaded for this chapter.

FIGURE 6.10 The added values for the `FlashVars` tag will set just the `urlList` variable for the `login_advanced.swf` file.

```html
<html xmlns="http://www.w3.org/1999/xhtml" xml:lang="en" lang="en">
<head>
<meta http-equiv="Content-Type" content="text/html; charset=iso-8859-1" />
<title>login_advanced</title>
</head>
<body bgcolor="#ffffff">

<object classid="clsid:d27cdb6e-ae6d-11cf-96b8-444553540000"
codebase="http://fpdownload.macromedia.com/pub/shockwave/cabs/flash/swflash.cab#version=8,0,0,0"
width="550" height="400" id="login_advanced" align="middle">

<param name="allowScriptAccess" value="sameDomain" />
<param name="movie" value="login_advanced.swf" />
<param name="quality" value="high" />
<param name="bgcolor" value="#ffffff" />

<param name="FlashVars"
       value="urlList=schemas/urls.xml" />

<embed src="login_acvanced.swf"

       flashVars="urlList=schemas/urls.xml"

       quality="high" bgcolor="#ffffff"
       width="550" height="400"
       name="login_advanced" align="middle"
       allowScriptAccess="sameDomain"
       type="application/x-shockwave-flash"
       pluginspage="http://www.macromedia.com/go/getflashplayer" />
</object>
</body>
</html>
```

STEP 5 ▼
Applying the ActionScript

The ActionScript for this project is nearly 300 lines of code. Open the finished version of `login_advanced.fla`, located in the `finished_source` folder you downloaded for this chapter. Then select the first keyframe, open the Actions panel, and copy all the ActionScript. Go to the first keyframe of *your* working version of the `login_advanced.fla` file and paste the copied code into the Actions panel.

Let me give you a tour of the code for the `login_advance.fla` file. The primary variables are listed in lines 13–21. The `urlLookup` variable is the actual contents of `urls.xml`. The `gateway` variable is an instance of my custom class defined in `XMLGateway.as`. That class simply handles the asynchronous operations of sending and receiving XML and lets you use the standard `addEventListener` model for all server calls. Lines 45–60 assign listeners to the various events each component triggers. Then all the *responders*, the functions invoked by the components, are listed in lines 67–124. There are only so many things the user can do: First, she can edit the `TextInput` fields by entering a username and password; second, she can click the `loginButton` or the `newUserButton`; and third, she can select a quiz from the `List` component and click the `goButton`.

Lines 148–216 involve the `XMLGateway` class. In lines 215–216, the listeners are set up, and they point to just two responders: `onFault` (line 211, for when a fault is returned) and `onResult` (line 151, for when data arrives). The gateway lets you pass parameters

wrapped in a `LoadVars` instance and trigger remote methods. When the `onResult` method is called, a single parameter contains an event object, much the same as listeners for V2 components do. This event object is an ActionScript object with properties for `methodName`, the original method name; `value`, the string returned from the server; and `tracker`, an arbitrary value you pass in the second parameter when invoking the `XMLGateway.trigger()` method. The `tracker` property gives you a way to track simultaneous calls. The first trigger occurs on line 220 when the movie loads, and it just loads the `urlList`. The gateway is also triggered in line 94 after the user clicks the Login button or New User button. When those results arrive successfully (line 167), the `getQuizzes()` function triggers the final call to `getAllQuizIDs` (line 272). The results from `getAllQuizIDs`, arriving on lines 185–206, are used to populate the `quizList List` component.

Finally, when the user clicks the Go button, the `getURL()` on line 115 jumps out to `quiz_html_simple.html` with a query string containing `userID` and `quizID`. (See the following sidebar for another option.)

You can save `login_advanced.fla` and then select Control, Test Movie to produce `login_advanced.swf`. Finally, launch the `login_advanced_html.html` file on an actual web server to test everything. The files you'll need to upload are listed here:

- ▶ `login_advanced_html.html`
- ▶ `login_advanced.swf`
- ▶ `quiz_html_simple.html`
- ▶ `quiz.swf`

You'll also have to post a schemas folder and the following files within it:

- urls.xml

- quiz.xml

- saveUserResults.xml

- requestLogin.xml

- makeNewUser.xml

- getAllQuizIDs.xml

In addition, if you want to run the quiz, you'll need all the template .swf files referred to in the quiz.xml file's <question> nodes.

Project: APIs for the Admin Assessment Tool

The quiz.swf you built in Chapter 5 was already sending a userID and quizID when it loaded the quiz.xml file. But because that was a static file, the parameters were ignored—the same content of quiz.xml was returned regardless of what userID and quizID were used. However, there's already an established programming interface (API): The getQuiz method accepts parameters for userID and quizID and returns a .xml document with question nodes designed to match the various question types developed in Chapter 5. To build the server-side code to accept userID and quizID, you and the server-side programmer must establish and agree on an API. In this project, we declare the APIs more formally, create static .xml documents for the methods we've already used (getQuiz, requestLogin, and so on), and create the additional methods needed to

build an administrator tool to review all the quiz results.

The static .xml files serve two purposes. First, the .xml files let us build the Flash side before the application server is complete and running. That is, if we read in the contents of a .xml file, it's the same thing as receiving that string from an application server. Second, the .xml files provide a target for the server-side folks. If the server-side method generates an XML string in the same form as our static files, we know the system should work. It's sort of like how you might trace a large pipe leading to your sink and then bring that piece of paper to a store and match it to a replacement screw.

An API is simply a list of methods, the parameters they pass, and the results that are returned. The names of the methods, their parameters, and form of the results are all arbitrary, although there's definitely an art to doing it well. Ultimately, an API is a document that defines how both the Flash person and the server-side person will communicate. For each feature you want to add to your Flash application (say, saving users' results), you need to think about which variables the server-side person needs (in this case, the actual answers, the userID, and probably the quizID) and the form those variables will take (most commonly name/value pairs or XML). In addition, you have to think about which values need to be returned to Flash (if nothing else, a confirmation that the data was received). These three elements—structure, parameters, and return values—are consistent with any programming language. Check out the ActionScript 2.0 Language Reference built in to Flash 8's help system. Each method has its signature, the parameters, and the return value, if any. We'll follow this same form for the APIs defined in this project. Although you've already done the work for steps 1–4, I include them here to present them all in one place.

> ### 📌 NOTE
>
> It might be interesting to you that I designed all these APIs for this project before I built the underlying code and long before the PHP was written. The point is that this is the logical order: Establish the APIs, let both the Flash and server-side folks develop simultaneously, and meet in the middle when you're done. Sure, you'll often need to make some tweaks at the end, but I don't want anyone to think this sequence was abnormal.

STEPS▼

1. Defining how to get quiz data
2. Defining how quiz results are saved
3. Defining how users can log in
4. Providing a way to retrieve all the `quizID`s
5. Defining an API to retrieve all `userID`s
6. Defining an API to retrieve all `quizID`s for one `userID`
7. Defining an API to retrieve all scores for a quiz
8. Defining an API to retrieve detailed quiz results

STEP 1▼
Defining How to Get Quiz Data

```
getQuiz({userID:String, quizID:String }):XML
```

Parameters: A single `LoadVars` instance with properties for `userID` and `quizID`.

Returns: An XML document represented in the static `quiz.xml` file. Basically, the main node is quiz (with a `quizID` attribute) and then as many question nodes as needed. Each question has attributes for type, questionID, and—optionally—correctAnswers. (More about this in Chapter 5, where you built the quiz.xml files by hand.)

You don't have to do anything for this API because you already have a listing in the urls.xml and the static quiz.xml file. However, for reference, here's one representative <question> node:

```
<question type="multipleChoiceSingle"
          questionID="oregonCaptital"
          questionText="What's the capital
                        of Oregon?">
  <possible label="Salem"/>
  <possible label="Eugene"/>
  <possible label="Portland"/>
</question>
```

<question> nodes—one for each question the user answered—that contain attributes for <questionID> and <theirAnswers>. This structure is shown in Listing 6.4.

Returns: An XML file with a single node, success, with a node value of true. Optionally, you can design this return value to contain the user's score (remember from Chapter 5 that this entire XML string is sent to the results.swf file).

You can see a static version of this return value in the file saveUserResults.xml in the finished_source/schemas folder you downloaded with this project, as well as here:

```
<?xml version="1.0"?>
<success>true</success>
```

STEP 2▼
Defining How Quiz Results Are Saved

saveUserResults(results:XML):XML

Parameters: A single XML string with nodes for <userID> and <quizID>. Also, a node for <details> inside of which there are

For the outgoing value, I think it's worth seeing it in a text file. That is, my quiz.fla file already generates the outgoing parameter as XML but the server-side folks might want to see what it looks like. Listing 6.4 shows the contents of the saveUserResults_OUTGOING.xml file that's in the finished_source/schemas folder you downloaded for this chapter.

LISTING 6.4 This Is the Form of the Parameter Sent to the saveUserResults Method

```
<results>
<userID>userID</userID>
<quizID>quizID</quizID>
<details>
    <question questionID="oregonCapital" theirAnswers="0" />
    <question questionID="fruits1" theirAnswers="1,2" />
    <question questionID="pickSafetySwitch"
              theirAnswers="191,148" />
    <question questionID="flash101" theirAnswers="0,1,2,3" />
</details>
</results>
```

You can also trace this string by uncommenting the last line in the submitResults() function of the quiz.fla file in the finished_source folder (line 175).

STEP 3▼
Defining How Users Can Log In

```
requestLogin( {username:String,
password:String} ):XML
```

Or for new users:

```
makeNewUser( {username:String,
password:String} ):XML
```

Parameters: A single LoadVars instance with properties for username and password.

Returns: An XML string with the success node and a node value of either true or false. When false, an attribute for errorcode appears; when true, an attribute for userID appears.

If you didn't complete the preceding project, "Advanced All-Flash Login," return to step 3 to add both the requestLogin method and makeNewUser method to the urls.xml file and to build the static XML documents for requestLogin.xml and makeNewUser.xml.

STEP 4▼
Providing a Way to Retrieve All the quizIDs

```
getAllQuizIDs ( [ {userID:String} ] ):XML
```

Parameters: A single LoadVars instance with an optional property for userID. (The square brackets indicate that the parameter is optional.)

Returns: An XML string with quiz nodes, containing attributes for id and name, for all the available quizzes. If no userID is passed, then all the quizzes are returned; if a userID is passed, only those quizzes available to that user are returned. Deciding which quizzes are available to a particular user must be handled on the server side.

For details about the form of the returned XML, refer to the getAllQuizIDs.xml document created in step 3 of the preceding project.

STEP 5▼
Defining an API to Retrieve All userIDs

```
getAllUserIDs():XML
```

Parameters: None.

Returns: An XML string with user nodes, each of which contains attributes for id (the userID) and name (the user's full name).

Here's the static form of what is returned (also found in the document getAllUserIDs.xml):

```
<?xml version="1.0"?>
<results>
    <user userID="userid1"
          name="Phillip Kerman"/>
    <user userID="userid2"
          name="Joe Smith"/>
    <user userID="userid3"
          name="Bob Jones"/>
</results>
```

The urls.xml file also needs the following node:

```
<url methodName="getAllUserIDs"
     path="schemas/getAllUserIDs.xml"/>
```

In the advanced admin application that appears later in this chapter, this method provides a roster of all the students. This way, I can select one student and then, using additional methods, look at that student's results. In addition, I can compare the results of all students (again, with another method).

STEP 6▼
Defining an API to Retrieve All quizIDs for One userID

```
getUserQuizIDs( {userID:String} ):XML
```

Parameters: A LoadVars instance with a property for userID.

Returns: An XML string with a single results node containing a comma-separated string of quizIDs.

Here's the static form of what is returned (also found in the document getUserQuizIDs.xml):

```
<?xml version="1.0"?>
<results>quizid1,quizid2,quizid3</results>
```

The urls.xml file also needs the following node:

```
<url methodName="getUserQuizIDs"
     path="schemas/getUserQuizIDs.xml"/>
```

In the advanced admin application that appears later in this chapter, this method provides a list of quizIDs for any student I select.

STEP 7▼
Defining an API to Retrieve All Scores for a Quiz

```
getQuizPercentages( {quizID:String} ):XML
```

Parameters: A LoadVars instance with a property for quizID.

Returns: An XML string with detail nodes that contain attributes for userID and percentage.

Here's the static form of what is returned (also found in the document getQuizPercentages.xml):

```
<?xml version="1.0"?>
<results>
    <detail userID="userid1"
            percentage="100"/>
    <detail userID="userid2"
            percentage="0"/>
    <detail userID="userid3"
            percentage="50"/>
</results>
```

The `urls.xml` file also needs the following node:

```
<url methodName="getQuizPercentages"
     path="schemas/getQuizPercentages.xml"/>
```

In the advanced admin application that appears later in this chapter, this method provides an overview look at the results for a single quiz. That is, it presents a list of a single quiz's scores for each `userID`. (The `userID` can be mapped to a username using the data returned to the `getAllUserIDs` method.)

STEP 8▼

Defining an API to Retrieve Detailed Quiz Results

`getQuizResults( {quizID:String} ):XML`

Parameters: A `LoadVars` instance with a property for `quizID`.

Returns: An XML string with `questionDetail` nodes that contain attributes for `questionID` and `correctAnswers`. It also includes, for every user who took the quiz, a child `userAnswer` node that has attributes for `userID` and `theirAnswers`.

Listing 6.5 shows the static form of what is returned (this code is also found in the document `getQuizResults.xml`).

LISTING 6.5   This XML Shows the Form Returned from the `getQuizResults` **Method**

```
<?xml version="1.0"?>
<results>
    <questionDetails questionID="fruits1"
                        correctAnswers="1,2">
        <userAnswer userID="userid1" theirAnswers="0,1"/>
        <userAnswer userID="userid2" theirAnswers="0,3"/>
    </questionDetails>

    <questionDetails questionID="oregonCapital"
                        correctAnswers="0">
        <userAnswer userID="userid1" theirAnswers="1"/>
        <userAnswer userID="userid2" theirAnswers="0"/>
    </questionDetails>

    <questionDetails questionID="pickSafetySwitch"
                        correctAnswers="300,190">
        <userAnswer userID="userid1" theirAnswers="200,190"/>
        <userAnswer userID="userid2" theirAnswers="300,190"/>
    </questionDetails>

    <questionDetails questionID="flash101"
                        correctAnswers="1,2,0,3">
        <userAnswer userID="userid1" theirAnswers="3,0,1,2"/>
        <userAnswer userID="userid2" theirAnswers="1,2,0,3"/>
    </questionDetails>
</results>
```

The `urls.xml` file also needs the following node:

```
<url methodName="getQuizResults"
     path="schemas/getQuizResults.xml"/>
```

In the advanced admin application that appears later in this chapter, this method provides a detailed view of every question—and every user's answer—for a particular quiz.

Project: API Tester

Given the beautiful APIs we designed in the preceding project, you might think it's time to jump in and build an admin tool. Before we do that, however, it's best to write starter code that tests every method. You'll use this API tester application to ensure that all the connections to the external data are hooked together properly. This application is suitable for testing locally (with static XML files) as well as remotely when the server-side application is built to support the APIs listed in the preceding project.

Go into the folder called `finished_API-tester-app` you downloaded for this chapter and open the file `tester.fla`. Select Control, Test Movie. After you click the Get urlList button, you will see the interface shown in Figure 6.11.

You can test everything from this application. You can enter a username and password (in the upper-left corner) and execute code that's identical to the "Advanced All-Flash Login" project earlier in this chapter. You can request a quiz's content by

clicking the getQuiz button in the upper-right corner. The column of buttons on the middle left are all fairly simple: They just exercise some the administrative methods, listed on the button labels.

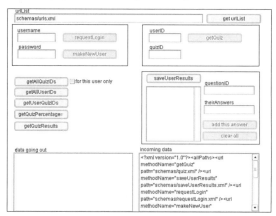

FIGURE 6.11 This tester application might not be much to look at, but it's the best way to test all your APIs.

The `saveUserResults` method needs some user answers before it can execute. The area on the middle right lets you add answers by first entering properties for `questionID` and `theirAnswers`. This is the only method that generates XML for the outgoing parameter, so the code is more involved. For example, say you wanted to create results for the multiple choice question with a `questionID` of `"oregonCapital"`. You'd simply enter oregonCapital in the `questionID` field and enter 0 in the `theirAnswers` field (as if the user had selected the first option). Click the Add This Answer button. You can continue adding answers in this manner. When you click saveUserResults, you'll see the following outgoing XML string in the Data Going Out field:

```
<results>
    <userID>myID</userID>
```

```
  <quizID>myQuiz</quizID>
  <details>
   <question questionID="oregonCapital"
             theirAnswers="0" />
  </details>
</results>
```

You'll need to enter a userID and quizID into the fields at the upper right for the first two child nodes to appear like this sample.

The fields at the bottom of the screen let you see the parameters going out and the raw results returned for every method you call.

Note that the default value for the urlList field at the top of the screen points to the local copy of urls.xml. You can modify this address to point to your server (that is, before you click the Get urlList button).

Project:
Simple Admin Tool

This project puts a practical face on the API tester application shown in the preceding project. In fact, the simple administrator tool you create in this project calls only a few of the methods available in the API tester application—just the methods necessary to give an administrator (the boss or teacher, for example) a view of all the students' results.

Open the folder called finished_ admin-simple that you downloaded for this chapter and open the admin_simple.fla file. Select Control, Test Movie and then select one of the users. You will see the interface shown in Figure 6.12.

FIGURE 6.12   The administrator can select any user to see all results for that user or any quiz to see all users' results.

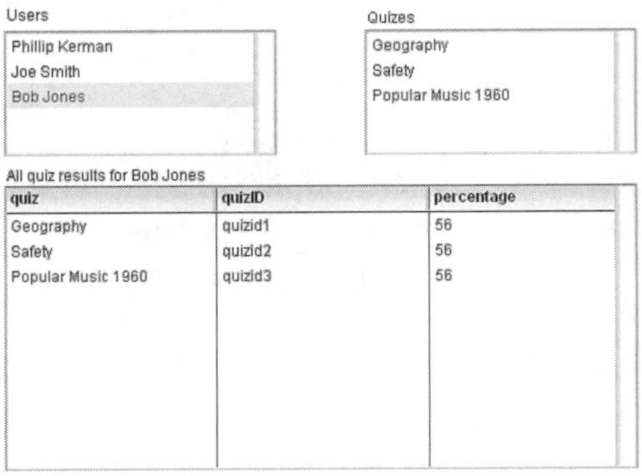

Here's an overview of how this application works. First, it loads the urlList, the value of which can be passed in via FlashVars. Then it makes two calls: to getAllUserIDs and to getAllQuizIDs. The results from these two calls populate the two List components at the top of the screen. When the administrator selects a quiz from the list at the upper right, we call getQuizPercentages and populate the DataGrid with the results. When the administrator selects a user, the sequence is a bit more complicated: First, we call getUserQuizIDs to find the quizIDs available for that user; then we call getQuizPercentages multiple times, once for each of the quizIDs returned. As the results arrive, we look through all the percentages to find just the one with a userID that matches the currently selected userID and append that result to the DataGrid. Remember that getQuizPercentages returns all the results but we want to know only one user's results.

explained in the preceding project. For one thing, the more advanced tool plots the users' results on a graph so you can select them by name or from a list. Also, because it calls the `getQuizResults` method, you can walk through the original quiz and see each user's answer. The coolest part is that the question appears exactly as it did originally because this application uses the same question templates (see Figure 6.13).

There are also some fancy maneuvers, such as caching results and not making unnecessary server calls. For example, if a particular quiz's results were already requested, the tool uses the old values instead of making another request. It might not be worth trying to deconstruct this tool in this book, but I think it's a valuable tool for two reasons: It shows you what's possible and it proves that the overall architecture (quiz, quiz templates, and APIs) is working.

Using the Full-featured Admin Tool

I built a more elaborate administration tool, which you can find in the `finished_admin-advanced` folder you downloaded for this project. It's quite useful. This application has several features in addition to what you'll find in the `admin_simple.fla` tool

FIGURE 6.13 The advanced administration tool plots all the users' results (on the bottom left) and even gives you a view of the quiz they took (on the right).

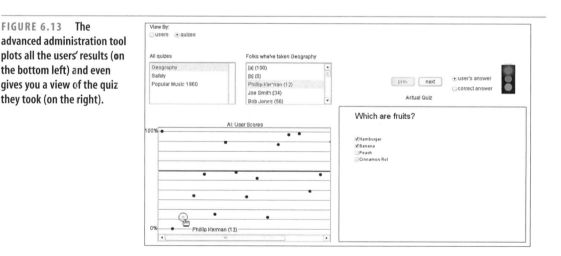

Final Thoughts

The quiz templates you built in Chapter 5 were pretty cool. But when you add the various login options and server-side APIs we built in this chapter, this quiz engine is both useful and extensible if you need to take it further.

About the Projects

In this chapter, you build a PowerPoint-style slide presentation that you can use over and over whenever you need speaker support material. When you finish this project, you can customize it for anyone in your organization. The finished project is a simple .swf file and a configurable .xml document plus one .swf file for each screen type you design (such as bullet points or a photo with a caption)—these are the templates you'll build in this chapter. You can also make your presentation display external media files including videos, images, and sound. You will be able to modify the .xml that drives the presentation by selecting from several screen types, customizing the actual content that appears, and selecting from a variety of feature preferences.

Prerequisites

Experience with XML and CSS is a definite advantage in this project, but it is not absolutely required.

@work resources

Download the chapter_7_downloads.zip file for this chapter from the accompanying CD-ROM.

Planning the Projects

Flash is great for customized presentations. There's really no limit to how you can present an idea. The problem with jumping right into the timeline to create a creative presentation is that all your work is focused on a one-off presentation—and you get to do it all over again the next time you want to create a presentation. In this project, you'll create templates based on common PowerPoint-type features you've come to expect in slide presentations, such as bulleted lists, transitions, and navigation controls. This way, you can recycle the skeleton for a new project by swapping out the content.

When planning this project, you should focus on structure, not specific content. A template needs to work for a variety of uses—many that you won't think of until after it's built—and it should adapt to any situation. If you want to incorporate features you've seen in other presentations, be sure to ignore all specific content that applies only to the old presentation.

Understanding the Presentation Features

The end product for this chapter is a presentation that displays the content you specify in a `.xml` file (`slide_data.xml`). You can edit the `slide_data.xml` file to produce additional presentations. The `slide_data.xml` file specifies not only the content of your presentation (such as the text or images that appear on the stage), but it also specifies a template type that affects how that data is presented.

Each slide in the presentation can use any available template type. The same template can appear multiple times within a single presentation because the content changes with every slide. In this chapter, you'll build a few templates from which to choose. One is a simple photo with a text caption, one has before and after photos that cross fade, and one displays a bulleted list of text. Inside the `slide_data.xml` file you'll create a `<slide>` node for each page in the presentation where you specify the type of template to use. The structure is open to you adding templates that I haven't thought of.

Presenters can navigate the presentation in several ways: They can jump to the next or previous slide, step forward or back to the next step, or right-click the mouse to reveal a context menu where they can jump to any slide. The number of `<slide>` nodes determines how many slides appear in the presentation. (You can think of slides as pages, although I'm calling them slides.) Within a single slide you might have multiple *steps*. For example, the bulleted list first appears with just at title, but as the presenter steps forward, the first bullet is revealed followed by as many additional bullets as are specified in the `slide_data.xml` file. Stepping forward goes through each step and then advances to the next slide; stepping backward does the reverse. Realize, however, that stepping backward from a slide's first step jumps you to the previous slide's *last* step. For example, if you're on the first step of slide 2 and step back, you're taken to the last step in slide 1.

When presenters press the right-arrow key on the keyboard, they step forward. When they press the down-arrow key, they jump to the next slide regardless of which step they are on. Similarly, the left-arrow key takes them to the previous step, or the last step of the preceding slide if they're already on the first step. And the up-arrow key goes to the first step of the previous slide. Figure 7.1 shows the navigation features. A simple click doesn't cause any navigation because I thought you might want interactive elements in your templates that would necessarily conflict with such a feature.

FIGURE 7.1   The presenter can step forward through all of a slide's steps or page forward to the next slide.

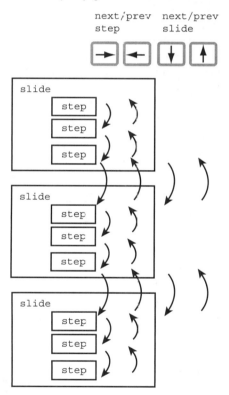

You won't have to program the main navigation, but it's important to understand this hierarchy as you develop content for your own custom presentations.

Understanding the Template Requirements

As you'll see, each template you build has several common features. In fact, they're both features and requirements because the main presentation engine won't work unless your templates contain a minimum set of features. You can separate these features into two categories: the features your template must implement (that is, the interface the presentation can rely on) and the features and utilities your template can employ (that is, the set of APIs available to each template to make your coding easier). Let me explain both:

► **Common interface**—Your templates must always include the functions init(), nextStep(), prevStep(), getStep(), and getTotalSteps(). You'll learn in much more detail how each of these functions works, but let me give you the highlights. Your init() function is where the template assembles its initial display. The init() function is passed all the information it needs to configure itself (most importantly, the value of its <slide> node). The nextStep() and prevStep() functions are sent to your template when the presenter wants to step forward or back; here you write code to change the onscreen content. For example, when the presenter steps forward in your bullet list template, you would display the next bullet. The two functions `getStep()` and `getTotalSteps()` return a number. These functions help the main presentation know whether it's time to go to the next slide or simply go to the next step.

> **NOTE**
>
> Like I say, you'll get much more detail, but every template must support these functions. Those who are experienced in object-oriented programming (OOP) can see that these functions are formally declared in the interface file `ISlide.as`.

▶ **APIs**—I said you'll get all the information you need in the arguments sent to your `init()` function. In addition to the `<slide>` node, you're given a reference to the `SlideHolder` class. In the code samples, I call this parameter owner, and you use it to access the following small library of support functions (the API) I built especially for this project:

  ▶ `selectSingleNodeValue` `(from:XMLNode, path:String)` returns a single node's value using an XPath string.

  ▶ `selectSingleNode(from:XMLNode, path:String)` returns an entire XML node so you can grab its attributes.

  ▶ `selectNodeList(from:XMLNode, path:String)` returns an array of nodes, which is useful when there is more than one node with the same name (such as the bullets in the `bullet_list.swf` template

that appears later in this chapter).

  ▶ `getCSS()` returns a reference to the style sheet that is imported from the `styles.css` text file. (You'll see how to use this text file in the last two projects.)

All the methods supported in the `SlideHolder` class (the owner reference) are formally defined in the interface `ISlideHolder.as`, which the `SlideHolder` class implements.

> **NOTE**
>
> XPath is a library of utility functions that provide an intuitive way to access nodes, arrays of nodes, or node values contained in your XML. For example, instead of saying something anonymous like `my_node.firstChild.childNodes[2]`, you could instead say `XPathAPI.selectSingleNode ( my_node, "presentation/slide")`. Although you can access XPath directly, I added the functions to the API for all templates so you wouldn't have to install support for XPath, which involves copying the `DataBindingClasses` from the Classes Common Library into each template.

You'll get more details in the projects that follow. This overview, however, helps you identify the consistencies among the templates—information you might not otherwise get until after you have built a few.

Formatting the Presentation Data

A key requirement for this presentation project is that the content appearing onscreen is drawn from a data file. This way, you (or anyone else) can make edits without reopening Flash. The exact format of that data must be designed. On the surface, this format is subjective and—provided that all the information is present—doesn't really matter. But the structure you come up with should take into consideration several issues discussed later in this section.

Depending on who is going to use the tool you're building, you need to think about the way users create and save the presentation. Can these users safely open a text file and edit XML? Or do you need to build another tool that generates the XML? Often a flat text file is easier for people to edit, but it still takes only one character out of place to break your *parsing* code. Although XML is obviously the best choice because it provides a structure that can easily accommodate additions, a novice user might not feel comfortable editing text formatted as XML.

I often start with how I'd like the data files formatted from the perspective of the person creating those files. The priority needs to be on ease of editing, while attempting to leave room for extensibility. So, don't worry about how you're going to parse the data because you can always extract the data from any logical format. The code that does the parsing is written only once, but every time a new presentation is built, that content data must be written.

The data format used in this project is clear and easy to edit if you understand *XML*.

Designing Templates

You can go wild designing any sort of slide template you want. In fact, the structure of the presentation engine you'll use here makes it easy to add more template types. However, it's best to generalize as many seemingly unique features into a single template. You don't need one template to support three bullet points and another for four bullet points. On the other hand, a slide design with a single quotation placed on top of a photograph would need to be a different template from the bullet points. Make as many unique template designs as you want, but try to consolidate the designs where you can.

The best way to design new slide types is to think about a use-case. Suppose you work for a construction company that often takes before and after photographs of the work sites. It'd be useful to have a template that allows the presenter to fade between the two images. But a template that cross-fades two images is nothing but eye candy without a specific use—in this case, to show how the work at the site is progressing. Think about the reason you need a template and how you plan to use it, and then design it for that purpose.

In addition to the fun part of creating the visual design and layout for your templates, you also need to know about the set of attributes every template will share. That is, the main presentation engine treats each slide equally. The engine always allows the user to go to the next slide and expects each slide to have a name so the presenter can jump to a particular slide using the right-click context menu. Similarly, because many template designs support the idea of taking a mini-step, it makes sense to require that all the slide templates support stepping. For example, a bulleted slide goes from one bullet point to the next in a series of steps.

After the last step, you need to automatically jump to the next slide. Even though some templates won't have mini-steps, you can act as though they do—just figure they're already on the last step.

The specific functional requirements I've designed for this project are that each slide will have a name, each slide must track its current step and the total number of steps it uses, and each slide must support next-step and previous-step functions. Beyond that, you can add any unique features you want to your templates. These basic functions are all defined in the ISlide interface.

Effective Transitions

Although Flash's special effects (call them gratuitous) are more customizable than those found in PowerPoint, the purpose of most presentations is not (and should not be) to dazzle and distract the viewers, but rather to help the presenter deliver her ideas. When you customize the templates we build here, keep the special effects to a minimum. The most effective transitions should reflect your message and not *be* your message. For example, fading down and then fading back up can help demonstrate the passing of time, but spinning text that flies in from various sides of the screen might be more of a show than the actual words themselves.

Deployment Options

Provided your presentation tool is a huge success, you might want to plan for—or at least leave open the possibility for—large-scale deployment options. For example, your company's sales representatives might want an easy to way to download and use presentations built by others in the field. They also might want to extract slides from various presentations to build their own customized versions. Although some of these ideas would require rebuilding the core presentation engine you downloaded for this chapter, you should always keep such ideas in mind. It's easier to add features later if they were in the back of your mind while building the first version.

The Point of a Presentation

Finally, remember why people are attending your presentation: They want to hear you speak! A powerful slide presentation supplements the speaker; it doesn't replace the human or cover up her nervousness. Having said all this, a good slide presentation can help the presenter organize her ideas and stay on topic. For more about what's wrong with PowerPoint presentations and how to more effectively display complex information, check out the writings by Edward R. Tufte (www.edwardtufte.com), especially *The Cognitive Style of PowerPoint*.

> ### ✒ NOTE
>
> This chapter details the process of creating and customizing templates for the presentation engine I built. Provided that the core features of this engine are acceptable, you'll never need to touch the engine. You'll learn to add new slide types for any sort of content. This is where the projects begin—in the middle, if you will. You're welcome to jump to the last section in this chapter, "Exploring the Class Files," for an overview of how the engine was built.

Project:
Simple Photo Caption Template

The first template you'll build is simple: It's just a photograph and a caption displayed on the slide. In this project, the caption's font, size, and style are locked to however you lay it out. (The actual words in the caption are loaded at runtime, as is the photograph itself.) But the text formatting is hardwired. In later projects, such as the bullet and the pull-quote templates, you'll learn how Flash can apply styles stored in an external .css file, enabling you to change the font attributes without returning to Flash.

STEPS▼

1. Setting up the document
2. Laying out the photo holder
3. Laying out the caption text
4. Adding the customized ActionScript
5. Editing the XML and testing the template

STEP 1▼
Setting Up the Document

Create a new working folder and copy into it, from the starter_files folder you downloaded for this chapter, that folder's contents, including the images folder. In a new file, select Modify, Document (or press Ctrl+J) and set the Dimensions to 800 × 600 pixels; this is the size of the slide you will use for all the template files in this project.

STEP 2▼
Laying Out the Photo Holder

Draw a white rectangle the size and shape of the expected photo size. Select the entire shape and select Modify, Convert to Symbol (or press F8). Click the Movie Clip option and be sure you select the upper-left Registration option, as shown in Figure 7.2. Name the symbol **Photo Holder** and click OK. Then give the clip the instance name **photo_mc**.

FIGURE 7.2 Use the upper-left registration point because that's where the loaded image's upper-left corner will appear.

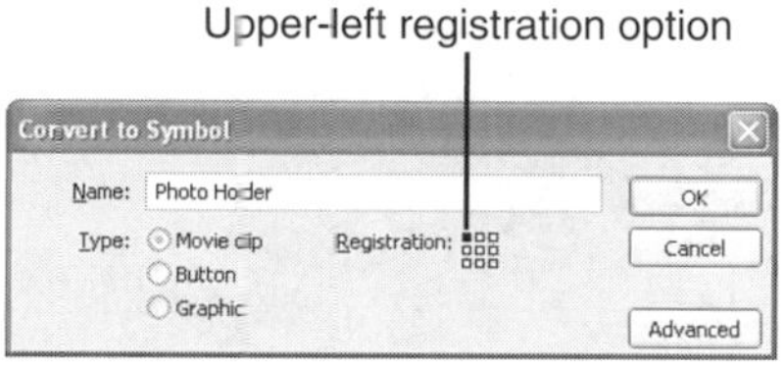

Upper-left registration option

STEP 3▼
Laying Out the Caption Text

Create a dynamic text field with the instance name **caption_txt**. Type some dummy text and then set the margins and select the font and style you want to see in the final slide. Select any font except the first three listed (_sans, _serif, or _typewriter). Make sure that the text field is not selectable (there's a Selectable option in the Properties panel; disable it). Finally, click the Embed button, select the Basic Latin (95 glyphs) option, and click OK. This way, the presenter doesn't have to have the same font you specified for the caption text installed on her computer (see Figure 7.3).

FIGURE 7.3 By embedding the caption's font into the template, presenters won't need to have that font installed on their computers.

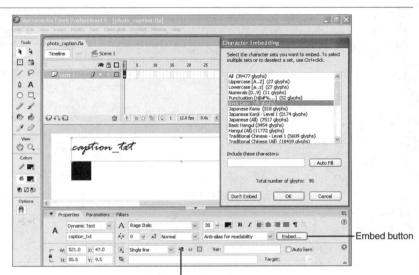

Selectable option

Embed button

STEP 4▼
Adding the Customized ActionScript

Select the first keyframe and open the Actions panel. Type the code shown in

Listing 7.1. (You can find this code in the photo_caption.fla file in the finished_source folder you downloaded for this chapter.)

LISTING 7.1   This Code Displays a Photograph and Caption

```
var owner:MovieClip;
var slideData:XMLNode;
var startAtBeginning:Boolean;

function init( p_owner:MovieClip,
              p_data:XMLNode,
              p_startAtBeginning:Boolean ) {
   owner = p_owner;
   slideData = p_data;
   startAtBeginning = p_startAtBeginning;
   var caption = owner.selectSingleNodeValue( slideData,
                                      "slide/caption" );
   var filename = owner.selectSingleNodeValue( slideData,
                                      "slide/photo" );
   photo_mc.loadMovie(filename);
   caption_txt.text = caption;
}
```

LISTING 7.1   Continued

```
function nextStep() {
}
function prevStep() {
}
function getStep():Number {
   return 0;
}
function getTotalSteps():Number {
   return 0;
}
```

The init() function is triggered by the main presentation engine after this template .swf loads. The first three lines are the three variables given to each slide: owner (a reference to the SlideHolder class), slideData (the entire XML node for this slide, as you'll see in the next step), and startAtBeginning (either true or false, indicating whether the presenter came into this slide from a previous slide (true) or from a later slide (false). The selectSingleNodeValue() function is one of the XPath utilities available in the SlideHolder class. Here we're using it to intuitively parse both the <caption> and <photo> nodes' values from inside the <slide> node, received as the p_data parameter in the init() function. The XPath utilities are part of the custom API I built for all slides, as described in the "Planning the Projects" section at the beginning of this chapter.

The last four functions—nextStep(), prevStep(), getStep(), and getTotalSteps()—are there because they're required by the ISlide.as interface. The main presentation.swf relies on each slide supporting these functions. Although these function are designed for templates that

support multiple steps, as you'll see in the next template project, I include them here as a good practice, even though this template does not use steps.

> **📌 NOTE**
>
> When applications provide a way for other programmers to access internal features, they build an interface (specifically called an application programming interface [API]) that is a predefined list of methods used to perform various tasks. For example, an API is available to get detailed information from the photo-sharing site flickr.com. You could easily display all the photos matching a particular keyword inside your application. In this case, the SlideHolder class I built for this presentation engine has an API that includes the selectSingleNodeValue() method, as well as others listed at the end of the next project.

Before moving on to the next step, save your file as **photo_caption.fla** in your working folder. Select Control, Test Movie to generate the photo_caption.swf file. You won't see anything onscreen except the instances caption_txt and photo_mc, but this template is ready for content, which you'll add using the XML file.

Editing the XML and Testing the Template

Open the `slide_data.xml` file already copied into your working folder in a text editor. Add the following code after the first two lines in the file (the first line starts with `<?xml` and the second line starts with `<presentation`):

```
<slide name="Dog"
       type="photo_caption.swf">
   <caption>My dog Grettle</caption>
   <photo>images/dog.jpg</photo>
</slide>

<slide name="Cat"
       type="photo_caption.swf">
   <caption>My cat Fido</caption>
   <photo>images/cat.jpg</photo>
</slide>
```

This code adds two slides to the beginning of the presentation that use the template named `"photo_caption.swf"`, which is the file you're about to generate. The two photos named `dog.jpg` and `cat.jpg` are already in your `images` folder. You can also change the values for the `<photo>` nodes to include the paths and filenames of two image files you want to use. Be sure to save the `slide_data.xml` file.

Now that the template file (`photo_caption.swf`) is created and the `slides_data.xml` file identifies the content and template type, we're ready to see it work. Simply double-click the `slideshow.swf` file in your working folder. That file will read the `slides_data.xml` file and both load and populate the `photo_caption.swf` file (see Figure 7.4). You can press your keyboard's

right-arrow key to page forward to the second slide, the cat photo. Note that even though you created only one template (`photo_caption.swf`), it is used as many times as there are `<slide>` nodes in the `slides_data.xml` file that point to this template (in this case, two times).

📌 **NOTE**

There are several illegal characters you should not use when writing XML. You can imagine that if you want a caption that reads, literally, "Fido doesn't understand `<nodes>`", the XML parser would get confused. This is what the CDATA keyword is for. Simply put `<![CDATA[` before and the characters `]]>` after the text that contains the special characters. For example, you could modify one of the `<caption>` nodes in the code given previously with:

```
<caption><![CDATA[
Fido doesn't understand <nodes>
]]></caption>
```

FIGURE 7.4 Your `photo_caption.swf` template appears with content when you launch the `slideshow.swf` file.

My dog Grettle

There's a lot of magic going on behind the scenes that we haven't discussed yet. Basically, `slideshow.swf` parses the XML, loads the specified `template.swf`, and then triggers the template's `init()` function so it can display its content—in this case, the caption and the photo.

Advanced Before-and-After Photo Template

A single presentation can include several `photo_caption.swf` templates or a mix of other templates. In this project, you'll build a completely different template you can include in your presentations where appropriate. This template supports stepping through a before-and-after pair of photos. First, the before image appears; then it dissolves to the after picture; and finally both appear at once. The procedure to create this template is nearly identical to that used in the previous project.

STEPS▼

1. Creating the document and layout
2. Writing the code to support stepping
3. Writing the XML for this template

STEP 1▼
Creating the Document and Layout

Start with the `photo_caption.fla` file you created in the last project and select File, Save As. Alternatively, you can start with the `photo_caption.fla` file in the `finished_source` folder. Rename the file **before_after.fla**. You can leave the Dynamic Text field (`caption_txt`) as is. For this template, we need two clip instances, so select the `photo_mc` instance and rename it **before_mc**. Then select the renamed instance, copy and paste it, and name the duplicate instance **after_mc**. Make sure that `after_mc` is stacked above `before_mc`—that is, make sure it's in a higher layer. This way, the `after_mc` can overlay as it fades in over the `before_mc` instance. Position the `before_mc` instance where you want the first photo to appear, as shown in Figure 7.5.

FIGURE 7.5 The `before_mc` instance is stacked under the `after_mc` instance. Only `before_mc` must be positioned where you want it to appear because `after_mc` will overlay `before_mc`.

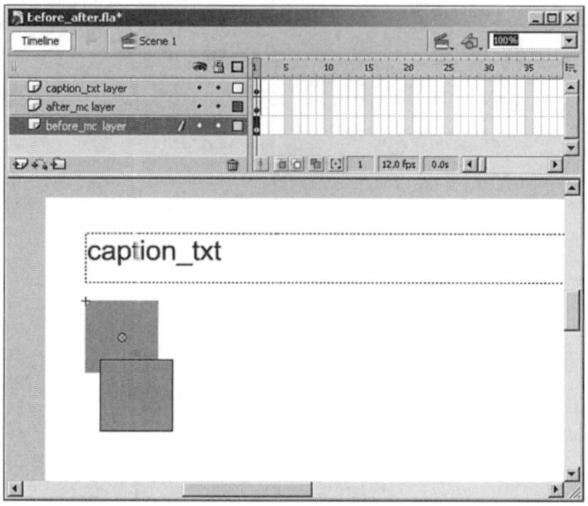

STEP 2▼
Writing the Code to Support Stepping

Select the first frame of the movie, open the Actions panel, and type the code shown in

---

Listing 7.2. This code can be found in the before_after.fla file you downloaded for this chapter if you want to copy and paste it instead of typing it manually.

LISTING 7.2   This Code Displays and Cross-Fades the Before and After Photos

```
1    var owner:MovieClip;
2    var slideData:XMLNode;
3    var startAtBeginning:Boolean;
4
5    //for this class
6    var currentStep:Number;
7    var caption_before:String;
8    var caption_after:String;
9    var fade:mx.transitions.Tween;
10
11   function init( p_owner:MovieClip,
                     p_data:XMLNode,
                     p_startAtBeginning:Boolean ){
12      owner = p_owner;
13      slideData = p_data;
14      startAtBeginning = p_startAtBeginning;
15
16      //get captions
17      caption_before =
         owner.selectSingleNodeValue( slideData,
                           "slide/caption_before" );
18      caption_after =
         owner.selectSingleNodeValue( slideData,
                           "slide/caption_after" );
19                                    *
20      //see if we start at beginning or end
21      if( startAtBeginning == true ){
22         currentStep = 0;
23      }else{
24         currentStep = 2;
25      }
26
27      //get the images to load:
28      var filename1 =
         owner.selectSingleNodeValue( slideData,
                           "slide/photo_before" );
29      var filename2 =
         owner.selectSingleNodeValue( slideData,
                           "slide/photo_after" );
30
31      //use the movie clip loader
32      var mcl:MovieClipLoader = new MovieClipLoader();
33      var clipsToLoad:Number = 2;
34      var listener = new Object();
```

LISTING 7.2 Continued

```
35    listener.onLoadInit = function( target ){
36        clipsToLoad--;
37        if( clipsToLoad == 0 ){
38            //now we're ready to show the photos!
39            showPhotos();
40        }
41    }
42    mcl.addListener(listener)
43    mcl.loadClip(filename1, before_mc);
44    mcl.loadClip(filename2, after_mc);
45 }
46
47 function nextStep(){
48    currentStep++;
49    showPhotos();
50 }
51
52 function prevStep(){
53    currentStep--;
54    showPhotos();
55 }
56
57 function getStep():Number{
58    return currentStep;
59 }
60
61 function getTotalSteps():Number{
62    return 2;
63 }
64
65 function showPhotos(){
66    switch(currentStep){
67        case 0://show only the "before" part
68            fade.stop();
69            after_mc._alpha = 0;
70            caption_txt.text = caption_before;
71            break;
72
73        case 1://fade "after" on top of before
74            after_mc._y = before_mc._y;
75            after_mc._x = before_mc._x;
76            caption_txt.text = caption_after;
77
78            var duration = 2;
79            fade=new mx.transitions.Tween( after_mc,
                                           "_alpha",
                        mx.transitions.easing.None.easeNone,
```

continues

LISTING 7.2   Continued

```
                                            0,
                                          100,
                                     duration,
                                        true );
80              break;
81
82          case 2://put "after" to the right of "before"
83              fade.stop();
84              caption_txt.text = caption_before +
                                    " (left) " +
                                    caption_after +
                                    " (right)";
85              after_mc._alpha = 100;
86              var padding = 10;
87              after_mc._y = before_mc._y;
88              after_mc._x = before_mc._x +
                                before_mc._width +
                                padding;
89              break;
90      }
91  }
```

Lines 6–9 are just some variables needed for this template—the currentStep variable is important in the stepping process. Notice that currentStep is incremented and decremented in the nextStep() and prevStep() functions (which, by the way, are called from the presentation engine when the presenter presses the right- or left-arrow key). Every time the currentStep variable changes we trigger the showPhotos() function on line 65, which handles all the display work. Inside the init() function, notice that line 21 decides whether to start currentStep at 0 or 2. If the presenter is backing into this slide—coming from a later slide—we need to start on the last step, which is step 2. In this template, I'm using the MovieClipLoader to manage the two photos that are loaded for one important reason: We don't want to trigger the showPhotos() function until both clips are loaded, which occurs on line 39 after the two clips have loaded. You can't ascertain the height of a loaded image until it's fully loaded. Finally, notice lines 17, 18, 28, and 29. These expect the supplied XMLNode to contain values for the nodes <caption_before>, <caption_after>, <photo_before>, and <photo_after>. These are simply the values for nodes I arbitrarily decided to add when building this template. (You'll see all four nodes in the XML you add in the next step.)

Before moving on to the next step, select Control, Test Movie to generate the before_after.swf file. You won't see much onscreen except your text and clip holders.

STEP 3▼
Writing the XML for This Template

Open the slide_data.xml file and, after the first two lines, add the node that appears in Listing 7.3.

You can replace both the before.jpg and after.jpg image files currently in the images folder if you want. Save this .xml file and launch the slideshow.swf file. Be sure that you can step through the images by pressing the right- and left-arrow keys. You can see the sequence of before and after images in Figure 7.6.

LISTING 7.3 The <slide> Node for the before_after.swf Template

```
<slide name="Construction Progress" type="before_after.swf">
    <caption_before>Construction Site</caption_before>
    <photo_before>before.jpg</photo_before>
    <caption_after>After Construction</caption_after>
    <photo_after>after.jpg</photo_after>
</slide>
```

FIGURE 7.6 This template shows the before image, then transitions to the after image, and finally shows the two images next to each other.

Before

Construction Site

Transitioning

FIGURE 7.6   Continued

After

After Construction

Construction Site (left) After Construction (right)

Project:
CSS Support in a Pull Quote Template

The main presentation engine (slideshow.swf) not only loads the slide information from slide_data.xml, but also reads in the file styles.css (CSS stands for Cascading Style Sheets). A .css file is a text file that includes custom definitions for text and layout styles, including font face, font size, style (such as bold or italic), color, and more. You can then *tag* HTML text with the custom styles in your .css document. When you use CSS, the definitions for how the text looks are defined externally. That means you or anyone using this presentation can change the text style without returning to the .fla file.

This project shows you how to build a template that displays a pull quote and a caption centered on a full-screen image; the pull quote appears using a text style you add to the styles.css file. In the end, we'll have a new template style called pullquote.swf that draws from a new <slide> node where you specify a background image, a large quote (the pull quote itself), and an optional caption to provide an attribution for the quote. You can assemble a presentation that includes several pages using this template along with pages using the other templates you build in this chapter.

STEPS▼

1. Creating the CSS styles
2. Designing the slide node
3. Embedding the fonts
4. Writing the code for the pullquote.swf template

STEP 1▼
Creating the CSS Styles

Locate your copy of the styles.css file you downloaded for use with this chapter (originally in the starter_files folder but now in your working folder). Open it with a text editor. We're going to add two style definitions, so after line 6 in the styles.css file, add the following text:

```
.pullquote {
    font-family: "Arial";
```

```
    font-size: 56px;
    color: #000000;
    text-align: center;
}

.quotecaption {
    font-family: "Arial";
    font-size: 24px;
    color: #663300;
    text-align: right;
    font-style: italic;
}
```

I selected the Arial font because most people have that font installed on their computers; if you don't have that font, select a font you do have installed.

Save the styles.css file.

STEP 2▼
Designing the Slide Node

This template and its corresponding <slide> node has three basic pieces: the main pull quote, an optional caption (for use as an attribution for who said the quote), and an optional background image. Open the slide_data.xml file in a text editor and add the code from Listing 7.4 after the first two lines in that file.

LISTING 7.4 The <slide> **Node for the** pullquote.swf **Template**

```
<slide name="Mission Statement"
       type="pullquote.swf"
       backgroundImage="images/penny.jpg">
    <pullquote>A Penny Saved is a Penny Earned</pullquote>
    <quotecaption>Benjamin Franklin</quotecaption>
</slide>
```

When designing new slide templates, you have the freedom to add to the `<slide>` node's format. As long as the node is called `slide` and has the `name` and `type` attributes, you can add any attributes or children nodes you want. In this case, I wanted two text values for the quote and the caption, so I added nodes called `<pullquote>` and `<quotecaption>`. In addition, I decided to add the `backgroundImage` attribute. Ultimately, the nodes I added are arbitrary because I could have added anything. The key here is that my template must parse out the elements it needs.

> **NOTE**
>
> You might have noticed that in this project you're beginning by designing the data structure (the XML file). In the first two projects in this chapter, you started by laying out the display inside Flash. You really can do it in either order because, ultimately, you have to do both. It makes sense to start with the data as long as you have an idea where you're headed. You'll see that most projects in this book start with designing the data structure.

STEP 3 ▼
Embedding the Fonts

Open a new file and immediately select File, Save As. Name the new file **pullquote.fla**, and set the document dimensions to 800 × 600. Instead of placing text on the stage using the Text tool, we'll trigger code in my `utils.as` class that uses the `createTextField()` method. Using `createTextField()` to place text on the stage has advantages over the manual approach. For one thing, you can create as many fields as needed, the number

of which you might not know while authoring. This will be the case when you build the `bullet_list.swf` template because it supports an unrestricted number of bullet points. In any event, there's one important step required for such a dynamically generated field, and that's for it to support the embedded font feature. We'll embed the font so the presenter's machine won't need that font installed. However, with dynamically generated text, there isn't a field on the stage—you'll manually place a field on the stage to ensure that the font exports with your `.swf`.

> **NOTE**
>
> Embedding fonts into a dynamic text or input text field means that your `.swf` file will display the font correctly on any person's machine, even if that user doesn't have the font installed. The side effect is that embedding fonts adds to the movie's file size, which is probably not an issue for this project (I suspect most presenters will run the presentation off their hard drives).

There are two ways to embed a font for use in dynamically generated fields. One way is to place a dummy dynamic text field offstage. Do this by using the Text tool to create two dynamic text fields positioned offstage: one for the `.pullquote` style and one for the `.pullquotecaption` style. For reference, type **Arial** into one field and **Arial Italic** into the other. Be sure to select the Arial font for these two fields. For the italic version, be sure to enable the Italic button in the Properties panel, as shown in Figure 7.7.

FIGURE 7.7   You'll need to
select the font and appropriate style using the Properties
panel.

Embed button

Italic option

Another important step is that you also click the Embed button on the Properties panel and select the characters your text field can display from the Character Embedding dialog box that appears. Select both fields and then click the Embed button. Select the Basic Latin (95 Glyphs) option as was shown previously in Figure 7.3.

Another way to embed fonts for the dynamically generated text is to create a *font symbol.* (However, you don't have to do it this way because you already added the dummy fields.) Open the Library window and select New Font. From the Font drop-down list in the Font Symbol Properties dialog box shown in Figure 7.8, select the font you defined in the styles.css file. In addition, you must ensure that the font exports with the movie. To do that, select the font you just added to the Library and select Linkage from the Library's menu. Enable the Export for ActionScript check box and make sure that the Export in First Frame option is also enabled (as shown in Figure 7.9). Repeat this process for each font you want to embed— one font for each of the styles .pullquote and .quotecaption.

FIGURE 7.8   Another way to embed fonts is to create a new font symbol.

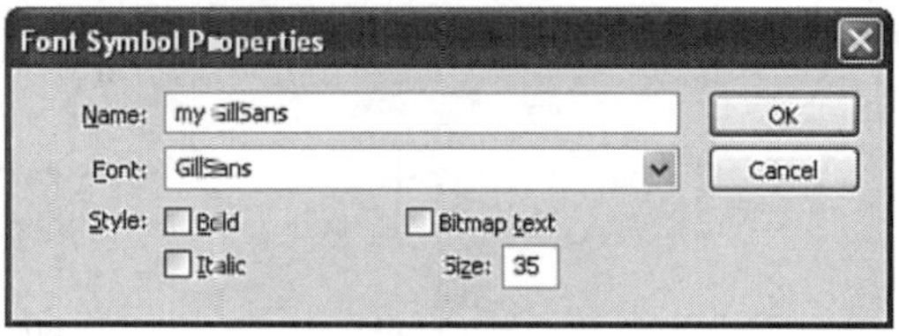

FIGURE 7.9   To ensure that your font symbol exports with the movie, set its linkage options as shown.

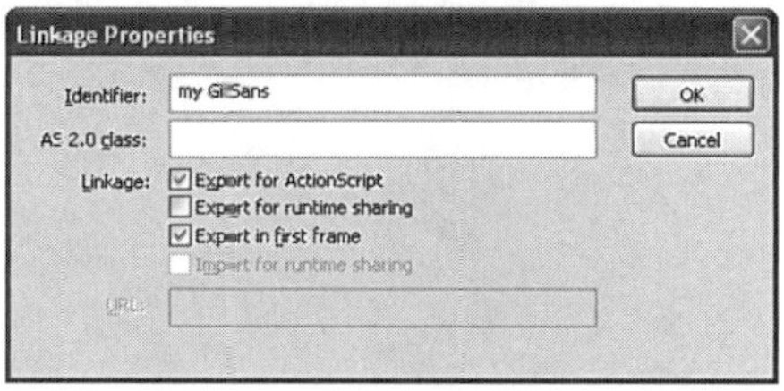

STEP 4▼
Writing the Code for the pullquote.swf Template

Select the first keyframe in the pullquote.fla file, open the Actions panel, and enter the code shown in Listing 7.5. You will also find this code in the pullquote.fla file in the finish_source folder you downloaded for this chapter.

LISTING 7.5   **This Code Displays and Centers the Pull Quote's** <slide> **Node**

```
1    var owner:MovieClip;
2    var slideData:XMLNode;
3    var startAtBeginning:Boolean;
4    var STAGE_WIDTH:Number = 800;
5    var STAGE_HEIGHT:Number = 600;
6
7    function init( p_owner:MovieClip,
                    p_data:XMLNode,
                    p_startAtBeginning:Boolean ){
8       owner = p_owner;
9       slideData = p_data;
10      startAtBeginning = p_startAtBeginning;
11
12      var backgroundImage =
        slideData.attributes.backgroundImage;
13      if( backgroundImage != undefined ){
14         var background_mc:MovieClip =
           createEmptyMovieClip ("background_mc",0);
15         background_mc.loadMovie(backgroundImage);
16      }
17      /*  for reference:
18          utils.makeText( scope:MovieClip,depth:Number,
19                          style:String,
20                          styleSheet:TextField.styleSheet,
21                          text:String,
22                          instanceName:String,
23                          x,
24                          y )
25      */
26      var pullquote_txt:TextField = utils.makeText(    this,
                                                         1,
                                                       ".pullquote",
                                                    owner.getCSS(),
        owner.selectSingleNodeValue(slideData, "/slide/pullquote"),
                                                    "pullquote_txt",
                                                         0,
                                                         0 );
27      var quotecaption_txt:TextField = utils.makeText( this,
                                                         2,
                                                     ".quotecaption",
                                                    owner.getCSS(),
        owner.selectSingleNodeValue(slideData, "/slide/quotecaption"),
                                                  "quotecaption_txt",
                                                         0,
                                                         0 );
28
29      //set pullquote margins
30      var padding = 50;
```

LISTING 7.5 **Continued**

```
31    pullquote_txt._width = STAGE_WIDTH - (padding * 2);
32    pullquote_txt.multiline = true;
33    pullquote_txt.wordWrap = true;
34
35    //center pullquote
36    pullquote_txt._x = padding;
37    pullquote_txt._y = STAGE_HEIGHT/2 -
                        pullquote_txt._height/2 -
                        padding;
38
39    //position quotecaption:
40    quotecaption_txt._x =
        pullquote_txt._x + pullqucte_txt._width;
41    quotecaption_txt._y =
        pullquote_txt._y + pullqucte_txt._height;
42    quotecaption_txt._x -=
        quotecaption_txt._width;
43    }
44
45    function nextStep(){
46    }
47    function prevStep(){
48    }
49    function getStep():Number{
50        return 0;
51    }
52    function getTotalSteps():Number{
53        return 0;
54    }
```

A few notes about the init() function in this code are in order. Notice that line 13 first checks to see whether there is a backgroundImage attribute before attempting to load it. One assumption I'm making here is that the background image fills the stage. You can certainly write some code to center a smaller image if you want. See the text-centering code on lines 36 and 37; also refer to the "Advanced Before-and-After Photo Template" project earlier in this chapter to see how the MovieClipLoader waits for the onLoadInit event to trigger before ascertaining the image's dimensions.

Lines 26 and 27 call the utils.makeText() method to create, populate, and stylize the blocks of text. The rest of the code is all about centering the text. Specifically, the pullquote_txt has its margins set to 50 pixels shy of the left and right edges of the stage. Then lines 36 and 37 center the pullquote_txt. Remember that the CSS style for .pullquote declared this text is center justified, so we don't have to deal with that here. You'll see the code text-align: center; in the styles.css file. Finally, lines 40–42 position captionquote_txt at the bottom-right corner of the pullquote_txt, wherever that ends up landing.

With the code in place, select Control, Test Movie to generate the `pullquote.swf` file. You'll see a blank screen when you test the movie. If you launch the `slideshow.swf` file, you should see the screen shown in Figure 7.10.

FIGURE 7.10   The pull quote template presents a background image and two blocks of formatted text.

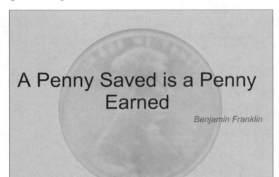

A Penny Saved is a Penny Earned

Benjamin Franklin

Project:
Bullet List Template

The primary focus of this bullet list template is to show you how to support the common delivery technique of topics followed by subtopics as bullet points. Because the exact number of bullets varies with each topic, the slide node has to support any number of bullet points. (Good thing we're using XML because that makes it easy.)

In the end, you'll have a new template named `bullet_list.swf` and a corresponding `<slide>` node that can be added to a presentation that includes various other templates.

STEPS▼

1. **Designing the XML structure**
2. **Adding the styles to the CSS document**
3. **Embedding the fonts**
4. **Writing the template code**

STEP 1▼
Designing the XML Structure

Each slide based on the bullet template will have a title and as many bullets as needed. Open the `slide_data.xml` currently in your working folder (originally copied from the `starter_files` folder). Listing 7.6 shows the XML you should insert after the second line in the `slide_data.xml` file.

Notice that I stuffed the `effect` attribute into the `<slide>` node in addition to the required `name` and `type` attributes. The `effect` attribute specifies how each bullet is revealed. That is, each bullet will appear with an effect, such as sliding in from the left side of the stage or dissolving. We'll create a library of a few effects using Flash's `TransitionManager` class as well as homemade code. This way, each page that contains the `bullet_list.swf` template can use any effect you choose. Also note that the `title` and `bullet` nodes each has a `style` attribute. I added this attribute for two reasons: First, I want to be sure that you understand how to extract attributes from nodes *within* the slide. Second, I'd like the CSS style to be independent of the template. That is, in the `pullquote.swf` template, we hard-wired the two styles for the pull quote and the quote caption. The design for this template (`bullet_list.swf`) allows a single template to support any number of styles for the `<title>` and `<bullet>` nodes.

LISTING 7.6 The `<slide>` **Node for the** `bullet_slide.swf` **Template**

```
<slide name="Flash 8 Benefits"
       type="bullet_list.swf"
       effect="dissolve">
    <title style=".headline1"  >Flash 8 is...</title>
    <bullet style=".smallbullet" >Fast</bullet>
    <bullet style=".smallbullet" >Powerful</bullet>
    <bullet style=".smallitalicbullet" >Cool</bullet>
</slide>
```

Save the `slide_data.xml` file.

STEP 2▼
Adding the Styles to the CSS Document

Open the `styles.css` file so you can add styles for, at a minimum, `.headline1`, `.smallbullet`, and `.smallitalicbullet`. These are the styles you specified in the `slide_data.xml` file in step 1. Each slide will have a headline (`.headline1`) that stays onscreen as well as bullet points that appear in sequence. The bullets we've added so far use either the `.smallbullet` style or the `.smallitalicbullet` style. Here's the code for the styles I added—you should be sure to pick a font that's installed on your Flash workstation:

```
.headline1 {
    font-family: "Arial";
    font-size: 56px;
    color: #FF0000;
}

.smallbullet {
    font-family: "Arial";
    font-size: 24px;
    color: #000000;
}

.smallitalicbullet {
```

```
    font-family: "Arial";
    font-size: 24px;
    color: 000000;
    font-style: italic;
}
```

You're welcome to list a different font than Arial, but be sure you pick one that's installed on your machine. Save the `styles.css` file.

STEP 3▼
Embedding the Fonts

Create a new Flash file; select File, Save As; and give the file the name **bullet_list.fla**. Select Modify, Document and set the dimensions to 800 × 600. Next, embed the fonts you referenced in the `styles.css` file in step 2. To do this, simply create one dynamic text field for each font you referenced. Create one block using Arial and another block of Arial with its italic setting enabled in the Properties panel, to support the `.smallitalicbullet` style. For each text field, click the Embed button in the Properties panel and select the Basic Latin (95 glyphs) option in the Character Embedding dialog box (shown earlier in Figure 7.3).

STEP 4▼
Writing the Template Code

So that you can easily see the main strategy for this template, let's first look at everything except the `init()` function. Select the first keyframe in the `bullet_list.fla` file, open the Actions panel, and enter the code shown in Listing 7.7. You can copy and paste it from the `bullet_list.fla` file in the `finished_source` folder.

LISTING 7.7 This Code Displays and Transitions the Bullet Points

```
1    import mx.transitions.*;
2    import mx.transitions.easing.*;
3    import flash.filters.*;
4
5    var owner:MovieClip;
6    var slideData:XMLNode;
7    var startAtBeginning:Boolean;
8    var currentStep:Number;
9    var totalSteps:Number;
10   var thisTimeline:MovieClip = this;
11
12   function nextStep(){
13      currentStep++;
14      goStep(currentStep, true);
15   }
16   function prevStep(){
17      currentStep--;
18      goStep(currentStep, false);
19   }
20   function getStep():Number{
21      return currentStep;
22   }
23   function getTotalSteps():Number{
24      return totalSteps;
25   }
26
27   function goStep( n:Number, withEffect:Boolean ){
28      for(var i = 0; i < totalSteps; i++){
29         thisTimeline["bullet_"+i]._visible = (n>i);
30      }
31      if( n == 0 || withEffect == false) return;
32
33      var lastBullet:MovieClip =
         thisTimeline["bullet_" + Number(n-1)];
34
35      switch(slideData.attributes.effect){
36         case "slide":
37            var TRANSITION_DURATION = 0.5;
38            var startX = 0 - lastBullet._width;
```

LISTING 7.7   Continued

```
39              var endX = lastBullet._x;
40              lastBullet._x = startX;
41              new Tween( lastBullet,
                            "_x",
                            Elastic easeOut,
                            startX,
                            endX,
                            TRANSITION_DURATION,
                            true );
42          break;
43
44      case "blinds":
45          var TRANSITION_DURATION = 0.5;
46          TransitionManager.start( lastBullet,
                                {type:Blinds,
                            direction:Transition.IN,
                        duration:TRANSITION_DURATION,
                            easing:None.easeNone });
47          break;
48
49      case "dissolve":
50          var TRANSITION_DURATION = 0.5;
51          var sections = 50;
52          TransitionManager.start( lastBullet,
                                {type:PixelDissolve,
                            direction:Transition.IN,
                        duration:TRANSITION_DURATION,
                            easing:None.easeNone,
                                xSections:sections,
                                ySections:sections });
53          break;
54
55      case "blur":
56          var TRANSITION_DURATION = 0.25;
57          var startingBlur = 50;
58          var blur:BlurFilter =
                new BlurFilter(startingBlur, startingBlur, 1);
59          lastBullet.filters = [blur];
60
61          var updateFrequency = 50;//milliseconds
62          var totalSteps = Math.round(
                            (TRANSITION_DURATION*1000)/
                                    updateFrequency   );
63          var blurChange = startingBlur/totalSteps;
64          var tempInterval =
                setInterval(function(){
65                      blur.blurX -= blurChange;
```

continues

LISTING 7.7   Continued

```
66                              blur.blurY -= blurChange;
67                              totalSteps--;
68                              lastBullet.filters = [blur];
69                              if(totalSteps == 0){
70                                  lastBullet.filters = [];
71                                  clearInterval(tempInterval);
72                              }
73                              updateAfterEvent();
74                              updateFrequency);
75
76                  break;
77          }
78      }
```

This code is fairly straightforward despite being long. We maintain a currentStep variable, and we know the value of the totalSteps variable because we set it, in the init() function that appears later, based on how many <bullet> nodes are found in the <slide> node. Every time the currentStep variable is changed in either the nextStep() or prevStep() function, the goStep() function is triggered (lines 14 and 18). The goStep() function begins by going through all the bullet clips, which are generated in the init() function that appears later, and either makes them visible or not, depending on the step number we're up to. You can see the code that sets the _visible property on lines 28–30. All the bullets are present at all times but, if you have five total bullets and are only on step 3, the last two bullets are invisible.

When the user is stepping backward, there's no transition applied. Line 31 skips the rest of the goStep() function if that's the case. Lines 33–77 handle the transition on the last visible bullet in the list. First, line 33 gets a

reference to the last bullet displayed; then the switch statement on line 35 figures out which effect to apply based on the effect attribute in the slideData—that's the <slide> node, again set inside the init() function. When you're on the first step, the first bullet is the "last" bullet, so it has a transition effect applied. When you go to the next step, the "last" step is the second bullet, so it also has a transition effect applied. This process continues, always applying the effect to the last bullet.

You'll see code for four effects: slide, blinds, dissolve, and blur. The slide effect uses the Tween class, whereas the blinds and dissolve effects use the new TransitionManager class. Finally, the blur effect is just a homemade solution using Flash's setInterval() function. Your <slide> nodes can use any of these four effects.

Listing 7.8 shows the init() function.

LISTING 7.8 The init()
function Completes the Code
for the bullet_list.swf
Template

```
81    function init( p_owner:MovieClip,
                     p_data:XMLNode,
                     p_startAtBeginning:Boolean ){
82        owner = p_owner;
83        slideData = p_data;
84        startAtBeginning = p_startAtBeginning;
85
86        var allBullets =
          owner.selectNodeList(slideData, "/slide/bullet");
87        totalSteps = allBullets.length;
88
89        var spacer = 20;
90        var left = 20;
91        var top = 20;
92
93        //make the title:
94        var title_txt = utils.makeText( thisTimeline,
                                          0,
          owner.selectSingleNode( slideData,
                             "/slide/title").attributes.style,
                                owner.getCSS(),
          owner.selectSingleNodeValue( slideData,
                             "/slide/title"),
                                "title_txt",
                                       left,
                                        top );
95
96        //track the top of the last piece of text
97        top += title_txt._y + title_txt._height;
98
99        for(var i = 0; i < totalSteps; i++){
100           top += spacer;
101           var thisBulletClip =
              thisTimeline.createEmptyMovieClip ("bullet_"+i,i+1);
102           var thisBullet = utils.makeText( thisBulletClip,
                                               0,
                           allBullets[i].attributes.style,
                                owner.styles,
                           allBullets[i].firstChild,
                                       "_txt",
                                         left,
                                          top );
103           top += thisBullet._height;
104        }
105
106       if( startAtBeginning == true ){
107           currentStep = 0;
```

continues

LISTING 7.8	Continued	108	`}else{`
		109	`    currentStep = totalSteps;`
		110	`}`
		111	
		112	`goStep(currentStep, startAtBeginning);`
		113	`}`

A few notes are in order. First, this code begins on line 81 because it's a continuation of Listing 7.7. On line 86, we grab all the `<bullet>` subnodes and save the `totalSteps` value in the next line. Starting on line 89, a few local variables are used to space out bullets (`spacer`) and identify where the title appears (`top`, `left`). The `top` variable is increased after every block of text is drawn (lines 94 and 102). I use the `utils.makeText()` method to draw all the text, but notice that the text for all the bullets is placed into a text field named `_txt`, which is nested inside its own movie clip (*"bullet_n"* on line 101). Recall that in the `goStep()` method, we reveal or hide a bullet by setting the `_visible` property, meaning we create all the bullets in the `init()` function but the `goStep()` method handles showing (or hiding) the bullets. Although text fields support the `_visible` property, we can apply filters and other effects to movie clips only when using the `TransitionManager` class.

Lastly, notice that we set the `currentStep` variable based on whether we're starting at the beginning. The `goStep()` method also accepts the `currentStep` parameter because, when stepping backward, you don't need to reanimate the last bullet.

With the code in place, select Control, Test Movie to generate the `bullet_list.swf` template file. You'll just see a blank screen when you test the movie. If you launch the

slideshow.swf, you should see the screen shown in Figure 7.11.

FIGURE 7.11 The `bullet_list.swf` template presents animated bullets in sequence.

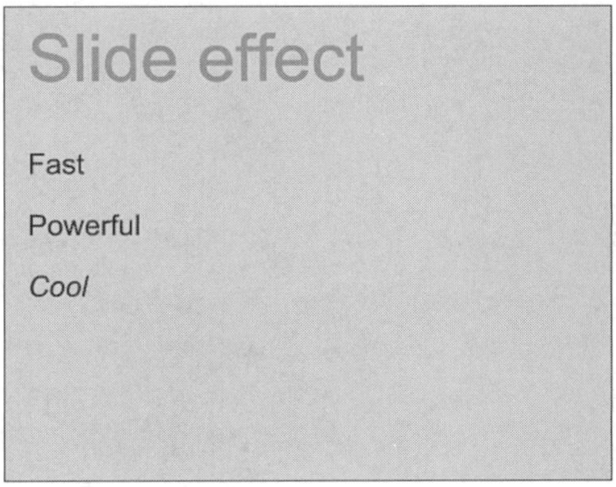

Project: Slideshow Distribution

Because not everyone has the Flash stand-alone player (SAPlayer), a couple of easy steps are necessary to distribute a slideshow presentation as a Flash *projector*. Follow the steps in this project to distribute the slideshow, complete with the presentation engine and all the slide data, that you created in this chapter.

STEPS▼

1. **Choosing distribution options**
2. **Creating a projector**
3. **Collecting the necessary distribution files**

CHAPTER 7: Creating a PowerPoint-style Slide Presentation

STEP 1▼
Choosing Distribution Options

There really aren't a lot of options available when you're distributing a Flash projector. In Chapter 8, "Creating a CD-ROM Front End," you'll learn about several available third-party tools that give you additional options. For this slideshow presentation, however, you might want to add a feature that is supported in Flash. Namely, the ability to make the presentation take up the full screen. Normally, if your screen resolution is greater than 800 × 600, the presentation we created in this chapter runs in a window. There are two variations you can make:

▶ If you want the presentation to overtake the entire screen, add this line of code at the top of the Actions panel for each of your templates—well, at least the template for the first slide in the presentation:

```
fscommand("fullscreen", "true");
```

This code also scales your content to fit whatever screen resolution you're using. Although this line of code works great for vector graphics, any photographs you have included in the slideshow will get stretched and look grainy. To compensate for that, you can add another line of code:

```
Stage.scaleMode="noScale";
```

This second statement ensures that everything appears at 100%. The space around the outside of your stage will be solid white.

▶ If you need to change the overall dimensions of the slideshow from the default 800 × 600 we set initially, you'll need to change all your templates, as well as the source `slideshow.fla` file, and then republish it as `slideshow.swf`.

STEP 2▼
Creating a Projector

This step is easy: Launch the `slideshow.swf` file and select File, Create Projector. If the menu is gone because you're at full screen, just press Esc to return your screen to the 800 × 600-pixel window size. When you select Create Projector, you'll be prompted to save the projector; do so in a new folder called `Distribution`. Name the file **presentation.exe** (or anything you prefer).

STEP 3▼
Collecting the Necessary Distribution Files

There are other files you need to work with the projector—namely, all the `.swf` template files you created, the `slidedata.xml` file, the `styles.css` stylesheet file, and any support image files (the `images` folder in your working folder). You don't have to distribute any of the `.as` files or the `.fla` files or the `slideshow.swf` file. Copy all the `.swf`, `.css`, and `.xml` files from your working folder into the `Distribution` folder. Also copy the `images` folder into the `Distribution` folder. Finally, delete the `slideshow.swf` file that's in your `Distribution` folder—it's embedded in the `.exe` you produced in the step 2.

Figure 7.12 shows a tidy folder with the appropriate files.

Now you can copy the Distribution folder onto the presenter's computer. Tell the presenter to double-click the projector .exe file to run the presentation.

Exploring the Support Classes

You might take this presentation engine as is and successfully build a collection of diverse, powerful, and effective templates for years to come. However, you also might want to make a change to the core structure of the engine, which will require modifying the underlying presentation.fla. You might simply want to dig into the engine and see how it was built. It's really not terribly intense, but the process of understanding it is more productive if I give you the following tour.

Although I didn't build the core engine entirely from the inside out, I did start with two basic objectives: First, I knew that the main slideshow.swf file would import the styles and slide data. When the user tried to navigate, slideshow.swf would load in the appropriate template .swf file. Second, I knew that each template .swf would receive an XML node with all the information it needed. Because I knew that most templates would want to parse their slide node plus have access to the loaded CSS from the styles.css file, I created a set of methods in their shared parent, the SlideHolder class. Also, each template needed to support a common set of stepping methods, listed in the ISlide interface.

The class diagram in Figure 7.13 shows the overall design of the slideshow presentation project.

Here's a quick tour that might be worth revisiting after you view the code. After the slideshow.swf file loads in the CSS and XML, it creates two variables: slideHolder (which is really an attached MovieClip, based on the SlideHolder class) and slideData (based on the regular object class SlideData). When creating the slideData instance, we pass a reference to the slideHolder. In turn, slideData contacts slideData using the refToSlideData() method so they both can have a reference to each other. Although the SlideData class doesn't do too much, it's decoupled from SlideHolder. To get any XML data, slideHolder must trigger one of SlideData's get methods.

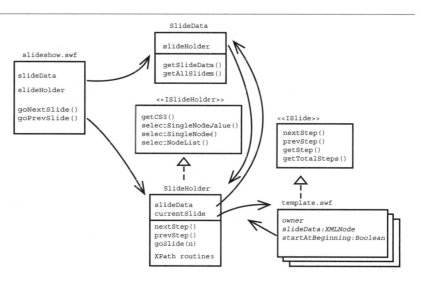

FIGURE 7.13 This architectural view shows the classes with their key properties and methods. The solid outlines show classes that extend `MovieClip`; the marks `<<` `>>` surround interface class names; the plain arrows show the class to which reference variables refer (so-called "has a" relationships); and the dashed arrows point to the interface a class implements (so-called "is a" relationship).

Final Thoughts

This presentation engine can be used for any number of projects because you can build your own templates (as long as each template includes a certain minimum set of features). I've included a couple extra templates in the downloadable files for this chapter. For example, designing a template that plays a `.flv` Flash video in a slide was easy. See the `video_slide.fla` and corresponding `video_slide.swf` template in the `finished_source` folder—there's *very* little code. Even so, I certainly didn't think of every possible need you might have. I plan to post additional templates on my website for this book, so if you come up with a template you'd like to share, please email it to me.

The core engine is something that can be improved; however, there's not a lot there to go wrong. Do note that the Flash context menu has a few limits. For one thing, you're limited to 13 entries, not including the two I added for Next Slide and Previous Slide. In addition, you can't get rid of the About Flash or Settings entries. Finally, you can't have two entries with the same name, so make sure that each `<slide>` node's name attribute is unique.

As great as I think this presentation engine is, I realize there's a lot you can add. For example, it wouldn't be much work to reorganize the file structure so that everything except the projector is placed in a folder—perhaps called data. Doing this gives the presenter an even easier way of finding the `presentation.exe`. A more involved feature is to give the presenter a selection from several presentation files. Right now, the engine just looks for `slide_data.xml`. You could give presenters a list of several presentation templates to choose from immediately after launching the `presentation.exe` file.

Additionally, if you have an application server (and the requisite skills), you could build a separate tool that generates `slide_data.xml` files. You can even give presenters the ability to share and modify `slide_data.xml` files from others in your organization. Sometimes, a decent engine like this can spark more ideas for projects (and work) you can produce.

CHAPTER 8: Creating a CD-ROM Front End

About the Project

In this project, you use Flash to create an interface to content you distribute on CD-ROM. For most CD-ROM front ends, you're effectively just slapping a pretty display onto a directory structure of files. However, the front end you create in this project will do more than simply spice up a list of files.

Prerequisites

To deliver a customized application, you'll need to own one of the third-party swf2exe projector-making tools listed in the section "Planning the Projects." Projectors created with these tools add many features not available in standard Flash projectors.

Planning the Projects

In this project, you use Flash to create an interface to content you distribute on CD-ROM. You'll make the files easier to find by organizing the list into sections and by using graphics that can be read faster than words. You'll also let users download files—really copy them from the CD to their hard drives. Finally, you'll let users launch native files in the file's associated application, such as opening .pdf files in Acrobat. Like many projects in this book, you'll be creating templates that work within the framework I built. However, this time you'll be able to modify that framework more than usual.

This kind of solution is popular for sharing large files with a select audience. For example, a manufacturer might want to provide high-resolution images to its distributors for use in local newspaper ads. Or a voice talent agency might want to send out samples to casting agents.

> **📌 NOTE**
>
> This project is built for delivery only on Windows machines, not Macintosh. If you need to deliver to Macintosh, there is a version of Zinc that can produce Macintosh OS X projectors. This chapter doesn't cover that particular product, though.

Ultimately it will be your content files (say, a bunch of .pdf files or .tif images) that you'll select and organize for this project. You'll also have to make many decisions about exactly how the files will be presented and how the users should gain access to them. The following sections discuss the primary considerations for this kind of project.

Why Not Create a Flash Projector?

To deliver a customized application, you'll need to own one of the following third-party swf2exe projector-making software products:

- ▶ SWFStudio V3 (www.northcode.com)

- ▶ Screenweaver (http://osflash.org/doku.php?id=screenweaver)

- ▶ Zinc V2 (www.multidmedia.com/software/zinc/)

- ▶ mProjector (www.screentime.com/software/mprojector/)

You can use any product (or even write a custom Flash shell with C++, Macromedia Director, or a similar tool) to deliver a custom application, provided you write a class that implements the IProduct.as interface discussed later. I've supplied code for only the four products listed, but that code can be adapted for other products.

As you know, Flash itself can also make *projectors*. Any project can benefit by working on your user's machine without the need for the Flash Player web plug-in. However, the Flash projector doesn't offer nearly the control you have with these third-party products. Pretty much anything you've seen in any desktop application is possible when you use one of these products to create your projector: copying files, changing the user's sound level, launching or installing other applications, and so on. In fact, you can even create nefarious applications. That's why projectors make sense only for limited distribution where the user trusts you.

NOTE

In case you're wondering why we're even making a projector, first realize that the premise in this project is that you're distributing the file to run on a user's desktop, not posting a .swf that runs on your website. If you simply distributed a .swf, only those people with the Flash player (the SAPlayer.exe file that is installed with Flash 8—the authoring tool) could run the file. Also, projectors can do different things than .swf files can. For one thing, they don't have the same web-only or local-only playback security rules .swf files do. Plus, you can do things such as display at full screen, which you can't do with .swf files.

The two features you'll build in to the CD-ROM front end in this project, in addition to displaying the CD's contents, are letting users copy files to their hard drives and opening native files. Also, depending on which third-party tool you use, you'll be able to first check whether the user has the necessary software to, say, view .pdf files. There's a lot more you can do with this application, but even these seemingly nominal features are possible only with a third-party (or custom) tool.

I think the features I've selected for this project are the most commonly used—certainly from my experience. However, if you want to add more features, you can base your solution on how these two core features are implemented here.

Designing a Workable and Organized File Structure

If your front end is well organized and easy for the user to navigate, it probably doesn't matter how you organize the support files (that is, all the .pdf files or whatever you're storing on the CD). However, I like to put only a minimum number of files in the root of the CD—for example, just the projector's .exe file—and then nest everything else inside one or two other folders. For example, you could have one folder called flash that contains all your .swf files and another called content that contains all the files for the user. The primary focus in organizing the CD's content is to make the organization neat. Second, it's also nice to make it relatively easy for users who prefer to navigate the folders to find what they want. If nothing else, the content folders must be organized in a manner that works well for you, the author.

The projector should be nothing more than a *stub* that immediately jumps to your main.swf file using the loadMovie() or similar function. So, you make a stub.swf that you convert into a projector using the third-party tool. After you have the projector .exe file, you can make updates to the main.swf file without having to re-create the projector .exe. If you had to build a new .exe as often as you do a test movie, you'd surely be frustrated because it is time-consuming and just plain unnecessary work.

All this effort organizing folders and making a stub projector revolves around making the CD-ROM's file layout neat. However, a perplexing side effect is that your main.swf might appear to get mixed up with relative paths. That is all the relative paths depend on—a base path or starting point. This base path is the folder in which the first file you launch resides. Consider what happens when you launch main.swf, or even when you select Control, Test Movie from a .fla file. You can load the adjacent image image.jpg or an image file that's in a folder named images you'd use images/image.jpg. These are *relative paths*. The problem arises when the first file launched is the stub.exe projector (up one level from main.swf). If the code in your main.swf file says images/image.jpg, it expects to find the images folder adjacent to the stub.exe—not adjacent to the main.swf. Naturally, you need to understand how your file structure affects relative paths. Figure 8.1 shows how the main.swf file can reference the photo.jpg image using images/photo.jpg but, even after the stub.exe jumps out to the main.swf (inside the data folder), it refers to the photo.jpg file by using data/images/photo.jpg.

FIGURE 8.1 Keeping the stub.exe outside the data folder makes a cleaner layout but can change how relative paths work.

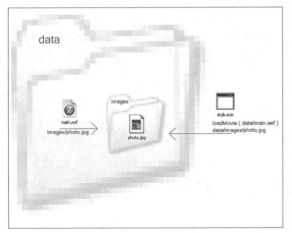

Because relative paths can mix you up, it's critical that you set up an environment where you can still test main.swf while authoring and the paths all work the same as they will in the final version. The way we'll approach this project is to make sure the stub.exe either changes its base path to match the main.swf or simply uses hard-wired paths instead. The key here is that we need to ensure that the main.swf works when we

choose the Test Movie command as well as in the final project.

Making Custom Icons

Unless you like generic icons, such as stub.exe's icon shown in Figure 8.1, you'll probably want to replace it with a custom icon. Any decent swf2exe tool will let you add a custom icon to the projector you create. You should realize that, depending on the version of the Windows operating system you're using (XP, Windows 98, or Windows 2000), there are different sets of icons. So, you won't be creating just one icon. A large icon appears when the window view is set to Icons; a small icon appears in the taskbar, one appears in the title bar, and another icon appears when you press Alt+Tab to move between open applications. The size of the icons Windows uses range from 16×16 pixels to 48×48 pixels. The bottom line is that your icon creation person must make several versions of the projector icon.

I can recommend a moderately priced and very handy icon and cursor creation tool called Microangelo Creation (www.microangelo.us/). This tool also lets you easily create multiple icons based on a single icon.

📌 TIP

If you like making icons, you can also make one for the CD itself that shows up in place of the default CD drive letter icon.

Autorun

A lot of people seem to want to add a feature to their CD-ROMs called *autorun*. Autorun means you identify the file (probably your

CHAPTER 8: Creating a CD-ROM Front End

stub projector) that you want to automatically launch when the CD is inserted into the computer. Personally, I find this feature annoying because I figure that if a person can insert a CD, he probably knows how to navigate to the CD-ROM drive on his computer. Also, if a CD has an autorun file, any time a user manually navigates to and double-clicks the CD-ROM drive he won't explore the disc's contents as you'd expect, but rather relaunch the stub.exe (later you'll see that creating an autorun file is as easy as creating a text file).

Perhaps even more persuasive than my personal aversion to autorun is the fact that autorun applications can silently install software you don't want. Some audio CDs, for example, install software that attempts to prevent you from copying the music. Other malware installs spyware or adware. Caution about all this secret installation of software has lead many people to turn off the Auto-Play feature for their CD-ROM drives or to simply hold down the Shift key when they insert a CD to temporarily disable Auto-Play.

After all this negative commentary about the autorun feature, I'll still show you how to implement it in this project (it's really easy) because I know many clients require it. (But please at least try to educate your clients as to the issues I just outlined.) Realize too that for the users who don't have the Auto-Play feature enabled, you'll want an easy way for them to find and run your projector.

Full Screen, Title Bars, and Quitting

Quit buttons were common in the glory days of the CD-ROM but are practically extinct now. You just don't think of needing one on a website because the user can just browse away anytime she wants. It makes sense to consider creating your own Quit button for this project—especially if you choose to make your presentation appear full screen. That is, if you choose to display the standard title bar with buttons for maximize, minimize, and close, you don't have to include your own Quit button. It doesn't hurt, however, to give users more than one way to quit. A full-screen application should definitely include a Quit button because many users won't know to press Ctrl+Q or Alt+F4 or Esc (some of which might or might not work for the particular swf2exe tool you choose).

Displaying your project full screen is a nice way to control the entire visual experience. However, it might not be appropriate if users commonly need access to other applications while they're running yours. Also, you should design your project with a stage size you're confident can be supported by all your users. For example, a stage size no larger than 800 × 600 is a pretty safe bet. Finally, also realize that, if you're including a title bar, the viewable part of your project is slightly less tall than the user's screen resolution. The title bar therefore eats away at part of the screen. If you assume that your users have 1024 × 768 monitor displays, you might design your stage at 1024 × 768. If you want to include the title bar, you'll need to change the stage size to something like 1024 × 750 to accommodate the title bar. To make matters worse, depending on the user's computer preferences, the title bar can vary in size, as Figure 8.2 shows. The safest bet is to be conservative and always create as small a window size as possible.

FIGURE 8.2 The title bar from the same application running on Windows XP (top) is 7 pixels taller than when it runs on Windows 2000 (bottom).

Decoupling the Front End, Data, and System-level Calls

It might not be terribly surprising that the front end application you'll build in this chapter is completely decoupled from the content. So, you'll be able to update the content without revisiting the Flash files. What might be less obvious is that the code necessary to perform the system-level functions, such as opening and copying files, is kept separate from the main Flash files. Consequently, the main file will say "third-party tool, open this file" but—depending on *which* third-party tool you're using—the code that follows will vary.

I wanted this project to work regardless of which third-party tool you're using. (Each product uses a different *API*.) It was also impossible to write code for every product; plus, you can build your own *custom shell* in place of these third-party tools. The way this project remains decoupled is that the calls from main.swf are always the same, triggering methods called openFile(), doSaveAs(), and doQuit(). These calls are channeled to a class written for whichever third-party tool you're using. I've written several classes to support the products listed earlier. As long as each class implements the same interface (that is, supports those three methods), then everything works because the main.swf doesn't care which product you're using.

Pieces You'll Build in This Chapter

For the most part, the projects in this chapter all lead to producing a single CD-ROM. The one exception is the "Section Templates" project in which you build several templates. That project is the most similar to the other chapters in this book because there you develop a variety of section.swf templates. However, you'll end up using only one of those templates in this final project. You'll see that the section.swf templates have the most significant impact on the overall look and feel of the CD-ROM. The idea of making more than one template is to give you a few styles from which you can choose when creating additional CD-ROMs.

Each of the other projects in this chapter has just one objective: to build specific elements that are needed in the final project. Specifically, you'll build the following pieces for this project:

- An XML file that lists all the files on your CD-ROM

- The main.swf file that eventually is converted to a projector

Then, after you build a few templates, you'll perform a few more activities:

- You'll tie the main.swf to a selected section.swf template.

- You'll integrate the third-party swf2exe tool.

- You'll prepare the CD-ROM for final delivery.

I think the best way to get an idea of where you're headed in this chapter is to first explore each of the files that begin with

CHAPTER 8: Creating a CD-ROM Front End

"main_" in the `finished_runtime` folder you downloaded for this chapter. Individually launch each of these `.swf` files to see how users will be able to navigate the final CD-ROM. Each file uses a different `section.swf` template.

Project:
XML Document That Identifies All Files

Before Flash can let the user copy or view an external file, you need to supply that file's name. Many third-party projector products can dig into a folder at runtime and gather all the filenames. However, we're still going to create an XML text file that lists the filenames that exist on the CD-ROM. This way, we can add information such as a nice descriptive name instead of displaying only the filenames—something you can't do with an automated solution.

The organization of the XML file we'll create is based on sections full of items. Each item corresponds to a single file. You can think of this as files in folders but not folders within folders. You can have as many sections as you want and, within a section, as many items as you want. (Note that you can store the actual files in any folder structure you want, but onscreen and in the XML, its hierarchy is one level deep.)

At the end of this miniproject, you'll have a single XML file that references all the files you're including on the CD-ROM.

STEPS▼

1. Creating the skeleton XML file
2. Adding and modifying the `Item.as` class
3. Adding and modifying the `Section.as` class
4. Copying the data folders

STEP 1▼
Creating the Skeleton XML File

Open a text editor such as `Notepad.exe`, create a text file named **data.xml**, and save it in your working directory. Type the code in Listing 8.1 into the file (or copy it from `data_min.xml`, located in the `finished_source` folder you downloaded for this chapter).

LISTING 8.1 **The Skeleton** `data.xml` **File**

```
<?xml version="1.0"?>
<main>

    <section name="Photographs" basepath="photos/" >
        <item name="My Dog" filename="dog.jpg"/>
        <item name="Sunset at the beach" filename="sunset.jpg"/>
    </section>

    <section name="Documents" basepath="" >
        <item name="1040 SE Form"
            filename="govforms/f1040sse.pdf"/>
        <item name="1040 SE Instructions"
```

continues

LISTING 8.1 Continued

```
                              filename="instructions/i1040sse.pdf"/>
                    <item name="1040 EZ Form"
                        filename="govforms/f1040ez.pdf"/>
                </section>

            </main>
```

Later you can modify this text for your content. For example, the `name` and `filename` attributes in the `<item>` nodes will refer to your own content. In fact, you'll also be able to change the `name` attributes for your `<section>` nodes. However, for now I recommend just entering the code as shown in Listing 8.1.

To save some typing, I added the `basepath` attribute to each `<section>` node. That is, the two photos in the first section are contained in a subfolder called `photos`. However, because the documents in the second section are stored in different folders (`govforms` and `instructions`), I left the `basepath` attribute empty. When we need to find the file for the second section, we'll always prepend the filename with the `basepath`, as I do here with the code `filename="instructions/i1040sse.pdf"`.

In step 2, you'll see how to add attributes to the `<section>` and `<item>` nodes. For example, maybe you want to add a caption attribute to each `<item>` node so that when the user selects the item, you can display a caption so the user can decide whether to copy the file.

STEP 2▼
Adding and Modifying the Item.as Class

Copy the file `Item.as` from the `finished_source` folder into your working directory, where you have saved the `data.xml` file you created in step 1. In this step, I'll show you how you can add attributes to the item node, but realize that you don't have to modify the `Item.as` class. The task here is only to copy the `Item.as` file into your working folder. But while we're here, I'll show you how you can add support for additional attributes in the `<item>` node in your `data.xml` file. Each attribute in the `item` node shows up later as a property (of the same name) in each `Item` object that is created.

Take a look at the `Item.as` class file, reprinted in Listing 8.2, so that I can point out a couple places where you can modify it.

LISTING 8.2 The `Item.as` Class File

```
1   class Item {
2
3       //add as many more expected attributes that you want
4       public var name:String;
5       public var filename:String;
6
7       //for the node value:
8       public var value:String;
9
```

LISTING 8.2   **Continued**

```
10     //created here:
11     public var extension:String;//e.g. "pdf", "swf", ".jpg"
12
13     function Item(data:XMLNode){
14
15        //turn the attributes into class variables
16        for (var i in data.attributes ){
17           this[i] = data.attributes[i];
18        }
19
20        //create a new property:
21        extension =
     this.filename.substr( this.filename.lastIndexOf(".") + 1 );
22
23        //grab the node value:
24        value = data.firstChild.nodeValue;
25
26        //do serialization such as this example:
27        //someAttribute = Number(someAttribute);
28
29     }
30  }
```

Notice that lines 4 and 5 match the two attributes already in your data.xml file: the name and filename attributes. Also, the extension property on lines 11 and 21 is calculated automatically by extracting the three-letter extension from the value of the filename attribute. That's it for the Item.as tour. There's no modification necessary unless you want to add more data to your XML's <item> nodes. For example, you might want to let the user view more than simply an item's name and filename, or you might want to include a caption or other data such as the size or date of the file.

There are two steps if you want to add more attributes to the <item> nodes in your XML file. First, add the attributes to the XML file. For example, if you want each <item> to include a caption attribute, add it to the <item> node in your XML as shown here:

```
<item name="My Dog"
   filename="dog.jpg"
      caption="This is my dog's caption"/>
```

The second step is to create a property in the Item.as class of the same name (for this example, caption). Basically, you just insert a new line of code below line 5 in Listing 8.2, as follows:

```
public var caption:String;
```

That's really all you have to do to add attributes to the <item> nodes. (And let me remind you that you don't have to add anything to the <item> nodes.) There are, however, two other variations you might want to consider. First, you might want to add a value to each <item> node that includes characters that aren't legal within a node's attributes. For example, if you wanted to include HTML tags to add italic text in your caption, you can't do that in an attribute. However, you can store it as CDATA (character data) within a node value. Here's how you could do it in the XML:

```
<item name="My Dog" filename="dog.jpg">
    <![CDATA[I <i>love</i> my dog]]>
</item>
```

The <item> node value (I *love* my dog) will appear in the Item class's value property (lines 8 and 24 in Listing 8.2). There's really nothing else you have to do; just store the content in the <item> node's value and realize that it will show up in a property called value.

Finally, the last bit of tweaking you might want to do if you're adding to the <item> nodes is serializing. *Serializing* is simply converting data in one type (such as a string) to another data type (such as numbers). This is common with XML because everything that arrives from the XML file is treated as a string. For example, serializing is necessary if you want to store a date in each <item> node. That is, you can store a string version of the date in the XML, but then you'll need to serialize it into a Flash Date class instance once inside the Item.as class. The XML might look like this:

```
<item name="Graduation Day 1983"
  filename="cap-gown.jpg"
      date="424076400000"/>
```

That's the date I graduated from high school using the Date.getTime() method, which I think is easier than making separate attributes for day, month, and year—although that's another way you could do it.

Because you're adding a new attribute, you'll have to add a new property to the Item.as class as we just discussed. You'd add the following line of code after line 6 in Listing 8.2:

```
public var date:Date;
```

You'd also have to serialize that string ("424076400000"). Notice line 27 in Listing 8.2 because it provides an example of how you can serialize particular attributes after they're extracted from the XML. To turn the string ("424076400000") into an actual date, you'd add a line of code after line 27 that reads as follows:

```
date = new Date(date);
```

In summary, you can add any attributes you want: Just add them to the XML and to the Item.as class. You can't use the reserved properties extension or value. If you want add a node value, it will appear in the Item.as's value property.

STEP 3 ▼
Adding and Modifying the Section.as Class

Copy the file Section.as from the finished_source folder you downloaded for this chapter into your working directory. In case you want to add more attributes to the section node, you can do so using the same technique you used to add to the <item> node in step 2. You just can't use the name items—that's a property that will contain an array of items. In addition, because the node value of a <section> node is the array of <item> nodes, you can't store CDATA in the section node (the way I showed in step 2 is to use CDATA inside the `<item>` node's value).

There's really no limit to the types of attributes you might want to add to the `<section>` nodes. You could have a `backgroundMusic` attribute that specifies a `.mp3` to play while the user is in a particular section. Or you might have a `backgroundColor` attribute and change the interface when the user is in that section. The idea is that anything you add to the `<section>` node would relate to the entire section of content.

STEP 4▼
Copying the Data Folders

Copy the three folders (`govforms`, `instructions`, and `photos`) from inside the `finished_source` folder and put them into your working directory. These include the linked media files (the `.pdf` and `.jpg` files). So far, you should have the following items in your working folder:

- ▶ `data.xml`
- ▶ `Item.as`
- ▶ `Section.as`
- ▶ `photos` (folder)
- ▶ `govforms` (folder)
- ▶ `instructions` (folder)

Project:
The main.fla File

The `main.fla` file displays a list of sections with the items each contains. Naturally, this means the `main.fla` will import and parse the `data.xml` file produced in the first project. (I wrote a simple class, `utils.as`, to handle the parsing.)

When users click a section, all the contained items appear. When they click an item, they see options to download or view the selected item. Interestingly, the look and feel of the sections and their contained items is based on a separate `section.swf` that you'll create in the next project. Here you'll assemble the main file that loads those section templates. You'll define how the sections appear, including their sizes and spacing. In addition, you'll write the code that responds to a user selecting a section or an item. You might want to immediately download a selected item, or you might want to display preview information first. The exact behavior is defined here in the `main.fla` file.

STEPS▼
1. Adding the `SectionMaker.as` and `utils.as` class files
2. Creating the `main.fla` file
3. Writing the code

STEP 1▼
Adding the SectionMaker.as and utils.as Class Files

Copy the files `SectionMaker.as` and `utils.as` from the `finished_source` folder you downloaded for this chapter and place copies of the files in your working directory. The `SectionMaker.as` class file handles loading the `section.swf` templates, which you'll create in the following project, and the `utils.as` class file helps parse the `data.xml` file, which you created earlier in this chapter.

STEP 2 ▼
Creating the main.fla File

Open Flash and create a new Flash document. Save it as **main.fla** in your working directory. Onstage, draw a rectangle to visualize where the sections will appear. Although we have only two sections in this sample project, we can support many more. The rectangle can take up most of the stage, but leave room around the sides, top, and bottom of the rectangle for user interface elements such as buttons for Quit, Launch File, and Copy File—which we'll get to later.

Select the rectangle and open the Info panel. Make sure that the upper-left registration option is selected by clicking the upper-left square in the grid of nine squares, as shown in Figure 8.3. Make a note of the x, y, width, and height values of the rectangle as reported by the Info panel; you'll need these values for step 3.

FIGURE 8.3   **The Info panel helps you figure out the exact dimensions of a drawn rectangle.**

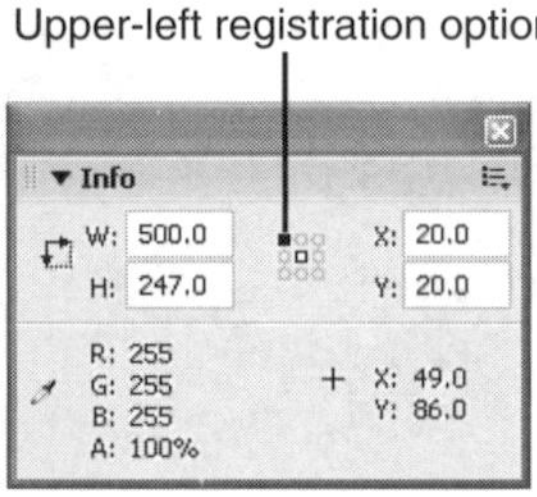

Upper-left registration option

STEP 3 ▼
Writing the Code

Four main tasks are handled in the code of the main.fla file: loading and parsing the XML; creating a SectionMaker instance that displays the sections; capturing and responding to the user interactivity, such as when the user clicks a button; and sending messages to the third-party tool. We'll do the first two—loading and parsing the XML and creating a SectionMaker instance—now. In the next two projects in this chapter, you'll add the second two items: capturing and responding to the user interactivity and sending messages to the third-party tool.

Select the first keyframe, open the Actions panel, and type the code shown in Listing 8.3 (which you can copy from the main_project2.fla in the finished_source folder you downloaded for this chapter).

Line 11 begins loading the XML file and then, when the XML is loaded, line 8 calls the utils.parseXML() method. The results of the XML are turned into an array (fileData) full of Section.as objects, each of which contains an item array full of Item.as objects.

When the XML is finished loading, the proceed() function creates the holder movie clip and then creates an instance of the SectionMaker class. You can see that there are 10 parameters—notice that the all-uppercase variable parameters describe the visual layout for the sections. The first parameter is simply the movie clip that will contain the sections, and the second parameter is the fileData array full of sections extracted from the XML. Notice that the third parameter, CONTENT_AREA, is a Rectangle instance that should match the dimensions and position of the rectangle you drew in step 2. In this example, my values in line 17 (20, 20, 500, and 247) are for a 500 × 247 rectangle whose upper-left corner is at position 20x,20y. The SectionMaker class lays out the sections to fit within this rectangle. The rest of the uppercase parameters provide additional details to the SectionMaker class, as shown in Figure 8.4. Note that Figure 8.4 diagrams a situation that has 9 sections. It also demonstrates how a MAX_ROWS_PER_COLUMN value of 5 will make the second column start after 5 sections. The SectionMaker class is smart enough to know when it has to start a new column, but the MAX_ROWS_PER_COLUMN parameter lets you control the maximum number of rows per column and thereby control how many columns appear. For example, if there were 6 <section> nodes in your XML file, you might want 2 columns of 3 sections instead of 1 column of 6 sections; in that case, you could set MAX_ROWS_PER_COLUMN to 3. In Listing 8.3 and Figure 8.4, the SectionMaker class would have placed six sections in the first row because that's how many would fit in the given rectangle. However, because we set the MAX_ROWS_PER_COLUMN variable to 5, the second column started with the sixth section.

LISTING 8.3 This Code Loads the XML and Tells the SectionMaker Class How to Assemble the Main Screen

```
1   var sectionMaker:SectionMaker;
2   var fileData:Array;
3
4   //XML===========
5   var myXML:XML = new XML();
6   myXML.ignoreWhite = true;
7   myXML.onLoad = function(success:Boolean) {
8       fileData = utils.parseXML(this);
9       proceed();
10  };
11  myXML.load('data.xml');
12
13  //SECTION MAKER: ===========
14  function proceed() {
15      delete myXML;
16      var CONTENT_AREA:flash.geom.Rectangle =
17      new flash.geom.Rectangle(20, 20, 500, 247);
18      var COLUMN_WIDTH:Number = 240;
19      var SPACE_BETWEEN_COLUMNS:Number = 20;
20      var SPACE_BETWEEN_ROWS:Number = 2;
21      var ROW_HEIGHT:Number = 30;
22      var MAX_ROWS_PER_COLUMN:Number = Number.MAX_VALUE;
23      var TRANSITION_SPEED:Number = 0;
24      var holderClip:MovieClip =
        createEmptyMovieClip("holderClip", 0);
25      sectionMaker = new SectionMaker( holderClip,
26                                       fileData,
27                                       CONTENT_AREA,
28                                       COLUMN_WIDTH,
29                                       SPACE_BETWEEN_COLUMNS,
30                                       SPACE_BETWEEN_ROWS,
```

continues

LISTING 8.3   Continued

```
31          ROW_HEIGHT,
32          MAX_ROWS_PER_COLUMN,
33          TRANSITION_SPEED,
34          "section_simple.swf" );
35   }
```

Finally, notice that the last parameter, `section_simple.swf`, is the `section.swf` template that we'll create in the next project. After you create additional `section.swf` templates, you can replace this value so it points to any `.swf` template you create.

Save your `main.fla` file.

Project:
Section Templates

Initially, each `section.swf` appears in its collapsed form with just the section name showing. When the user clicks the section name, it expands to display the contained items. You can customize these section and item names in any way you want. For example, you don't have to display the section and item names as text; you can use graphics instead. The `section_animated.swf` template you build in this project displays an icon next to each item that matches its extension (`.pdf` or `.jpg`). The `SectionMaker` class handles most of the display for each `section.swf` template. It also ensures that the content in the section doesn't appear outside the content area by using the `scrollRect` property, which is equivalent to masking. Your `section.swf` templates simply have to support the minimum set of methods defined in the formal interface file, `ISection.as`, that each template must implement. Those required methods are `init()`, `expand()`, `collapse()`, `getExpandedHeight()`, and `getCollapsedHeight()`, and they appear in the code samples for this project.

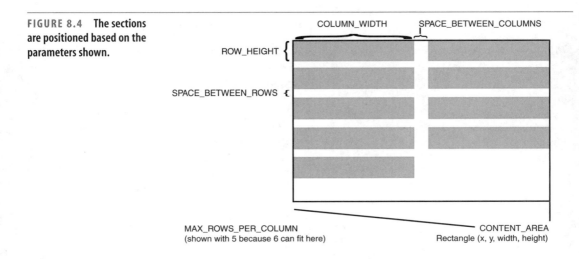

FIGURE 8.4   The sections are positioned based on the parameters shown.

COLUMN_WIDTH   SPACE_BETWEEN_COLUMNS

ROW_HEIGHT

SPACE_BETWEEN_ROWS

MAX_ROWS_PER_COLUMN
(shown with 5 because 6 can fit here)

CONTENT_AREA
Rectangle (x, y, width, height)

STEPS▼

1. **Assembling the** `section_simple.fla` **file**
2. **Writing the code**
3. **Testing the simple template**
4. **Creating the** `section_animated.swf` **template**
5. **Modifying the code in** `section_animated.fla`
6. **Modifying** `main.fla` **to point to** `section_animate.swf`
7. **Designing the** `section_static.swf` **template**
8. **Building the** `section_static.swf` **template**
9. **Writing the code for the** `section_static.fla` **file**
10. **Modifying** `main.fla` **to point to** `section_static.swf`

STEP 1▼
Assembling the section_simple.fla File

For each section you'll need to create the text and layout, a button for the user to click that expands and collapses the section, plus a button for each contained item. Create a new Flash movie and save it as **section_simple.fla** in your working directory. Select Modify, Document and set the dimensions of the stage to 200 × 50. The dimensions are actually unimportant because the `SectionMaker` class resizes the `section.swf` templates to fit

their allotted space. However, setting your `.fla` file's dimensions close to what you expect the final size to be makes it easier to lay out the text and graphics.

Use the Text tool to create a block of text that will contain the name of the section, close to the upper-left corner of the stage. Use the Properties panel to set the text type to Dynamic Text and the instance name to **section_txt**. Be sure that the Selectable option is disabled, as shown in Figure 8.5.

Now we'll create the background for the section. It will be a filled rectangle the user will be able to click to expand or collapse the section. Draw a rectangle shape with no stroke. Select the rectangle and then select Modify, Convert to Symbol. Name the symbol **section_back** and make sure that the Movie Clip option is selected and that the upper-left registration option is selected; then click OK. Use the Properties panel to give the instance, now on the stage, the instance name **section_back**—there's nothing wrong with an instance name that matches the symbol's name. With the `section_back` instance still selected, choose Modify, Arrange, Send to Back. (You could also create additional layers to achieve the same result—just make sure that the `section_back` instance is behind the text.)

FIGURE 8.5 The `section_txt` **Dynamic Text** field is not selectable; if it were, that would turn the cursor into an I-beam and conflict with users trying to click the button.

Selectable option disabled

To graphically show which section is currently expanded, we'll create a triangle that either points to the right (when the section is collapsed) or points down (when the section is open). In a blank area of the stage, draw a triangle that points to the right. Select it and select Modify, Convert to Symbol. Name the symbol **arrow**, make sure that the Movie Clip option is selected, and then click OK. Position it to the left of the `section_txt` field; then double-click the arrow to edit its contents. Click frame 2 and insert a keyframe by pressing F6. Select the triangle shape in frame 2 and use the Free Transform tool to rotate it so that it's pointing down. Return to the main Timeline and be sure to give the arrow the instance name **arrow**.

That's it for how the user views and interacts with the section. Now we can assemble a clip that behaves as an item. Select Insert, New Symbol and name the new symbol **item**. Make sure the Movie Clip option is selected. Before you click OK, select the Export for ActionScript check box from the Linkage area (if that portion of the dialog box is not visible, click the Advanced button). The Export in First Frame option is also selected, which is what you want. The Identifier field should also read item, as shown in Figure 8.6. Click OK.

You'll be taken inside the `item` symbol. Draw a filled rectangle and use the Info panel to set its height to 18, its width to something larger than the column width (which was 240 in line 18 of Listing 8.3), and its x and y values both to 0. Use the Text tool and create a block of text within the rectangle shape. Use a font size around 10 points. Make sure that this text field is set to Dynamic Text and has an instance name of **item_txt**. Also ensure that the text's Selectable option is *not* enabled.

FIGURE 8.6 The `item` symbol must have the Export for ActionScript option enabled and have an identifier of `item`.

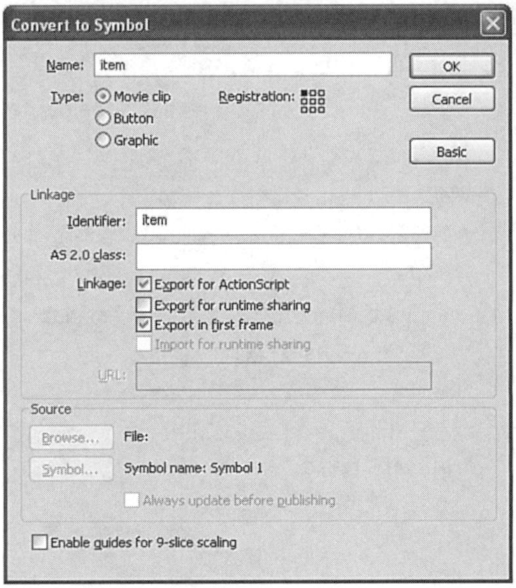

That's it for assembling the `section_simple.fla` file. You don't need to drag an instance of the `item` symbol onto the stage because that is handled using the `attachMovie()` method in the next step.

STEP 2▼
Writing the Code

Make sure you're in the main timeline of the `section_simple.fla` file and select the first keyframe. Open the Actions panel and type the code in Listing 8.4, which can also be found in the `section_simple.fla` file in the `finished_source` folder you downloaded for this chapter; you can copy and paste the code from that file to your working version of `section_simple.fla` if you want to avoid typing.

```
1    var controller:SectionMaker;
2    var section:Section;
3    var myWidth:Number;
4    var myHeight:Number;
5    var expandedHeight:Number;
6
7    section_txt.autoSize = true;
8    section_txt.text = "";
9    arrow.stop();
10
11   //required
12   function init( p_controller:SectionMaker,
13                  p_section:Section,
14                  p_width:Number,
15                  p_height:Number){
16
17      controller = p_controller;
18      section = p_section;
19      myWidth = p_width;
20      myHeight = p_height;
21
22      var itemClip:MovieClip =
         createEmptyMovieClip( "itemClip", 0 );
23      var ITEM_HEIGHT = 18;
24      var total = section.items.length;
25      for(var i = 0; i<total; i++){
26         var thisItem:MovieClip =
            itemClip.attachMovie( "item", "item" + i, i );
27
28         //stuff the data into the clip:
29         thisItem.itemData = section.items[i];
30
31         //layout/populate the clip:
32         thisItem._y = myHeight + (i * ITEM_HEIGHT);
33         thisItem.item_txt.autoSize = true;
34         thisItem.item_txt.text = section.items[i].name;
35
36         //set up callbacks
37         thisItem.onPress = function(){
38            controller.pickItem(this.itemData);
39         }
40         thisItem.onRollOver = function(){
41            controller.rollItem(this.itemData);
42         }
43         thisItem.onRollOut = function(){
44            controller.rollItem(undefined);
45         }
```

continues

LISTING 8.4   Continued

```
46      }
47
48      //figure out max height:
49      expandedHeight = thisItem._y + thisItem._height;
50
51      //populuate the section
52      section_txt.text = section.name;
53
54      //resize the section
55      section_back._width = myWidth;
56      section_back._height = myHeight;
57
58      //callbacks for the back
59      section_back.onPress = function(){
60          controller.pickSection(section);
61      }
62      section_back.onRollOver = function(){
63          controller.rollSection(section);
64      }
65      section_back.onRollOut = function(){
66          controller.rollSection(undefined);
67      }
68  }
69  //required
70  function expand(){
71      arrow.gotoAndStop(2);
72  }
73  //required
74  function collapse(){
75      arrow.gotoAndStop(1);
76  }
77  //required
78  function getExpandedHeight():Number{
79      return expandedHeight;
80  }
81  //required
82  function getCollapsedHeight():Number{
83      return myHeight;
84  }
```

I suppose that this code is a tad involved, considering this is the "simple" version—the more advanced templates build on this code. The init() function is called by the SectionMaker when this clip is fully loaded, and the SectionMaker class loads as many instances of the section.swf template as you have sections. The parameters received are saved because they all contain important information—namely, a reference to the SectionMaker class (controller), the instance of the Section.as class chocked full

CHAPTER 8: Creating a CD-ROM Front End

of information (`section`), and the width and height allotted to this `section.swf` template (`myWidth` and `myHeight`). After saving the parameters, I create a single clip called `itemClip` in line 22. All the instances of the `item` symbol (one for each item in the section) appear inside `itemClip`. The `for` loop started on line 25 does the following for each item: It creates an instance of the item symbol (line 26), stuffs the entire `Item.as` object into a homemade property called `itemData` (line 29), positions the item based on the height specified in line 23, and populates the `item_txt` field. Finally, a callbacks are set to tell the `controller` which item was clicked or rolled over. Lines 51–67 affect the `section_text` and `section_back` instances in a similar manner as the items.

Before moving on to the section name, notice what happens on line 49: Saved into the `expandedHeight` variable is the total height of the `itemClip` (or the `_y` value for the bottom of the last item attached to the `itemClip`). This is important because the `SectionMaker` calls `getExpandedHeight()` and `getCollapsedHeight()` when it positions all the different sections. Each `section.swf` template has to tell the `SectionMaker` how much height is needed for it to display itself.

Finally, the `expand()` and `collapse()` methods are called by the `SectionMaker` as well. That is, the `SectionMaker` class tells this `section.swf` template when it's being opened or closed. This `section.swf` template simply changes the appearance of the arrow symbol you made in the previous step. So, when expanded, the arrow points down; when collapsed, the arrow points to the right (see Figure 8.7).

The Photographs section is expanded so you see the contained items plus the arrow pointing down.

Before moving on to the next step, select Control, Test Movie to generate the `section_simple.swf` template file. You won't see anything special yet: just the arrow and the `section_back` instance.

STEP 3 ▼
Testing the Simple Template

All you need to test the template you just created is to open `main.fla` and select Control, Test Movie. You can click a section to reveal the contained items and click again to close the section (refer to Figure 8.7). You should also notice that clicking one section closes the other section if it's open. (You'll find a copy of `main.fla` in the `finished_source` folder you downloaded with this chapter.)

Play around with the uppercase parameters in the `SectionMaker()` constructor (lines 16–23 of `main.fla`). You can also see what the template looks like if you add more sections. Just edit the `data.xml` file by copying and pasting more `section` nodes.

All you can do with this template is expand and collapse the sections. In the next project, you'll write code that reacts to when the user selects a section or an item. Already, the section_simple.swf is sending events to the main.fla file when the user interacts; however, the main.fla file just isn't set up to listen for those events yet.

There are still two more section.swf templates I want to show you how to build: one that animates when the section opens or closes and one that uses graphics instead of text.

STEP 4▼
Creating the section_animated.swf Template

Open the section_simple.fla file you created in the first two steps and save it at as section_animated.fla. You're going to make two changes: You'll change the arrow into an animated arrow and a place a graphic icon next to each item that represents its file type.

Double-click the arrow instance so you're editing the timeline of that symbol. You're going to make an animation that, in the first 10 frames, has the arrow rotate from pointing right to pointing down. Then in frames 11–20, the arrow will rotate back. There are many ways to achieve this effect; I'll show you one way. First, right-click frame 2 and select Remove Frames from the context menu. Because we want this animation to be a motion tween and that requires you have a movie clip on the stage, select the arrow shape and press F8 to convert it to a movie clip called arrow shape. Then click frame 10 and inserted a keyframe by pressing F6; click frame 20 and insert a keyframe there by pressing F6 again. Back in frame 10, rotate the arrow shape instance. Select frame 1 and use the Properties panel to set the Tween drop-down menu to Motion. Because we want the animation to stop automatically when it gets to frame 10 (in the middle, where it's pointing down) as well as when it returns to frame 1 after animating from frames 11–20, put a stop() action on the keyframes in frame 1 and frame 10.

For the icon that will appear next to the item's name, select File, Import, Import to Library and select two .jpg files in the source_media folder (acrobat.jpg and photo.jpg). Open the Library window and select the acrobat.jpg item and then either right-click the item and select Linkage from the context menu or use the Library panel's options menu to select Linkage. Select the Export for ActionScript check box, which automatically selects the Export in First Frame option. Set the Identifier option to pdf. Click OK and repeat this step for the photo.jpg item, setting its linkage identifier to jpg. The code to place the icons next to the item text will use Flash 8's new attachBitmap() method. Before Flash 8, you had to place each bitmap into a movie clip before dynamically placing it on the stage.

STEP 5 ▼
Modifying the Code in section_animated.fla

Return to the first frame inside your section_animated.fla file. Select the first keyframe open the Actions panel, and find the expand() method on line 70. Change just that method to read as shown in Listing 8.5. (You can find this code on line 74 in the section_animated.fla file in the finished_source folder you downloaded for this chapter.)

LISTING 8.5 This Replacement Version of the expand() Method Makes the Arrow Animate

```
74   function expand(){
75       arrow.gotoAndPlay(2);
76       var speed = 1;
77       new mx.transitions.Tween( itemClip,
                                    "_alpha",
         mx.transitions.easing.Regular.easeOut,
                                              0,
                                            100,
                                          speed,
                                           true );
78
79       var speed = 0.5;
80       var total = section.items length;
81       for(var i=0; i<total; i++){
82           new mx.transitions.Tween(itemClip["item" + i],
                                        "_x",
                mx.transitions easing.Regular.easeOut,
                                              -30*i,
                                                  0,
                                              speed,
                                               true );
83       }
84   }
```

This code does three things: First, it makes the arrow clip play from frame 2—remember that it stops on its own when it gets to frame 10. Then it starts an alpha tween on the whole `itemClip` symbol, fading it from 0% to 100% opaque. Finally, for each item in the section, it starts a horizontal tween to make the items zoom on from the left. Because the starting point (the fourth parameter in the `Tween()` on line 82) varies (`-30*i`), the top items appear to arrive earlier even though they really all arrive at the same time—some just have a longer trip to their final location.

Also change the `collapse()` method to read as follows to make the arrow un-rotate:

```
function collapse(){
    arrow.gotoAndPlay(11);
}
```

Finally, displaying the icon for each file takes very little code, as shown in Listing 8.6.

Type the three lines in Listing 8.6 anywhere in the `init()` method's `for` loop after the `thisItem` clip is created (namely, after line 26).

Before you continue with step 6, select Control, Test Movie to generate the `section_animated.swf` file to which you'll point to from the main file.

STEP 6▼
Modifying main.fla to Point to section_animate.swf

Open `main.fla`, select the first keyframe, open the Actions panel, and find where you're currently pointing to `section_simple.swf` (line 34). Change that line to read "**section_animated.swf**". (Don't forget that the filename is inside quotation marks.)

Also, set the `TRANSITION_SPEED` parameter on line 23 to `0.5`. Finally, select Modify, Document and set the frame rate to something high, such as 31 fps, so the animation plays more smoothly. Test the movie. You can experiment with different values for the `TRANSITION_SPEED` variable, and you can tweak the speed variable values inside the `section_animated.fla` file's `expand()` method (edited in step 5). There are three animation speeds: the time it takes for the sections to move out of the way (`TRANSITION_SPEED`), the time it takes for the items to fade on (the first speed in `expand()`), and the time it takes for the items to zoom on (the second speed in `expand()`).

You'll find a finished version of this `main.fla` in the `finished_source` folder named `main_project3_uses_animated.fla`.

LISTING 8.6 This Code Attaches the Appropriate Bitmap to Each Item in a Section

```
import flash.display.BitmapData;
var linkage = section.items[i].extension;
thisItem.attachBitmap( BitmapData.loadBitmap(linkage), 0 );
```

Designing the section_static.swf Template

Within your `section.swf` template, you can display the section names and items however you want—even without text (that is, using graphics in place of text labels). As a simple example, recall that you generated the icon graphic dynamically in the `section_animate.swf` template. The template variation you'll make in this step uses graphics for everything. The template is hard-wired in that the `section.swf` template will need to know which sections and items are possible. So, you'll build a graphic for the Photos section and one for the Docs section, as shown in Figure 8.8. If you want to also support additional sections, such as an audio section, you'll have to create that graphic and match it to a specific expected section.

FIGURE 8.8 The static template lets you customize the look for each section. Here, the Photos section is expanded to reveal thumbnails for each item in that section.

STEP 8▼

Building the section_static.swf Template

Open the `section_animated.fla` you created in steps 4 and 5, or grab the one in the `finished_source` folder you downloaded for

this chapter. Select File, Save As and name the copy `section_static.fla`. Delete the text instance `section_txt`. Next, create the graphic for the Photographs section; for now you can just use the Brush tool and write the word *Photos* above the stage. Scale it to be no taller than 30 pixels. In the `main.fla` file, you had set `ROW_HEIGHT` to 30; you can draw your section title larger provided you adjust the `ROW_HEIGHT` value in `main.fla`. Select the Photos drawn shape and either select Modify, Convert to Symbol or press F8. Name the symbol **Sections**, select the Movie Clip option, and then click OK. Use the Properties panel to give the instance of the Sections symbol, now on the stage, the instance name **section_graphic**. Position the symbol at 0x,0y; then double-click the instance of the Sections symbol (`section_graphic`) so you can edit its contents. Click frame 1 and use the Properties panel to give it the label **Photographs**. Click frame 2 while still inside the Sections symbol, and press F7 to insert a blank keyframe. Use the Brush tool to draw the word *Docs* in frame 2. Select the second keyframe and use the Properties panel to give it a frame label of **Documents**. Now the two labels match what's in the XML file.

> **★ NOTE**
>
> If you have many sections, you might consider adding an attribute to the `section` node of the XML file, as shown in step 3 of the first project in this chapter, "XML Document That Identifies All Files." For example, you might want to add an attribute called `framenum`, where you can specify which frame in the Sections symbol to use. That way, you won't have to label every frame.

From the Library panel, double-click to edit the contents of the `item` symbol. Select the item_txt field and delete it. Next, select the background rectangle and use the Properties panel to set its height to 100 pixels. Name the sole layer **background** and lock that layer. Insert a new layer and name it **icons**. Select File, Import, Import to Stage and select all the images in the source_media folder with names starting with icon_. Position the thumbnails of the sunset and the dog anywhere you like on top of the background rectangle. I recommend keeping the dog icon on the left because it's listed first in the XML file simply to make troubleshooting easier. (Don't go farther to the right than the COLUMN_WIDTH you plan on using in the main.fla, which is currently 240 pixels.) Select the other icons (not the dog and sunset); select Edit, Cut (or press Ctrl+X); click frame 2 of the icons layer; and press F7 to insert it. Now select Edit, Paste or press Ctrl+V. Position these icons anywhere on the rectangle, although it's easiest if the order in which you arrange the icons matches the order they're listed in the XML: f1040sse, i1040sse, and f1040ez.

Select the cell in frame 2 of the background layer and press F5 to insert a frame. Lock all the layers and then add a third layer named **buttons**. Next, we'll create an invisible button to place on top of each item thumbnail. In frame 1 of the buttons layer, draw a square shape. Select it and select Modify, Convert to Symbol. Name the symbol **Invisible** and be sure to select the Button option (not the Movie Clip option); then click OK. Double-click the invisible button symbol you just made to edit its contents, and then move the shape to the Hit frame by clicking once on the first keyframe. Click again, drag to the right, and let go on the hit state. The invisible button's frames should look like those shown in Figure 8.9.

FIGURE 8.9   A button with nothing except a shape in its Hit frame is an invisible button.

Return to the contents of the item symbol by clicking item or the left-pointing blue arrow in the Edit bar. You should see an instance of the Invisible button as a translucent blue square. Position and resize it to cover the dog thumbnail icon. Use the Properties panel to give this button an instance name **b0**. Copy and paste the button, position the duplicate on top of the sunset thumbnail icon, and name this button instance **b1**. Click frame 3 of the buttons layer and press F6 to insert a keyframe. Adding a keyframe copies the two invisible buttons you just aligned in frame 1. Those two invisible buttons are probably not aligned with the first two document thumbnails, so line them up. Also, copy the Invisible button to make a third instance on the third document; name the third instance **b2**.

The last step is to make frame labels to match the section names. Select any keyframe in frame 1 and use the Properties panel to specify a frame label of **Photographs**. Give frame 2 the frame label **Documents**.

That was a lot of mousing around. The idea, really, is that you can hard-wire any graphics you want into the template file.

STEP 9▼
Writing the Code for the section_static.fla File

Make sure you're in the main timeline of section_static.fla. Select the first keyframe, open the Actions panel, and type the code shown in Listing 8.7. (You might want to copy the code from the section_static.fla in the finished_source folder you downloaded for this chapter and paste it into your working version of the section_static.fla file.)

LISTING 8.7 This Code Presents the Hard-wired Sections and Items

```
1   var controller:SectionMaker;
2   var section:Section;
3   var myWidth:Number;
4   var myHeight:Number;
5   var expandedHeight:Number;
6
7   section_graphic._visible = false;
8   arrow.stop();
9
10  //required
11  function init( p_controller:SectionMaker,
                   p_section:Section,
                   p_width:Number,
                   p_height:Number ){
12
13      controller = p_controller;
14      section = p_section;
15      myWidth = p_width;
16      myHeight = p_height;
17
18      var itemClip:MovieClip =
        attachMovie("item", "itemClip", 0);
19      itemClip._y = myHeight;
20      //jump to the section frame with the thumbnails:
21      itemClip.gotoAndStop(section.name);
22
23      //define the button behaviors:
24      var total = section.items.length;
25      for(var i = 0; i<total; i++){
26          //reference the button we know is there:
27          var thisButton = itemClip["b"+i];
28          //stuff the data into the button:
29          thisButton.itemData = section.items[i];
30
31          thisButton.onPress = function(){
32              controller.pickItem(this.itemData);
```

continues

LISTING 8.7 Continued

```
33              }
34              thisButton.onRollOver = function(){
35                  controller.rollItem(this.itemData);
36              }
37              thisButton.onRollOut = function(){
38                  controller.rollItem(undefined);
39              }
40          }
41
42          //figure out max height:
43          var ITEM_HEIGHT = 100;
44          expandedHeight = myHeight + ITEM_HEIGHT;
45
46          //section graphic
47          section_graphic._visible = true;
48          section_graphic.gotoAndStop(section.name);
49
50          //section back
51          section_back._width = myWidth;
52          section_back._height = myHeight;
53          section_back.onPress = function(){
54              controller.pickSection(section);
55          }
56          section_back.onRollOver = function(){
57              controller.rollSection(section);
58          }
59          section_back.onRollOut = function(){
60              controller.rollSection(undefined);
61          }
62      }
63      //required
64      function expand(){
65          arrow.gotoAndPlay(2);
66          var speed = 1;
67          new mx.transitions.Tween( itemClip,
                                       "_alpha",
        mx.transitions.easing.Regular.easeOut,
                                           0,
                                           100,
                                           speed,
                                           true );
68      }
69      //required
70      function collapse(){
71          arrow.gotoAndPlay(11);
72      }
73      //required
74      function getExpandedHeight():Number{
75          return expandedHeight;
```

LISTING 8.7	Continued	76	}
		77	//required
		78	function getCollapsedHeight():Number{
		79	return myHeight;
		80	}

Let me point out the differences in this code from that of previous projects. First, we don't create an empty clip and attach a bunch of `item` symbols to it; rather, we attach one `item` symbol (line 18) and go to the frame that matches the section name (line 21). The loop started on line 25 simply defines the behavior for all the buttons (b0–b*n*). The `expandedHeight` is calculated on lines 43–44 based on the fact that we set the `item` symbol to be 100 pixels tall. Instead of populating the `section_txt` field, which is gone in this version of the template code, we just jump to the appropriate frame in the `section_graphic` instance (line 48).

The only other difference is that the `expand()` method applies a tween only to the `itemClip`—and not to the individual items.

Before you go on to the next step, be sure to select Control, Test Movie to generate the `section_static.swf` file, which you'll point to from the main file.

STEP 10 ▼
Modifying main.fla to Point to section_static.swf

Open `main.fla`, select the first keyframe, open the Actions panel, and find where you're currently pointing to `section_animated.swf` (line 34). Change that line to read **section_static.swf**. (Don't forget that the filename is inside quotation marks.)

Again, you can tweak the parameters. For example, the `Sections` symbol in my `section_static.fla` file was 50 pixels tall, so I had to modify the `ROW_HEIGHT` parameter to equal 50.

You'll find a finished version of this `main.fla` in the `finished_source` folder named `main_project3_uses_static.fla`. Figure 8.10 shows what I see when I test `main.fla` with my rough section graphics.

FIGURE 8.10 Although my example is messy, the `section_static.swf` template lets you customize the section and items within a section.

Now that you've made three `section.swf` template variations, check out a couple more variations I produced— `section_static_custom.fla` and `section_custom.fla`. Both are found in the `finished_source` folder you downloaded for this chapter. The `section_static_custom.fla` template is similar to the `section_static.fla` you just produced, except it's much more graphically pleasing (refer to Figure 8.8). The `section_custom.fla` template uses the

BevelFilter class to make the buttons stand out. It also highlights the currently selected item. That's the template used in the opening figure at the top of the chapter.

Project:
Listeners in the main.fla File

The projects we've worked on so far in this chapter have created code that makes the sections open and close to reveal and hide the list of the items each section contains. All the code for rollovers and clicks executed by the user of the CD-ROM front end in the `section.swf` templates are directed to their *controller* (that is, to the `SectionMaker` class). The `main.fla file` can also listen for those user events if you add event listeners to the `main.fla` file. By making the main file listen for mouse clicks and rollovers, we can do something when the user selects a section or an item.

In this project, you'll add a text prompt area that changes as the user rolls over sections and items. In addition, when the user clicks an item, you'll display buttons for launch and copy. When we finally add the swf2exe code in the next project, it will be a piece of cake to make those buttons really launch or copy external files.

STEPS▼

1. Adding user interface elements to `main.fla`
2. Writing ActionScript that listens for user events
3. Adding code to respond to user events

STEP 1▼
Adding User Interface Elements to main.fla

In the `main.fla` file, use the Text tool to add three dynamic text fields with the following instance names: **currentSection_txt**, **download_txt**, and **launch_txt**. Both `download_txt` and `launch_txt` should be set to Multiline in the drop-down on the Properties panel. Also, none of the three text fields should be selectable. See Figure 8.11 for the layout I used. The main objective is simply to place these user interface elements outside the rectangle where the sections will appear.

FIGURE 8.11 You can add user interface elements around the outside of the rectangle where all the sections appear.

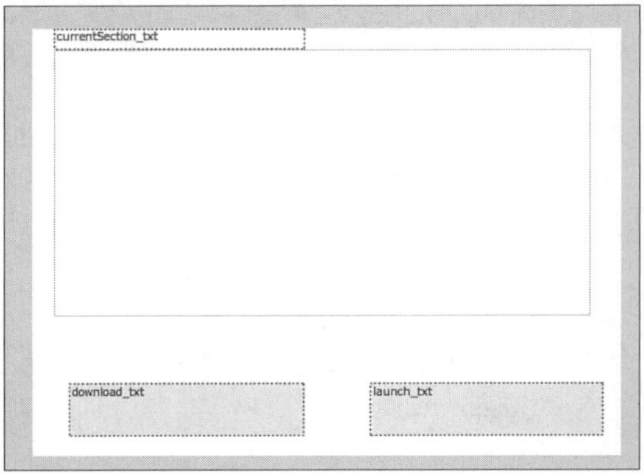

Create an invisible button as you did in step 8 of the preceding project (refer to Figure 8.9). Position the invisible button on top of the `download_txt` field; name the button instance **download_btn**. Drag another instance of the invisible button and place it on top of the `launch_txt` field. Name this instance of the invisible button **launch_btn**. When the dynamic text fields change to read something like click here to download the file, the user can click these invisible buttons.

rollItem—all of which are broadcast from the SectionMaker class. In the next step, you set up the functions that handle those four events.

STEP 2▼
Writing ActionScript That Listens for User Events

You can add event listeners to the SectionMaker after you have an instance of the class. Select the first keyframe in main.fla and open the Actions panel. Find the proceed() function and insert the code in Listing 8.8 at the end of the function, after you call the new SectionMaker() constructor.

This code sets up listeners for four events—pickSection, pickItem, rollSection, and

STEP 3▼
Adding Code to Respond to User Events

Type the code in Listing 8.9 after all the existing code in the main.fla file (you can find this code following line 40 in the main_project4.fla file, located in the finished_source folder if you want to copy and paste it instead of typing it all from scratch).

LISTING 8.8 This Code Adds Four Listeners to the sectionMaker **Instance**

```
sectionMaker.addEventListener("pickSection",this);
sectionMaker.addEventListener("pickItem", this);
sectionMaker.addEventListener("rollSection", this);
sectionMaker.addEventListener("rollItem", this);
```

LISTING 8.9 This Code Handles Displaying Text for Rollovers and Buttons

```
41   //UI STUFF   (added in project 4)
42   var rollover_fmt:TextFormat = new TextFormat();
43   rollover_fmt.font = "Arial";
44   rollover_fmt.size = 12;
45
46   var rollover_txt:TextField =
     createTextField("rollover_txt",1,0,0,0,0);
47   rollover_txt.setNewTextFormat(rollover_fmt);
48   rollover_txt.autoSize = true
49   rollover_txt.selectable = false;
50   rollover_txt.background = true;
51   rollover_txt.backgroundColor = 0xFFFFCC;
52   hideTooltip();
53
54   launch_btn._visible = false;
55   launch_txt.text = "";
56
```

continues

LISTING 8.9   **Continued**

```
57      download_btn._visible = false;
58      download_txt.text = "";
59
60      currentSection_txt.text = "";
61      var currentBasePath:String;
62
63      function rollSection(evt) {
64          if ( evt.data == undefined ){
65              hideTooltip();
66          }else{
67              showTooltip("section: "+evt.data.name);
68          }
69      }
70      function pickSection(evt) {
71          launch_btn._visible = false;
72          launch_txt.text = "";
73
74          download_btn._visible = false;
75          download_txt.text = "";
76
77          if( evt.data == undefined ){
78              currentSection_txt.text = "";
79          }else{
80              currentSection_txt.text = evt.data.name;
81              //hold base path now...
82              currentBasePath = evt.data.basepath;
83          }
84      }
85      function rollItem(evt) {
86          if ( evt.data == undefined ){
87              hideTooltip();
88          }else{
89              showTooltip("item: "+evt.data.name);
90          }
91      }
92      function pickItem(evt) {
93          launch_btn._visible = true;
94          launch_txt.text = "launch: "+evt.data.filename;
95          launch_btn.onPress = function(){
96              trace( "LAUNCHING "+
                          currentBasePath+evt.data.filename);
97          }
98
99          download_btn._visible = true;
100         download_txt.text = "download: "+evt.data.filename;
101         download_btn.onPress = function(){
102             trace( "DOWNLOADING "+
                          currentBasePath+evt.data.filename);
103         }
```

CHAPTER 8: **Creating a CD-ROM Front End**

LISTING 8.9 Continued

```
104    }
105    function hideTooltip(){
106        rollover_txt._visible = false;
107    }
108    function showTooltip(theText:String){
109        rollover_txt._visible = true;
110        rollover_txt.text = theText;
111        rollover_txt._x = _xmouse + 5;
112        rollover_txt._y = _ymouse + 5;
113    }
```

Lines 41–51 create the `rollover_txt` field dynamically, which is necessary to make it appear above the `holderClip` in level 0—the clip into which the `SectionMaker` class creates instances of your `section.swf` template. You can see the `hideToolTip()` and `showTooltip()` methods at the end in lines 105–113.

The primary functions are `rollSection()`, `pickSection()`, `rollItem()`, and `pickItem()`. They're triggered whenever the `SectionMaker` receives notices from the `section.swf` template. The roll functions simply result in displaying or hiding the ToolTip. Clicking a section causes the buttons `launch_btn` and `download_btn` to hide and the `currentSection_txt` field to display the name of the current section. We also save the section's basepath in line 82 so that it's available later when the user clicks an item.

Test the movie and you'll see that, when the `pickItem()` method is called, the `launch_btn` and `download_btn` buttons are revealed, along with text that explains what will happen when the user clicks either of them (see Figure 8.12). The `trace()` statements on lines 96 and 102 will be replaced with calls to our swf2exe tool in the next project, but currently they only trace what should happen.

FIGURE 8.12 The project looks more complete with the added interface elements.

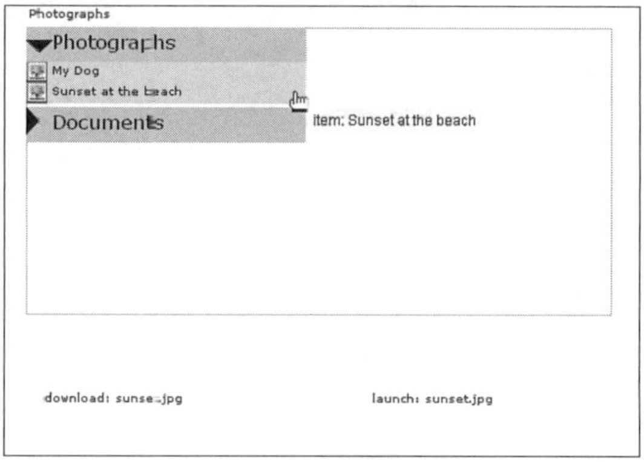

Project: Third-party Product Integration

Perhaps it's ironic that we're getting to the third-party products this late in the chapter, but when you see how little work is necessary to implement them, I think you'll agree that all the ground work we did in the projects leading up to this point was worth the effort.

STEPS▼

1. **Copying the support files**
2. **Instantiating the** `ThirdParty.as` **class**
3. **Triggering the** `ThirdParty` **class's** `openFile()` **and** `doSaveAs()` **methods**

STEP 1▼
Copying the Support Files

Go into the `finished_source` folder and copy the following six files, which you downloaded for this chapter:

▶ `ThirdParty.as`

▶ `IProduct.as`

▶ `SWFStudio.as`

▶ `Screenweaver.as`

▶ `Zinc.as`

▶ `mProjector.as`

Paste these files into your working directory. If you plan on using a different third-party

swf2exe maker, you'll have to make a class for that tool that implements the interface file `IProduct.as` (as do the four product classes `SWFStudio.as`, `Screenweaver.as`, `Zinc.as`, and `mProjector.as`). In addition, you should add a case statement inside the `ThirdParty.as` class file's constructor. See the "Exploring the Class Files" section at the end of this chapter for more information.

STEP 2▼
Instantiating the ThirdParty.as Class

Inside your `main.fla` file, select the first keyframe, open the Actions panel, and type the code in Listing 8.10 at the end of all the existing code (you can find this code in the `main_project5.fla` file in the `finished_source` folder if you want to copy and paste the code instead of typing it all from scratch).

LISTING 8.10 **This Code Creates an Instance of the** `ThirdParty` **Class**

```
124    var thirdParty:ThirdParty =
       new ThirdParty( "SWFStudio", this );
125
126    thirdParty.addEventListener("isExtensionRegistered", this);
127
128    var canSupport = new Object();
129    function isExtensionRegistered(evt){
130        canSupport[evt.parameter] = evt.result;
131    }
132    thirdParty.isExtensionRegistered("pdf");
133    thirdParty.isExtensionRegistered("jpg");
134
135    quit_btn.onPress = function(){
136        thirdParty.doQuit();
137    }
```

Amazingly, if you're only going to call *synchronous* operations (those that can happen instantly), you only need the first line of code! In the case of the code in Listing 8.8, I'm using SWFStudio V3, which is why that first parameter is `"SWFStudio"`. You can change that to `"Screenweaver"`, `"Zinc"`, or `"mProjector"` because all three are supported in the `ThirdParty.as` file.

If the user clicks the Quit button, notice how the `quit_btn` makes the application quit. You have to make an invisible button with the instance name `quit_btn` and a text label that reads *Quit*, as I did in the `main_project5.fla` file in the `finished_source` folder. The quit statement reads `thirdParty.doQuit()` (line 136). Depending on which third-party tool you're using, the exact code inside the class that implements the `IProduct` interface will vary, but our main file doesn't care—it just says "doQuit()".

Each third-party product must support four methods: `doQuit()`, `openFile()`, `doSaveAs()`, and `isExtensionRegistered()`. The only method that's *asynchronous* is `isExtensionRegistered()`. So, you can't just call this function in the following way:

```
result = thirdParty.
isExtensionRegistered("pdf");
```

Instead, you must have a *listener* that waits for the result. That's why line 126 adds the event listener, which appears in lines 129–131. Lines 132 and 133 check to see whether .pdf and .jpg files are supported on the user's machine. You can add more file types, such as .xls Excel files. When the results are returned to the listener, the `canSupport` object is populated; this variable will look like this if the user can view both file types:

```
{pdf: true, jpg: true}
```

What's cool, though, is that you can just check the value for `canSupport["pdf"]`; if it returns `true`, the user can view Acrobat files.

STEP 3 ▼
Triggering the ThirdParty Class's openFile() and doSaveAs() Methods

Find the code in the `main.fla` file where you're currently tracing instead of actually launching or copying files. Inside the `pickItem()` function are two `onPress` declarations. Modify the `pickItem()` method to appear as shown in Listing 8.11.

LISTING 8.11 This Updated Version of the pickItem **Function Directs Clicks to the** thirdParty **Instance**

```
function pickItem(evt) {
    if ( canSupport[evt.data.extension] ){
        launch_btn._visible = true;
        launch_txt.text = "launch: "+evt.data.filename;
        launch_btn.onPress = function(){
            trace('LAUNCHING '+currentBasePath+evt.data.filename);
            thirdParty.openFile(currentBasePath+evt.data.filename);
        }
```

continues

LISTING 8.11 Continued

```
                                          }else{
                                              launch_txt.text = "Your system can't support " +
                                                                 evt.data.extension +
                                                                 " files";
                                          }

                                          download_btn._visible = true;
                                          download_txt.text = "download: "+evt.data.filename;
                                          download_btn.onPress = function(){
                                              trace("DOWNLOADING "+currentBasePath+evt.data.filename);
                                              thirdParty.doSaveAs(currentBasePath+evt.data.filename);
                                          }
                                      }
```

Now the `thirdParty` instance's `openFile()` and `doSaveAs()` methods are triggered when the user clicks the Launch or Download button. However, the user won't even see the `launch_btn` unless her computer can support that file type.

None of the third-party code actually does anything while you're testing, which is a good reason to leave in the trace statements. You can select Control, Test Movie to see this functionality working. Notice the additional trace statements that appear because I added them to the various support files.

Be sure to select Control, Test Movie to generate your final `main.swf file`. Figure 8.13 shows how this version populates the Launch and Download buttons.

FIGURE 8.15 Now the user will see a Download and a Launch button, provided the file type is supported on her computer.

Project: Stub Application

In this project, you'll build a `stub.exe` file that does nothing more than immediately jump to your `main.swf` neatly stored in a folder named `data`. You'll be able to distribute this `stub.exe` to anyone, even if they don't have the Flash player. Plus, the `stub.exe` will enable the third-party tool you're using to support additional features not in Flash—namely, copying and launching external files.

1. Preparing the file structure
2. Creating the `stub.fla` **file**
3. Building the projector

STEP 1▼
Preparing the File Structure

Create a new folder named **ROOT**; this will become the root of the CD-ROM you burn. Inside ROOT, create a folder named **data**. Copy (don't move) your working files into the data folder. You don't need the .fla or .as files, but you do need the main.swf file, whichever section.swf template you're using, the data.xml file, and the folders of data files (photos, govforms, and instructions).

Obviously, you don't need to distribute your source files on the CD-ROM. It's nice to have duplicates of all your .swf files inside the ROOT/data folder because if you need to edit the source, you can make changes, do as many test movies as you need to, and then finally overwrite the corresponding .swf file with the final version of the file in the data folder.

STEP 2▼
Creating the stub.fla File

The exact code to get from the stub.fla file for a specific third-party product to your main.swf file in the data folder varies by product. I've included a stub file for each of the four third-party products listed at the beginning of this project. Find the appropriate stub_*PRODUCTNAME*.fla file for the product

you are using in the starter_files folder you downloaded for this chapter and copy it to the ROOT folder—not inside the data folder. Rename the file **stub.fla**.

Open the stub.fla file and select Control, Test Movie to produce the stub.swf file.

> 📌 **NOTE**
>
> The stub.fla **file basically just jumps into the** main.swf **file in the** data **folder. However, it also resets the base path so that calls made from your** main.swf **file resolve to the** data **folder (and not one folder up to the** ROOT **folder). For situations in which relative paths still fail, the** stub.fla **file also sets the variable** _global.rootURL **to the full path of the** data **folder. This arrangement is required by several third-party tools when they copy a file from the CD because they need a full path. Most of the time, this path is** D:\data\ **because** D **is the CD-ROM drive letter.**

STEP 3▼
Building the Projector

Open your third-party swf2exe program and select the stub.swf file as the main file. You can also replace the default .exe icon by pointing to the projector_icon.ico file inside the starter_files folder (or one that you produce yourself). As discussed at the beginning of this chapter, the swf2exe tools supported by this project have a lot of other options such as displaying in full screen and so on.

Build the project to generate a projector with the filename stub.exe. You can rename that file if you want. For example, in SWF Studio you click the Build button as shown in Figure 8.14.

FIGURE 8.14 The final
step is building a projector
using your third-party tool.

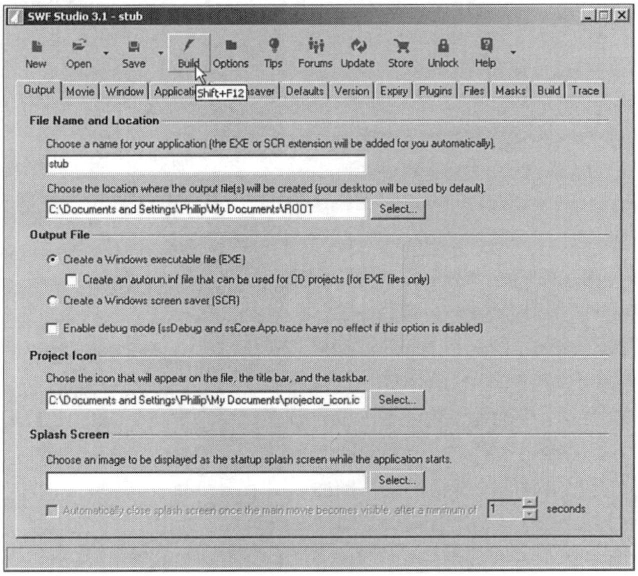

Copy the entire ROOT folder to another
machine if you can, or just burn a CD-ROM
and test the application extensively.

Project:
Auto-play Functionality

This is probably the easiest project in the
whole book. Here I'll show you how to make
the stub.exe file run as soon as the user
inserts the CD-ROM into his drive, provided
that the user hasn't disabled the auto-run
feature on his computer.

STEPS▼

1. **Creating the** autorun.inf **file**
2. **Copying the files**

STEP 1▼
Creating the autorun.inf File

Use Notepad to create a text file, name it
AUTORUN.INF, and save in the ROOT folder adjacent to the stub.exe file. In the AUTORUN.INF
file, enter the following text:

```
[autorun]
open=stub.exe
icon=cd_icon.ico
```

STEP 2▼
Copying the Files

Create your own icon file or copy the
cd_icon.ico file from the starter_files
folder and paste it in the ROOT directory. You
don't have to rebuild your stub.exe, just

include these two files (AUTORUN.INF and cd_icon.ico) in the root of the CD-ROM you burn. Figure 8.15 shows the file layout.

FIGURE 8.15 The AUTORUN.INF file gives the user's CD-ROM drive the icon in the cd_icon.ico file and automatically launches stub.exe when the user inserts the CD-ROM.

AUTORUN.INF   stub.exe   cd_icon.ico   data

Exploring the Class Structure

There's a lot going on in the various support files for this chapter. Check out Figure 8.16 as I discuss the features.

These class diagrams are supposed to make things clearer. This example is busy only

because it shows so many things in a single figure. Let's start with the parts you actually built in this project: the main.swf file and the section.swf template. The fileData array is created by the utils.parseXML() method. That method creates an array of Section instances, and each Section instance has an array of items in its items property. Basically, that's the ActionScript version of the data.xml file.

The main.swf file also creates an instance of the SectionMaker class, which handles creating instances of your section.swf templates. Notice that each section.swf template implements the ISection interface. Each section.swf template also has the properties controller (the sole SectionMaker instance) and section (a single instance of the Section class—specifically the Section for which the section.swf is displaying).

FIGURE 8.16 This class diagram shows where your main.swf and section.swf templates fit.

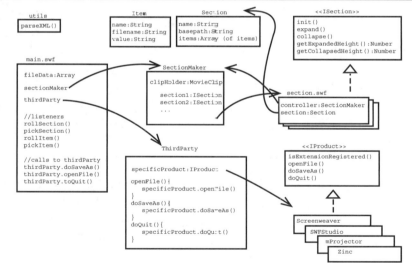

The `main.swf` file creates an instance of the `ThirdParty` class. This is actually a proxy class that channels all methods to an instance of one of the various `IProduct` classes—Screenweaver, SWFStudio, mProjector, or Zinc—depending on which swf2exe you're using. That is, when the `main.swf` file first creates the `ThirdParty` instance, it tells it which product to use. Then the `ThirdParty` class saves in its `specificProduct` property one of the product-specific classes. All those product classes implement the same interface (`IProduct`). This way, when the `main.swf` file says `thirdParty.doSaveAs()`, the `ThirdParty` class redirects that call to `specificProduct.doSaveAs()`. This structure is based on the formal design pattern called Factory. There are other projects in this book where I should have used the Factory pattern, but I tended to use monolithic classes so you would have fewer files to tote around.

Final Thoughts

It's sort of amusing that about 75% of this chapter was about how to implement the `SectionMaker` class and very little was about the third-party swf2exe tools. But that was actually by design. Those tools only supplement what's possible in Flash. You should be able to make your Flash application do all the stuff you want; however, when you require a feature that's not possible to accomplish in Flash (such as copying files from disk), you can use a swf2exe tool to help you. The focus shouldn't be on the tool.

The framework that keeps the swf2exe tasks separated also lets you easily convert your `main.swf` to work online, provided you use only those features supported in the Flash Player. Inside the `pickItem()` method, change the call `thirdParty.openFile(currentBasePath+evt.data.filename)` to instead read `getURL(currentBasePath+evt.data.filename)`, and the browser will jump to those files. You don't need the `stub.swf` file if you're running this application from the Web. Similarly, if you want to trigger different methods available to the swf2exe tool you're using, you already have a nice gateway built in the `ThirdParty.as` class, which lets `main.swf` make the calls indirectly.

There are lots of other variations that you can do with very little work. For example, if your CD-ROM is full of .mp3 files for users to either copy or simply listen to, you can modify the `pickItem()` method to create an instance of the `Sound` class and play a .mp3 with just two lines:

```
var s:Sound = new Sound();
s.loadSound( currentBasePath +
            evt.data.filename, true);
```

You can do something similar with your image files by giving users a preview of the .jpg files included on the CD-ROM. That is, any media source files Flash supports (.jpg, .gif, .png, .swf, .flv, or .mp3) can either be displayed or played right inside your project.

Finally, I want to make one more comment about the download feature you built in this chapter. It was really just a "copy from CD" feature. In Chapter 10, "Building a Photo Share Application," you'll build a similar application that works online without any third-party products to actually download—and upload—image files. It's a totally different application, but the copying files aspect is similar.

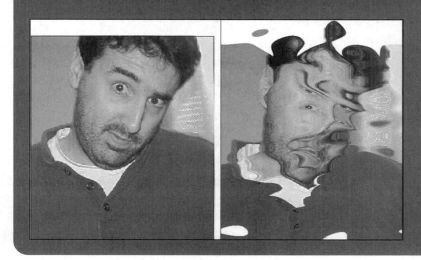

About the Project

This "project" is unlike any other in the book. In fact, it is really about a dozen disconnected miniprojects. Each little project explores how to create a particular special effect ranging from visual changes to a single image to animated effects over time. The techniques presented here also range from effects that are free of all code (that is, they're built by hand in the timeline) to effects created entirely using ActionScript. I suspect you'll think that some effects are cheesy and others impressive.

Prerequisites

Flash Professional 8—not Flash Basic 8—is required for many of the projects in this chapter. Those that take advantage of the new, impressive, and file-size-saving blends and filters effects are available only in Flash Professional 8. In fact, you can apply these effects using Flash Basic 8—but only through ActionScript, not while authoring.

@work resources

Download the `chapter_9_downloads.zip` file for this chapter from the accompanying CD-ROM.

Planning the Projects

In the multiple projects in this chapter, I'll try to show you practical uses for the effects in this chapter. Making something that's just really cool might be fun to look at (and might even impress your friends), but unless the effect adds something to your core message, it most definitely detracts from it. Effects should supplement your project, not simply spice it up. Having given you that warning, I can say that these projects are also fun to create.

I've broken the projects into three categories: timeline (no code), one-off classes (in which the code is written for just one effect), and a class library of code to animate any filter you choose. The first four projects fall into the timeline category, the next four projects are one-off classes, and the last two projects use the class library.

There are a lot of considerations to take into account when building a special effect. The general tips that follow should help you efficiently create powerful special effects.

Think About Impressions, Not Effects

The reason some special effects work is that they communicate an idea. Rarely does the viewer focus on the technical effect itself but rather how it affects them. You want to impress an idea on the user, not call attention to the effect itself. One key is to try to be subtle.

When you design a special effect, think first about the feeling or impression you want the user to have. For example, if you want to show a bus speeding past the screen, think about how you experience a bus in real life. It's loud, for one thing, so a sound effect in this case might be more powerful than an image. The fact is that all animation is a lie—you're not really showing a bus but trying to give the impression of a bus in motion.

Although this suggestion to focus on impressions and not on real-life physics is very general, I think it helps even when you're drawing a still image or creating a simple animation.

Start with the End in Mind

One of the most common tricks of timeline animation is that you start with your ending keyframes and then work backward to define how the graphics look in earlier frames. For example, if you want to animate a ball from the left to the right side of the stage and then back, you create the last keyframe first (where the ball is back at the beginning) and then create the middle keyframe and move the ball to the right. With this approach, the first and last keyframes line up.

Timeline Versus Scripted Effects

A lot of programmers pooh pooh the idea of using the timeline, but there are many cases where it's not only acceptable but also desirable. In addition, it can be very quick, which is useful when you're just exploring variations on an effect before building it for real. The downsides include that when you use your timeline for an animation, you sort of paint yourself into a corner. For example, you can't change the frame rate without affecting every timeline animation in your movie. Also, every small change to a timeline animation is a manual change. On the other hand, the fact that you can make manual changes can sometimes be a benefit. If you need to add one odd keyframe in the middle of a tween, you can do so easily when it's in the timeline.

Scripted animation is nice because it's completely decoupled from your timeline layout—and even from the frame rate. You can use the setInterval() function, along with the updateAfterEvent() function, to control the timing of an animation regardless of the movie's frame rate. Also, if you use an algorithm to describe the motion, you can make subtle changes by modifying just a few numbers. Finally, by keeping the programming separate from the graphics, you can recycle the code on future projects.

It's not always easy deciding which situations are best for each type of animation. Ultimately, use what you're comfortable with. I often start by studying the motion using the timeline and then writing a script modeled after that motion. In this chapter, you'll see both techniques.

Justify Everything

Saying "if it's not adding to your message, it's most certainly detracting from it" is more than just a catchy phrase—it's true. For every blip, splash, or beep you add to your Flash movie, be sure that you can answer the question, "What's this for?" Everything should have a purpose. With a purpose, it's easy to determine whether an effect is working because it either achieves its purpose or doesn't. A bunch of clutter and unnecessary effects simply get in the way of your core message. It's hard enough communicating

an idea without having to compete with special effects for the user's attention.

Project:
Continuous Loop

In this project, you'll see how to create a looping movie clip where the last frame lines up perfectly with the first frame. Just think of the old cartoons that use a repeating background, and you'll have an idea of what you'll build here.

STEPS▼

1. **Creating one cycle**
2. **Matching the end with the beginning**
3. **Making the animation**
4. **Touching up the animation**

STEP 1▼
Creating One Cycle

Create a new Flash document and start by using the Pencil tool with a thick stroke to draw a jagged horizontal line that's wider than the whole stage; this represents a horizon of mountains. You can add clouds or whatever you want to this scene using other tools. When you're done, use the Line tool to draw a vertical line somewhere to the left of your mountains. Select just the vertical line and then select Modify, Group so that it won't merge with your drawing when the line is positioned on top of the mountains. (This is the case only when you're in the default Merge Drawing mode, but grouping the line first is always a good safeguard.) Nudge the line to the right so that it just overlaps your mountains, as shown in Figure 9.1. Select everything on the stage and select Modify, Convert to Symbol. In the dialog box, enable the Movie Clip option and name the symbol **Looping Background**.

STEP 2▼
Matching the End with the Beginning

Double-click the `Looping Background` instance so you can edit its contents. Use the Arrow tool and select everything in your mountain line from the left edge to some-where over the vertical line you drew. It's

okay if you select the entire mountain line (for example, if it was grouped), but you only need part of it, as Figure 9.2 shows. If the mountains are a group or Drawing object, you must first break them apart.

Copy the selection by pressing Ctrl+C and then select Paste in Place by pressing Ctrl+Shift+V. While the pasted graphics are still selected, press and hold the right-arrow key to position the selected portion all the way beyond the right end of the mountains, as shown in Figure 9.3. Hold down the Shift key when you press the arrow key to move more quickly.

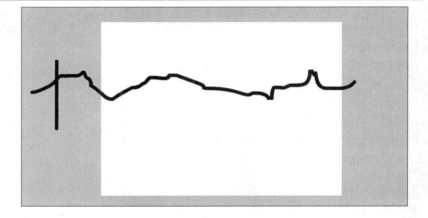

FIGURE 9.1 **The vertical line, in its own group, over-lapping part of the skyline serves as a reference point.**

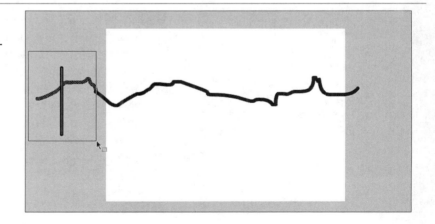

FIGURE 9.2 **Select enough of the skyline to overlap the vertical registra-tion line.**

CHAPTER 9: Creating Special Effects

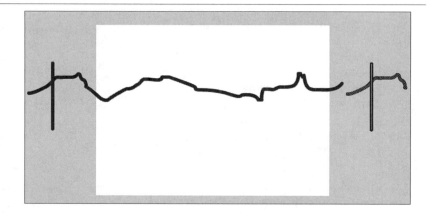

Draw a line to connect the right edge of the original mountains to the new shape on the right side. You can modify the look of the right end of the original skyline, but just don't modify anything to the right of the vertical line.

STEP 3 ▼
Making the Animation

Select everything inside your `Looping Animation` symbol and select Modify, Convert to Symbol. Name the symbol **One Cycle** and

select the Movie Clip option. Insert a keyframe in frame 30 of the `Looping Animation` symbol. While in frame 30, select the `One Cycle` instance; select Edit, Copy; and then select Edit, Paste in Place. Select just one of the two instances on top of each other and use the left-arrow key to move it way off to the left such that the vertical line on the right side of the instance you're moving lines up with the vertical line on the left side of the instance underneath, as shown in Figure 9.4.

FIGURE 9.4　**In frame 30, move a copy of the `One Cycle` instance to the left so that its right side lines up with the left side of the duplicate.**

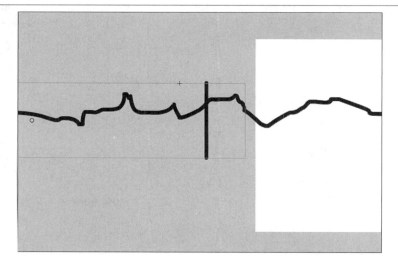

Select the instance you didn't move—the one that's in the middle, not on the left side—and select Edit, Cut. (Don't forget that you have an instance of One Cycle in your clipboard.) Select frame 1 and use the Properties panel to set the Motion Tween option. At this point, you have a tween that moves the One Cycle clip to the left so that its beginning and end match but the mountain line runs out and you see nothing to the right of it. To see a second "One Cycle Animation" on the heels of this animation, we'll create another motion tween, which always requires a second layer.

Lock the sole layer by clicking the dot underneath the padlock. Select Insert, Timeline, Layer; then select Edit, Paste in Place. Because this is going to the end of our second animation, click the cell in frame 30 of the new layer and insert a keyframe by pressing F6. Now the end frame has an instance of One Cycle in its proper ending position. Go back to frame 1 by clicking frame number 1; the red current frame marker moves all the way to the left. Select the mountains, still in your second, unlocked, layer, and use the right arrow to move the instance all the way to the right so the left vertical line in the instance you're moving lines up with the right vertical line of the instance underneath, as shown in Figure 9.5.

Select frame 1 in the unlocked layer and select the Motion Tween option in the Properties panel.

Select Control, Test Movie. Other than the annoying vertical line, which you'll get rid of in a minute, try to note what's not right about the animation.

FIGURE 9.5 The beginning of the mountains in the second layer must line up with the right side of the original mountains.

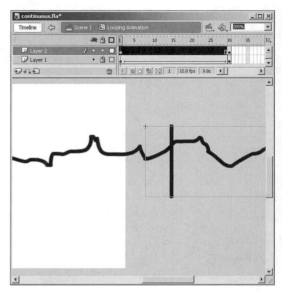

STEP 4▼
Touching Up the Animation

Our animation is perfect in that the first frame is the same as the last frame. But if the user sees the last frame and then the first frame, that means he sees the same frame twice in succession. There are two ways to fix this repetition problem. You can select the last frame in the animation, open the Actions panel, and type this code:

```
gotoAndPlay(1);
```

The reason that works is the code executes before the user sees what's in the last frame.

Although this solution works great, because I said this was a "no code" project, I'll show you another way to make the animation work. Click the cell in frame 29 on either layer and insert a keyframe by pressing F6. Do this for both layers. Now we'll remove frame 30 by clicking its keyframe and pressing Shift+F5 to remove the frame. Do this for both layers. The reason this solution works is that you're inserting a keyframe on an already-interpolated frame (frame 29).

The last step is to go inside the One Cycle symbol and remove those two vertical lines. Now the animation will play without appearing to pause on the last frame.

Project:
Jitter Effect

The effect you'll learn in this project should be familiar because it has been used in many Flash cartoons. Basically, all the elements in your animation will continuously jitter. It's an easy effect to build and, despite becoming a bit cliché, it can be an effective way to add a living quality to otherwise slow-moving animations.

STEPS ▼

1. **Drawing the base elements**
2. **Adding the jitter**

STEP 1 ▼
Drawing the Base Elements

Draw your animated character; Mr. Stickman is fine for this exercise (see in Figure 9.6). Often people create body parts, such as an arm, a leg, a head, and so on, and animate them independently. You can do that, too;

you'll just have to add the jitter to each element. Convert your character into a movie clip symbol, or convert each of the character's body parts into a movie clip symbol.

FIGURE 9.6 A line-drawn stick man is a fine way to start this exercise.

STEP 2 ▼
Adding the Jitter

To create the jitter, you're just going to add multiple frames to the character and cycle those frames. Double-click the symbol instance to edit its contents. Click frame 2 and insert a keyframe by pressing F6. Select everything and click the Smooth button in the Tools panel. Alternatively, select Modify, Shape, Smooth. By smoothing a drawn line, Flash simplifies the shape. This results in a shape with fewer kinks or corners.

Continue to add keyframes sequentially in frames 3, 4 5, and so on by pressing F6; each time, smooth the character a little bit more. Figure 9.7 shows Mr. Stickman over four frames.

FIGURE 9.7   Mr. Stickman is getting smoother over time.

You can do your own adjustments, such as changing the thickness of strokes or just modifying the shape by hand. For more jumpiness, just add kinks to the lines or change their thickness. Basically, you can add your own style of jittering depending on the exact effect you want.

Select Control, Test Movie; your character should jitter. If you animate a movie clip that contains multiple (jittering) frames, the jitter will appear while the animation plays. You can see some of the samples I created in the Project2_jitter folder in the finish_source folder you downloaded for this chapter.

Project:
Magnifier Lens Effect

This magnifier lens effect is pretty cool and only requires using layers and masks. In this case, the Mask layer contains a round shape that reveals a large version of some text, which has the effect of looking magnified because it's larger than the original text in a lower layer.

STEPS ▼

1. Creating the large movie clip
2. Creating the small movie clip
3. Adding the mask
4. Animating the mask
5. Adjusting the motion
6. Adding a layer for the reflection

STEP 1 ▼
Creating the Large Movie Clip

Use the Text tool to create a very large text field with just one line of text (say, a line of text reading Magnifier Effect). Use the Properties panel to ensure that the text is set to Static Text and is not selectable. This will be the large (magnified) version, so it can be wider than the stage if you want. Use the Rectangle tool and draw a white rectangle at least as large as the text—you don't need a stroke. Position the rectangle shape underneath the text. Use the Arrow tool to select both the rectangle shape and the text and then select Modify, Convert to Symbol. In the Convert to Symbol dialog box, select the Movie Clip option and click OK.

> ### 📌 NOTE
>
> It makes sense to start by creating the enlarged symbol first and then scale the small one down. It's not as critical if you're creating the graphic inside Flash. However, if you plan to use a raster graphic that you import, be sure to import the graphic at the size you want the large (magnified) symbol to appear; you can make a scaled-down version for the small (nonmagnified) symbol. If you import a small graphic and enlarge it, the symbol will appear grainy at the larger size.

STEP 2▼
Creating the Small Movie Clip

You should have an instance of your symbol on the stage. Align it so that the left edge of the symbol corresponds to the left edge of the stage. Select the symbol instance and copy it by pressing Ctrl+C. Name the sole layer **Large** and lock the layer. Also, to make alignment easier, set the Large layer to View Layer As Outlines by clicking the colored square in that layer. Select Insert, Timeline, Layer and name the new layer **Small**. Select Edit, Paste in Place to paste the copy of the original symbol instance in the Small layer.

Use the Free Transform tool and hold down the Shift key while you scale down the duplicate instance in the Small layer. Align the left edge of the Small layer with the left edge of the Large layer underneath, as shown in Figure 9.8.

FIGURE 9.8 The large version's layer is set to View Layer As Outlines, enabling you to see through and align the two clips.

STEP 3▼
Adding the Mask

Drag the Small layer below the Large layer, and then select Insert, Timeline, Layer. Name the new layer **Magnifier** and make sure that it's

above all the other layers. In the Magnifier layer, use the Oval tool to draw a filled circle at least as tall as the large text. Make sure that the circle has a stroke for the final touch we'll add later. Select the circle shape and select Modify, Convert to Symbol (or press F8). Name the symbol **Magnifier** and select the Movie Clip option. Move the circle to the left edge of the stage, or at least to the left edge of the two instances containing the text.

Double-click the page curl icon for the Magnifier layer or select Modify, Timeline, Layer Properties to open the Layer Properties dialog box. Set the symbol's layer properties to Mask, as shown in Figure 9.9, and click OK.

FIGURE 9.9 The Layer Properties dialog box lets you turn the Magnifier symbol into a mask.

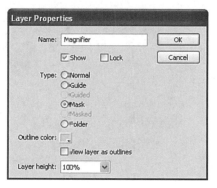

This property change will likely cause the Large layer properties to change to Masked, which is what you want. You'll see that the Large layer's page curl icon changes to a blue/green checkerboard to represent that it's set to Masked. If the Large Layer Properties dialog box does not have the Masked option selected, manually select it now. Ensure, too, that the Small layer's Type is still set to Normal.

STEP 4▼
Animating the Mask

Click the cell in frame 30 of the Magnifier layer and insert a keyframe by pressing F6. Unlock the Magnifier layer and make the Large layer invisible. Hold down the Shift key while you drag the Magnifier instance in frame 30 all the way to the right of the small text.

Select the keyframe in frame 1 of the Magnifier layer. Use the Properties panel to select the Motion Tween option.

Make all the layers visible and lock all the layers. You can judge the effect so far by scrubbing—click and drag left and right on the frame numbers. You'll see the large text only where the circle shape moves to. You should notice two areas that need improvement:

- ▶ The animation starts off okay, but by the end of the animation, the large text seems too far to the right.

- ▶ You can't see the magnifier circle at all—a real magnifying glass has a frame and reflections in the glass.

STEP 5▼
Adjusting the Motion

As the Magnifier layer moves to the right, the large text should move to the left. Unlock the Large layer and set it to show outlines only by either clicking the little square on the right side of the layer or accessing the Layer Properties dialog box and selecting the View Layer As Outlines check box.

Click the cell in frame 30 of the Large layer; then insert a keyframe by pressing F6. In frame 30, use the left-arrow key and nudge the large instance of the text over to the left. You want to line up the right edges of both the large and small versions of the text. Return to the keyframe in frame 1 of the Large layer and use the Properties panel to set a motion tween. Turn off the View As Outlines option in the Layer Properties dialog box and lock all the layers; then scrub the timeline again to see the results. This time the large text moves to the left while the magnifier moves to the right.

STEP 6▼
Adding a Layer for the Reflection

Although Flash 8 now supports 8-bit masks, they're not needed or appropriate for this effect. That is, the standard 1-bit mask employed by Mask layers is good for this project because we want the Magnifier layer to completely reveal the large text, but we also want to see the frame of the magnifying glass. An 8-bit mask has 256 levels of transparency, whereas a 1-bit mask is either on or off.

Open the Library and double-click the Magnifier symbol to edit its contents. Select the fill and use the Color Mixer panel to select the default white-to-black radial gradient. We'll edit this gradient to go from 0% *alpha* white to 100% alpha black. With the fill of the magnifier still selected, click the color proxy arrow for the white end of the gradient, as shown in Figure 9.10.

FIGURE 9.10   Change the white end of the gradient to 0% alpha by first clicking the mixer's color proxy arrow.

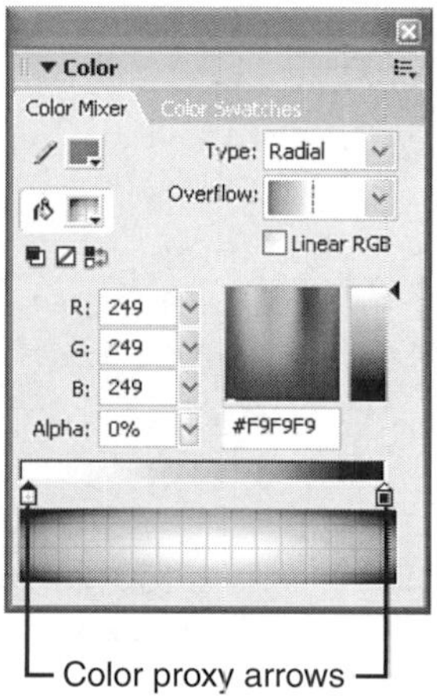

Color proxy arrows

Drag the Alpha slider all the way down to 0%. You can use the Gradient Transform tool to modify additional subtleties in the gradient, but for our purposes 0% white to 100% black is fine.

Return to the main timeline and notice that the change made to the Magnifier symbol had no impact on the effect that the magnifying glass has on the Large layer because layer masks are either on or off and gradients are not supported by masks.

Select all the frames in the Magnifier layer by clicking the layer name. Select Edit, Timeline, Copy Frames, and then insert a new layer above all the other layers. Click the first keyframe in the new layer and select Edit, Timeline, Paste Frames. (If the new layer has more than 30 frames, select the excess frames and press Shift+F5 to remove those frames.) Open the Layer Properties dialog box for the new layer and make sure that the Normal option—not the Mask option—is selected. Select Control, Test Movie. Now a shaded version of the magnifying glass appears on

top of the zooming text, as shown in Figure 9.11.

FIGURE 9.11   The finished project should look believable.

Project:
Blends and Filters

This project is really a few miniprojects that use blends and filters. I wanted to point out some neat tricks using the often-underappreciated blend feature. Some of the effects are very simple. Blends let you control how the colors from layered clips can be combined with each other, whereas filters let you add special effects such as drop shadows and blurs (although here we'll use them just to modify colors).

STEPS▼

1. Using the layer blend for accurate transparency
2. Making a spotlight effect using the Alpha blend
3. Making a black-and-white photo
4. Making a sepia-toned photo

STEP 1▼
Using the Layer Blend for Accurate Transparency

Applying the Layer blend to a single clip instance is powerful on its own. This blend retains the clip's visual appearance while you change its alpha. Simply use the Properties panel to set a clip's blend to Layer. Any time a clip contains multiple layered clips or raster graphics and you change its alpha, you can see through its contents at varying degrees—but not if you first set the clip's blend to Layer, as shown in Figure 9.12.

FIGURE 9.12 Both flowers' alpha is set at 50%, but the flower on the right also has its blend set to Layer, thus avoiding the skeleton effect.

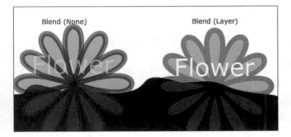

STEP 2▼
Making a Spotlight Effect Using the Alpha Blend

While the Layer blend is useful on its own, it's also a necessary component to using the Erase or Alpha blend. The Erase and Alpha blends are a bit tricky because they work only when you apply one to a clip that's nested inside another clip. Clips with Erase or Alpha blends either hide or reveal the colors of the clips underneath. Erase erases more where its clip is opaque and less where it's clear; Alpha erases more where its clip is clear and less where it's opaque. The catch is that you apply Alpha or Erase to a clip that's inside another symbol and the parent clip must have its blend set to Layer. So, you can apply the Erase or Alpha blend to an instance of a clip that itself is nested within another instance. The parent clip must have the Layer blend

applied; otherwise, you won't see the effect of the Erase or Alpha blend.

Import a photograph; select it; and select Modify, Convert to Symbol. In the Convert to Symbol dialog box, select the Movie Clip option and name the symbol **Photo**. Select the Photo instance and select Edit, Copy; then select Edit, Paste in Place. With the instance on top selected, select Modify, Convert to Symbol again. Once again, select the Movie Clip option and name this instance of the symbol **Dark Photo**. Double-click the Dark Photo instance, and you will find an instance of Photo inside. Select that instance of the Photo symbol and use the Properties panel to set the Color Style drop-down menu to Brightness; then set the slider to –75% or so. Draw a filled circle somewhere on the stage other than on top of the photo. Set the circle's fill to a radial gradient going from white to black with the white's alpha at 0%, as shown in Figure 9.13.

FIGURE 9.13 This gradient goes from a clear (0% alpha) white to solid black.

Select the circle and select Modify, Covert to Symbol (once again, click the Movie Clip check box and name this symbol **Circle**).

Position the Circle instance on top of the dark instance of Photo. In fact, you can put the circle on its own layer and do a motion tween inside the Dark Photo symbol. Select the Circle instance and use the Properties panel to set the Blend to Alpha, meaning that where the Circle layer is clear, the entire Dark Photo symbol will be transparent. Return to the main timeline and set the Dark Photo instance's blend to Layer so you can see the impact from the Circle instance's Alpha blend. Figure 9.14 shows the finished arrangement.

FIGURE 9.14   With a clip set to Alpha, nested inside another clip set to Layer, you can create a spotlight effect.

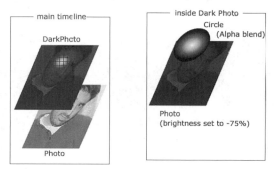

STEP 3▼
Making a Black-and-White Photo

This effect is lame unless you don't know how to do it: Import a photo; select it; and select

Modify, Convert to symbol. Open the Filters panel, click the plus button, and then select Adjust Color. Drag the Saturation slider all the way to the left, and adjust the Brightness and Contrast if you want.

STEP 4▼
Making a Sepia-toned Photo

This effect is not nearly as simple as the black-and-white photo effect described in step 3. Import a photo; select it; and select Modify, Convert to Symbol. Open the Filters panel, click the plus button, and then select Adjust Color. Start by setting the dials as shown in Figure 9.15: Brightness 14, Contrast 18, Saturation –100 (the value of Hue doesn't matter).

Use the Properties panel to set the Color Style to Advanced, and then click the Settings button. Adjust the dials in the Advanced Effect dialog box as shown in Figure 9.16: Red 96% and 23, Green 100% and 0, Blue 98% and –33, and Alpha 100% and 0.

These are just starter values; you'll likely want to use the Adjust Color filter to modify the Brightness and Contrast, depending on your photograph.

FIGURE 9.15   You'll need to desaturate and adjust the brightness and contrast for part of the sepia effect.

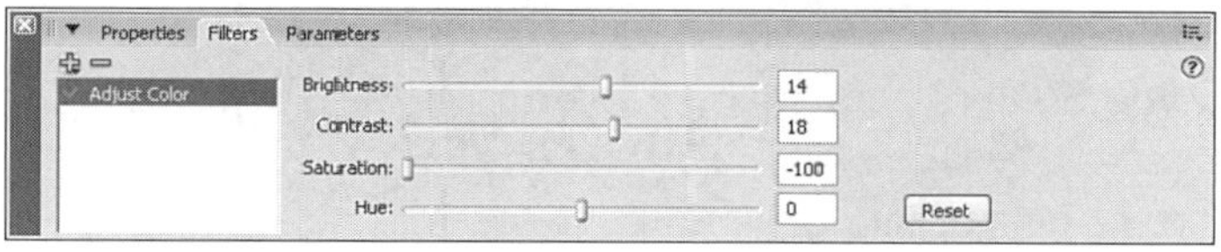

NOTE

I'll show you how to create both the black-and-white and sepia-toned photo effects using code in the next project.

Project:
Matrixes for the ColorMatrixFilter

Anything you can do with blends, filters, and color styles, you can do with code. This project introduces you to using the ColorMatrixFilter class that ships with Flash 8. This class lets you create color filters using ActionScript. Basically, it's a filter you can apply to any clip using the following form:

```
myClipInstance.filters =
[ myColorMatrixFilterInstance ];
```

Notice that the filters property is set to an array of filters—in this case, we apply just one filter, but the array lets you apply multiple filters, just as the Filters panel lets you apply more than one filter on the stage. This

approach works for any of the filters in the flash.filters package (such as BlurFilter or DropShadowFilter). In the case of the ColorMatrixFilter, you need to create a matrix that describes the effect you want. Don't worry, I'm not going to attempt to explain how the matrixes work. But I have two simple applications for coloring a clip just as we did in the previous two projects.

STEPS▼
1. Making a photograph black and white using code
2. Making a photograph sepia using code

STEP 1▼
Making a Photograph Black and White Using Code

Import a color photograph; select it; and select Modify, Convert to Symbol. Select the Movie Clip option in the Convert to Symbol dialog box and click OK. Use the Properties panel to give it an instance name of **photo** (this is not the same thing as naming a symbol).

Select the first keyframe and paste this code in the Actions panel (you can also grab the code from the file project5_e1_ blackandwhite.fla located in the finished_source folder you downloaded for this chapter):

```
var bwFilter =
new flash.filters.ColorMatrixFilter ();

bwFilter.matrix = new Array (
     0.3086, 0.609, 0.282, 0, 0,
     0.3086, 0.609, 0.282, 0, 0,
     0.3086, 0.609, 0.282, 0, 0,
     0,      0,     0,     1, 0);
photo.filters = [ bwFilter ];
```

It's not required that you space out the array as I did here, but because the array is four rows by five columns, spacing the values out helps. Test the movie!

STEP 2▼
Making a Photograph Sepia Using Code

In a new file, import a color photograph; select it; and select Modify, Convert to Symbol. Select the Movie clip option in the Convert to Symbol dialog box and click OK. Use the Properties panel to give it an instance name of **photo** (this is not the same thing as naming a symbol).

Select the first keyframe and paste this code into the Actions panel:

```
var sepiaFilter =
new flash.filters.ColorMatrixFilter ();

sepiaFilter.matrix = new Array (
          0.393, 0.769, 0.189, 0, 0,
          0.349, 0.686, 0.168, 0, 0,
          0.272, 0.534, 0.131, 0, 0,
          0,     0,     0,     1, 0);
photo.filters = [ sepiaFilter ];
```

Test the movie and you'll see that the photo now has a sepia-toned effect.

Project: Film Dirt

This project uses a class I created (FilmDirt.as) that randomly displays a single frame from a clip full of "dirt" that you draw. Most likely you'll use this effect with a video clip to make the video look all scratched up, like an old home movie. In fact, you can apply the sepiaFilter ColorMatrixFilter effect from the preceding project to compound the visual impact of this Film Dirt project. For example, if you have a FLVPlayback component with the instance name myFLVPlayback, you could say myFLVPlayback.filters = [sepiaFilter] to give the entire video a sepia tone.

STEPS▼

1. Copying the required files
2. Creating the dirt
3. Entering simple code
4. Setting up a file to put dirt on a video
5. Entering code to show dirt while video plays

STEP 1▼
Copying the Required Files

Copy the `FilmDirt.as` file from the `classes\FilmDirt` folder you downloaded for this chapter and place the copy in your working folder. Open Flash and create a new document; then save the `.fla` file in the same working folder.

STEP 2▼
Creating the Dirt

Select Insert, New Symbol. Select the Movie clip option, name it **scratches**, and click the Export for ActionScript check box as shown in Figure 9.17. (You might have to click the Advanced button if your dialog box doesn't display all the options shown here.) Enter **scratches** in the Linkage Identifier field, and leave the Export in First Frame option selected. Click OK.

You should be taken inside the **scratches** symbol. Now you'll draw a different speck or scratch on each keyframe. Use the Pencil tool to draw a little squiggly, as shown in Figure 9.18.

FIGURE 9.17 The scratches symbol must have its linkage identifier specified as shown.

FIGURE 9.18 This innocuous-looking squiggle will become a random piece of dirt on top of a video.

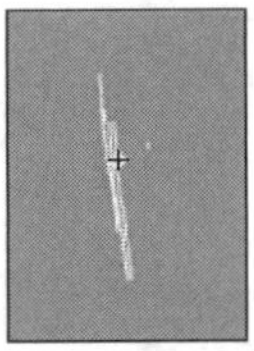

Press F7 to insert a blank keyframe, and then draw another piece of dirt. I find that drawing mostly white specks works best for video noise, but mix in a few black marks, too. Because these "scratches" will be positioned randomly on the real video clip, keep the marks centered around the clip's center point (indicated with a plus sign). If you want to ensure that a scratch extends to the full height of your video, make the line twice the height of your video. For example, if your video is 240 pixels tall, make sure that the scratch line reaches from –240 y down to 240 y. You make the scratch twice the height of the video display because the code randomizes the location by plus or minus 240 pixels when the video is 240 pixels tall. Also, even though each speck stays onscreen for only a fraction of a second, you can create a movie clip with a few frames of the same speck moving up or rotating. Place that multiframe movie clip on a single frame inside the scratches symbol. See my finished version of the scratches file in the finished_source folder for some ideas. Just make sure that you have something on every frame of the scratches symbol. You need only a few frames, but the more you have, the more random the shapes will appear.

STEP 3 ▼
Entering Simple Code

Just so that you can see the minimum functioning code, go back to the main timeline in your .fla file, select the first keyframe, open the Actions panel, and enter the code shown in Listing 9.1.

Test the movie. You can come back and vary the value for dirtFactor, although I recommend not going over 20 for performance reasons. The higher the dirtFactor value, the more pieces of dirt the user will see at any one moment. Also, because updateFrequency represents how frequently the dirt is moved in milliseconds, I wouldn't set that lower than 20 (a higher value makes the updates less frequent and therefore perform better).

The FilmDirt constructor takes five parameters:

▶ targetClip—A clip instance where you want the dirt to appear. Basically, my class needs a clip to draw into.

▶ linkageID—The linkage identifier for the clip containing the dirt.

▶ rect—The Rectangle (x, y, width, height) that specifies the shape within which you want to draw dirt. In the example in Listing 9.1, it's the whole screen, but we'll make that space smaller in the next example so the rectangle just covers the video clip.

▶ dirtFactor and updateFrequency— Values you can tweak, as described previously.

LISTING 9.1 This Code Makes the Dirt Appear in a 550 × 400 Rectangle

```
var targetClip = createEmptyMovieClip( "scratchClip", 0 );
var linkageID = "scratches";
var rect = new flash.geom.Rectangle( 0, 0, 550, 400 );
var dirtFactor = 5;
var updateFrequency = 20;
var fd = new FilmDirt( targetClip,
                       linkageID,
                       rect,
                       dirtFactor,
                       updateFrequency );
fd.start();
```

Notice that the dirt doesn't start to appear until you call the start() method. In the next step, you'll see methods for pause() (to freeze the dirt) and clear() (to remove all the dirt).

STEP 4▼
Setting Up a File to Put Dirt on a Video

Start a new file and save it in your working directory next to the FilmDirt.as file. Copy the sample.flv file from the source_media folder you downloaded for this chapter into your working directory. In your Flash file, drag onto the stage a FLVPlayback component from the Components panel (open the panel by pressing Ctrl+F7). Use the Properties panel to give the component an instance name **myFLVPlayback**.

STEP 5▼
Entering Code to Show Dirt While Video Plays

Select the first keyframe, open the Actions panel, and type the code shown in Listing 9.2.

LISTING 9.2 This Code Makes Dirt Appear on the Video While It Plays

```
var myFLVplayback:mx.video.FLVPlayback;
myFLVplayback.contentPath = "sample.flv"

var targetClip = createEmptyMovieClip( "scratchClip", 0 );
var linkageID = "scratches";
var rect = new flash.geom.Rectangle( myFLVplayback.x,
                                     myFLVplayback.y,
                                     myFLVplayback.width,
                                     myFLVplayback.height );
var dirtFactor = 5;
var updateFrequency = 20;
var fd = new FilmDirt( targetClip,
                       linkageID,
                       rect,
                       dirtFactor,
                       updateFrequency );

function paused(){
    fd.pause();
}
function playing(){
    fd.start();
}
function rewind(){
    fd.pause();
}
myFLVplayback.addEventListener( "paused", this );
myFLVplayback.addEventListener( "playing", this );
myFLVplayback.addEventListener( "rewind", this );
```

There are two differences in this code from the code in Listing 9.1: The `Rectangle` is based on the `FLVPlayback` component's size, and the dirt doesn't start appearing until the video's playing event fires. With this second version of the file, if you stop and start the video, the dirt also stops and starts. Figure 9.19 shows how the dirt appears on top of a video.

FIGURE 9.19   You can add as much dirt to your video as you want.

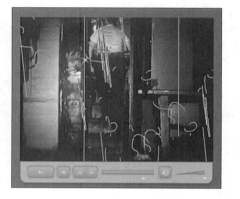

Project: Tracers

I find that many new Flash developers get so excited about the *onion skin*, only to be let down when they realize it's available only while authoring. The onion skin feature is a cool effect that keeps copies of an animating clip on the screen after its frame has passed (see Figure 9.20). But it only works while authoring.

The `TraceClip.as` class I supplied for this chapter lets you identify any clip and start adding tracers any time you want. You can select how many leftover copies to display (a

higher number makes the trail longer) and when to turn off the effect.

FIGURE 9.20   The onion skin feature lets you see the preceding frames of this bouncing ball animation, but only while authoring.

STEPS▼

1. Creating an animation
2. Copying the support files
3. Tracing while the mouse is down
4. Making tracers appear in specific parts of the animation

STEP 1▼
Creating an Animation

In a new file, draw any shape, such as a circle; then select what you've drawn and select Modify, Convert to Symbol. Select the Movie Clip option and click OK. Use the Properties panel to give the symbol instance the instance name **targetClip**. It's important that you name the instance before you add more keyframes. Make a simple animation of the clip moving across the screen. For example, one by one, click frames 20, 30, and 40 and insert a single keyframe by clicking the cell and pressing F6. Move the instances in frames 20 and 30 to different locations. Select all the frames and use the Properties panel to set Tween to Motion. Save your .fla file in a working directory.

STEP 2▼
Copying the Support Files

Copy the TraceClip.as file from the classes\TraceClip folder you downloaded for this chapter, and put it into your working directory.

STEP 3▼
Tracing While the Mouse Is Down

Select the first keyframe in your .fla file, open the Actions panel, and enter the code shown in Listing 9.3.

Let me explain the three parameters for the TraceClip() constructor:

▶ clipToStoreCopies—A clip where my class is free to draw copies. In this case, we just pass an empty movie clip.

▶ clipToTrace—The clip to make copies; that is, the thing you're animating (in this example, targetClip).

▶ framesToLive—How many copies should appear trailing the target clip. A higher number means more copies and therefore a longer tail.

In this code sample, the traces appear only while the user holds down the mouse button.

> **📌 NOTE**
>
> By the way, the startTracing() method accepts an optional parameter to temporarily change the framesToLive parameter. So, if you want to make the tracing appear with 10 copies trailing, just call startTracing(10).

LISTING 9.3 This Code Tells the TraceClip Class to Make Duplicates of the Target Clip While the User Holds Down the Mouse Button

```
var clipToStoreCopies:MovieClip =
createEmptyMovieClip("historyClip",0);
var clipToTrace:MovieClip =  targetClip;
var framesToLive:Number = 5;

tc = new TraceClip( clipToStoreCopies,
                    clipToTrace,
                    framesToLive );

onMouseDown = function(){
    tc.startTracing();
}

onMouseUp=function(){
    tc.stopTracing();
}
```

CHAPTER 9: Creating Special Effects

Because the animation is in the main time-line, all the code in the first keyframe executes every time the movie loops. That overwrites the tc TraceClip instance. You can simply select the last frame in your animation, insert a keyframe, and enter the code gotoAndPlay(2). Another alternative is to create your animation inside another movie clip instead of inside the main time-line. You'll find this solution in the traceClip_inAClip.fla file inside the finished_source/Project7_TraceClip folder.

STEP 4▼
Making Tracers Appear in Specific Parts of the Animation

Suppose that your animation is of a man running from frame 1 to 20, he jumps from frame 20 to 30, and then he keeps running again. It's easy to make the tracers appear only while the man is in the air. Remove the onMouseDown and onMouseUp code from the first frame, but leave the rest of the code in that frame. Then, on frame 20, where you want the tracers to start, select the keyframe (make a keyframe in a new layer if there isn't one there already); then type this code:

```
tc.startTracing();
```

Then, on frame 30, where you want the tracers to stop, enter this code:

```
tc.stoptTracing();
```

Figure 9.21 shows the result, which you can investigate yourself in the traceClip_atCertainFrames.fla file inside the finished_source/Project7_TraceClip folder.

FIGURE 9.21 You can make tracers appear only while Mr. Stickman is leaping.

Project: VU Meter

Although the tracer effect you created in the last project is pretty cool—and quite versatile—it's probably not as practical as this very specific project. Often you need a way to show the user that audio is playing. The VUMeter.as class lets you create your own clip for the graphics of a volume unit (VU) meter and then, with just a few lines of code, make the VUMeter animate, pause, or turn off (where it animates back to its initial position). Figures 9.22 and 9.23 show both the digital style and analog versions that you'll make for this project.

STEPS▼
1. Planning your VU meters
2. Creating the digital VU meter symbol
3. Copying the support files
4. Building a test bed application

5. Entering starter code

6. Making an analog version

STEP 1▼
Planning Your VU Meters

You'll create a single movie clip containing the graphics for your VU meter and then tell the VUMeter.as class how many of those clips you want on stage. For example, for something that looks like a multichannel graphic equalizer (as shown in Figure 9.22), you'll use several digital VU meters. For an old-style analog VU meter (like the one shown in Figure 9.23), you'll use only two dials.

FIGURE 9.22 Multiple digital VU meters create a multi-channel graphic equalizer meter.

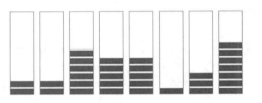

FIGURE 9.23 Two analog VU meters create an old-style meter.

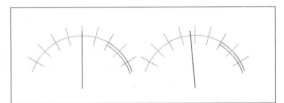

STEP 2▼
Creating the Digital VU Meter Symbol

In a new Flash file, draw a rectangle with no fill that's 40 pixels wide and 138 pixels tall.

Select it and select Modify, Convert to Symbol. Name the symbol **bars**, select the Movie Clip option, and click the Export for ActionScript option (which automatically selects the Export in First Frame option as well). Confirm that the Linkage Identifier text box reads bars. Before you click OK, make sure that the upper-left registration option is selected as shown in Figure 9.24.

FIGURE 9.24 For the bars symbol, you need to set the linkage identifier and select the upper-left registration option as shown.

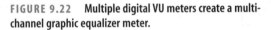

Double-click the bars symbol to edit its contents. Lock the current layer and then insert a new layer. Into the new layer, draw a filled rectangle that's 40 pixels wide and 10 pixels tall. Position the filled rectangle so its bottom-left corner aligns with the bottom-left corner of the rectangle outline you just drew. Add new keyframes, creating an additional filled rectangle for each frame. That is, frame 1 has one rectangle, frame 2 has two rectangles, and so on. Each new rectangle should be separated from the preceding rectangle by 2 pixels, so that by the 12th frame, the 12th rectangle touches the top of the outline, as shown in Figure 9.25.

FIGURE 9.25   The small bar at the top of the 12th frame should line up with the top of the unfilled rectangle.

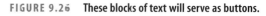

TIP

In my source file (`digitalVUMeter.fla`, which you downloaded for this chapter), you'll see that I put all 12 filled rectangles in frame 1 but had a mask that revealed only the first rectangle. Then I added keyframes *for* the mask and moved it to reveal 1 more rectangle every frame. It doesn't matter how many frames you use to draw your filled rectangles, but don't add extra frames unless you draw into those frames.

Save this file in your working directory.

STEP 3▼
Copying the Support Files

Copy the `VUMeter.as` file from the `classes\VUMeter` folder you downloaded for this chapter, and put it into your working directory.

STEP 4▼
Building a Test Bed Application

In this step, you'll build a testing application that lets you explore the various methods

supported in the `VUMeter` class. In the end, you'll have six buttons that let you trigger six methods to test how the `VUMeter` class works with your `bars` symbol.

Back inside your `.fla` file, remove any instances on the stage. The `bars` symbol is safely stored in your Library. Draw a rectangle that will become an invisible button. Select the shape; select Modify, Convert to Symbol; and name the symbol **Invisible**. Select the Button option and then click OK. Double-click the instance on the stage and click once to select the first keyframe in the button. Click again and drag the keyframe to the Hit frame. Return to your main timeline and look for an instance of your `Invisible` button, which will appear in a semitransparent cyan.

Use the Text tool to create six text fields, as shown in Figure 9.26. Make six instances of the `Invisible` button and position them on top of the six text fields. Name the instances of the buttons the same as what the text is in Figure 9.26 (**start_btn**, **freeze_btn**, and so on).

FIGURE 9.26   These blocks of text will serve as buttons.

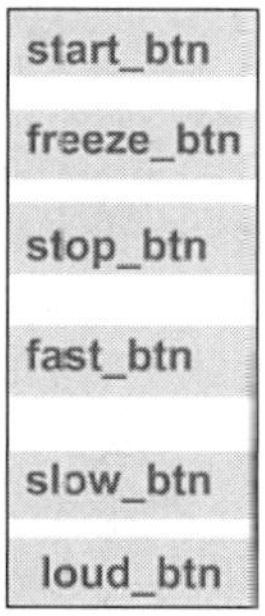

start_btn
freeze_btn
stop_btn
fast_btn
slow_btn
loud_btn

STEP 5▼
Entering Starter Code

Select the first keyframe, open the Actions
panel, and enter the code shown in
Listing 9.4.

LISTING 9.4 This Code
Lets the Six Buttons Exercise
the Features of the VUMeter
Class

```
1   var holderClip:MovieClip = createEmptyMovieClip("vu",0);
2   var linkageID = "bars";
3   var numberOfBars = 8;
4   var spaceBetweenBars = 10;
5   var initialVariability = 3;
6   var initialVolume = 50;
7   var updateFrequency = 50;
8   var optionalWidth = undefined;
9   vu = new VUMeter( holderClip,
10                    linkageID,
11                    numberOfBars,
12                    spaceBetweenBars,
13                    initialVariability,
14                    initialVolume,
15                    updateFrequency,
16                    optionalWidth    );
17
18  start_btn.onPress = function(){
19      //reset the variability
20      var optionalStartupVariability = 3;
21      vu.start(optionalStartupVariability);
22  }
23  freeze_btn.onPress = function(){
24      vu.freeze();
25  }
26  stop_btn.onPress = function(){
27      vu.stop();
28  }
29  fast_btn.onPress = function(){
30      vu.setVariability(20);
31  }
32  slow_btn.onPress = function(){
33      vu.setVariability(4);
34  }
35  loud_btn.onPress = function(){
36      vu.setVolume(100);
37  }
38  loud_btn.onRelease = loud_btn.onReleaseOutside = function(){
39      vu.setVolume(50);
40  }
```

The `VUMeter` constructor needs to know the following pieces of information:

- `holderClip`—The clip where multiple instances will be created (see lines 1 and 9). Incidentally, if you want to move where the VU meter appears, just move that clip either manually if it's already on stage or with code as in `holderClip._x = 100` for example.

- `linkageID`—The symbol's linkage identifier. In this case, it's `bars`, as shown in line 2 because that's what you named it in step 2.

- `numberOfBars`—How many copies of the bars symbol you want created (see line 3).

- `spaceBetweenBars`—This is for spacing out the multiple `bars symbols` (see line 4).

- `initialVariability`—This controls how active the meters will appear. I set it to 3 on line 5. A higher variability makes the VU meter take bigger jumps when it changes direction.

- `initialVolume`—The starting "volume"; set it to 0–100. A value of `50` in line 6 means the VU meter starts off at the midpoint.

- `updateFrequency`—The number of milliseconds between updates. The default is 100 milliseconds, or updates every 1/10 of a second. Feel free to experiment with other values (see line 7).

- `optionalWidth`—This is optional, so you can just leave it out, which has the same effect as assigning it the value of `undefined`. If you do pass a value, the spacing is based on this width. When it's `undefined` (as I left it on line 7), the spacing is based on the actual clip's width. I added this option because your VU meter might contain masked shapes, which will contribute to the width and can throw off the spacing. Basically, you can squeeze things together by providing a value less than the visible width.

After you have created the vu instance in line 9, you can do stuff to it any time you want! For example, you can make it start animating with the `vu.start()` method or you can use the `vu.start(3)` call to reset the variability in case the `fast_btn` changed it. Check out how the `vu.stop()` method makes the bars slowly move down versus how the `vu.freeze()` method holds the current values.

Test the movie to play around a bit. To apply this effect to your own application, you might add code to actually play a sound along with the code in `start_btn`. That is, the VU meter doesn't really show the volume of a sound—in fact, there's no direct way to do that in Flash 8. Imagine, though, if on frame 1 you create the vu instance to display the bars; on frame 10, you start a sound and issue `vu.start()`; then on frame 130, you issue `vu.setVolume(100)` because you know that's where the sound gets loud. Again, these meters just simulate the sound activity.

STEP 6▼
Making an Analog Version

In the same file, you can create an analog version of the VU meter by making another movie clip that contains an animation of a line rotating through an arc. See Figure 9.27 for the timeline from my version of the analog meter.

FIGURE 9.27 The line rotates about an axis at its base during a motion tween inside the analogVUMeter symbol.

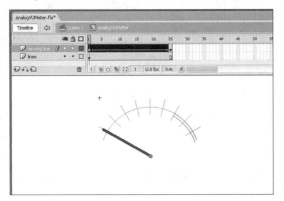

The symbol properties for the analog symbol must be set to Export for ActionScript and Export in First Frame. Also, you need to set a unique linkage identifier for this symbol. For example, I used the identifier analogVUMeter. Then simply change the code in Listing 9.4 where it reads:

```
var linkageID = "bars";
var numberOfBars = 8;
```

To instead read:

```
var linkageID = "analogVUMeter";
var numberOfBars = 2;
```

By the way, there's no rule that says your VUMeter symbol has to look like a real VU meter! You can have an animation of someone dancing or whatever you want. For example, the character simply needs to go from very calm in the first frame to totally wild in the last frame. In the first frame, make the character sitting down. Then in the last frame make it standing up with its arms stretched out. Draw gradations of this range in the in-between frames.

Project:
DualFilter Classes

Using Flash's Filters panel is intuitive. You can select a movie clip instance, apply filters, and even tween between two keyframes. It's not much more difficult to store a filter in a variable and apply that variable to a movie clip instance at runtime. For example, the following two lines of code apply a blur to a clip instance named myClip:

```
myFilter = new flash.filters.BlurFilter();
myClip.filters = [ myFilter ];
```

Making a filter effect animate using code isn't as easy as applying a basic filter. Basically, you create a new version of the filter on every frame where you want a change to appear, like this:

```
import flash.filters.BlurFilter;
var blurAmount = 0;
onEnterFrame = function(){
   myFilter = new BlurFilter( blurAmount,
                              blurAmount );
   myClip.filters = [ myFilter ];
   blurAmount = blurAmount + 1;
}
```

This code isn't that terrible, but it gets tiring when you have to build a similar block of code for all the common filter types, such as BevelFilter, BlurFilter, DropShadowFilter, and GlowFilter. I built a fairly simple collection of classes that all use the same interface, formally defined in IDualFilter.as.

To use any of the classes that implement IDualFilter.as, you simply create an instance by passing two filters of the same type that you want to tween from and to. For example, you can pass one BlurFilter instance with a blurX and blurY of 0 and another BlurFilter instance with a blurX and blurY of 100. Then you can call getNextStep() to generate an animated filter that's interpolated between the start and end

filters (0%, 1%, 2%, and so on up to 100%). This means you can make animations that automatically tween between any beginning and ending filter states.

Alternatively, you can call getFiltersAtPercentage() and pass a percentage to get the interpolated filter for a specific percentage. This way, you can make a slider that jumps to a specific portion in a filter tween. Figure 9.28 shows how you can easily get any interpolated filter after you have a beginning and an end filter.

FIGURE 9.28 Classes that implement IDualFilter let you interpolate any beginning and end filter by percentage.

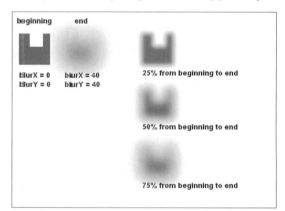

Before I show you some code samples, let me remind you that the advantage of using ActionScript for filter effects is that you don't have to dedicate a portion of your timeline to these animations. Plus, only code lets you create an animation that behaves differently based on dynamic information, such as the user's mouse movement or weather information pulled from a web service.

1. **Selecting the start and end filters**
2. **Creating two filter instances**
3. **Copying the support files**
4. **Passing a start and end** BlurFilter **to the** DualBlurFilter **class**
5. **Combining filter effects**
6. **Using the** WavyFilter **class**

STEP 1▼
Selecting the Start and End Filters

I find the easiest way to select your filter settings is by simply using the Flash authoring tool. You create a movie clip instance and play around with the Filters panel. When you find a setting you like, simply note the values in all the fields, as Figure 9.29 shows for the Drop Shadow filter.

Start by gathering the values for two Blur filter effects: one that doesn't blur very much and one that is very blurred. The Blur filter is a good one to start with because there are only three settings. From the Filters panel, note the values for Blur X, Blur Y, and Quality for both Blur effects.

✦ NOTE

Although the Filters panel shows the Strength value for a filter as a percentage, you must convert that value into a factor when you create a filter. That is, if you want 100% strength, the ActionScript value will be 1. The same goes for alpha, such as when specifying a color's transparency. An alpha value of 100% is represented as 1 when using code.

STEP 2▼
Creating Two Filter Instances

In a new file, draw a simple shape such as a square. Select it and convert it to a symbol by pressing F8. Select the Movie Clip option and click OK. Use the Properties panel to give the box an instance name, such as **box**. Don't apply any filters using the Filters panel. Rather, open the Actions panel for this symbol and type the code shown in Listing 9.5.

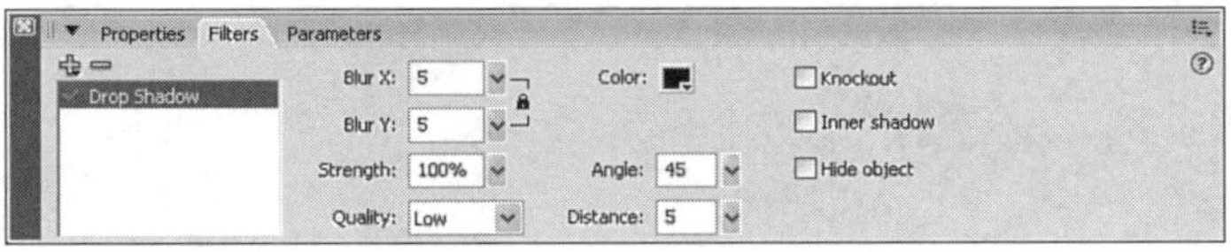

FIGURE 9.29   You can collect a filter's settings straight from the Filters panel.

LISTING 9.5   This Code Creates Two BlurFilter **Instances**

```
import flash.filters.BlurFilter;
var bf1:BlurFilter = new BlurFilter( 0, 0, 1 );
var bf2:BlurFilter = new BlurFilter( 100, 50, 1 );
```

The first line simply lets you type BlurFilter instead of flash.filters.BlurFilter in every instance throughout the code. The bf1 instance has a blurX and blurY of 0 and a quality of 1. The bf2 instance has a blurX of 100 and blurY of 50. Notice that if you simply type BlurFilter(), you immediately see the ToolTip that helps you enter the parameters in the correct order.

To see the effect of one of these filters on your box movie clip instance, you need at least one more line of code:

```
box.filters = [ bf2 ];
```

When you test the movie, you will see the bf2 instance of the Blur filter applied to the box symbol. Save the .fla file in a working directory. Naturally, that's just one filter and we want to animate the two filters, which involves interpolation.

STEP 3▼
Copying the Support Files

Find the classes\IDualFilter folder you downloaded for this chapter and copy all the files into your working directory. (For this part of the exercise, you really need only the IDualFilter.as, utils.as, and

DualBlurFilter.as files, but you should grab the others for the next few steps when you use other filters.)

STEP 4▼
Passing a Start and End BlurFilter to the DualBlurFilter Class

Return to the code you wrote in Listing 9.5 and modify it to read as shown in Listing 9.6.

After you create the dbf DualBlurFilter instance, you can call getNextStep() and it cycles from the start filter to the end filter and back again. If you want it to make bigger jumps, just pass a numeric value to the function. For example, specify getNextStep(5) to jump 5% of the way each time.

Instead of automatically changing the filter on every cnEnterFrame, as the code in Listing 9.6 does, an alternative is to change the filters when the user does something such as moving the mouse. For example, you can remove the last three lines from Listing 9.6 (beginning with onEnterFrame = function...) and use the code on the next page instead:

LISTING 9.6 **This Code Interpolates the Two** BlurFilters **As the Movie Plays**

```
import flash.filters.BlurFilter;
var bf1:BlurFilter = new BlurFilter(0,0,1);
var bf2:BlurFilter = new BlurFilter(100,50,1);

var dbf = new DualBlurFilter( bf1, bf2 );

onEnterFrame=function(){
    box.filters =  dbf.getNextStep() ;
}
```

```
onMouseMove=function(){
    var p = _xmouse/Stage.width;
    box.filters =
    dbf.getFiltersAtPercentage( p*100 );
    updateAfterEvent();
}
```

Creating the same types of effects with other filters simply involves using other classes that implement IDualFilter—those that start with Dual. For example, you can create a tweenable DropShadowFilter with the code in Listing 9.7.

STEP 5▼
Combining Filter Effects

You've probably noticed that, when setting a clip's filters property, you're providing an array. That's because one clip can have several filters applied at once. All my IDualFilter.as class files supply an array instead of a single filter variable. If you want to have a tween that both blurs and changes its DropShadow, or that employs any combination of filters, here's the way to do it: Make multiple DualFilter instances, grab the first item in the array that each one returns, and use those items to create an array that you apply to your clip.

For example, check out the code in Listing 9.8, which is really just a combination of the last few steps with a small change in the last line.

Notice that I'm calling getNextStep() on both DualFilters and grabbing just the first item ([0]) and stuffing the two filters into the array to which the filters property is being set.

> 📌 **NOTE**
>
> It might seem arbitrary and annoying that I am passing an array instead of a filter to the getNextStep() and getFiltersAtPercentage() methods, but I did this to be consistent with the ListAnim class from the final project in this chapter, which also implements IDualFilter.as.

STEP 6▼
Using the WavyFilter Class

This class implements the IDualFilter.as interface, but the construction is totally different. So, you don't simply provide a beginning and ending filter; rather you supply different parameters entirely. However, this project makes using Flash's new DisplaymentMapFilter very easy, and the result is really cool.

LISTING 9.7 This Code Interpolates the Two DropShadowFilters As the Movie Plays

```
import flash.filters.DropShadowFilter;
var ds1 = new DropShadowFilter( 100, 45, 0xFF0000, 0 );
var ds2 = new DropShadowFilter( 100, 45, 0x00FF00, 100 );
var dsf = new DualDropShadow ( ds1, ds2 );
onEnterFrame=function(){
    box.filters =  dsf.getNextStep();
}
```

LISTING 9.8 **This Code**
Applies Both a Blur **and a**
DropShadow **Filter to a Clip**
As the Movie Plays

```
import flash.filters.DropShadowFilter;
import flash.filters.BlurFilter;

var ds1 = new DropShadowFilter( 100, 45, 0xFF0000, 0 );
var ds2 = new DropShadowFilter( 100, 45, 0x00FF00, 100 );
var dsf = new DualDropShadow ( ds1, ds2 );

var bf1:BlurFilter = new BlurFilter( 0, 0, 1 );
var bf2:BlurFilter = new BlurFilter( 100, 50, 1 );

var dbf = new DualBlurFilter( bf1, bf2 );

onEnterFrame=function(){
    box.filters =  [ dsf.getNextStep()[0] ,
                     dbf.getNextStep()[0]  ];
}
```

Create a new file and save it in your working directory. Import a photograph; place it on the stage; select it; and select Modify, Convert to Symbol. In the dialog box, select the Movie Clip option and click OK. Use the

Properties panel to give the symbol an instance name of **photo**. Select the first keyframe for the clip, open the Actions panel, and type the code in Listing 9.9.

LISTING 9.9 **This Code**
Uses the WavyFilter **Class**
to Make the Photo **Instance**
Appear to Melt

```
1    var tempClip:MovieClip = createEmptyMovieClip( "tempClip", 0 );
2    tempClip._visible = false;
3
4    var bitmapWidth = photo._width;
5    var bitmapHeight = photo._height + 40;
6    var baseX = 100;
7    var baseY = 50;
8    //these are optional:
9    var minX = 0;
10   var maxX = 0;
11   var minY = 0;
12   var maxY = 100;
13
14   wf = new WavyFilter( tempClip,
15                        bitmapWidth,
16                        bitmapHeight,
17                        baseX,
18                        baseY,
19                        minX,
20                        maxX,
21                        minY,
```

continues

LISTING 9.9   **Continued**

```
22                           maxY );
23
24    onEnterFrame = function(){
25      photo.filters = wf.getNextStep()  ;
26    }
```

Because Flash's `DisplacementMapFilter` class requires a movie clip to base its displacement on, my `WavyFilter.as` class needs a clip to draw into (*tempClip*). Comment out the second line to see the Perlin Noise that is drawn into that clip.

> **NOTE**
>
> Perlin Noise is an algorithm that generates organic-looking patterns. You can vary several parameters to affect how random or consistent the pattern appears. Interestingly, the algorithm was developed for the 1982 movie *Tron* by Professor Ken Perlin (see http://mrl.nyu.edu/~perlin/) who won an Academy Award for it!

The second and third parameters most often match the width and height of the clip you're filtering, but you usually need to make these slightly larger than the clip to accommodate for the fact the clip will expand past its borders when distorted. Notice line 5: Based on the other parameters I'm passing, the image would get cut off at the bottom if I didn't add those extra 40 pixels.

The parameters *baseX* and *baseY* are used in the `perlinNoise` property of the `BitmapData` class. You can vary these to make for very different-looking patterns. Both pairs *minX*, *maxX*, and *minY*, *maxY* affect the animation. Remember the two filters in the other `DualFilter` examples? Well, if you make *minX*

and *maxX* equal and *minY* and *maxY* equal, you won't see any animation—but the noise filter keeps moving! These four parameters specify how much influence the Perlin Noise has on your photo. You can still have a wild effect on the photo even if it doesn't animate over time. Just play around with these variables. Figure 9.30 shows a few combinations I found interesting.

> **NOTE**
>
> Although I think my `IDualFilter.as` interface to these classes is very simple, it's also ultimately a bit limited. It doesn't support easing, for example. For a more advanced set of code, check out the `ColorMatrix` class written by Grant Skinner at www.gskinner.com/blog. This class enables you to integrate filter effects with other tween engines such as Zigo/Fuse (www.mosessupposes.com/Fuse/) and the Macromedia transitions classes.

Project:
Offline ListAnim Filter Class

The examples that implement my `IDualFilter` class all require that you create a start filter and an end filter (and then the class tweens the difference). However, sometimes frame-by-frame animations are more appropriate than tweens. For this reason, I built the `ListAnim` class, which also implements `IDualFilter`.

FIGURE 9.30 These six variations show the range of effects possible using the `WavyFilter` class.

Original

Base X: 100
Base Y: 10
Max X: 10
Max Y: 50

Base X: 100
Basy Y: 50
Max X: 0
Max Y: 100

Base X: 5
Base Y: 10
Max X: 10
Max Y: 10

Base X: 5
Base Y: 5
Max X: 50
Max Y: 50

Base X: 100
Base Y: 10
Max X: 100
Max Y: 10

The way the `ListAnim` class works is that you start in a working file by animating a clip in the timeline—you can use any filter or filter combination you want. Then, while the clip plays, you run a script that gathers all the filters applied to your clip and outputs an XML string. You paste that XML code into a text file; then you can load that XML into another file. At runtime, the filters are applied to any clip you specify, in much the same way as with any of my `IDualFilter` examples. However, instead of passing a start filter and an end filter, you pass the contents of that XML file.

The key to this project is that you have both an "offline" working file, where you create the animation and generate the XML using the `FilterMonitor.as` class, and the real "online" version, where you load the XML and send the results to the `ListAnim` class, which re-creates the filters you can apply at runtime.

STEPS▼

1. **Creating the offline animation**
2. **Copying the support files**
3. **Running the** `FilterMonitor.as` **class to gather the filter values**

STEP 1▼
Creating the Offline Animation

In a new file, create a movie clip and give it an instance name of **targetClip**. It's important that the clip has an instance name before you add any keyframes. Make an animation in the main timeline, applying any filter or filter combinations you want to the `targetClip` instance. Create as many keyframes as you want; use tweens or just do everything frame-by-frame.

Save the animation file in a working folder.

STEP 2▼
Copying the Support Files

Find the `classes\IDualFilter` folder you downloaded for this chapter and copy all the files into your working directory. For this part of the exercise, you need only the `FilterMonitor.as` file, but you'll need `ListAnim.as`, `utils.as`, and `LongHex.as` for the online version.

STEP 3▼
Running the FilterMonitor.as Class to Gather the Filter Values

In your offline animation `.fla` file, select the first keyframe, open the Actions panel, and type the code shown in Listing 9.10.

Select Control, Test Movie; when the animation completes, your Output panel displays the filter data collected. It's an XML string with all the filters and filter settings you applied to the `targetClip` in your timeline.

Select all the text that appears in your Output panel, right-click it, and select Copy from the context menu (alternatively, you can use the Output panel's Option menu to select Copy). Open a text editor such as Notepad and paste (press Ctrl+V) the long string of XML data into the text editor. Save the text file in your working directory with the filename **myAnimation.xml**.

LISTING 9.10 This Code Gathers the Filters Applied to a Clip

```
var fm = new FilterMonitor();
//add one for this frame:
fm.addToList( targetClip );

onEnterFrame=function(){
    //add one for this frame
    fm.addToList( targetClip );

    //see if we're done
    if(_currentframe == _totalframes ){
        trace (  fm.getXML().toString() );
        delete onEnterFrame;
        stop();
    }
}
```

STEP 4▼
Creating the Online Version

Create a new .fla file and immediately save it in your working directory. Create a movie clip and give it an instance name of **targetClip**. Don't apply any filters to this movie clip instance. Select the first keyframe, open the

Actions panel, and type the code shown in Listing 9.11.

This code first loads the XML and passes the contents when it triggers the init() function. Test the movie; when you move your mouse, an array of filters is calculated and applied to the targetClip instance.

LISTING 9.11 This Code Loads in the XML Data and Uses It to Animate a targetClip

```
var la = new ListAnim();

x = new XML();
x.ignoreWhite=true;
x.onLoad = function(){
    la.init(this);
}
x.load("myAnimation.xml");

onMouseMove=function(){
    var p = _xmouse/Stage.width;
    targetClip.filters = la.getFiltersAtPercentage( p*100 );
    updateAfterEvent();
}
```

You can also use the getNextStep() method. However, both the getNextStep() and getFiltersAtPercentage() methods are based on going from 0 to 100%. If your original animation is not exactly 100 frames, the percentage and actual frame number won't match (my code simply finds the closest one). To enable you to play the animation exactly as it was gathered, I added a few additional methods. Namely, getFiltersOnFrame(*frameNumber*), getFrameCount(), and getFilterList() (to get the whole array of frames).

With those methods, you can make the animation play once, from start to finish, every time the user clicks by using the code in Listing 9.12.

Now, each time the user clicks the code finds the total frames, sets step to 0, and starts grabbing filters for each frame number—one step at a time.

Final Thoughts

This chapter was all over the map. It was fun because you got to do lots of individual effects. However, there's one big step that wasn't covered in detail: applying the effects to larger projects. Let me give you a few ideas of how I've used the various effects in real projects.

LISTING 9.12 This Code Applies the Saved Filter Animation Every Time the User Clicks

```
var la = new ListAnim();

x = new XML();
x.ignoreWhite=true;
x.onLoad = function(){
   la.init(this);
}
x.load("myAnimation.xml");

onMouseDown = function(){
   var total = la.getFrameCount();
   var step = 0;
   onEnterFrame=function(){
      step++;
      if( step < total ){
         targetClip.filters = la.getFiltersOnFrame( step );
      }else{
         targetClip.filters = [];
         delete onEnterFrame;
      }
   }
}
```

It seems that the timeline effects show up in various forms on every project. Coincidentally, after writing this chapter, I had a project where I needed to add a continuous loop containing a strip composed of cloud photographs. It brought an otherwise static image to life because the clouds slowly moved across the background. By the way, the seam where the clouds repeated was simply a portion of the sky with no clouds, as you can see in Figure 9.31.

FIGURE 9.31   Using two identical images with photos of clouds made a project come alive.

Loops can be more than just a linear strip that moves left or right. Even a simple rotating wheel should loop properly, with the last frame lining up with the first.

The magnifier effect has shown up in several of my projects—although never exactly as shown in this chapter. For example, back in the dark ages of the Internet (1999), I programmed the m3 snowboards website (now archived at www.deepplay.com/sites/m399) where users could zoom in on portions of the snowboards, as shown in Figure 9.32.

Although making the magnifier follow the mouse (as in the case of m3 website) requires ActionScript, the approach is the same as the Magnifier Lens Effect project in this chapter. You can learn more about adding ActionScript to this effect by downloading the source at www.phillipkerman.com/actionscripting/workshopsmx/workshop_5.htm.

FIGURE 9.32   I used the magnifier effect we used earlier in this chapter in this site to let users see details of snowboard designs.

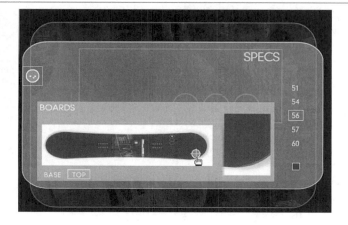

I've only started using Flash 8's blends and filters on real projects, but they really save time and file size! For example, in the past, to create both a black-and-white and color image, you had to import two bitmaps. The other comment I want to make is that filters and blends are not only for wild "special effects." For example, Figure 9.33 shows a practical example using the BevelFilter that creates raised tiles and sunken targets and the DropShadowFilter that makes the tile the user drags appear to float over the stage.

version. That's the same as how the ListAnim class works and how the recording application for the VUMeter class in the downloaded files works. I've seen programmers spend a ton of time working up complex mathematical algorithms for a scripted animation when it's much easier to simply work up an offline prototype animation in the timeline and then write a script that gathers the values. I've used this approach in many projects. The part to remember is that you can write code to help you assemble the project—not just code that executes at runtime.

FIGURE 9.33 **Filters can do more than create gratuitous effects.**

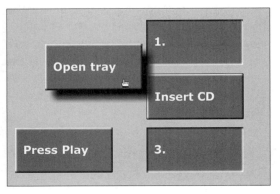

Finally, the approach taken in the "Offline ListAnim Filter Class" project is quite valuable. That is, you produce an animation using traditional techniques, gather the coordinates and filter settings, and then use the values gathered in the online version. In fact, we took a similar approach in Chapter 3, "Creating a Video with Synchronized Captions," when using gathering_tool.swf to collect cue points while the video played. In offline mode, you watched the video and clicked to "record" the cue point times and then used those recorded values in the online

CHAPTER 10: Building a Photo Share Application

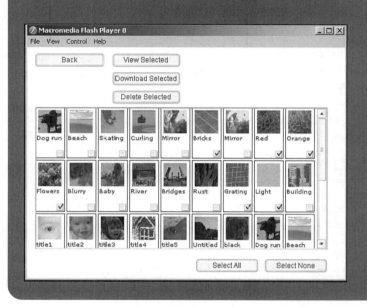

About the Project

This project lets your users upload images, associate tags with those images using keywords, and then browse all the hosted images. On the surface, it's a mini version of photo sharing sites such as www.flickr.com; however, you can modify it to support any file format. In a lot of ways, it's the same as the photo portfolio from Chapter 4, "Creating a Portfolio," but this photo sharing application adds support for downloading files (not just viewing them) as well as optional support for uploading files. To support these features, you'll need an application server and an online database tool.

Prerequisites

You'll need an application server that can handle both the file uploads and the database management. I've included scripts for doing it in PHP and a concise application programming interface (API) for the server-side component. Finally, you'll need Flash Professional 8 to use the DataGrid component, although I have included an alternative version that uses the List component—available with Flash Basic 8.

@work resources

Download the chapter_10_downloads.zip file for this chapter from the accompanying CD-ROM.

Planning the Projects

When you allow users to add to the content that drives your application (in this case, letting them upload photos), you open a giant can of worms. Naturally, you can't let an unlimited number of users upload an unlimited number of files because you'll run out of disk space. You need to monitor or restrict how much content users can upload. In addition, there are legal issues when sharing copyrighted material as well as inappropriate content. I've seen implementations of this kind of project where no uploaded file is available for public viewing until after it goes through a manual review process in which one person looks at every uploaded file.

This section covers the more down-to-earth considerations such as which features we'll be adding to our project and how all the pieces we'll build fit together. In this chapter, you'll build each screen that appears in the photo share application, adding the features you want to support. This section covers which screens are available and which features each screen can support.

> ### 📌 NOTE
>
> This project was designed around the new `FileReference` class that lets you upload or download files. Normally, you start with an objective and then find the tool to solve it. However, this new capability in Flash 8 is so useful that I had to include a project that uses it. It's not that this project is impractical, but it does give you only a taste of what's possible with this new feature.

Features for This Project

This section is an overview that introduces the main interface elements you'll build in this project.

There are three main screens:

- ▶ **Selection**—This is where the user narrows her image search by selecting keywords before advancing to the Thumbnail screen.

- ▶ **Thumbnail**—This is a screen where all matching image thumbnails are displayed. The user selects one or more images to download, delete, or view full screen.

- ▶ **Zoom**—This is where the user sees her selected image(s) and can individually download or make edits to the image's keywords.

In addition, this project uses two modal screens that are more like dialog boxes that must be completed before the user can return to the screen she was on:

- ▶ **Upload**—This begins with a browse dialog box where the user selects an image to upload. The actual upload process doesn't begin until after the user selects an image and confirms it by clicking the Upload button. Immediately after a successful upload, the user is taken to the Edit screen (to add details about the image she uploaded) and then back to the Selection screen.

- ▶ **Edit**—This is where the user enters keywords for each image she uploads, as well as other optional tags.

After you make at least one .swf version of each of the screens just listed, you'll create a very simple *main* file that does two main things: specifies the filename of each screen .swf you want to include and instantiates the PhotoShare class, which you downloaded for this chapter. The PhotoShare class handles loading the various screens and sending messages between the screens.

The first thing I did was to build a prototype. Check it out by launching prototype.swf, in the prototype folder you downloaded for this chapter. That should give you an even better idea of how the project will flow. In addition, Figure 10.1 shows how the user can navigate the final project.

FIGURE 10.1 This flow-chart gives you an overview of how the user will use the final project.

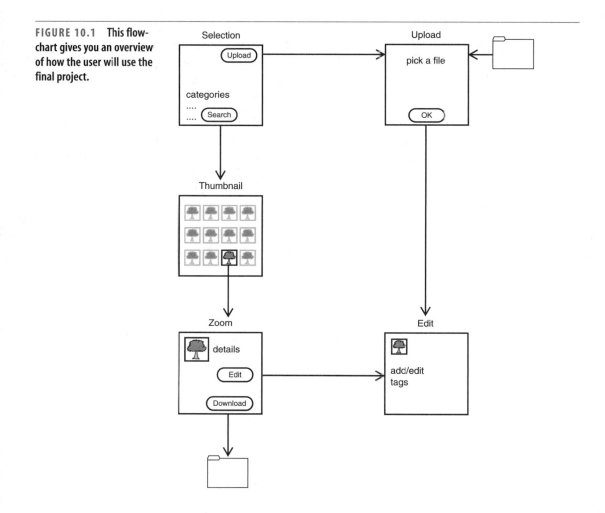

Additional Tags

Users can tag their images with as many *keywords* as they like. They can also give the images a category. (Originally, I thought to place a limit of one category per image, but later I removed that limit.) The result is that keywords and categories are different only in practice—that is, I suspect that users will tag their images with many more keywords than categories.

Here's an example: Suppose you have photos of a gray cat, a black cat, a black dog, and a child. Consider these tags:

▶ The gray cat is given the category pets and the keywords gray and cat.

▶ The black cat is given the category pets and the keywords black and cat.

▶ The black dog is given the category pets and the keywords black and dog.

▶ The child is given the category kids and the keywords boy, tommy, and 6 years old.

After the photos are uploaded, the user can select the category pets and receive a list of three images: the two cats and the dog. The user could also select the keyword black and see the black dog and black cat images. Ultimately, the way this feature is used is entirely based on how users create tags for the images they upload. They are given a chance to edit the tags in the edit screen when they first upload the image, but they can also return to edit the tags later.

When Flash sends image information to the server, or when the server returns image information to Flash, each image is described by an XML node named <image>. Consider the <image> node in Listing 10.1.

LISTING 10.1 This Data Represents a Typical Image

```
<image imageID="idog987df"
       title="black dog"
       thumbnail="dog-t.jpg"
       image="dog.jpg">

    <keywords>
       <keyword name="black"/>
       <keyword name="dog"/>
    </keywords>

    <categories>
       <category name="pets"/>
    </categories>

    <additional_details>
       <detail name="photographer"
               type="string">Phillip Kerman</detail>
       <detail name="date"
               type="number">930857</detail>
    </additional_details>
</image>
```

To make this project as adaptable as possible, the objects that contain all the image information (an XML node named <image> with the child nodes <filename>, <title>, <category>, and <keywords>) are not fixed to a given format. For example, Listing 10.1 shows an extra node called <additional_details>. Each <image> node is required to have an imageID attribute, but beyond that, you can customize the schema as you want. The support files relay the <image> nodes as is. So, if you decide that each image should have a photographer attribute, you can easily write the ActionScript code to extract that information from the <image> node that is sent to the particular screen you're building. This approach makes more sense than having me try to think of all the possible tags readers will want. I'm pointing out the extensibility of the <image> node for two reasons—first, so you understand how you can extend this project, and second, as a general strategy that (when possible) you should leave room for extension.

Limits of the FileReference Class

The flash.net.FileReference class is relatively straightforward. After you have an instance of the FileReference class (say, in a variable myRef), you can issue the myRef.browse() method and the user will see a standard file selection dialog box, shown for Windows XP in Figure 10.2. You can listen for any event, such as onSelect and onCancel, and then upload the selected file using the myRef.upload("myuploadScript.php") function.

A key to understanding the limits of the FileReference class is to remember that the name is File*Reference*, meaning you can only work with a reference to the file the user selects. You can access its filename, modification date, and size, but not much else. You can't access the file's full path, which means you can't load the selected file directly into a .swf file—for example, using the loadMovie() or loadSound() method. Of course, if the .swf file is on your server, you can't load images that reside on the user's hard drive even if you do know their full paths. These seeming limitations are in place to ensure that the Flash player remains secure.

The basic idea for this project is that users can upload images, tag them with keywords, and browse or search all existing images that are online for optional download. Browsing, sorting, and downloading turns out to be very easy. However, although Flash has existing mechanisms for talking to a database (primarily through the LoadVars and XML classes), the new FileReference.upload(url) method available with Flash 8 has only one way to send data along with the file you're uploading. Namely, you can tack on a short query string to the url where your server-side script resides. That query string is limited to 255 characters, so you can't add many keywords—certainly not enough to make this approach very workable. A second issue is that the user should view the image while he sets the image's keywords. But, as I mentioned previously, the user must first upload the file before you can display it. This means you'll have to first upload the image and then issue loadMovie() to view that uploaded image inside the photo share tool so the user can enter tags. If it were possible, it would be more intuitive for you to let the user pick a file, view it while he adds tags, and then click Upload and be done with it. Alas, for the reasons mentioned, we won't do it this way.

Ideally, the server-side script that accepts the uploaded image file would immediately return an ID that your Flash application could use to request the image. But even that would be too easy! Instead, the approach I ended up with for this project works like this: When the user selects a file to upload, I first ask the server for a unique imageID which, in turn, I use in the query string when finally issuing the upload() command (like uploadScript.php?imageID=123). This way, after the image is uploaded, I can immediately request to download the same image

using the known imageID when issuing the loadMovie() method that gives the user a preview while he adds tags. Figure 10.3 shows the sequence of events necessary to upload an image.

Uploading and Downloading from a Server Only

It's important to understand that the FileReference class lets you download from and upload to only a web server. This limitation makes testing locally more difficult, but not impossible. You'll see that the first project in this chapter simply configures a work environment; you can take this first project much further and also configure a web server depending on how you're planning to deploy your project. The main point I want to make here is that the FileReference class works only from the Web—not a from a CD or your local file system. Although you can test using the Control, Test Movie command from Flash, files can only be uploaded to a web server or downloaded from a web server (not your local file system). Refer to Chapter 8, "Creating a CD-ROM Front End," for a similar project that lets users copy files from a CD-ROM.

FIGURE 10.3 When a user wants to upload an image, we first get a unique ID from the server (A); then we upload the image using that ID in the query string (B). When the image is uploaded, we get all the information about that image (C), including an attribute for image and an attribute for thumbnail, which is used in the loadMovie() method call (D).

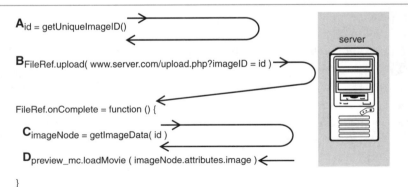

Project:
Work Environment

You should be able to build and test this project locally before having an application server up and running. Naturally, some of the features won't function fully while you're working locally, such as uploading images, which requires a server. But other features can be simulated very effectively. For example, we can stock a static .xml file that returns the expected results from a keyword search. The results won't be dynamic without connecting to a real database, but this test environment lets you build all the interface screens for the project.

You can easily convert the project to work with a live server, after it's up and running, by editing a single lookup table. The application uses a lookup table (the file named urls.xml) to find the actual names for the server-side methods. That lookup table can reference methods on a live server, or it can point to static XML files that contain data in the same format you expect to receive from the server. When you're ready to go live, you just edit that lookup table. We used the same approach in Chapter 6, "Saving and Evaluating Quiz Results," to build and test the quiz review application in lieu of the finished server.

STEPS▼

1. Setting up the static XML files
2. Setting up a starter folder of images
3. Copying the support files

STEP 1▼
Setting Up the Static XML Files

Create a working folder and copy into that folder the folder named schemas, which you can find in the finished_source folder you downloaded for this chapter. Using Notepad or your favorite text editor, open the urls.xml file.

Our project always begins by reading that urls.xml file. The first url node sets a basePath as shown here:

```
<url methodName="basePath"
    path="images/" />
```

The path value (images/) is appended to the beginning of every image or thumbnail file-name. For example, if the server says to load the image myPhoto.jpg, our project changes that filename reference to images/myPhoto.jpg. Therefore, the myPhoto.jpg file must reside in a folder called images right next to the main project .swf file. You can change the value for path to an explicit address on your server, such as http://www.example.com/images/. Alternatively, if you expect the server to include a full path to every image it references, you can set the path attribute to an empty string, using path = "". You'll see, however, that using this base path approach keeps the results from various server calls less wordy because every image and every thumbnail won't have to include a long, explicit file path. When you use this path attribute, the project always looks for images in the folder you specify.

The rest of the urls.xml file is nothing more than a list of where all the server-side methods reside. For example, look at the first `<url>` node:

```
<url methodName="getCategories"
     path="schemas/getCategories.xml"/>
```

When our application needs to get a list of all the existing categories, it calls the `getCategories` method. I'll talk more about how this particular method is used in the initial selection screen to create the list of available categories, but what's important now is to see how Flash determines where to find any server-side method. The `getCategories` method is just being used here as an example. Flash looks at the `path` attribute associated with the `<url>` node whose `methodName` is `"getCategories"`, or, in this case, simply a static XML file called `getCategories.xml`. That's the file we'll read in during testing. When you configure your server, you can change that path to match where the live `"getCategories"` script resides. It can be named anything you want—just list it in the `path` attribute. When our project needs to "get categories," it uses the path we specify here instead of referring to a value hard-coded in the Flash file.

Realize that the static file `getCategories.xml` only simulates the results our server would normally provide. The live server dynamically generates an equivalent XML string with up-to-date values, but we'll just use the hard-coded version during the initial production phase.

Peruse the comments in the `urls.xml` file because they serve as an overview of all the server-side methods our application will need. You can also view the various static XML files to see the values that are normally returned from a live server. The `urls.xml` file and corresponding static `.xml` files serve as an inline API listing. For example, here's the comment for `getCategories` in `urls.xml`:

```
getCategories
params: none
returns: categories/category @name @total
description: called initially to get a
list of all categories
```

The format shown here for the return value should make more sense when you look at the `getCategories.xml` file, shown here:

```
<?xml version="1.0"?>
<categories>
    <category name="Animals" total="1344"/>
    <category name="Buildings" total="1344"/>
    <category name="Music" total="1344"/>
</categories>
```

Notice that the comment in the `urls.xml` file says *categories/category*. That means there's a `<categories>` node that contains child nodes named `<category>`. Then the comment says *@name @total*, which means the `<category>` node has attributes for *name* and *total*.

STEP 2 ▼
Setting Up a Starter Folder of Images

Because we won't be testing the upload feature until the server-side component is running, we'll need to prepopulate the database with references to images. In fact, the database is already stocked. Look in the file getImages.xml and you'll see that every request to "get images" results in the same list of 8 images—that's 16 images total when you consider the thumbnails.

Place a copy of the images folder (from the starter_files folder you downloaded for this chapter) into your working directory.

STEP 3▼
Copying the Support Files

Copy all the .as files from the finished_source folder into your working directory. You really only need the PhotoShare.as file, the IPhotoShare.as interface it implements, plus the XMLGateway.as file. The others are interface files that help formalize the methods you need to implement in the templates you'll build for each screen type. Figure 10.4 shows the completed working folder.

FIGURE 10.4   Your working folder needs these files and folders present.

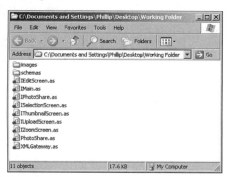

Your first project is complete. Really all you did was copy files into your working folder. The important part of this project, however,

was taking a tour of the various files that will come into play during the subsequent projects.

Project:
Basic Photo Share Project

This project might be "basic," but it's fully functional and pretty complex. There are five screens (selection, upload, thumbnail, zoom, and edit), each of which can be customized. I'm calling this the basic project because, although it is complete, each screen includes the minimum set of features. I'll walk through each one so you can get it up and running. The next project shows ways to modify these screens.

In this project, you'll create a single .swf file for each screen; you'll also create a main file that instantiates an instance of the PhotoShare support class.

Be sure you examine the prototype.swf file (in the prototype folder) so you have a good sense of what the five screens do.

STEPS▼

1. **Creating the main file**
2. **Creating the** selection.swf **template**
3. **Creating the** upload.swf **template**
4. **Assembling the** thumbnail.swf **template**
5. **Applying the code for** thumbnail.swf
6. **Creating the** zoom.swf **template**
7. **Creating the** edit.swf **template**
8. **Testing it**

STEP 1▼
Creating the Main File

The main file simply creates an instance of the PhotoShare class and tells it where the urls.xml resides and which template.swf files to use for the five screens. The PhotoShare class handles all the heavy lifting.

In Flash, create a new file and save it as **main.fla** in your working directory. Use the Text tool to create a text field with very wide margins at the bottom of the screen. Use the Properties panel to set the text's type to Dynamic and its instance name to **prompt_txt**. This text field lets you display various messages that instruct the user.

Because the PhotoShare class uses *XPath* to parse the XML, your main.fla file needs the DataBindingClasses symbol in its Library. Select Window, Library to open the main.fla file's Library panel and then select Window,

Common Libraries, Classes. Drag the DataBindingsClasses symbol from the classes.fla file's Library to the main.fla file's Library, as shown in Figure 10.5.

Select the first keyframe in the main.fla file, open the Actions panel, and type the code in Listing 10.2. You can also find this code in the main.fla file in the finished_source folder you downloaded with this chapter.

FIGURE 10.5 Including the DataBindingClasses symbol in your main.fla file enables this project to use XPath for XML parsing.

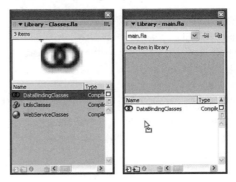

LISTING 10.2 This Code Instantiates the PhotoShare Class and Specifies the Names for Each Screen		

```
1   var urlList:String; //path to urls.xml
2   //This value can be set via FlashVars,
        //but just in case set a default:
3   if(urlList == undefined){
4       urlList = "schemas/urls.xml";
5   }
6
7
8   var scope = this;
9   var selectionScreen = "selection.swf";
10  var uploadScreen = "upload.swf";
11  var thumbnailScreen = "thumbnail.swf";
12  var zoomedScreen = "zoom.swf";
13  var editScreen = "edit.swf";
14  var controller:PhotoShare = new PhotoShare( scope,
15                                              urlList,
16                                              selectionScreen,
17                                              uploadScreen,
```

LISTING 10.2 Continued

```
18                                              thumbnailScreen,
19                                              zoomedScreen,
20                                              editScreen );
21
22   setPrompt("");
23   function setPrompt(toWhat){
24       prompt_txt.text = toWhat;
25   }
```

There are only two things going on in Listing 10.2. The parameters are defined and sent to the PhotoShare constructor, and a setPrompt() method defines how the prompt_txt field is populated. The urlList variable is set up so that, if it already has a value (set in the FlashVars tag of the HTML file), it's left alone. Otherwise, it's set to point to the urls.xml file in the schemas folder. The various screen .swf filenames are specified in lines 8–13, which makes it easy to change later. Say that you want to make a version of this project where the selection.swf doesn't include an Upload button. You can either replace the selection.swf file, which we'll build in the next step, or point to a different filename in line 8.

Save the main.fla but don't bother publishing at this point because the five screen .swf files don't exist yet.

STEP 2 ▼
Creating the selection.swf Template

In this step, you'll assemble the selection screen by placing components on the stage that let the user view all the categories or all the keywords. In addition, the user can navigate away from the selection screen in two ways: by selecting a listed category or keyword and clicking the Get Thumbnails button, or by clicking the Upload button that lets the user select an image to upload. You'll implement the ActionScript to support all this activity, even though the actual thumbnails screen and upload dialog box are built in later steps.

Create a new Flash file and save it in your working directory as **selection.fla**. Select Window, Components and drag onto the stage the following components: two RadioButton components, two Button components, and one DataGrid component. Lay them out as shown in Figure 10.6, and use the Properties panel to give them the instance names **categoryRB**, **keywordRB**, **getThumbnailsButton**, **uploadButton**, and **dg** (for the DataGrid). Set the instance names for the components to match the labels shown in Figure 10.6; you don't have to set the labels, though.

Open the version of selection.fla in the finished_source folder, select the first keyframe, open the Actions panel, and copy all the code you find there. Return to your working version of the selection.fla file and—with the first keyframe selected—paste the code into the Actions panel. The bulk of the code handles the processing of the components. Check out the code following line 100, which is reprinted in Listing 10.3 for your convenience.

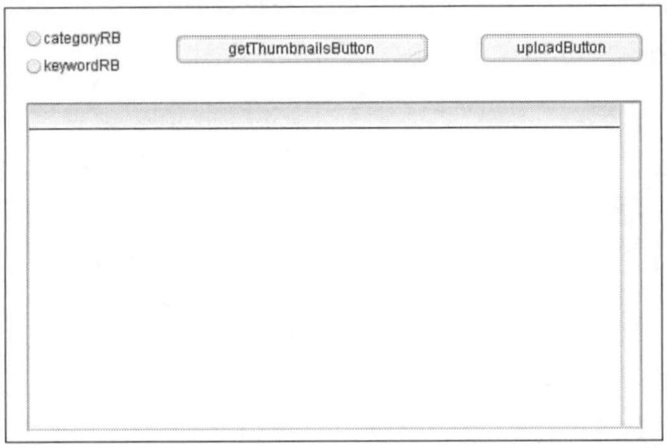

FIGURE 10.6   The selection screen includes the components positioned as shown.

LISTING 10.3   This Excerpt Shows How the Selection Screen Parses the Data It Receives to Configure the Display

```
100   var controller:PhotoShare;
101   var categories:Array;
      //of <category name="Animals" total="1344"/>
102   var keywords:Array;
      //of <keyword name="Animals" total="1344"/>
103
104   //required by interface
105   function init( p_controller:PhotoShare,
                     p_categories:Array,
                     p_keywords:Array ){
106      controller = p_controller;
107
108      categories = new Array();
109      var total = p_categories.length;
110      for(var i = 0; i < total; i++){
111         categories.push( {Category:
                                 p_categories[i].attributes.name,
112                              Total:
                                 p_categories[i].attributes.total });
113      }
114      keywords = new Array();
115      var total = p_keywords.length;
116      for(var i = 0; i < total; i++){
117         keywords.push( {Keyword:
                               p_keywords[i].attributes.name,
118                           Total:
                               p_keywords[i].attributes.total });
119      }
120
121      //simulate pressing the button:
122      categoryRB.selected = true;
```

LISTING 10.3   Continued

```
123      clickRadio({target:categoryRB});
124      show();
125  }
126  //required by interface
127  function hide(){
128     this._visible = false;
129  }
130  //required by interface
131  function show(){
132     this._visible = true;
133  }
```

Every selection screen must implement these three methods: init(), hide(), and show(). These are also defined formally in the ISelection.as interface file. The hide() and show() methods simply to let the PhotoShare class control when the selection.swf is visible. The init() method is called after the PhotoShare class receives a list of all the categories and keywords, after calling getCategories and getKeywords as defined in the urls.xml file.

Both the p_categories and p_keywords parameters are arrays full of the nodes that contain name and total attributes. Notice that the init() method populates the categories and keywords arrays with ActionScript objects by extracting the name and total attributes.

Finally, it's worth looking at the two ways this screen will direct messages to the PhotoShare class, referenced in the init() method's p_controller parameter. When the user clicks the Upload button, the PhotoShare instance's public function goToUpload() is triggered as this code (from line 45 in the selection.fla file):

```
45  function goToUpload(){
46      controller.goToUpload();
47  }
48  uploadButton.addEventListener("click",
                              goToUpload);
```

After the user selects one or more values in the dg (DataGrid instance), she can click the getThumbnailsButton button and PhotoShare's getThumbnails() method will be triggered on line 67, as shown in Listing 10 4.

```
67  function getThumbnails(evt){
68      var valuesToSearch = new Array();
69
70      //grab the selected data from dg
71      var ar = dg.selectedIndices;
72      for(var i=0; i< ar.length; i++){
73          valuesToSearch.push ( dg.getItemAt(ar[i])[mode] );
```

continues

LISTING 10.4   Continued

```
74        }
75        var param = new Object();
76
77        if(mode=="Category"){
78            param.categories = valuesToSearch;
79        }
80        if(mode=="Keyword"){
81            param.keywords = valuesToSearch;
82        }
83        controller.getThumbnails(param);
84    }
85    getThumbnailsButton.addEventListener("click", getThumbnails);
```

Notice that the PhotoShare's getThumbnails() method is passed an ActionScript object (param) that contains an array of categories or keywords based on what's currently selected in the dg DataGrid. The mode variable is set to either "Keyword" or "Category", depending on which radio button—categoryRB or keywordRB—was clicked last. Notice that the param object has either a keywords or a categories property set, but not both. You're welcome to use both categories and keywords properties (for example, if the user wants to search a category and some keywords). The design set up in this project is such that the DataGrid displays either all the categories or all the keywords.

Select Control, Test Movie to generate selection.swf, which the main file needs when we test it in step 8.

STEP 3▼
Creating the upload.swf Template

This upload screen is simple: The user browses to a file and clicks Upload (or she

can click Cancel). You'll just need to assemble a few components and write some basic code in this step.

Create a new Flash file and save it in your working directory as **upload.fla**. Select Window, Components and drag a TextInput component and two Button components onto the stage. Position the components on the stage as shown in Figure 10.7, and use the Properties panel to give them the instance names **filenameField**, **uploadButton**, and **cancelButton**.

FIGURE 10.7   The upload screen includes the components positioned as shown.

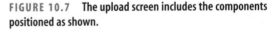

Because this screen acts as a modal dialog box that appears on top of the selection screen or another screen from which the user can select to upload, we need to cover the rest of the screen. The clip used to cover the rest of the screen can be semitransparent but—above all else—it must have an onPress function defined so users can't activate any buttons underneath. We'll also set the cover's useHandCursor property to false.

Create a new layer and use the Rectangle tool to draw a filled rectangle in that layer that covers the whole stage. Select the entire shape and select Modify, Convert to Symbol. In the Convert to Symbol dialog box, select the Movie Clip option, name the symbol **Cover**, and click OK. Use the Properties panel to give the clip the instance name **cover**. Finally, arrange the layers so the layer containing the cover instance is below the layer containing the UI components created earlier.

Open the version of the upload.fla file located in the finished_source folder you downloaded for this chapter, select the first keyframe, open the Actions panel, and copy all the code you find there. Return to your working version of upload.fla, select the first keyframe, and paste the code into the Actions panel. Listing 10.5 shows some excerpts from that code for discussion.

The init() function is required, along with the show() and hide() functions, by the IUpload.as interface. The PhotoShare class calls init() when it's time for the user to select a file to upload—that is, when the user clicks the uploadButton instance in the selection.swf. The main things to note in this init() method are that we store a reference to the PhotoShare class in the controller variable and that we trigger the browse() method on a variable instance (fileRef) of the flash.net.FileReference class (instantiated earlier in the code, on line 40, and not shown in Listing 10.5).

LISTING 10.5 This Excerpt Shows How the Upload Screen Initializes Itself

```
63    cover.onPress = null;
64    cover.useHandCursor = false;
65
66
67    //required by interface
68    function init( p_controller:PhotoShare ) {
69        controller = p_controller;
70        filenameField.text = "";
71        uploadButton.enabled = false;
72        cancelButton.enabled = true;
73        fileRef.browse( [ { description:"Image Files",
                            extension:"*.jpg;*.gif;*.png"} ] );
74        show();
75    }
76    //required by interface
77    function hide() {
78        this._visible = false;
79    }
80    //required by interface
81    function show() {
82        this._visible = true;
83    }
```

You'll notice that, in fact, the only `FileReference` work going on here is the `browse()` call. There are listeners that respond to the user canceling or selecting a file from the standard file browse dialog box, but even after the user confirms by clicking the `uploadButton` instance, the `PhotoShare` reference handles the actual uploading of the file. In fact, everything is channeled back to the instance of the `PhotoShare` class; there are two public functions in the `PhotoShare` instance (the variable `controller`). These are `cancelUpload()` and `doUpload()`, as the following excerpt shows:

```
18    //_____
19    //----------cancel button:
20    //_____
21    function cancelUpload() {
22        controller.cancelUpload(fileRef);
23    }
24    cancelButton.addEventListener("click",
                                   cancelUpload);

26    //_____
27    //----------upload button:
28    //_____
29    function doUpload() {
30        controller.doUpload(fileRef);
31        uploadButton.enabled = false;
32        cancelButton.enabled = false;
33    }
34    uploadButton.addEventListener("click",
                                   doUpload);
```

Finally, the code in Listing 10.6 listens for events from the `FileReference` instance (`fileRef`).

LISTING 10.6 This Code Responds to the User Selecting a File or Canceling the Selection of a File

```
40    var fileRef:flash.net.FileReference = new FileReference();
41    var controller:PhotoShare;
42
43
44    //_____
45    //----------FileReference listener:
46    //_____
47    var listener:Object = new Object();
48    listener.onSelect = function( selectedFile:FileReference ) {
49        filenameField.text = selectedFile.name;
50        uploadButton.enabled = true;
51    };
52    listener.onCancel = function() {
53        //call the same method as if they clicked cancel
54        cancelUpload();
55    };
56    fileRef.addListener(listener);
```

Notice that nothing really major happens when the user selects a file except that the `filenameField` is populated and the `uploadButton` is enabled. If the user cancels out of the standard browse dialog box, we trigger the `cancelUpload()` function in the same way as when the user clicks the `cancelButton`. If the user clicks the `uploadButton` instance, the `doUpload()` method is called on the `PhotoShare` class, shown in the preceding code excerpt on line 30. The `PhotoShare` class actually uploads the file, but not until after the server provides a unique ID for the image—as discussed in the "Limits of the `FileReference` Class" section of "Planning the Projects," earlier in this chapter.

Select Control, Test Movie to generate `upload.swf`, which the main file needs when we test it in step 8.

STEP 4▼
Assembling the thumbnail.swf Template

The thumbnail screen is probably the most complex template in this project. After a set of thumbnails is delivered to the client and displayed in a scrolling window, the user can select some or all of the thumbnails and then choose to view, download, or delete the full-size images on the server.

Create a new Flash document and save it in your working directory as **thumbnail.fla**. Select Window, Components and drag onto the stage six `Button` components, a `ProgressBar`, and a `ScrollPane`. Position the components on the stage as shown in Figure 10.8, and

use the Properties panel to give the buttons the following instance names: **backtoSelection**, **viewButton**, **downloadButton**, **deleteButton**, **selectAllButton**, and **selectNoneButton**. Name the `ProgressBar` instance **progressBar** and name the `ScrollPane` **sp**.

FIGURE 10.8 The thumbnail screen includes the components positioned as shown.

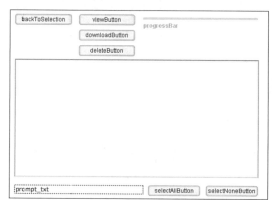

Use the Text tool to create a block of text with wide margins. Use the Properties panel to set the text type to Dynamic Text and give it the instance name **prompt_txt**. This area will display information about whichever thumbnail is under the user's mouse pointer as it hovers over the thumbnails.

There are two more steps before we get to the code. To dynamically add content (the thumbnail images) to the sp `ScrollPane`, we need an empty movie clip with a linkage identifier. Select Insert, New Symbol. In the Create New Symbol dialog box, set the symbol's name to **empty** and select the Export for ActionScript option, as shown in Figure 10.9; then click OK. The Linkage Identifier text box should also read **empty**.

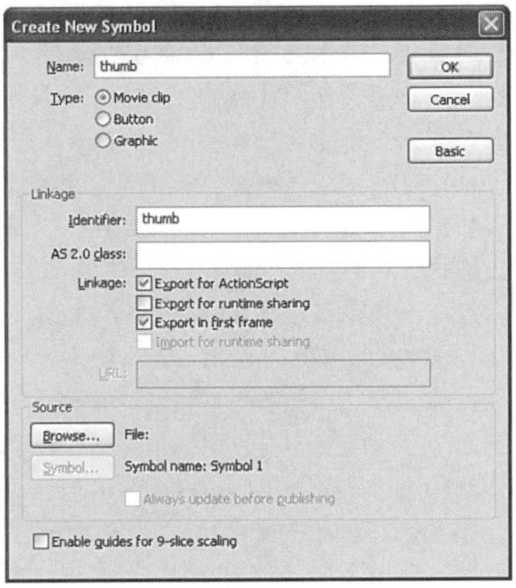

You'll be inside the `empty` symbol, but don't draw anything; instead, return to editing the main document by clicking Scene 1 in the Edit bar or by pressing Ctrl+E.

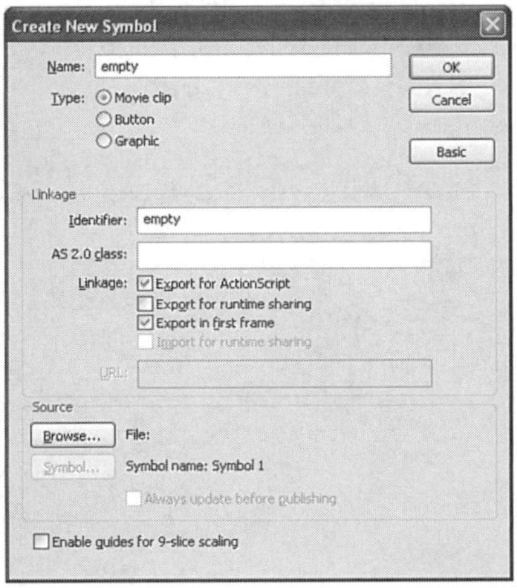

Next, we'll create a clip that holds a thumbnail, its title, and a check box so the user can select the thumbnail to view, download, or delete its full-size equivalent. Select Insert, New Symbol. In the Create New Symbol dialog box, set the symbol's name to **thumb** and select the Export for ActionScript option, as shown in Figure 10.10; then click OK.

Inside the `thumb` symbol, we'll draw some interface elements. The thumbnails we're using are each 40 × 40 pixels. Use the Rectangle tool to draw a rectangle filled with white. Select the drawn rectangle (stroke and fill) and then select Window, Info. First, confirm that you're looking at the upper-left coordinates by clicking the upper-left box in the Info panel as shown in Figure 10.11. Then set W to 50, H to 88, X to 0, and Y to 0.

FIGURE 10.11 The Info panel reflects the upper-left coordinates of the selected shape only when the upper-left registration option is selected.

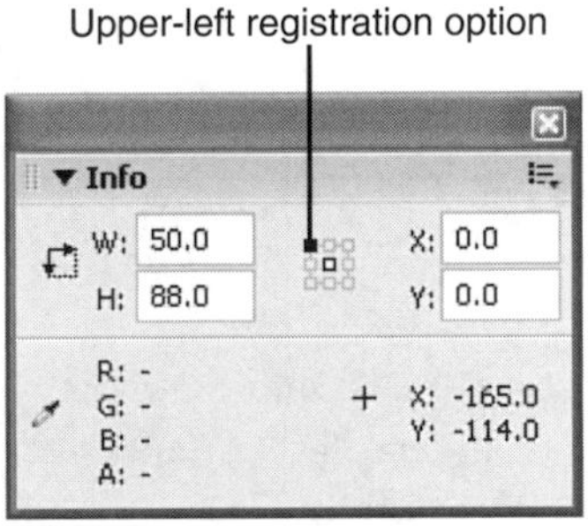

Upper-left registration option

Next, use the Text tool to create a block of text. Use the Properties panel to set the text type to Dynamic Text, the line type to Multiline, the font size to 8, and the instance name to **_txt**. Because this text is small, set the Font Rendering method to Bitmap Text. Use the Properties panel to set the _txt instance's X position to 0 and its Y position to 45 (now that we know the coordinates are reflecting the upper-left position). Finally, resize the _txt instance's margins and height using the text handles, not the Properties panel. You want the text to fill as much space as possible without extending past the drawn rectangle's borders, as shown in the extreme close-up in Figure 10.12.

FIGURE 10.12   Maximize the text, but don't go past the rectangle's edges.

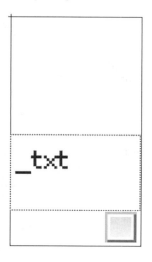

Finally, select Window, Components and drag an instance of the CheckBox component into the thumb symbol. Use the Properties panel to give this CheckBox an instance name of **cb**. With the cb instance selected, open the Parameters tab and delete the value for label. Position the cb instance in the bottom-right corner of the drawn rectangle, as shown in Figure 10.12.

Return to the main timeline by pressing Ctrl+E.

STEP 5▼
Applying the Code for thumbnail.swf

Open the version of thumbnail.fla in the finished_source folder that you downloaded for this chapter, select the first keyframe, open the Actions panel, and copy all the code you see. Return to your working version of thumbnail.fla, select the first keyframe, and paste the code into the Actions panel. Listing 10.7 shows some excerpts from this code for discussion.

LISTING 10.7   This Code Shows How the Thumbnails Screen Places All the Thumbnails Inside the ScrollPane Component

```
201   //_____
202   //----------makeNewHolder
203   //           called after each init() to clear out
      //           the holder clip's content
204   //_____
205   function makeNewHolder(){
206     holder = createEmptyMovieClip( "holder", 0 );
207   }
208   makeNewHolder();
209
210   //required by interface
211   function getImageHolder():MovieClip{
212     return holder;
```

continues

LISTING 10.7 **Continued**

```
213      //can return undefined if you don't want the PhotoShare
         //to download thumbnails
214    }
215
216    //required by interface
217    function init( p_controller:PhotoShare, p_images:Array ){
218      //save off some vars
219      controller = p_controller;
220      images = p_images;
221
222
223      //create a clip inside the sp ScrollPane:
224      var realHolder:MovieClip =
         sp.content.createEmptyMovieClip( "realHolder", 0 );
225
226      var MAX = 9;//per row (or, think "number of columns")
227      var WIDTH = 50+4;//"thumb" symbol's width plus spacer
228      var HEIGHT = 88+4;//"thumb" symbol's height plus spacer
229
230      var OFFSET:Matrix = new Matrix();
231      OFFSET.translate(5, 5); //how far down and to the right
                                 //the little thumbnail should
                                 //appear within the thumb symbol
232
233      //go through each <image> node in the images array
234      var total = images.length;
235      for( var i=0; i<total; i++ ){
236        var row = Math.floor( i / MAX );
237        var thisImage = images[i];
238        //attach the thumb symbol:
239        var thisThumb:MovieClip =
           realHolder.attachMovie( "thumb", "thumb"+i, i );
240        //position the thumbnail
241        thisThumb._x = (i * WIDTH)  - (row * WIDTH * MAX);
242        thisThumb._y = (row * HEIGHT);
243        //set label:
244        thisThumb._txt.text = thisImage.attributes.title;
245        //attach custom properties for tracking
246        thisThumb.mainTimeline = this;
247        thisThumb.selected = false;
248        thisThumb.index = i;
249
250        //assign press and rollover handlers
251        thisThumb.onPress = function(){
252          this.mainTimeline.doPress(this);
253        }
254        thisThumb.onRollOver = function(){
255          this.mainTimeline.doRollOver(this.index);
256        }
```

LISTING 10.7   **Continued**

```
257        thisThumb.onRollOut = function(){
258          this.mainTimeline.doFollOver(-1);
259        }
260
261        //copy the bitmap data loaded by PhotoShare
262        //FROM holder["image_"+i]  TO  thisThumb
263        var copy:MovieClip = holder["image_"+i];
264        var bd:BitmapData =
           new BitmapData( WIDTH, HEIGHT, true, 0x00000000 );
265        bd.draw( copy, OFFSET );
266        thisThumb.attachBitmap( bd, 0 );
267
268      }//end for
269      //disable all buttons
270      viewButton.enabled = false;
271      deleteButton.enabled = false;
272      downloadButton.enabled = false;
273
274      //clear old holder because we're done taking the bmps
275      makeNewHolder();
276      //update the sp ScrollPane
277      sp.redraw(true);
278      //make this clip visible
279      show();
280    }
281    //required by interface
282    function hide(){
283      this._visible = false;
284    }
285    //required by interface
286    function show(){
287      this._visible = true;
288    }
```

The init() function is bit long, but let me first point out an additional required function, getImageHolder() on line 211. This function exists so that the PhotoShare class can handle the preloading of all thumbnails. All you do is create an empty MovieClip instance and return it to the PhotoShare class. It preloads all the thumbnails before calling your init() function. If you don't want to take advantage of this feature, just return a value of undefined from the getImageHolder() function—but realize that

you'll ther have to write the code to load all the thumbnails here. Because we're supplying the PhotoShare with a holder clip, we know that by the time init() is called, that holder will contain clips for every loaded thumbnail (with the instance name image_X, where X is the index in the array of matching thumbnails).

The approach this init() function takes is to first create a movie clip inside the sp ScrollPane (line 224). Then it loops through all the image nodes received in the p_images parameter and attaches an instance of the thumb symbol you created in the previous step. Lines 235–268 handle positioning the thumbnail in its proper row and column; filling in the _txt field; and then assigning handlers for onPress, onRollOver, and onRollOut. Those handlers (doPress() and doRollOver()) are defined above the code segment shown in Listing 10.7 (on lines 170 and 184). To easily track which thumbnail is which and whether it's selected, I tacked onto each thumbnail instance the homemade properties for index and selected (lines 247 and 248).

Finally, the cool part: Lines 263–266 create a BitmapData instance (bd) and use the draw() method to copy the pixels from the clip created by the PhotoShare class inside the holder clip. The feature to automatically load images only loads the images, so we have to copy their contents into the thumb instances we're creating. This is quicker than making another call to issue a loadMovie() method for each thumbnail. Because the PhotoShare instance already loaded the images before the init() function is called, there's no reason to do it again. However, the PhotoShare instance loaded the images into the MovieClip instance holder, not into the ScrollPane instance's content.

There's a fair bit more code, but Listing 10.8 highlights the places where the thumbnail.swf needs to talk to the PhotoShare class instance (controller).

LISTING 10.8 This Excerpt Shows the Places Where the Thumbnail Screen Triggers Code in the PhotoShare Class (the Thumbnail's Controller)

```
38   //----------back to selection button:
39   //_____
40   function gotoSelection(evt){
41      //clear this because you will necessarily need
        //to reload images if you come back
42      //sp.content.realHolder.removeMovieClip();
43      controller.goto( "selection", "thumbnail" );
44   }
45   backToSelection.addEventListener( "click", gotoSelection );
46
47
48   //_____
49   //----------viewButton
50   //_____
51   function viewSelected(evt){
52      controller.getImages(selectedThumbnails);
53   }
54   viewButton.addEventListener( "click", viewSelected );
55
56
57   //_____
58   //----------deleteButton
59   //_____
```

LISTING 10.8	Continued	60	`function deleteSelected(evt){`
		61	`   controller.deleteImages(selectedThumbnails);`
		62	`}`
		63	`deleteButton.addEventListener( "click", deleteSelected );`

Each of these examples is simple in concept: The buttons tell the controller to do something. `goto()`, `getImages()`, and `deleteImages()` are public methods in the `PhotoShare` class. Each screen can talk to the `PhotoShare` class by way of its public methods that are defined in the `IPhotoShare.as` interface, which `PhotoShare` implements.

This code references a `selectedThumbnails` variable that is defined earlier in the `doPress()` function (line 184). The `doPress()` method, which is called anytime the user clicks a thumbnail, loops through every clip in the sp `ScrollPane` and—if its `selected` value is `true`—adds its `imageID` to the `selectedThumbnails` array. The main thing I want to point out is that the `PhotoShare` can delete one or more images given an array of `imageID`s. Similarly, you can pass an array of `imageID`s to the `getImages()` method, and the `PhotoShare` will present those in the zoom screen, which you'll create next.

Select Control, Test Movie to generate `thumbnail.swf`, which the main file needs when we test it in step 8. You won't see anything here except all the buttons and a blank `ScrollPane`.

STEP 6 ▼
Creating the zoom.swf Template

After the user selects one or more thumbnails, he can navigate to the zoom screen. Here the user can view a full-sized image along with details about that image. The user can download the image or navigate to the edit screen to modify the tags. If the user selected multiple thumbnails, he can page through all of them in the zoom screen.

Create a new Flash file and save it in your working directory as **zoom.fla**. Select Window, Components and drag five `Button` components, one `ScrollPane` component, and two `ProgressBar` components onto the stage. Position the components on the stage as shown in Figure 10.13, and use the Properties panel to give the buttons the following instance names: **backToThumbnail**, **downloadButton**, **prevButton**, **nextButton**, and **editButton**. Name the `ProgressBar` instances **progressBar** and **imageProgressBar**. Name the `ScrollPane` instance **sp**.

Use the Text tool to create a large block of text (about 200 × 300 pixels) be sure to drag the text handles to resize it—don't use the width and height fields in the Properties panel. Use the Properties panel to set the text type to Dynamic Text and give it the instance name **details_txt**. This field will contain information about the selected image.

FIGURE 10.13 The zoom screen includes the components positioned as shown.

FIGURE 10.13 The zoom screen includes the components positioned as shown.

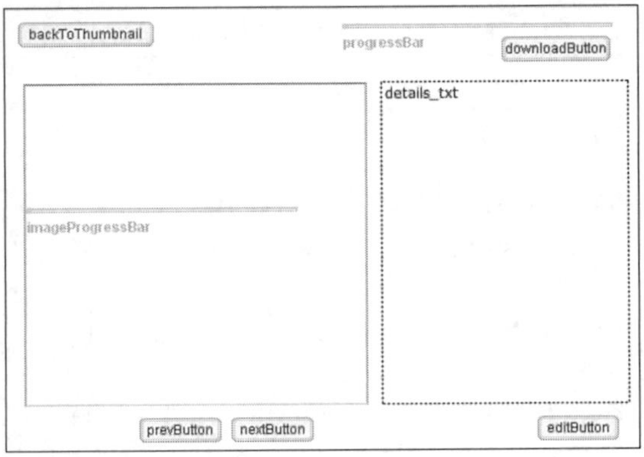

The code for this template is relatively simple. Open the version of zoom.fla located in the finished_source folder that you downloaded for this chapter, select the first keyframe, open the Actions panel, and copy all the code you see. Return to your working version of zoom.fla, select the first keyframe, and paste the code into the Actions panel. Listing 10.9 shows some code excerpts for discussion.

LISTING 10.9   The Main Initialization Code for the Zoom Screen

```
171    //required by interface
172    function getImageHolder():MovieClip{
173      return undefined;
174    }
175
176    //required by interface
177    function refreshImage(){
178      goPage(0)
179    }
180
181
182    //required by interface
183    function init( p_controller:PhotoShare, p_images:Array ){
184      //save off some vars
185      controller = p_controller;
186      images = p_images;
187
188      prevButton._visible = images.length>1;
189      nextButton._visible = images.length>1;
190
191      currentPageNum = 0;
192      goPage(0);
193      show();
194    }
```

Notice that the getImageHolder() function (line 172) returns a value of undefined. Although the PhotoShare can preload all the images, as we did with the thumbnails.fla screen template, I chose to not take advantage of that feature here for two reasons. First, the user will be viewing only one image at a time on this screen, so I just use the MovieClipLoader.loadClip() method inside our homemade goPage() function (shown next in Listing 10.10) when it's time to display the image. Second, the time it would take to download all the full images could be quite long. In this case, the user simply endures a short delay every time he clicks the Next or Previous button instead of one long delay at the beginning.

Notice, too, the additional required refreshImage() function on line 177. The PhotoShare class calls this function after an image's data is updated after visiting the edit screen, which you'll create next. Basically, if the details change, we just reload the current image to get the up-to-date details.

The init() function (line 183) should look simple this time. All it does is hide the Next and Previous buttons if there's only one image to show, set the homemade currentPageNum variable to 0, and trigger the goPage() method. In Listing 10.10, you'll see that clicking the Next button triggers goPage(1) and clicking Previous triggers goPage(-1). By triggering goPage(0), you can load the current image without changing the currentPageNum.

LISTING 10.10 The goPage() Function Displays a New Photograph	

```
65   function goPage(evt){
66      details_txt.text = "";
67      var direction = 0
68      if(evt.target == prevButton ) direction = -1;
69      if(evt.target == nextButton ) direction = 1;
70
71      currentPageNum += direction;
72      if(currentPageNum < 0) currentPageNum = images.length-1;
73      if(currentPageNum > images.length-1) currentPageNum = 0;
74
75      //load a new image:
76      imageProgressBar._visible = true;
77      imageProgressBar.setProgress(0,100);
78      var imageHolder:MovieClip =
            sp.content.createEmptyMovieClip( "imageHolder", 0 );
79      mcl.loadClip( images[currentPageNum].attributes.image,
                      imageHolder );
80   }
81   prevButton.addEventListener( "click", goPage );
82   nextButton.addEventListener( "click", goPage );
```

Both the Next and Previous buttons trigger the same method, but the `direction` variable is set according to which button was clicked. Then the `currentPageNum` updates and the `MovieClipLoader` instance `mcl` issues a call to the `loadClip()` method. The image is loaded into a movie clip that we create inside the `sp` `ScrollPane` instance on lines 78 and 79. Notice that the `images` array (saved originally in the `init()` function) contains all the `<image>` nodes sent from the `PhotoShare` class. To figure out the filename of the current image, we grab the `currentPageNum` index from inside the `images` array and then dig into its `image` attribute with the code `images[currentPageNum].attributes.image`.

Finally, the two ways that the `zoom.fla` file directs messages to the `PhotoShare` controller are shown in Listing 10.11.

The `gotoThumbnail()` method calls the `goto()` method in the same manner as how

the thumbnail screen gets back to the selection screen. The `goGetImageData()` method is how the zoom screen launches the edit screen to modify details for a given image. You'll build the edit screen next.

> **NOTE**
>
> When the image finally loads, there's a fair bit of code to extract the details that appear in the `details_txt` field. See `imageListener.onLoadInit` on line 100 in the finished version of the `zoom.fla` file in the `finished_source` folder you downloaded for this chapter. Basically, it parses values from inside the `<image>` node for the current image. My code calls on the `PhotoShare` class to help do that parsing. Specifically, I call `controller.selectNodeList()`, which in turn calls `mx.xpath.XPathAPI.selectNodeList()`. The reason for this approach is just so that the various screens don't need to also import the `DataBindingClasses` the way we did in step 1.

LISTING 10.11 This Code Shows How the Zoom Screen Tells the `PhotoShare` Class to Go to a New Screen

```
43    //_____
44    //----------editButton
45    //_____
46    function goEdit(evt){
47      var imageData:XMLNode = images[currentPageNum];
48      controller.goEditImageData(imageData);
49    }
50    editButton.addEventListener( "click", goEdit );
51
52
53    //_____
54    //----------backToThumbnail
55    //_____
56    function gotoThumbnail(evt){
57      controller.goto( "thumbnail", "zoomed" );
58    }
59    backToThumbnail.addEventListener( "click", gotoThumbnail );
```

Select Control, Test Movie to generate zoom.swf, which the main file needs when we test it in step 8. You won't see much onscreen except for your various buttons.

STEP 7▼
Creating the edit.swf Template

The edit screen is where users can edit the various tags given to any single image. Users have two ways to access the edit screen: First, it automatically appears immediately after users upload an image, so they can supply the initial tags. Users can also navigate to the edit screen by clicking the Edit button on the zoom screen. Although the edit screen is similar to the zoom screen, the main difference is that users are given user interface controls that let them add or change the tags.

Create a new Flash file and save it in your working directory as **edit.fla**. Select Window, Components and drag three TextInput components, six Button components, and two List components onto the stage. Position the components on the stage as shown in Figure 10.14.

Use the Properties panel to give the TextInput components the instance names **titleInput**, **categoryInput**, and **keywordInput**. Name the Button instances **saveButton**, **cancelButton**, **addC**, **remC**, **addK**, and **remK**. Finally, give the two List components the instance names **categoryList** and **keywordList**. Use the Text tool to create static text blocks that read **Title**, **Categories**, and **Keywords** (also shown in Figure 10.14). Finally, use the Rectangle tool to draw a 40-x-40 pixel square. Select the square shape and select Modify, Convert to Symbol. Name the symbol **holder**, select the Movie Clip

option, select the upper-left registration option, and then click OK. Select the instance of the holder symbol and use the Properties panel to give it an instance name of **thumbnail_mc**.

FIGURE 10.14   **The edit screen includes the components positioned as shown.**

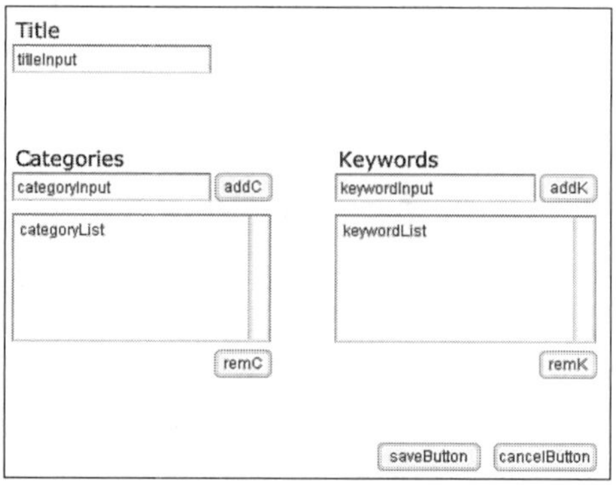

Just like the upload screen, the edit screen acts as a modal dialog box, so we need to cover the rest of the screen. Create a new layer and use the Rectangle tool to draw a filled rectangle into that layer that covers the whole stage. Select the entire shape and select Modify, Convert to Symbol. In the Convert to Symbol dialog box, select the Movie Clip option and click OK. Use the Properties panel to give the clip the instance name **cover**. Finally, arrange the layers so that the cover's layer is below the layer containing the UI components you've already placed on the stage.

Open the version of edit.fla in the finished_source folder you downloaded for this chapter, select the first keyframe, open the Actions panel, and copy all the code you see. Return to your working version of edit.fla, select the first keyframe, and paste the code into the Actions panel. Listing 10.12 shows some excerpts from this code for discussion.

LISTING 10.12 This Code Initializes the Edit Screen

```
177   function init( p_controller:PhotoShare,
                        p_imageData:XMLNode ){
178     //save off vars
179     controller = p_controller;
180     imageData = p_imageData;
181
182     categoryInput.text = "";
183     keywordInput.text = "";
184
185     thumbnail_mc.loadMovie( imageData.attributes.thumbnail );
186     titleInput.text = imageData.attributes.title;
187
188     categoryList.removeAll();
189     keywordList.removeAll();
190     addC.enabled = false;
191     remC.enabled = false;
192     addK.enabled = false;
193     remK.enabled = false;
194
195     //show keywords
196     var keywords:Array = controller.selectNodeList(imageData,
                                    "image/keywords/keyword");
197     var total = keywords.length;
198     for (var i=0; i<total; i++){
199       keywordList.addItem(
                        {label:keywords[i].attributes.name} );
200     }
201
202     //show categories
203     var cats:Array = controller.selectNodeList(imageData,
                                    "image/categories/category" );
204     var total = cats.length;
205     for (var i=0; i<total; i++){
206       categoryList.addItem({label:cats[i].attributes.name});
207     }
208
209     show();
210   }
```

Notice that the second parameter passed to the init() function, stored in the variable imageData, contains a copy of the <image> node for the image you're currently editing. The thumbnail_mc movie clip instance loads the image, which is in the thumbnail attribute. Then both List components are populated with labels matching the image's categories and keywords attributes.

The edit screen can say only two things to the controller: either cancel any changes that have been made or overwrite the image's details with new values, as shown in Listing 10.13.

```
70   //_____
71   //----------cancelButton:
72   //_____
73   function doCancel(evt){
74      controller.closeEditScreen();
75   }
76   cancelButton.addEventListener("click", doCancel);
77
78   //_____
79   //----------saveButtton:
80   //_____
81   function doSave(evt){
82      controller.overwriteImageData(imageData);
83   }
84   saveButton.addEventListener("click", doSave);
```

In the `overwriteImageData()` method, we simply send back the `imageData` values. The only tricky part is that, while the user makes changes to the `categories`, `keywords`, or image `title` attributes, the edit screen must update the `imageData` variable. The easy one is how the image's `title` attribute is updated, as this code shows:

```
function changeTitle(evt){
  imageData.attributes.title =
  evt.target.text;
}
titleInput.addEventListener( "change",
                     changeTitle);
```

You can find the more complex code that adds and removes category or keyword nodes in the two methods `addTag()` and `remTag()` (lines 92 and 137). These are triggered by the `Button` instances `addC`, `remC`, `addK`, and `remK`.

Select Control, Test Movie to generate `edit.swf`, which the main file needs when we test it in the next step.

STEP 8 ▼
Testing It

Confirm that your working directory has—at a minimum—the files and folders shown in Figure 10.15. When you finally deploy this project, you won't need any `.fla` or `.as` files on the server.

FIGURE 10.15 You're about to create the `main.swf` from the `main.fla` file; to do so, all the other files shown here must be present.

Open the `main.fla` file and select Control, Test Movie. The project should run, albeit in simulated mode. That is, it doesn't matter which keywords or categories you select, you'll always end up with the same thumbnails because we're not really searching an online database. Similarly, the images aren't really deleted when you click the Delete button because the application server has to do that. Finally, the edits you make don't appear to stick because, again, the database isn't being updated in this local test version. Despite all these limits, the current version does let you test all the Flash programming completed so far. Although there are many places where the coding can fail, at this point we're only testing the Flash side of things because we've removed the application server from the equation.

To make this application really work, you need to implement all the methods listed in the `urls.xml` file (except for `basePath` because that's not a method). For example, the `urls.xml` file has a `<url>` node with the `methodName` attribute equal to `"getCategories"`. Currently, the `path` attribute for that node is `"schemas/getCategories.xml"`—a static file. If you upload the `getCategories.php` script to www.example.com/php/getCategories.php, simply edit the path attribute in the `urls.xml` to point to that URL.

You'll find a working set of scripts that rely on PHP and MySQL in the `finished_php` folder. Because there are both PHP scripts and connections to a database of images, the installation process is a bit more involved. You'll find an overview of how to integrate these scripts on a PHP server in the `finished_php` folder. But let me remind you that the structure of this project enables you to integrate with any application server. There's a relatively simple API that Flash uses to send and receive data. Each method is defined inside the `urls.xml` file. Provided that your sever-side scripts can support these methods, you can use this project with any server.

Now that you have the basic project built, the following projects show you several variations for the five screens. Although these variations might be interesting for your particular needs, hopefully they will also introduce you to the many ways you can modify the screen templates.

Figures 10.16–10.21 show the sequence of a typical use for the photo share application.

FIGURE 10.16 From the selection screen, the user chooses to upload an image.

Testing the Download and Upload Features

You might notice that the download feature doesn't work while you're testing the main.swf file locally. However, you don't have to configure an application server to see that part work. Simply create a folder on a web server, such as http://www. phillipkerman.com/images, and upload all the images from your local folder to this web folder. Then open the urls.xml file and set the path attribute for the first <url> node (the one for basePath) to match your online images folder.

You need a database to see the images the user uploads in subsequent searches. However, there's a simple way to test the core upload feature without configuring a database. I've included the sample upload PHP script, which I renamed simple.php, from the Flash help files in the schemas folder. To make it work, do two things: Place the simple.php file on a PHP-enabled web server, and edit the urls.xml file so the <url> node with the methodName attribute reading "uploadImage" has its path attribute pointing to that file, as shown in this example:

```
<url methodName="uploadImage"
path="http://www.sample.com/simple.php"
/>
```

When you test the upload feature, the file you select appears in a folder called images adjacent to the simple.php file.

FIGURE 10.17 After selecting a photograph, the user clicks Upload on the upload screen.

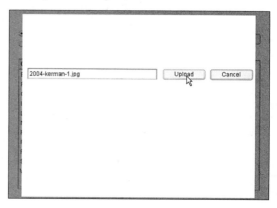

FIGURE 10.18 After the image uploads, the user adds tags in the edit screen.

FIGURE 10.19 Back at the selection screen, the user can choose to view images that match several categories.

Category	Total
Buildings	3
Flowers	13
Games	33
Insects	3
Landscapes	43
Music	4
People	10
Places	21
Planets	1
Sports	32
Walking	5

FIGURE 10.20 **FIGURE 10.20** The thumbnail images that match the selected categories appear, and the user can select which ones to zoom in on.

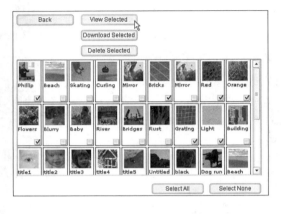

FIGURE 10.21 The zoom screen appears to reveal the full-sized image with its tags. From this screen, the user can download that image if desired.

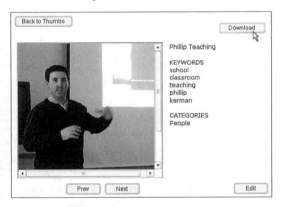

Project:
No Upload and Editing Features

Removing features is easy! In the case of this photo share application, removing some of the features presented in the basic project can also serve a practical need. For example, although you might want to let users view and download images, you might also want to prevent them from uploading their own images. One of the reasons to restrict or limit a user's uploading capability is a concern that your server might quickly become full of images and run out of disk space. You might also be concerned about legal issues if you allow users to share copyrighted or indecent images. For whatever reasons you might have, this project modifies the selection and zoom screens so that there is no upload button. You'll then use these replacement screens in the main project we just completed.

STEPS▼

1. **Modifying the selection screen**
2. **Modifying the zoom screen**
3. **Modifying the main screen**

STEP 1▼
Modifying the Selection Screen

Open the selection.fla file you created earlier, or copy the finished one from the finished_source folder you downloaded for this chapter. Select File, Save As and name it **selection_noupload.fla**. Select the uploadButton Button instance and delete it. Select Control, Test Movie to generate the selection_noupload.swf file.

STEP 2▼
Modifying the Zoom Screen

Chances are good that if you're not letting users upload images, you probably don't want them to make edits to the tag information either. However, I can see some cases where you might want to let people add comments. In any event, you can easily eliminate access to the edit screen if you want. Recall the two ways users can get to the edit screen are immediately after uploading an image (which we just disabled) and by clicking the Edit button from the zoom screen. Therefore we'll remove that button from the `zoom.fla` file.

Open the `zoom.fla` you created earlier, or the one in the `finished_source` folder. Select File, Save As and name the copy **zoom_noedit.fla**. Select the `editButton` instance and delete it. Select Control, Test Movie to generate the `zoom_noedit.swf` file.

STEP 3▼
Modifying the Main Screen

Now we need to change the main screen so that it tells the `PhotoShare` class to load our new `.swf` files.

Open the `main.fla` file you created earlier, or use the one in the `finished_source` folder you downloaded for this chapter. Select File, Save As and name the copy **main_noupload.fla**. Select the first keyframe and open the Actions panel. You need to change only a few lines of code—namely, replace lines 7–11 with the code on lines 7–12 shown in Listing 10.14. Listing 10.14 shows the completed code.

LISTING 10.14 This Code Tells the `PhotoShare` Class to Load the New Selection and Zoom Screens and Not the Upload or Edit Screen

```
1   var urlList:String; //path to urls.xml
2   //if no FlashVars set a default:
3   if(urlList == undefined){
4     urlList = "schemas/urls.xml";
5   }
6
7   var scope = this;
8   var selectionScreen = "selection_noupload.swf";
9   var uploadScreen = undefined;
10  var thumbnailScreen = "thumbnail.swf";
11  var zoomedScreen = "zoom_noedit.swf";
12  var editScreen = undefined;
13  var controller:PhotoShare = new PhotoShare( scope,
14                                              urlList,
```

continues

LISTING 10.14 **Continued**

```
15                                                      selectionScreen,
16                                                      uploadScreen,
17                                                      thumbnailScreen,
18                                                      zoomedScreen,
19                                                      editScreen );
20
21    setPrompt("");
22    function setPrompt(toWhat){
23      prompt_txt.text = toWhat;
24    }
```

The main difference is that we're now pointing to the new `selection_noupload.swf` and `zoom_noedit.swf` files (lines 8 and 11). Also, because we don't need the upload screen or edit screen, we pass `undefined` for those two (lines 9 and 12).

While still in the `main.fla` file, select Control, Test Movie. Check it out: Now you can't upload or make edits to the tags! By the way, you can still populate the database with images using the original version of `main.swf` that you created earlier. One deployment scenario I can imagine is that you put the original `main.swf` in a password-protected part of your website. Then only you can upload photos. You can then put the `main_noupload.swf` in a public area so users accessing that version can view the photos you've uploaded. It's common to create two interfaces to the same core code in this manner.

Project:
A Version That Downloads .pdf Documents

This project changes the feature that lets users download image files to a feature that lets them download Acrobat `.pdf` documents. Perhaps you have documents online that you want to let users download. In place of thumbnails and full-size images, you can create images of your documents' covers.

The main feature this project demonstrates is that you can add arbitrary child nodes and attributes to the XML and then parse it in any of the screens. That is, each `<image>` node in the results from server calls, such as `getImages`, can have additional nodes or attributes. You can design this however you want. In this example, we'll add a child node to the `<images>` node called `<additional_details>`. We'll also add a doc attribute to the `<image>` node. The zoom screen will have to change because it now extracts that doc attribute we added to the XML. The changes necessary on the Flash side are fairly easy because the `PhotoShare` class already passes entire `<image>` nodes to the various screens. If we add an attribute to the `<image>` node, `PhotoShare` doesn't care; it just forwards the whole node. When it arrives in our screens, we can parse out the values we need.

In the end, you'll have a project that's not meant for sharing photos but rather for giving users a way to access and download a library of `.pdf` documents.

STEP 1▼
Creating a New Working Folder

Create a new folder that will become your working folder. This new folder will keep you from getting mixed up with the files from the other projects. Open the `document_version` folder inside the `starter_files` folder you downloaded for this project, select all three folders, and copy them. Go to your new working folder and paste the folders. You'll also need to copy the following support files from the `finished_source` folder to your new working folder: `IPhotoShare.as`, `PhotoShare.as`, and `XMLGateway.as`.

Because we're only going to update the main file and the zoom screen, you need to grab finished versions of the `selection_noupload.swf` and `thumbnail.swf` screens. You can either use the ones you created in previous projects or use the copies found in the `finished_source` folder you downloaded. In either case, select those two files, copy them, and paste them into your

new working folder. Your completed working folder should have the files and folders shown in Figure 10.22.

STEP 2▼
Creating a New main.fla

Open the latest `main.fla` file you produced, or open the `main.fla` file in the `finished_source` folder you downloaded for this chapter. Immediately select File, Save As and save the copy into your new working directory as **main_document_version.fla**.

Select the first keyframe, open the Actions panel, and completely replace the code with what is shown in Listing 10.15. You'll find this code in the `main_document_version.fla` file in the `finished_source` folder you downloaded for this chapter.

FIGURE 10.22 These files are needed in your working folder—we'll add the main file plus a new zoom screen.

LISTING 10.15 This Code Tells the PhotoShare Class to Load the New Zoom Screen We're About to Build

```
1  var urlList:String; //path to urls.xml
2  //if no FlashVars set a default:
3  if(urlList == undefined){
4    urlList = 'doc_schemas/urls.xml';
5  }
```

continues

LISTING 10.15   Continued

```
 6
 7     var scope = this;
 8     var selectionScreen = "selection_noupload.swf";
 9     var uploadScreen = undefined;
10     var thumbnailScreen = "thumbnail.swf";
11     var zoomedScreen = "zoom_document_version.swf";
12     var editScreen = undefined;
13     var controller:PhotoShare = new PhotoShare( scope,
14                                                 urlList,
15                                                 selectionScreen,
16                                                 uploadScreen,
17                                                 thumbnailScreen,
18                                                 zoomedScreen,
19                                                 editScreen );
20
21  setPrompt("");
22  function setPrompt(toWhat){
23      prompt_txt.text = toWhat;
24  }
```

There are two differences between the code in Listing 10.15 and the code in the last version of the main.fla file you worked on: On line 4 the urlList variable is now pointing to a folder named doc_schemas, simply to draw attention to the fact that the two projects are different, and the zoomedScreen variable on line 11 is pointing to a yet-to-be-created file zoom_document_version.swf, which we'll make in a minute. We're not going to let users upload or edit the tags. That's why both variables on lines 9 and 12 are set to undefined. It's also why the sectionScreen variable (line 8) points to the selection_noupload.swf screen file.

STEP 3 ▼
Exploring the getImages.xml Schema

In your favorite text editor, open the getImages.xml file that is in your

doc_schemas folder. Notice two things about the slightly modified format of this XML file: Each <image> node has a doc attribute that points to a .pdf file, and each <additional_details> node has exactly two <detail> nodes—one with a name of "Author" and one with a name of "Description". We'll extract those values when displaying the full-size image in the zoom screen next.

STEP 4 ▼
Creating the zoom_document_version.swf File

Open the zoom_noedit.fla file you created in the last project. Alternatively, you can open the version of zoom_document_version.fla in the finished_source folder—it's simply a modified version of zoom_noedit.fla—and save it in your new working directory. In either case, you might want to open the zoom_document_version.fla (in the finished_source folder) so you can grab the code.

The only differences between this new document version of the zoom screen and the previous version of the zoom screen is what happens when the user clicks the Download button: In the new version, clicking the Download button downloads the <image> node's doc attributes. The other difference occurs when the full-size image loads: In the new version, the title, author, and description appear in the details_txt field.

First, make sure that the downloadImage() function grabs the doc attribute by making it read as shown in Listing 10.16.

Notice that the attributes.doc, which used to be attributes.image, now grabs the attribute for the doc. Also notice that we have to precede it with controller. getBasePath() because the value you set for basePath in the urls.xml is automatically added only to the attributes for thumbnail and image.

Second, completely replace the imageListener.onLoadInit function (line 100) to read as shown in Listing 10.17. (You can steal this code from the zoom_document_version.fla file in the finished_source folder.)

LISTING 10.16 **This Code Downloads a File Based on the doc Attribute**

```
144  function downloadImage(evt){
145      fileRef.download( controller.getBasePath() +
                             images[currentPageNum].attributes.doc);
146  }
```

LISTING 10.17 **This Code Displays Information About the Selected Document When the Image of It Loads**

```
100  imageListener.onLoadInit = function(target:MovieClip){
101
102      sp.redraw(true);
103
104      imageProgressBar._visible = false;
105
106      var imageData:XMLNode = images[currentPageNum];
107
108      //get the title
109      var title = imageData.attributes.title;
110
111      //get the author's name
112      var str =
             "image/additional_details/detail[@name='Author'";
113      var thisNode =
             controller.selectSingleNode(imageData, str);
114      var author = thisNode.firstChild.nodeValue;
115
116      //get the description
```

continues

LISTING 10.17   **Continued**

```
117      var str =
         "image/additional_details/detail[@name='Description']";
118      var thisNode =
         controller.selectSingleNode(imageData, str);
119      var description = thisNode.firstChild.nodeValue;
120
121      //populate the text field
122      details_txt.html = true;
123      details_txt.htmlText =  "<b>" + title + "</b>" + newline
124      details_txt.htmlText += "By  " + author + newline;
125      details_txt.htmlText += "<i>" + description + "<i>" ;
126    }
```

This function triggers when an image fully loads. We grab the title (line 109) the same as before. But then in lines 112–114, we grab the node value for the <detail> node whose name is "Author". Line 112 builds a search string for the XPath selectSingleNode() method that requires the found <detail> node to have a name attribute matching "Author". Lines 117–119 do the same to get a <detail> node whose name is "Description".

Finally, in lines 122–125, the details_txt field is populated with a title, author, and description.

For reference, Figure 10.23 shows both the original XMLNode and the rendered display_txt field on the stage, as you'll see when you test the main movie in the next step.

FIGURE 10.23   **The origi-nal XML (top) is formatted and presented as shown here (bottom).**

```
<image imageID="doc1"
       doc="docs/fire.pdf"
       title="Fire Safety"
       thumbnail="images/fire-t.jpg"
       image="images/fire.jpg">

    <additional_details>
            <detail name="Author"
                    type="string"> Phillip Kerman </detail>

            <detail name="Description"
                    type="string"> This document helps you identify
                                   hazards such as candles.  </detail>
    </additional_details>

</image>
```

Fire Safety
By Phillip Kerman
This document helps you identify
hazards such as candles.

Testing the PDF Download Project

Because the primary feature we added was downloading .pdf files, we need to place those files online to see the download feature work. Create a folder on a web server, say www.sample.com/data, and in that folder create two more folders: docs and images. Upload the local versions of the .jpg files and the .pdf files from the docs and images folders you downloaded for this chapter and now residing in your new working folder to the same folders online. Finally, open the urls.xml file in your doc_schemas folder and edit the first url node to point to your online folder, as in this example:

```
<url methodName="basePath"
    path="http://www.sample.com/data/"/>
```

Return to the main_document_version.fla file and select Control, Test Movie. You should be able to select any or all three thumbnails and see the appropriate titles, authors, and descriptions. In addition, when you're in the zoom screen, you can download the actual .pdf files, as shown in Figure 10.24.

FIGURE 10.24 The finished application displays different information n the zoom screen and lets users download documents.

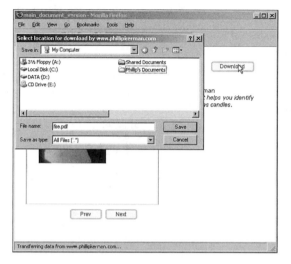

Project: List View for the Image Filenames

As cool as the thumbnail view is, it might not be appropriate for every project. For one thing, it takes up more screen space than if you displayed only a text-based list. In addition, the thumbnails are generated dynamically by the server as the support PHP scripts I've provided do. Therefore, the user doesn't upload both the main image and the thumbnail. In any event, this small project changes the thumbnail screen to present just a simple list of files.

STEP 1▼
Creating Another New Working Folder

Create a new folder that will become your working folder for this project. Go into the finished_source folder and copy all the .as files plus the folders images and schemas. Go to your new working folder and paste the files and folders. You should have the same starter files and folders as you did for the second project, shown previously in Figure 10.4.

Because we're concentrating on building only a replacement thumbnail screen and a new main file, copy the following finished .swf files you created in the "Basic Photo Share Project" section earlier in this chapter (if you didn't build that project, copy these files from the finished_source folder you downloaded for this chapter):

- ▶ edit.swf
- ▶ selection.swf
- ▶ upload.swf
- ▶ zoom.swf

Place these files into your new working folder. You can use other versions of these files you might have created in this chapter—such as the zoom_noedit.swf file—if you prefer; just remember to specify the correct filename in the main file you create in step 5 of this project.

STEP 2▼
Creating a New Thumbnail Screen

If you have an existing thumbnail.fla file you created with your own layout, open that file and save it into your working directory as **thumbnail_list.fla**. If you haven't created a thumbnail screen template, just copy the thumbnail_list.fla file from the finished_source folder and jump to step 4.

The only onscreen differences between the thumbnail screen you'll create for this project and the one you created for the basic project are that the ScrollPane component is replaced by a List (or DataGrid) and that the prompt_txt field is removed.

Select the sp ScrollPane instance onstage and delete it. Also delete the prompt_txt field. Select Window, Components and drag a List component onto the stage. Use the Free Transform tool to resize the list box, as shown in Figure 10.25. Then use the Properties panel to give the List an instance name of **itemList**.

the Actions panel, and copy all the code. Return to your version of the thumbnail_list.fla, select the first keyframe, open the Actions panel, and paste the code.

STEP 4▼
Analyzing the ActionScript

Let me discuss the key differences in the new ActionScript code you just pasted. First, notice that because we don't need or want the PhotoShare class to preload thumbnails, the required getImageHolder() method returns undefined:

```
188    //required by interface
189    function getImageHolder():MovieClip{
190        return undefined;
191    }
```

STEP 3▼
Applying the ActionScript to the Thumbnail Screen

Open the version of thumbnail_list.fla in the finished_source folder you downloaded for this chapter, select the first keyframe, open

Listing 10.18 shows the init() function.

LISTING 10.18 The init() **Function Populates a** List **Component with the Images' Titles and Filenames**

```
193    //required by interface
194    function init( p_controller:PhotoShare, p_images:Array ){
195        //save off some vars
196        controller = p_controller;
197        images = p_images;
198
199        selectedImages = new Array();
200
201        itemList.removeAll();
202
203        var basePath = controller.getBasePath();
204
205        //go through each <image> node in the images array
206        var total = images.length;
207        for( var i=0; i<total; i++ ){
208            var thisImage = images[i].attributes;
209
210            //get just the filename, minus any base path
```

continues

LISTING 10.18   Continued

```
211        var shortFilename = thisImage.image;
212        if( basePath != "" ){
213          shortFilename = shortFilename.split(basePath).pop();
214        }
215
216        var niceLabel =
           thisImage.title + " (" + shortFilename + ")";
217
218        itemList.addItem( {label: niceLabel,
219                             imageID: thisImage.imageID} );
220      }
221      //disable all buttons
222      viewButton.enabled = false;
223      deleteButton.enabled = false;
224      downloadButton.enabled = false;
225
226      //make this clip visible
227      show();
228    }
```

Here we save the p_images parameter into our images variable (line 197). In line 199, the selectedImages array is cleared. When the user makes selections to the itemList List component, this variable is updated (see the updateSelectedImages() function on line 97 of the complete code in the thumbnail_list.fla file).

The primary task of this code is to populate the itemList List component. In the for loop, the code on line 207 first grabs just the attributes from the current <image> node. Before adding text to the itemList component, we prepare the niceLabel variable. It would be easiest to simply use the title attribute when populating the itemList. However, I wanted to show the title followed by the filename in parentheses—as in Title (filename.jpg). That formatted string is put into niceLabel on lines 216–218. But the image attribute still contains the full path to the image! So, first we strip the basePath (grabbed from the PhotoShare class in line 203) from the beginning of the image attribute on line 213.

Eventually, we use the addItem() function in lines 218–219 to insert a label and an imageID into the itemList component. The label property is what the user sees (niceLabel), and the imageID property (that I made up) is conveniently stored within the itemList component. That way, when the user selects a row, we know which imageID she selected (the image's ID is needed when the user clicks the viewButton, downloadButton, or deleteButton).

With the new code in place, select Control, Test Movie to generate the thumbnail_list.swf file.

STEP 5▼
Creating a New Main File

Open the `main_list_version.fla` file in the `finished_source` folder and select File, Save As; save the copy into your working folder (using the same filename is fine). Select the first keyframe, open the Actions panel, and modify the code to point to your new `thumbnail_list.swf`, as shown in Listing 10.19.

You're welcome to modify the other screen .swf names; for example, you might want line 7 to point to your `"selection_noupload.swf"` version of the selection screen.

STEP 6▼
Testing the Thumbnail List Screen

While still in your `main_list_version.fla` file, select Control, Test Movie. You should be able to navigate to the thumbnails screen and see a list of matching files, as shown in Figure 10.26.

LISTING 10.19 This Code Makes the PhotoShare Class Load Our New `thumbnail_list.swf`

```
1    var urlList:String; //path to urls.xml
2    if(urlList == undefined){
3        urlList = "schemas/urls.xml";
4    }
5
6    var scope = this;
7    var selectionScreen = "selection.swf";
8    var uploadScreen = "upload.swf";
9    var thumbnailScreen = "thumbnail_list.swf";
10   var zoomedScreen = "zoom.swf";
11   var editScreen = "edit.swf";
12   var controller:PhotoShare = new PhotoShare( scope,
13                                               urlList,
14                                               selectionScreen,
15                                               uploadScreen,
16                                               thumbnailScreen,
17                                               zoomedScreen,
18                                               editScreen );
19   setPrompt("");
20   function setPrompt(toWhat){
21       prompt_txt.text = toWhat;
22   }
```

FIGURE 10.26 **The finished** `thumbnail_list.swf`
appears as shown.

Back	View Selected
	Download Selected
	Delete Selected

title1 (image1.jpg)
title2 (image2.jpg)
title3 (image3.jpg)
title4 (image4.jpg)
title5 (image5.jpg)
Untitled Image (sunset.jpg)
black dog (dog.jpg)
black cat (cat.jpg)

Select All   Select None

Exploring the Class Structure

An easy way to summarize the support classes for this project is to say, "It's all in the `PhotoShare` class." For a visualization of how the project is structured, take a look at Figure 10.27 while I provide the following overview.

The `main.swf` basically tells the `PhotoShare` class everything it needs to know: the names of the screen `.swf` files and the path to the `urls.xml` file. The `PhotoShare` class handles loading and displaying the various screens. Notice that each screen has a slightly different `init()` method depending on the variables it needs for its job. However, the first parameter in each screen's `init()` function is a reference to the `PhotoShare` class. This way, the screens have access to the public methods in the `IPhotoShare` interface. These methods include both utilities, such as XPath parsing, and navigation triggers such as `gotoUpload()`, which is how the screens can say it's time to go to the upload screen. (All the ways the screens can talk to the `PhotoShare` controller were detailed in the projects in this chapter.) Finally, notice that the thumbnail and zoom screens must support the `getImageHolder()` function that returns a reference to a `MovieClip` into which the `PhotoShare` class can preload images or thumbnails.

FIGURE 10.27 **The** `main.swf` **file tells the** `PhotoShare` **class which screens to include; the rest of the heavy lifting is handled by the** `PhotoShare` **class.**

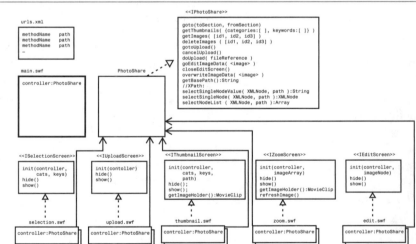

Final Thoughts

Because this project was a bit more complex than many others in this book, you might not be able to modify it quite as much as you've come to expect from the other projects. For this project, you always need to visit a selection screen and invoke a search; then you have to visit the thumbnail screen to select the images you want to download, view, or delete. Although the sequence of events is somewhat fixed, you can modify each screen however you want.

Modifying the screens means more than just changing the layout and graphics, although, of course, that's a good way to customize this project. You can also change the behavior of the screens. For example, if you don't like the way the upload screen we built immediately invokes the `FileReference.browse()` method, you can remove that line from the `init()` function (the line starting with `fileRef.browse`) and instead add a button the user must click before the browse dialog box appears. I built this variation in the file named `upload_delayed.fla`, located in the `finished_source` folder.

Finally, I picked the "photo share" idea for this chapter because it is visual. But the `.pdf` variation of the project shows you can easily modify the application to upload or download any file type. Although this project had a specific and practical purpose, I'm sure that you can think of more applications than simply a photo sharing tool.

PART III: Appendixes

Here's a collection of links I think you might find useful.

Configuration Folders

Perhaps it's odd to list folders on your own computer as resources, but the configuration folders generated by Flash 8 and the Flash 8 player are important. Adjacent to your installed version of Flash you'll find the FirstRun folder. Every time a new user launches Flash, the contents of the FirstRun folder are copied into a username-based configuration folder.

In Chapter 2, "Producing a Flash Project," I explained how Flash has a default class path that points to this configuration folder. That is, the classes in the configuration folder are available to every project you build in Flash.

I find myself exploring the configuration folders for two general reasons: If I want to quickly see the package paths and available classes, I can see all the folders and .as files inside the Classes folder (within the configuration folder). For example, I can see all the available programmatic tweens by looking inside the Classes\mx\ transitions\easing folder (and, therefore, I know that the class path is mx. transitions.easing). The second reason to use the configuration folder is to add your own utility classes. If you add a folder full of your own custom classes, they'll be available to every project you build.

You should add a shortcut to this folder to your desktop or your Favorites menu for quick access.

On Windows:

```
<drive letter>\
Documents and Settings\
<username>\
Local Settings\
Application Data\
Macromedia\
Flash 8\
<language>\
Configuration
```

On Macintosh:

```
<Macintosh HD>/
Users/
<username>/
Library/
Application Support/
Macromedia/
Flash 8/
<language>/
Configuration
```

- ◀ *<drive letter>* is your operating system boot drive.

- ◀ *<username>* is your login ID.

- ◀ *<language>* is your language code, such as en for English or es for Español.

- ◀ *<Macintosh HD>* is your Mac system hard drive's label.

The other folder to become familiar with (and consider making a shortcut to) is the Flash Player folder:

On Windows:

```
<drive letter>\
Documents and Settings\
<username>\
Application Data\
Macromedia\
Flash Player
```

On Macintosh:

```
<Macintosh HD>/
Users/
<username>/
Library/
Preferences/
Macromedia/
Flash Player
```

There are two reasons you might be in this folder: You need to inspect or clear out Local Shared Object files (.sol), or you want to manually edit the configuration files in the #Security folder. Local Shared Object files are basically like browser cookies and are stored in a randomly named folder inside the #Shared Objects folder. Each file is saved in a folder matching the domain that created it (websites read and write .sol files only in the folder matching their domain).

The #Security folder contains both the FlashAuthor.cfg file and the FlashPlayerTrust folder. This folder and file relate to a new restriction that limits .swf files published in Flash 8 from accessing the Internet when they're being played locally (that is, when they're not on a web server). Normally, the only folks doing this are developers testing their applications before posting them. But end users are also protected from any security issues if they do double-click a .swf or a local .html file hosting a .swf.

The FlashAuthor.cfg file was created when you installed Flash. By default, it is set to show the not-so-user-friendly dialog box shown in Figure A.1. For end users, any attempt to break the new security rules will simply fail. (If you want, you can edit the FlashAuthor.cfg file so you experience the same silent failure; however, you'll likely want to know if there is an issue with your application.)

If you're locally testing a .swf that needs to reach out to the Web, you should approve the operation by default. You could just post the .swf online every time you publish, but that would get old real fast. You can grant access to a file or folder by clicking the Settings button in the dialog box shown in Figure A.1, and you'll be taken to the Flash

Player Settings Manager shown in Figure A.2. (You can get directly to the Flash Player Settings Manager from this link: http://www. macromedia.com/support/documentation/en/flashplayer/help/settings_manager04a.html.)

FIGURE A.1 This dialog box appears when you break the local file access restrictions and you have Flash 8 installed on your system.

FIGURE A.2 One way to grant file access to a local .swf is through the Flash Player Settings Manager.

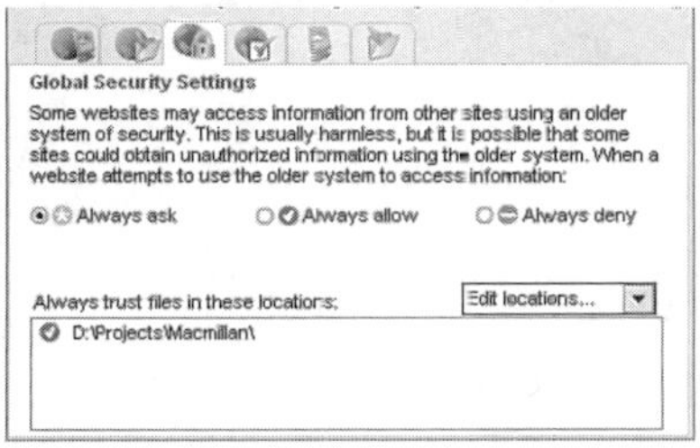

Another way to grant access is to create a text file you store in the FlashPlayerTrust folder that lists any files or folders where you'll be doing testing. For example, I put a text file in the FlashPlayerTrust folder containing the following string:

D:\Projects\Macmillan\

Any .swf files I launch from that project folder can access the Internet without restriction.

Macromedia Links

The Macromedia site has a lot of resources and some great technical articles. However, I find myself frequently returning to five specific links.

Flash Uninstaller

www.macromedia.com/go/14157

This technote includes a handy application that uninstalls the Flash player. This can be useful when testing what users who don't have Flash will experience when they visit your site.

Player Archive

www.macromedia.com/go/14266

Here you'll find an archive of the old Flash players. Use this resource to test how users with, say, Flash player 7 will experience your site.

Player Version

www.macromedia.com/go/15507

This simple swf displays the currently installed version of Flash player in case you get mixed up while installing and uninstalling various versions of the player.

LiveDocs

http://livedocs.macromedia.com/flash/8/main/

The livedocs are basically the same as your integrated help files, but it also includes comments by other users. Anyone can add helpful comments here.

Macromedia Labs

http://labs.macromedia.com/

This new site is where you can find out about new products Macromedia is working on. You can also download and test alpha versions of new software, such as the Flash player version 8.5.

Community Sites

Here are a few great Flash community and information sites that will get you started.

Full as a Goog

www.fullasagoog.com

This aggregator of Macromedia-related blogs will quickly link you to the rest of the Flash blogosphere.

Community MX

www.communitymx.com

This subscription-based information site also has many free articles of value. For example, you can find information about using cell renderers in the `DataGrid` and `List` components.

Chatty Fig

http://chattyfig.figleaf.com

Here you'll find links to subscribe to the most active Flash listservs around.

Open Source Flash

http://osflash.org

The folks at Open Source Flash lead several Flash-related projects and also maintain the FlashCoders WIKI.

Flashkit

www.flashkit.com

This is one of the oldest Flash community sites (along with the We're Here site, described next). Here you'll find both tutorials and an active forum. Let me respectfully mention that, like many sites where you can download Flash code, you should take care that you're getting samples created in the modern version of Flash. Although the old ways of doing things in, say, Flash 5, might be fun to look back on for the sake of nostalgia, they can also be confusing and counterproductive.

We're Here

www.were-here.com

Like www.flashkit.com, you'll find a long history of forums and tutorials at We're Here. Interestingly, for years, I thought the site was pronounced "were here" (as it's spelled), even though that makes no sense.

Ultrashock

www.ultrashock.com

This site is in the same genre as www.flashkit.com and www.were-here.com. Personally, I use all three sites equally.

Third-Party Products

Just as there's no shortage of information about Flash, there are also lots of ways to spend money on it. I'm sure there are additional great products out there, but the ones listed here are either well-established in the Flash world or tools I've used and can personally vouch for.

ActionScript Viewer

http://buraks.com/asv/

ActionScript viewer lets you view and recover elements contained in a .swf file. It's a great product that includes some invaluable plug-ins, such as the Shared Object Viewer. You'll also find a Flash video captioning tool, called Captionate, at this site.

Swift 3D

www.swift3d.com

Swift 3D is a full-blown 3D modeling, animation, and rendering product. The primary focus is to let you create .swf stills and animations with 3D that you can import into Flash. This site also has supporting tools for some other popular 3D creation tools.

Toon Boom Studio

www.toonboomstudio.com

Toon Boom Studio has its roots in conventional cell animation. Unique features include color styles (where you can replace all uses of a particular color), rotating the stage to help you draw (as in real life), and camera movements to simulate 3D. Plus, Flash can import source Toon Boom Studio work files.

Flix

www.on2.com

Although On2 happen to be the folks who created the VP6 codec added to Flash player 8, they also have a video encoder called Flix that produces .flv files.

Sorenson Media

www.sorensonmedia.com

Sorenson Media is well known for its video compression technologies and tools. It has a product called Sorenson Squeeze for Flash 4.2 that produces .flv files. Be sure to purchase its On2 VP6 Pro codec plug-in for Squeeze, too. Both Squeeze and On2's Flix will ultimately produce better quality .flv files than the Flash Video Encoder.

Techsmith's Camtasia

www.camtasia.com

This screen-capture tool effectively lets you make a video of your screen. You can output crystal-clear .swf or .flv files as well as .avi files using a custom codec.

Zoomify

www.zoomify.com

This product lets you display super-high-resolution photos in a Flash movie. I've always wanted a project that would give me a chance to use this product because I've seen some great examples, such as the atlas of the Theban Necropolis at http://www.thebanmappingproject.com/.

SWF Studio

www.northcode.com

This is the third-party swf2exe projector maker with which I'm most familiar. The rest of the products listed in this section (and discussed in Chapter 8, "Creating a CD-ROM Front End") fall into the same product category as SWF Studio.

M Projector

www.screentime.com/software/mprojector/

Arguably better or worse than the other swf2exe products—but definitely equivalent.

Zinc V2

www.multidmedia.com

Like the other swf2exe products.

Screenweaver

http://osflash.org/doku.php?id=screenweaver

A little bit different from the other swf2exe products because Screenweaver is now Open Source.

Content Site

I could probably dig up a few clip art or pay-per-photo sites for this section, but I'll list just one link that I find fascinating.

Moving Image Internet Archive

www.archive.org/details/movies

You'll find a range of content at this site—most of which is in the public domain. This is where I found the video excerpts for the video captioning project in Chapter 3, "Creating a Video with Synchronized Captions."

In this appendix, you'll receive basic training on how to use Flash *components*. Although components are supposed to make developing easier, they can be quite complex. The event model (based on the formal design pattern called Observer) is useful even when you're not using components. This book uses event listeners in the eight project-based chapters.

Except for a brief primer in Chapter 2, "Producing a Flash Project," many of the projects assume that you know how to use components. This appendix provides a complete overview of both how to use components and how to employ their event model.

Using V2 Components

Using components can be as easy as dragging an instance onto the stage and using the Parameters panel to populate values such as a Button component's label or the items that appear in a List component. However, you'll need to set up a listener to respond when the user clicks or interacts with a component. This section shows you how to set up listeners.

Simple Listener

Drag two instances of the Button component onto your stage. Give one the instance name aButton, and give the other the instance name bButton. Select the first keyframe, open the Actions panel, and type the code in Listing B.1 (which is also in the simple_listener.fla file contained in the downloads for this appendix).

> **📌 NOTE**
>
> Download the appendix_B_downloads.zip file for this appendix from the accompanying CD-ROM.

LISTING B.1 **This Code Configures Two** Button **Components and Sets Up a Listener (for When the User Clicks)**

```
1   import mx.controls.Button;
2
3   var aButton:Button;
4   var bButton:Button;
5
6   aButton.label = "a";
7   bButton.label = "b";
8
9   function click (evt:Object){
10      trace( "You clicked " +
11              evt.target +
12              " which has the label " +
13              evt.target.label );
14      trace( "The type was " + evt.type);
15  }
16
17  aButton.addEventListener( "click", this );
18  bButton.addEventListener( "click", this );
```

This example demonstrates a few useful things in addition to the listeners. The first line isn't necessary, but if you leave it out, you'll have to type two instances using the full path, as shown here:

```
var aButton:mx.controls.Button;
```

All that variable typing gets you is the code hints. For example, after lines 3 and 4, as soon as you enter the text aButton. you'll see a code-completion drop-down list with the button component's supported properties and methods (as shown in Figure B.1).

Consider the last lines in Listing B.1. When you trigger a component instance's addEventListener() method, you need to specify the string name of the component event you want to listen for, followed by the scope where it can find a function with the same name. This means "click" is an event supported by the mx.controls.Button class. Here's a trick to quickly find the available

events from a component: Select the component instance (say the aButton instance on stage), open the Actions panel, and type on(. A code-completion drop-down list appears with all the events this component can broadcast and that you can listen for. If you use this trick, just remember to remove all the code you typed because I recommend putting code in only keyframes (and this trick would attach code to the instance—which you don't want to do).

FIGURE B.1 **Typing variables helps trigger the code-completion drop-down list box.**

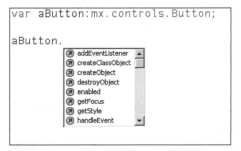

The second parameter in addEventListener() is the scope where events should be directed. By passing this for the second parameter (as I did in the code in Listing B.1), I was saying that there's a function in this scope (think timeline) named click(). Incidentally, you don't have to have a function that matches the event name (click()). Instead, you can use handleEvent(), which is triggered by all the events you add using addEventListener().

In the next section, I discuss the alternative of passing a homemade object as the second parameter. Then I show still another way that involves the utils.Delegate class.

Notice that both instances are channeled to the same .click() function. It's easy enough to sort out which button triggered the click() function because of all the information packed into the sole parameter (shown as evt). No matter where the click() function resides, when the component triggers it, it passes an object containing—at a *minimum*—properties for target and type. Check out the output from when I tested the sample code in Listing B.1 and clicked one of the buttons:

```
You clicked _level0.aButton which has the
label a
The type was click
```

The evt.target is a reference to the component instance itself (aButton). Using evt.target, I could get or set any property in that instance. For example, we're getting the component's label by using evt.target.label. (Realize that you can use any name you want for the parameter received; I just always use the parameter name evt, which is short for *event*.)

The fact that the evt parameter includes a type property might seem really silly considering that we're inside the click() method—and it *had* to be called click() to capture the "click" event based on the way we set up the addEventListener(). However, the type property is useful when you set up the addEventListener() .differently. For example, you might want to channel other event types to the same function. The following code sends both the focusIn and click events to the same myHandler function:

```
aButton.addEventListener( "click",
                          myHandler);
bButton.addEventListener( "click",
                          myHandler );
aButton.addEventListener( "focusIn",
                          myHandler );
bButton.addEventListener( "focusIn",
                          myHandler );
```

For this code to work, you need to define the myHandler() function. Simply change your click() function to read myHandler() if you just want to test it. I started by saying it was easy enough to use the evt.target to sort out which of the two buttons got you into the click() function. However, if you want to channel both focusIn and click to the same myHandler() function, you also need to sort out which event got you into that function. This process is similar to using the catchall handleEvent() function. Instead of using myHandler in the code just shown, use this instead. Then, both the click and focusIn events are channeled to a function you create named handleEvent().

Sometimes you might want to channel all the events from several components through a single handler. For example, it makes sense that a group of radio buttons all go through a single handler. However, if you want to handle the `click` event coming from several unrelated `Button` instances, you'll probably want to do the opposite and have a separate handler for each button. Check out the following variation (which you can find in the `simple_listener_variation.fla` file you downloaded for this appendix):

```
function aButtonClick(evt){
    trace( "you clicked a" );
}
function bButtonClick(evt){
    trace( "you clicked b" );
}
aButton.addEventListener( "click",
                          aButtonClick);
bButton.addEventListener( "click",
                          bButtonClick);
```

Notice that if you go this route, you don't even need to bother accessing the evt parameter because you only directed one component to trigger each function.

Before moving on, let me remind you that the second parameter in your `addEventListener()` call is a reference to the function. So don't put the extra parenthesis after `aButtonClick`, as in this example—which does not work:

```
aButton.addEventListener( "click",
                          aButtonClick() );
```

Using a Custom Object As a Listener

Using a custom object as a listener is similar to what I've shown so far. I first showed how passing `this` as the second parameter to `addEventListener()` makes the component broadcast the event to a function of the same name (as in `click()`). Then I showed an alternative in which you can pass a function reference (as in `aButton.addEventListener( "click", aButtonClick);`). Think about the first example using `this`. You're telling the component to look in `this` timeline for a function matching the event name. You can instead pass a homemade ActionScript object that happens to have a property matching that event name with a function for its value. The following code (from the `custom_object_listener.fla` file you downloaded for this appendix) shows a complete example equivalent to the one shown in Listing B.1 (but using a custom object as a listener this time):

```
import mx.controls.Button;

var aButton:Button;
var bButton:Button;

aButton.label = "a";
bButton.label = "b";

var myListener = new Object();

myListener.click = function (evt:Object){
    trace( "You clicked " +
           evt.target +
           " which has the label " +
           evt.target.label );
    trace( "The type was " + evt.type);
}

aButton.addEventListener( "click",
                          myListener );
bButton.addEventListener( "click",
                          myListener );
```

It's actually pretty simple. The myListener is where the component finds the `click()` function. It's just that myListener happens to be an object, and `click` is a property with a value set to a literal function. When we passed this in the Listing B.1, we were saying click() would be found in this timeline. Not only does the preceding code do the same thing, but it's the same concept (even if the code looks a bit different).

Using mx.utils.Delegate

When you add an event listener, the function that is called runs in the scope of the component calling it. For example, consider a Button instance named aButton nested inside a Movie clip instance named clip. Then consider the code in Listing B.2, which was placed in the main timeline (and in the file using_delegate.fla).

The myClickHandler is called, but it doesn't trigger nudgeClip using this.nudgeClip() because the "this" is the button itself and nudgeClip() is a function in the main timeline. (It turns out this isn't a huge deal when coding in the timeline because you can simply remove the "this" in front of nudgeClip(evt.target) and it will work.) The mx.utils.Delegate class lets you identify both the function you want triggered as well as the scope you want it triggered in. For

example, change the line where the addEventListener is assigned to read as follows:

```
clip.aButton.addEventListener("click",
    mx.utils.Delegate.create(this, myClick-
Handler));
```

Here the second parameter is the result of a call to the mx.utils.Delgate.create() method. The create() method's two parameters are the scope in which you want the function to get called (this, as in the main timeline) and the function you want called (myClickHandler—just like we had originally). Now, when the myClickHandler is called, the "this" will be the main timeline and not the button.

It turns out you'll probably never need to use the Delegate class outside of AS2 class files. But the class is useful to change the way functions are triggered. The general tip I have is that, when your listeners don't seem to be triggering properly, test them by placing the trace(this) statement in the handler—you might see a scope that's different from what you expected.

| LISTING B.2   This Code Demonstrates a Scope Issue with addEventListener |
```
function myClickHandler( evt ){
    trace("your scope is " + this);
    this.nudgeClip( evt.target );
}
clip.aButton.addEventListener( "click", myClickHandler );

function nudgeClip( whichOne ){
    whichOne._x = whichOne._x + 10;
}
```

Instantiating Components Dynamically

You can place components on stage dynamically using ActionScript. All V2 components effectively have a default Linkage Identifier, enabling you to use `attachMovie()` to place an instance on stage—provided the component is in your Library. However, you should use `createClassObject()` instead of `attachMovie()`. (The two methods are nearly identical in syntax.)

The key step to remember is that you must have a copy of the component in your Library. Check out the format (also found in the `using_createClass.fla` file you downloaded for this appendix):

```
import mx.controls.Button;
var ref:Button = createClassObject(Button,
            "myButtonInstance",
            0);
```

The first parameter is the class, the second parameter is the instance name you want to use, and the last parameter is the level to which your instance will be attached. Like `attachMovie()`, you can pass an optional fourth parameter containing a set of initial properties—for example, `{label:"click me"}`. Alternatively, you can just use the reference returned or the clip instance name itself as the last two lines of code, as this sample does:

```
import mx.controls.Button;
var ref:Button = createClassObject(Button,
            "myButtonInstance",
            0);
ref.label = "click me";
myButtonInstance.emphasized = true;
```

Like `attachMovie()` and its alter ego `removeMovieClip()`, you'll find that `destroyObject()` is the way to remove components created with `createClassObject()`. You simply pass a string matching the component's name:

```
import mx.controls.Button;
var ref:Button = createClassObject(Button,
            "myButtonInstance",
            0);
ref.addEventListener("click", this);

function click(evt){
    destroyObject(evt.target._name);
    //or:
    //destroyObject("myButtonInstance");
}
```

Finally, whether you're creating components dynamically or simply placing them on stage, it's best to avoid moving or resizing them using properties such as _x, _y, width, and height. (Yes, component instances have width and height properties as well as _width and _height properties, but the trend is toward properties without the underscore.) The way you should modify instances is by using the move() and setSize() methods. This way, the component author (in this case Macromedia) can write additional code to handle the change, such as if the graphics within the component need to be re-centered. Also, setSize() is more of a "request" than a command in that the component author might only want to support a minimum width.

Dispatching Events

I'm not going to detail the complete process to create your own components, but it's pretty easy to take advantage of the same event-dispatching model in your own code. I use this approach extensively in this book's projects.

After you have it set up, you can use addEventListener() on instances of your own custom classes. You can also create additional properties to send, along with the target and type properties received in the evt parameters that components use. There's just a little bit of ground work, but after you have it set up, you can make a class that parses XML and a specific value using code something as shown here (and as found in the using_MyClass.fla file you downloaded for this appendix):

```
var myListener:Object = new Object();
myListener.loadComplete = function(evt){
    trace (evt.filename +
            "'s contents:" +
            newline +
            evt.contents);
}
myInstance = new MyClass();
myInstance.addEventListener("loadComplete",
                            myListener);
myInstance.load("somefile.xml");
```

I just made up the event name loadComplete as well as the idea that it will pass properties for filename and contents. But if you're building the class, you really can do all that! Listing B.3 shows what the contents of the MyClass.as file look like.

LISTING B.3 How Your Own Custom Classes Can Dispatch Events to Any Listeners

```
1    import mx.events.EventDispatcher;
2
3    class MyClass {
4
5        var addEventListener:Function;
6        var removeEventListener:Function;
7        var dispatchEvent:Function;
8        var dispatchQueue:Function;
9
10       private var filename:String;
11
12       function MyClass(evt) {
13           EventDispatcher.initialize(this);
14       }
15
16       public function load(p_filename:String){
17           //save filename:
18           filename = p_filename;
19
20           var x:XML = new XML();
21           x.ignoreWhite = true;
22           x["target"] = this;
23           x.onLoad = function(success){
24               this.target.parseXML(success, this);
25           }
26
```

continues

```
27          x.load(filename);
28      }
29
30      private function parseXML (success:Boolean, contents:XML){
31
32          if( success == false ){
33              dispatchEvent({type:"error",
34                              target:this,
35                              message:"file load error"});
36              return;
37          }
38
39          dispatchEvent({type: "loadComplete",
40                          target:this,
41                          contents: contents.toString(),
42                          filename:filename});
43      }
44  }
```

The dispatchEvent() function takes only one parameter, but it's an ActionScript object, so you can add as many properties you want. You should be sure you set a type value to match the events you want to support, meaning the event names for which there might be listeners set up. You can see I'm dispatching both the loadComplete and error events. The code I showed you for the .fla was only listening for loadComplete. You could easily add another listener using addEventListener("error", myListener) as the using_MyClass.fla file does.

To dispatch events, you need to include the variables on lines 5–8, and be sure to call mx.events.EventDispatcher.initialize (this), as shown on line 13.

can do two additional cool things with components that I didn't cover here. Namely, skinning and making your own components from scratch. *Skinning* is where you can change the colors and styles (such as fonts) used in the component. In fact, you can often build replacement graphics for every element in the component. Related to skinning is the concept of *cell renderers*. A cell renderer is a custom movie clip you can make appear in place of a cell in the List or DataGrid components.

Where to Go from Here

The details in this appendix should ensure that you get the most out of the projects in this book that use components. However, you

Glossary

8-bit mask   A mask with 256 levels of transparency (that's 8 bits).

absolute path   *See* explicit path.

ActionScript   A programming language that is a way of expressing instructions your Flash application will follow when it runs. There's a formal set of rules for syntax and usage just like any other programming language.

address (*verb*)   To refer to a specific instance. It's the same meaning as how you address a judge with "your honor." In programming, you often need to address the object or instance you want to affect. That is, you don't say _x = 100; you first address a clip instance name and say myClip._x = 100.

accessibility issues   Considerations for users with various physical limits such as low vision or blindness, mobility issues, and hearing impairment. For the hearing impaired, you can add captioning to display the spoken dialogue in a video. When accommodating blind users who use a screen reader that reads aloud all the onscreen text, you can use the Accessibility panel to add a name and description for every pertinent object onscreen.

alpha channel   Defines which part of an image (or video) will be transparent. Every pixel in a 24-bit image includes 256 shades (that's 8 bits) of red, green, and blue. A 32-bit image has an additional 256 shades of transparency (or "see-through-ness"). Chroma key effect is when a character is shot against a solid background (usually green). Then the background is keyed out, meaning everything in that color is removed and becomes an alpha channel.

alpha transition   An animation in which the alpha of a clip transitions from 0 to 100% (or really, any change such as 100 down to 0).

API (application programming interface)   A set of public methods made available to an outside application. For example, Flickr.com has an API that lists all the ways you can search or perform other maneuvers on photos on its server. Many of the support classes for the projects in this book are not intended for your direct use; however, they can have an API of methods that are available.

application server   A standard web server needs only to let users browse to files over the Internet. An application server adds the capability to dynamically generate pages with timely information. For example, when a user requests a page called news.html, the application server can first draw on new sources and then generate the text for this page.

arguments   *See* parameters.

array   A variable that stores more than one value. Each value is stored in an index so you can access each item (to reveal or change it) by its position in the array. Arrays let you perform various manipulations, such as sorting all the contained items.

assignment   How you change the value of a variable or property. The equals sign always performs assignments as in myClip._x = 100. You can read the equals sign as "is now assigned a value of." Incidentally, the double equals (==) is not an assignment but rather a comparison.

asynchronous   Refers to certain method calls in Flash. When an asynchronous call is made, Flash continues to execute subsequent lines of code while the call executes. Methods that are asynchronous include those that must reach a remote server. You don't want these calls to be synchronous because your Flash application would freeze while the method executes. The tricky part with asynchronous methods is that you need to set up an event listener that responds to the method completing.

attributes   Available to XML nodes. These are effectively the same as properties of a movie clip.

authortime   Refers to when you're editing a .fla file. *See also* runtime.

auto run   A feature of CD-ROM drives whereby an application on the CD-ROM launches immediately after the user inserts the CD-ROM.

batch   A list of files or folders on which you want to perform the same procedure. For example, you might set up a batch to rename all the files in a folder.

blends   Compositing effects where the colors in one movie clip instance blend or interact with the colors of an underlying movie clip instance. You can apply only a single blend to any one movie clip instance.

captions Also called *open captions* and *closed captions*, these are simply text transcripts of the audio portion to a video or soundtrack.

category Used in the Photo Share project (in Chapter 10, "Building a Photo Share Application") as a variation of *keywords*. The concept is that each image could have several keywords but only a few categories. The only real difference from a category is how it was used in practice.

CBR (constant bit rate) A way of encoding video in which every frame is compressed the same amount. Generally, this results in a lower-quality video because bandwidth is wasted on frames that could otherwise be heavily compressed. However, CBR offers a slight advantage over VBR for the user who can just barely support the required bandwidth because CBR has no bandwidth spikes during playback.

cell A single frame in the timeline for a particular layer.

cell renderer A movie clip you use in place of the default text that normally appears inside a component. For example, you could create a graphic icon to supplement the text in a ComboBox component.

class Defines how a particular object type behaves. Classes can be internal to Flash, such as MovieClip and Sound, or they can be created by a programmer using ActionScript.

classpath A folder or set of folders Flash uses as its base or starting point when looking for classes referenced in your movie. That is, if you say import myClasses.myClass, Flash

needs to find the file myClass.as. It looks inside the folder myClasses, but that folder needs to be in the classpath. By default, the current folder where your .fla resides is part of the classpath so, in this case, you can place the myClasses folder there.

client side Anything that happens at the user's computer, including all the code inside a .swf file. Compare to server side.

codec Short for compressor/decompressor. It's the technology used on videos to first compress them to a small file that downloads quickly and then decompresses it when the user watches it (to reveal as much of the original detail as possible).

comment A line of code Flash ignores. It's a way to include notes inline with your code. You can comment out a single line by typing // at the beginning of the line. You can comment out several lines of code by starting with /* and ending with */.

component A self-contained movie clip containing all the code to perform a specific task. For example, some user interface components behave as buttons or list boxes. The developer using a component is insulated from the component's internal code.

composition A way of designing your ActionScript class in which that class is composed with a reference to another object. For example, the class might have a reference to a movie clip. You can say the class is composed of that movie clip, but the class isn't actually a movie clip itself.

constant   A variable that, by the way you use it, never changes. By convention, people name constants with all uppercase characters.

constructor   The function you use to instantiate any class. In use, it always appears after the keyword `new`, as in `new MyClass()`. Inside the class definition, the constructor is a function matching the class name, as in `function MyClass(){}`.

controller   Taken from the formal design pattern Model View Controller. In many of the projects in this book, an instance of a class serves as the controller. Often this class instantiates movie clips or `template.swfs` you create. Your templates might need to call on the controller to send information to other parts of the project.

crop   A technique in which you cut out portions of an image to reveal a smaller image. This way, you can remove excess image content that might distract the viewer.

CSS (Cascading Style Sheet)   A standard way of describing font and layout attributes such as font, size, and alignment.

cue points   Specific moments in a video or an audio clip when you want to have an event occur, such as displaying a caption.

custom shell   Comparable to any of the third-party swf2exe projects covered in Chapter 8, "Creating a CD-ROM Front End," and Appendix A, "Resources." However, you build the exe in a custom application in a tool such as Director or C++.

data type   The kind of data stored in a particular variable. The data type affects what you can do with the variable. For example, if your variable contains a 2 (that's the `Number` data type), you can do things such as add or subtract with that value. If your variable contains `Phillip` (a `String` data type), you can do things such as count the characters or change them all to uppercase.

deinterlace   An option when encoding video using Squeeze or Flix. It creates a much better result when your source video is created for television. Each frame of television video is made up of two fields, which are just frames containing either the odd scan lines or the even lines. The fields are played in sequence simply because the scanning ray gun can't move fast enough to scan every line. But because the fields are separated by 1/60 of a second, their content is not the same and you see horizontal lines if you simply combine the fields. You can correct this by selecting deinterlace when encoding.

drawing objects   Created in the new drawing mode called Object Drawing. In past editions of Flash, there was only Merge Drawing mode, in which every drawn shape resides in the same shared level. This means two shapes occupying the same space will merge. Now, when you select Object Drawing mode (from the Tools panel), you can create drawing objects that won't merge. Drawing objects are sort of like grouped objects, but you can continue to edit their contents.

easing   An option when Flash tweens that affects the acceleration or deceleration. *Ease in* means it starts slow and then picks up speed; *ease out* means the animation gradually comes to an end.

event listeners Can mean one of several approaches you take to make code execute only after a particular event occurs. For example, you might want to respond to a user's click by executing some code. You can set up an event listener that listens for a click.

events Things that happen when the user actively interacts with your project, such as when he clicks or moves his mouse. Other events are not tied to the user, such as onSoundComplete (which happens when a sound reaches the end). Many events occur while your project runs, and you might want to respond by executing specific code you wrote. For example, you might want to display a replay button when the onSoundComplete event occurs.

execute To perform the instructions in a piece of code. This always occurs during runtime, and it's always Flash that does the execution. When writing the code, you should always think about what happens when your code finally executes. A key consideration when writing your ActionScript is deciding precisely when the code should execute—when the user clicks, when the song ends...it's up to you.

explicit path Compare with *relative paths*. References to files that include the complete path from a drive letter, a hard drive name, or a domain. Examples of explicit paths are http://www.phillipkerman.com/index.html and c:\Program Files\Macromedia\Flash 8\ Flash 8.exe. The advantage of explicit paths it that they're not dependent on where the reference is made. However, if you change the folder hierarchy, explicit paths have to be updated. Often called *absolute path*.

export frame The frame where symbols with a linkage identifier download. When you want to use that symbol, it must have already downloaded in an earlier frame. Your actual class files have an export frame, too. By default, the export frame is frame 1.

expose A generic term I use to refer to methods in class files that are designated public.

filters A Flash 8 feature that includes several visual effects you can apply to movie clip instances and text. Filters include Drop Shadow, Blur, and Glow.

fire (*verb*) A generic term for describing when a particular block of code should execute. You could say, "when the user clicks, it's time to fire the code to change the screen."

FlashType A new technology for how fonts are displayed onscreen. Flash authors are given fine-tuning controls to make text appear as clear as possible.

FlashVars A way to send variables from the .html page that hosts a .swf to that .swf itself. All the variables identified as FlashVars are assigned their values before any of the code in the .swf executes.

FLVPlayback The name of a component that ships with Flash 8 and that can play external .flv video files. It also includes several skins to affect how the playback controls look.

font symbol A font you've included in the Library.

function   Used generally as an equivalent to *method*. More accurately, a function is a block of code that returns a value. That is, some methods just do something (like `play()`), but others are more like functions because they return a value (such as `getBytesLoaded()`).

gradient   An area of color that transitions from one color to another. A gradient can include multiple bands of color. Gradients are either linear or radial.

handle   A generic way of describing how you're going to respond to a particular event. For example, the way you might want to handle a mouse click is to pause a video. You can handle events however you want; you just have to write the code.

implement   A technical term from object-oriented programming. You can say one class will implement a particular interface. This means the class includes all the methods listed in that interface file. *See also* interface.

inheritance   A way of designing your ActionScript class in which the class extends another class. That is, it inherits all the attributes, including the properties and methods, from one class and, presumably, adds functionality to it. Generally, I recommend avoiding inheritance because it's only appropriate for certain cases. However, inheritance is appropriate and useful to extend the `MovieClip` class, as we do in this book.

instance   Usually refers to a movie clip instance on the stage, but you can instantiate many other data types by issuing the `new` statement. Think of a class is the blueprint and an instance as a copy based on the class.

instantiate   To create an instance. Usually, you create an instance using the `new` keyword, as in `new ClassName()`. You can also instantiate a movie clip by simply dragging a symbol onto the stage.

interface   The exact mechanism by which you interact with an object. The user interface is how the user interfaces with your project. Also, object-oriented programming uses the concept of an interface file to define the exact methods another class (which is said to *implement* the interface) will support.

Interface has two meanings. 1) An interface is like a class file but lists only methods that another class must include. The list of methods includes just the method names, their parameters, and return values (if any). The body of the methods are not defined in the interface. An interface is a contract that classes which implement it agree to support. 2) An interface is a term used to refer to the graphical user interface with which the user interacts—basically the screen.

interpolated   How Flash calculates the in-between frames of a tween. Interpolating 1–10 into three equal segments results in the values 1,5,10.

keyframe   A frame in which something new appears on the stage. An animation is made up of either a series of keyframes or keyframes separated by tweens. *See also* tween.

keyword   Usually a single word associated with an object, such as an image or music file. By tagging files with keywords, you can later search for all the files containing a particular keyword.

layer mask   Simply a layer that has its Layer properties set to Mask. It reveals only objects in layers underneath (set to Masked) where the layer mask has content.

layers   Part of the Flash timeline. Not only do objects in higher layers cover objects in lower layers, but each layer can maintain a separate motion tween animation. Also, layers can affect other layers through Layer properties such as Mask and Guide.

listener   Part of a design pattern called Observer. Code inside one object can broadcast an arbitrary event that another block of code is listening for. The listener is decoupled from the broadcaster, so the broadcaster simply broadcasts to any listeners what happened but the broadcaster doesn't need any direct knowledge of the listener.

mask   A way to reveal only part of another image. You can think of a mask like a costume mask you put over your face. However, where you place content in the mask defines which part of the object being masked is revealed. The mask is the holes for your eyes in the costume mask analogy.

matrix   An array of several numbers that together define how an object—usually a movie clip instance—has been modified or distorted. After a description of an object is stored in a matrix, you can perform modifications to that matrix and then apply the modified version to another object.

methods   Equivalent to functions, except methods always apply to a specific instance of a class. You can apply the play() method to one movie clip instance and only that movie clip instance will play. Methods optionally accept parameters in their parenthesis, but they always have parenthesis even if they don't accept parameters.

multipass   An option in video encoders to improve quality. However, it always takes about twice as long because the encoder first goes through the whole video to analyze it. Then, on the second pass, it encodes the video.

namespace   Has a more formal definition in other programming languages as well as ActionScript 3.0, but for the purposes of this book, a *namespace* is simply a convention where you can ensure your class names don't conflict with other, identically named classes created by another developer. It's simple: Instead of saying myClass, you say myDomain.myClass. That is, myDomain.myClass is not identical to otherDomain.myClass despite the fact the class name (myClass) is the same.

node   An XML document is made up of nodes that appear in the form <nodeName>value</nodeName> or simply <nodeName/>. A node's value can be a string or additional child nodes. In addition, nodes can contain attributes.

object   This has two meanings. 1) It's the class or data type on which every other class is based. If you don't specify a variable type for your variables (that is, if you don't type them), their data type defaults to Object. The simplest form is the ActionScript object, which is a variable in which you can set properties to any value you want. 2) It's just a generic way to refer to individual instances onstage as objects.

offline time   Refers to work you do outside of Flash or in Flash but outside your main .fla file. The term comes from video editing where offline editing is performed so editors don't actually make any cuts to the video but rather prepare to do so by making a list of edits to perform.

Onion Skin   An option that, while editing a .fla file, lets you view the contents of other frames. Normally, you see only the contents of the current frame. With the Onion Skin feature enabled, you can get a better sense of what comes before or after the current frame in your animation.

package   A group of classes organized in a single folder.

parameters   Additional details you pass to a function or that you include as properties inside an ActionScript object. In the example gotoAndPlay(1), the 1 is a parameter specifying which frame you to go.

parse   The process extracting just a portion of a larger block of text. When you import a large XML string, you need to parse out the pieces you want.

progressive download   The way files—including video—download from a standard HTTP web server. That is, it downloads the video from beginning to the end, progressively. This enables you to watch the beginning while the rest downloads. This is unlike the way a streaming video lets you seek to a later point in the video. *See also* streaming.

projector   A standalone .exe version of your project .swf. You can send a projector to anyone even if they don't have Flash, the Flash Player, or the Flash standalone player (SAPlayer.exe) and they'll be able to see your project.

property   An attribute of any instance such as the _width of a movie clip instance. You're allowed to change some properties, which often results in a visual change, but all properties are accessible so you can ascertain their values. Although several properties start with an underscore, that is by no means a requirement.

public methods   Methods available from outside a class. A class can refer to any of its methods—public or private—by simply triggering them with the form methodName(). From outside a class, you can trigger public methods using the following syntax: classInstance.methodName().

query string   A way for variables to be sent to a web application. A query string is a string of characters that appears after the web address. For example, index.html?myvar=test sends a variable named myvar with a value of test to the application index.html.

raster image   Any image format other than vector. A raster is a grid, and raster images have pixel information for every pixel in a grid equal to the image's width × height.

relative path   A way to refer to files where their location is dependent on where the reference is made. That is, if you say "next door" or "in the folder images," these are relative because you can only find the reference relative to where you are at one point. Relative paths won't break if you move all the files to a different server.

resize   A technique in which you change the width and height of an image to make it larger or smaller.

responders   A general term for code you write to respond to specific events.

rollover   The effect of the user moving his cursor over an object such as a button.

runtime   When your .swf plays in the Flash Player for the user. Features such as loading images at runtime are significant because you can load the images when the user requests them (perhaps loading an up-to-date photo from a traffic camera). If you load something at authortime, it's locked with the file.

scripts   The lines of code you type in the ActionScript language.

scrubber   A type of button the user clicks and drags, such as Flash's red-current frame marker.

server side   Anything (especially code) that runs on the server (compare to client side).

skinning   A process in which you change the visual look of a particular interface. In the case of a Button component, you might change the rectangle shape to have sharp corners instead of rounded corners.

streaming   A way files can be served from special media servers, such as the Flash Media Server. When a user requests a video, only the bits she requests download. Normally, users watch a video from beginning to end, but a streaming server enables a user to seek to a later part of the video and just that part begins to download.

stub   Has two meanings that I use: 1) A small .swf or .exe file that immediately jumps to the main files. This way, you can perform all the initialization in the stub and continue to make changes to the main files. 2) People also say you should start a complex project by "stubbing" your code.

This is writing just skeletons of each method you plan on creating. They're skeletons because they have no body or, at most, a trace statement.

stuff   As a verb, as in "stuff the i variable," it is a term I often use for when I dynamically create a custom property (usually on a movie clip instance) to store information.

style sheet   Synonymous with Cascading Style Sheet.

symbol instance   An instance of a symbol on the stage.

synchronization   Making graphics or events happen at precise times. If you're displaying captions for a video, you'll want these synchronized with the audio track.

synchronous   Compared with *asynchronous*, synchronous method calls complete before continuing to the next line of code.

syntax   The set of rules to which all ActionScript must adhere. Compared to many programming languages, ActionScript is *loose*, meaning the syntax rules can be broken. Ultimately, however, your scripts must have acceptable syntax; otherwise, your projects won't work.

tags   Additional details or keyword you associate with an object. For example, you can tag your images with a date tag or a photographer's name tag.

template   The term I often use for a .swf that you generate for use in the various projects in this book. The idea is that you can often create several variations of the same basic template. Each template is interchangeable.

trap   A generic term meaning to capture an event and, presumably, respond to it. Because most events don't have any impact, you need to trap the events you want. For example, you might want to trap when a user clicks the keyboard and determine when he typed.

trigger   The cause for how a particular block of code is executed. That is, you'll often want your code to trigger only when a particular event happens.

tween   Short for *between*, it's a term for how Flash can take two keyframes and interpolate the difference over time to create an animation.

variable   A way to store data so you can use it later. Every variable has a name and a value. You can also type a variable to declare that its value will be allowed to contain only a particular data type.

Variable bit rate (VBR)   A way of encoding video in which less compression is applied to more detailed frames, resulting in a higher bandwidth. But that added bandwidth is compensated with additional compression applied to other frames. In the end, a VBR video should be the same total size as a CBR video but have better quality where it matters: in the detailed frames. *See also* CBR (constant bit rate).

V2 Components   Components first introduced in Flash MX 2004 were the second generation of components and used an entirely new architecture, referred to as V2. The coding rules are consistent with all V2 components.

XML (Extensible Markup Language)   A string that follows a formal structure. The best way to think about XML is to realize that it's mainly a way to store content. But, by the nature of its format, the XML form adds meaning to the content. For example, a number such as 8005551212 has more meaning when placed in the format (800) 555-1212. (This isn't XML, but it demonstrates that structure can add meaning to the content.)

XPath   A set of APIs that makes parsing XML much easier and more intuitive. Instead of digging through nodes using `childNodes[z].childNodes[y]`, you can use the actual node names.

Index

Symbols and Numbers

A

classes

O

Object Drawing, 36

objects

custom objects as event listeners, 382-383

deselecting, 35

Drawing Objects, 36

Object Drawing, 36

PhotoController, 107-108

selecting, 34-36

offline time, 44-45

On2 Flix, 377

onion skin, 305

online resources. *See* resources

onLoadInit() method, 119

onMouseMove() function, 178

Open Source Flash website, 376

openFile() method, 281-282

overwriteImageData() method, 353

P

packages, 49

definition of, 22

flash.display, 22

flash.external, 24-26

flash.filters, 21

flash.geom, 22-24

flash.net, 26

parameters, 19, 63

parseXML() method, 260, 285

parsing code, 143

paths, 20

absolute, 193

explicit, 104

external paths to server-side methods, 192-194

FlashVars variable, 194

urls.xml file location, 193-194

urls.xml file, adding methods to, 192-193

relative, 104, 193, 251

.pdf documents, downloading, 358

getImages.xml file, 360

main.fla file, 359-360

testing, 363

working folders, creating, 359

zoom_document_version.swf file, 360-362

Perlin Noise, 318

photo captions

before-and-after photo template, 227-231

before_after.fla file, creating, 227

code listing, 227-230

<slide> node, 231

pull quote template

code listing, 235-238

CSS styles, creating, 233

embedded fonts, 234-235

<slide> node, 233-234

simple photo caption template

ActionScript code listing, 224-225

caption text, laying out, 223

document setup, 223

photo holder, laying out, 223

testing, 226-227

photo share application, 325

class structure, 368

edit.swf file, 351-353

canceling and saving changes, 353

initialization code, 352

list view, 363

getImageHolder() method, 365

init() method, 365-366

main_list_version.fla file, creating, 367

testing, 367

thumbnail screen, creating, 364

working folder, creating, 364

main screen modifications, 357-358

main.fla file, 334-335

.pdf documents, downloading, 358

getImages.xml file, 360

main.fla file, 359-360

testing, 363

working folders, creating, 359

zoom_document_version.swf file, 360-362

planning, 326

FileReference class limits, 329-330

keywords and categories, 328-329

screens, 326-327

uploading/downloading, 330

S

saveUserResults() method, 209-210

saving

    cue points in XML files, 65, 70-73

    quiz results. *See* application servers

Scale option (strokes), 10-11

scratches. *See* film dirt

Screenweaver, 378

scripted effects, 288-289

scripting, 30

scripts, 21, 30

scrubbers, 130

scrubTo() method, 83

section_animated.swf file, 268-270

Section instances, 285

<section> nodes, 259

section_simple.fla file, 263-268

section_static.swf file, 271-276

section templates (CD-ROM front end), 262

    section_animated.swf, 268-270

    section_simple.fla, 263-268

    section_static.swf, 271-276

Section.as class, 258-259

SectionMaker class, 259-261, 266, 285

#Security folder, 374

security, local, 167

seekToNextNavCuePoint() method, 63

seekToPrevNavCuePoint() method, 63

selecting objects, 34-36

Selection screen (photo share application), 326, 356

selection.swf file (photo share application), 335-338

    data parsing, 336-337

    navigation, 337-338

selectNodeList() method, 165, 220, 350

selectSingleNode() function, 166, 220

selectSingleNodeValue() function, 166, 220, 225

selectSingleNodeValue() method, 225

sepia-toned photos, creating, 299-301

serializing data, 258

server-side methods, external paths to, 192-194

    FlashVars variable, 194

    urls.xml file location, 193-194

    urls.xml file, adding methods to, 192-193

server-side tasks, 153

servers. *See* application servers

set scale() method, 56

setController() method, 109, 112-114

setInterval() function, 289

setPrompt() method, 335

setSize() method, 384

setTimeout() method, 27

shape tweens, 31

#Shared Objects folder, 374

show() method, 337

showImage() method, 109, 119, 147

showPhotos() function, 230

showText() function, 74-75, 86

sizeToRect() method, 115, 122-123, 136

sizing images, 102

skinning video, 69

skins, 12

skipping questions (assessment quiz), 161

<slide> nodes

    before-and-after photo template, 231

    pull quote template, 233-237

slide presentation, 217

    before-and-after photo template, 227-231

    before_after.fla file, creating, 227

    bullet list template, 238-244

        code listing, 240-242

        CSS styles, 239

        embedded fonts, 239

        init() function, 242-244

        XML structure, 238-239

    code listing, 227-231

    deployment options, 222

    design, 222

    distribution, 244-246

        choosing, 245

        distribution files, 245-246

        projectors, 245

urls.xml file

adding methods to, 192-193, 203-204

location, 193-194

utils.as class, 259

V

variables, 19

FlashVars, 194-195

reference, 52

typing, 19, 46

value variables, 52

vertical thumbnail templates, 140-141

video captions. *See* **captions**

videos, playing automatically, 79

VU (volume unit) meter, 307-312

analog version, 312

code listing, 310-311

digital VU meter symbol, 308-309

planning, 308

support files, 309

test application, 309

VUMeter() constructor, 311

W-X-Y-Z

WavyFilter class, 316-318

We're Here website, 376

websites. *See* **resources**

work environment (photo share application), 331-333

images folder, 332-333

static XML files, setting up, 331-332

support files, 333

workflow, 13-14

XML files

data.xml (CD-ROM front end)

folders, 259

Item.as class, 256-258

Section.as class, 258-259

skeleton file, 255-256

exporting, 72-73

saving cue points in, 65, 70-73

static XML files, creating, 204-205

XMLGateway.as file, 333

XPath, 220

Zinc V2, 378

Zoomify, 377

zoom_document_version.swf file (photo share application), 360-362

Zoom screen (photo share application), 326, 357

zoom.swf file (photo share application), 347-351

goPage() method, 349-350

initialization code, 348

messages, directing, 350